P. JULIO MEINVIELLE
DOCTOR OF THEOLOGY AND PHILOSOPHY

FROM KABBALAH TO PROGRESSIVISM

JULIO MEINVIELLE
(1905-1973)

Julio Meinvielle was an Argentine Catholic priest, theologian and philosopher known for his ultra-conservative stance and his opposition to communism and liberalism. Ordained in 1930, he wrote on Thomistic philosophy and defended a traditionalist Catholic view of society. His works include "Communism in the Anti-Christian Revolution" and "From Kabbalah to Progressivism". He was an influential and controversial figure in Catholic circles in Argentina.

FROM KABBALAH TO PROGRESSIVISM

De la Cabala al Progresismo

CALCHAQUÍ PUBLISHER, *Salta, Rep. Argentina* January 1970

Translated and Published by
Omnia Veritas Limited

www.omnia-veritas.com

© Omnia Veritas Ltd - 2024

All rights reserved. No part of this publication may be reproduced, distributed or transmitted in any form or by any means, including photocopying, recording or other electronic or mechanical means, without the prior written permission of the publisher, except in the case of brief quotations in critical reviews and other non-commercial uses permitted by copyright law.

FOREWORD 15
CHAPTER I... 21
   THE JUDEO-CATHOLIC TRADITION AND THE GNOSTIC-
   KABBALISTIC TRADITION THROUGHOUT HUMAN HISTORY 21
      The two oral traditions 21
      The Judeo-Catholic tradition... 23
      The three economies of the Judaeo-Catholic tradition. 26
      The Second Vatican Council recognises the three economies of the
      Judeo-Catholic tradition 27
      The Ancient Kabbalah of the Jews... 30
      Perversion of Jewish Kabbalah 31
      Content of the perverted Kabbalah 33
      The primordial tradition 37
      Fundamental content of the two Kabbalahs or traditions 40
      Stages of Jewish Perverted Kabbalah... 42
      The intermingling of traditions and peoples in the 6th century BC 43
      Brahmanic Gnosis 44
      The Iranian gnosis... 45
      Sumerian-Acadic Gnosis.. 46
      Egyptian gnosis 47
      Extracts from the Pyramid Texts... 47
      Hermetic gnosis... 48
      The Hebraic Gnosis... 49
      The Sefer-ha-Zohar 54
CHAPTER II 55
   THE VARIOUS INTERPRETATIONS OF THE KABBALAH............... 55
      l. THE CHRISTIAN INTERPRETATION OF THE KABBALAH...... 55
         1. The written law and the two oral laws: one legal, the other mystical
         or cabalistic... 57
         2. Main doctors of the Kabbalah. The Zohar............................... 58
         3. Treatises and books complementary to the Zohar 58
         True idea of the Kabbalah. Its use in the Synagogue........................ 59
         1. The emanation of the Kabalah and the ten sephiroth or splendours.
         The three supreme splendours 60
         2. The seven splendours comprised under the denomination of
         Knowledge or the Divine Attributes... 63
         3. The seven spirits of the Apocalypse, I, 4.................................. 64
         4. The seven dazzling lights in the Apocalypse, IV, 5, and the seven
         eyes of Jehovah in Zechariah IV, 10. 66
         5. The cabalistic tree. Et nolite tangere... 67
         6. Extracts from Kabbalistic books... 68
      II. NATURALISTIC INTERPRETATION OF THE CABBALA 77
         The Zohar 78
         The En-sof 79

The world of the Sephiroth 80
   Language, a divine symbol 81
   The divine self and the Chekina... 81
   God and nothingness.. 82
   Mysticism and dialectics.. 84
   The Wisdom of God and the Primordial Point................................... 86
   God, subject of the cosmic process... 86
   God, subject and object of the cosmic process................................... 87
   The pantheism of the Zohar 88
   Creation before Adam's sin 89
   Sexuality in the Zohar.. 89
   The Chekina as a female aeon.. 90
   Original sin... 91
   The origin of evil.. 91
   The doctrine of the soul 93
   Conclusion on the Zohar.. 94
   Kabbalah after the Zohar.. 94
   The doctrine of Tzimtzum.. 94
   The rupture of vessels 95
   God shapes Himself 97
   The Process of Restitution in God and in Man 97
   Metempsychosis.. 99
III. OCCULT INTERPRETATION OF THE KABBALAH 99
   Occultists' antiquity of the Kabbalah... 100
   Kabbalah's teachings on mankind 102
   Kabbalah's Teachings on the Universe... 104
   Kabbalah's Teachings on God 104
   Influence of the Kabbalah on Philosophy 106
   The world of the "quliphah" or demons.. 106
   The Sephiroth in the Five Worlds 108
IV. THE JUDEO-MASONIC-DIABOLIC KABBALAH 111
   Meurin's book... 113
   The Jews.. 113
   The instruments of destruction... 114
   The Judaeo-Masonic-Demonic Cabala 115
   The enthronement of the Jew 115
   Political application of the Kether-Malkhuth................................... 116
   Conclusion of this second chapter... 118
CHAPTER III **119**
THE EXISTENCE OF A JUDAIC GNOSIS SINCE THE 16TH
CENTURY BC 119
   The practice of the mysteries in Israel 127
   Egyptian Mysteries 129
   Exporting Egyptian Mysteries.. 130

CHAPTER IV 134
CHRISTIAN GNOSTICISM OR A CHRISTIANITY ALTERED BY KABBALAH 134
- Jewish origin of Christian Gnosticism 135
  - Jewish Gnosticism 137
- What is Christian Gnosticism? 139
  - Christian gnosis 139
- Development of Gnostic systems 146
  - The Simon Magician system 147
  - The Valentinian Gnosis 150
  - Theogony 151
  - Formation of the Spiritual Man 153
  - The final consummation 153
- Significance of Alexandria in the Gnostic polemic 157
  - The Christian school of Alexandria 160

CHAPTER V 162
THE KABBALISTIC INFLUENCE IN THE ANCIENT AND MIDDLE AGES 162
- Manichaeism 162
- The Arian Heresy 166
- From the Manichaeans to the Albigensians 169
  - Catharos 169
  - Bogomilas 169
  - Paulicians 170
  - Albigensians 170
  - The Templars 172
- John Scotus Eriugena 175
  - The concept of creation 178
  - The lower creation and man 180
  - Predestination of the wicked 181
  - The reintegration of humanity in God 181
  - General appreciation of Eriugena: 182
- Joaquín de Fiore 186
- General conclusion of this chapter 192

CHAPTER VI 193
CHRISTIAN METAPHYSICS AND THE PROBLEM OF GOD, THE WORLD AND MANKIND 193
1. Is there a Christian metaphysics? 193
2. What problems are involved in Christian metaphysics? 194
3. Christian metaphysics in the face of anti-Gnostic polemic 196
4. Development of Christian metaphysics 198
5. Culmination of Christian metaphysics in St. Thomas 200
6. The great theses of Thomistic metaphysics 201
7. The Creation of Man and Anthropological Problems 206

8. Man, through the gift of grace, participates in the divine nature. 207
Conclusions 207
CHAPTER VII **211**
PENETRATION OF THE KABBALAH INTO THE CHRISTIAN
WORLD 211
The beginnings of Christian Kabbalah in Spain 212
Pico della Mirandola and the Italian milieu of Christian Kabbalah 213
Jean Reuchlin 215
The Golden Age of Christian Kabbalah in Italy 218
The Development of Kabbalah in Germany 220
Christian Kabbalah in France 221
   The school of William of Postel 223
Christian Kabbalah in England 224
Kabbalah among Protestants 224
Christian Kabbalah and Occult Philosophy 226
CHAPTER VIII **228**
THE KABBALAH, ONCE INTRODUCED, WORKS IN THE
CHRISTIAN WORLD WITH BOEHME, SPINOZA AND LEIBNIZ 228
The precursors 228
God, Eternal Nothingness and Chaos 232
   A God Who Begets Himself 233
   Creation ex nihilo 234
   God's creation of evil 234
   The present world, a mixture of good and evil, can be explained by a
   cosmic fall 235
   Anthropology 235
   Adam did not resemble the present man in body. 236
   Man saves himself 236
   Man possesses absolute autonomy 238
   Judgement on Boehme's thinking 238
Baruch Spinoza 240
Gottfried W. Leibniz 246
Conclusion of the chapter 249
CHAPTER IX **250**
THE CABAL ACTS OPENLY THROUGH GERMAN IDEALISM 250
Fichte 250
Schelling 254
Hegel 254
   Creation would be an alienation and a development of God. 256
   Evil within the divine essence 257
   The passion of Christ is an alienation and reconciliation of the divine
   essence. 258
   The philosopher must relive this process of alienation and the return
   to himself of the divine substance in nature and history. 259

CHAPTER X **261**
 MODERN PHILOSOPHY ON THE ROAD TO THE NEGATION OF
 GOD AND THE DIVINISATION OF MANKIND................................. 261
  1. The principle of immanence.. 262
  2. The principle of immanence implies the negation of the principle of
  contradiction and atheism. 263
  3. Descartes introduces the principle of immanence as the first principle
  of philosophy. 265
  4. Spinoza introduces metaphysical immanence............................ 267
  5. The Metaphysical and Dynamic Immanence of German Idealism .. 268
  6. The drama of atheistic humanism 271
    Feuerbach and only Feuerbach... 272
  7. Nietzsche and the Death of God.. 273
    The madman 273
  8. The Principle of Immanence in Modern Politics......................... 274
    Eric Voegelin's approach 275
  9. The Modern Revolution 279
CHAPTER XI... **282**
 VARIOUS WAYS MANIFEST THE INVASION OF THE KABBALAH
 INTO THE CHRISTIAN WORLD 282
  1. The cabalistic lines of esotericism 282
    The notion of creation or chaos. 284
    Metaphysical realisation 284
  2. Hindu doctrines and the Christian West..................................... 288
  3. Occultism 291
  4. The Kabbalistic Line of Hegelian Philosophy 294
    Christian Doctrine Adulterated by Lutheranism........................ 296
  5. The Gnosis of the Communist Revolutionary Dialectic 300
  6. The Schopenhauerian Kabbalistic Line...................................... 304
  7. Nietzsche's Nihilism 306
  8. Freud and Jung, or the psychoanalytic current of the Kabbalah 308
  9. Heidegger's Kabbalist Line... 313
  10. Kabbalah and Mass Culture 315
CHAPTER XII **318**
 THE CABAL WITHIN THE CHURCH OR CHRISTIAN
 PROGRESSIVISM... 318
  1. Relativism in Revelation and Theology 318
  The historical character of Scripture is called into question. 322
  3. The theologians of the new theology made the Primum movens of the
  Church.. 325
    Cardinal John Heenan denounces current contempt for the
    magisterium 326
  4. Progressivism tends to weaken the firm truth of God's existence. ... 328
    A re-evaluation of atheism in progressivism 328

The proofs of God's existence 333
5. Some new theologians call into question the mystery of the Holy Trinity and the mystery of the Incarnation. 335
6. There is no lack of theologians who doubt the existence of Satan. ... 338
7. Original sin of origin is denied 338
8. An all too human image of the Person of Christ is constructed. 342
   The Image of Christ in Contemporary Theology 346
   Remarks on the image of Christ in contemporary theology 347
   Observations on the psychological knowledge of Christ's human nature in relation to the divine Self 349
9. Marian privileges, and in particular her virginity, are curtailed. 350
10. Downgrading the Character and Authority of the Church 351
11. The new theology also questions transubstantiation 356
12. The historical value of the Gospel accounts, including that of the Lord's resurrection, is questioned 362
13. Karl Rahner's anonymous Christianity 362
14. Justification in Karl Barth and Luther 365
15. Heaven and hell are questioned 367
16. Replacement of the traditional morality, based on theology and natural law, by a morality based on Christology and the situation of the world 367
17. The Secularisation of Christianity, even among Catholic Theologians 374
18. Worship and Prayer in a Secularised World 393
19. Some facts anticipating the new secularised Church 395

CHAPTER XIII **397**
  TOWARDS A KABBALISTIC CHRISTIANITY 397
    The Essence of Gnostic and Kabbalistic Error 400
    Extracts from the Pyramid Texts 401
     1. God is Nothing coming out of Nothing 402
     2. This Nothingness by evolution becomes the world and mankind. 403
     3. The sexual is fulfilled in God 404
     4. Evil is in God 405
     5. God perfectly fulfilled and realised culminates in the man of mankind 405
    The essence of the Gnostic error expressed equivalently by some predominant note 407
     The progressivism of theologians, a first stage of Christian Gnosticism 417
    The Gnosticism of the Dutch Catechism 421
    Karl Rahner's Gnosticism 425
     The Incarnation 428
     Redemption 429

The Trinity	430
The Eucharist	432
Theilhardism, a stage full of Gnosticism	433
CONCLUSION	**443**
Other titles	**451**

Quid habes quod non accepisti?

What do you have that you haven't received?

FOREWORD

This book sets out to demonstrate that, throughout human history, there are but two fundamental attitudes of thought and life: one, the Catholic, which is the tradition received from God by Adam, Moses and Jesus Christ, and whose unsurpassed expositor was St. Thomas Aquinas; the other, the Gnostic and cabalistic, which nourishes the errors of all peoples in gentility and in the apostasy of Judaism first and then in that of Christianity itself, and which is particularly true in the modern world.

In their primary origin, these traditions are not two but one, for there is only God and the good that proceeds from His beneficent hands. The perverse and cabalistic tradition originates in the good tradition, which is perverted by the malice of man, who, in turn, allows himself to be seduced and alienated by the devil. The great Gnostic temptation of "you shall be as gods" takes hold of the human race and loses it.

The essential nucleus of truths that comes from God revolves around the immutable mystery of the Unity and Trinity of God; the mystery from which the universe comes by creation and which is to constitute the object of vision of the blessed. Therefore, the first and fundamental of Catholic doctrine is the immutable and metahistory.

Such a principle governs history and time. This explains why St Thomas in his Summa Theologica *devotes himself in a particular way to explaining the aforementioned immutability and metahistory.*

Because they alone provide a reason for history. Aristotle had already warned that without the Act neither becoming nor change can be explained.

The evil Kabbalah, on the other hand, is based on pure change, which is called evolutionism, historicism, dialecticism or progressivism. Change is not to be found in the creature but in the Creator. God would become the universe and man. God would be History, Evolution, Dialectics and Progress. God would not be the Esse Subsistens, *in whose contemplation for eternity the blessed must find their joy, but* would be an incessant becoming, a becoming, a praxis, to whose making the creature must apply himself.

These two conceptions determine two diametrically opposed cultures: one, the Catholic culture, which is essentially contemplative, and in which man, in perfecting his faculties, tends to contemplate God and his works; the other, the modern culture, essentially magical, operative and manufacturing, and in which man exercises a predominantly transitive and transformative action, seeking the practical utility of things.

The second mystery of the Catholic tradition is that of the Incarnation, according to which the Logos, or the Second Person of the Blessed Trinity, communicates Himself as a gift to man so that he in turn can be raised up to the Creator. The Humanity of Jesus, which unites all the perfections of Creation, is united in hypostatic unity with the divine person of the Word and through this union raises all predestined humanity to the very depths of the Trinitarian life. It is the highest union, without confusion, of creature with Creator. Jesus Christ, in whom this union is fulfilled, redeems and saves sinful humanity.

In the perverse tradition or cabal, on the other hand, the human creature has the insolence to rise up to God, and, by his own effort, to obtain divinisation. It is not God who saves man in Jesus Christ, but man who completes and completes God.

The Catholic tradition is a culture of communication and service - a gift - which is given in humility, poverty and meekness as opposed to the kabbalistic culture which, with arrogance and greed, concentrates all powers. Hence the cabalistic conception conceives the things of the world as if they were the true motor of history. It absolutises the unimportant and sin. St. Paul, on the other hand, shows that the world of Christ and of the elect moves the world, even the world of the wicked, in its own function.

The Catholic tradition, which culminates in the Saints and in Christ, is a barely perceptible thread in the history of mankind. All the rest, however, has no other reason for being than that this imperceptible thread should shine through. The darkness of the Kabalistic tradition, in its gigantic vanity and grandeur, offers background and contrast to the luminous poverty of the Catholic tradition.

It remains for us to say a word about how the present book has been composed. The author confesses his limitation in the knowledge of Hebrew and related languages, such as Chaldee, whose knowledge *would have allowed him a more direct access to the sources of the Kabbalistic tradition. Moreover, he lacked very useful bibliographical resources, such as, for example, the "prínceps" edition of the Zohar, the Mantua edition of 1558-1560, or the Cremona edition of 1560. He had to content himself with consulting, here in Buenos Aires, apart from the usual articles in the main dictionaries, the following works:*

Sepher Ha-Zohar *(Le Livre de la Splendeur), Doctrine esotérique des Israelites - Traduit sur le texte chaldaïque par lean de Pauly. 1907-1911, Paris. Volumes II-VI (Volume I is missing).*

Sepher Ha-Zohar. *Esoteric Doctrine of the Israelites. Paris, 1906-11, 6 volumes.*

Zohar. *Translated by Harry Sperling, M. Simon and P. Levertofk. 5 vol. With introduction by J.*

Abelson. London, 1949.

Zohar. *The book of Splendor. Selected and edited by Gershom Scholem. New York, 1949.*

Le livre de Zohar. *Pages translated from the Chaldaic by J. de Pauly. Paris, 1925, 282 p. F. Rieder et Cie, Editeurs.*

The author has made special use of the Italian translation Le Grandi Correnti della Mistica Ebraica, *by G. Scholem, Casa Editrice de Saggiatore, 1965, Milan, and the French translation* Les Grandes Courants de la Mystique Juive, *Payot, Paris, 1968.*

And also:

Henri Serouya, La Kabbale, *Grasset, Paris, 1947.*

Siphra Di-Tzeniutha, *ouurage essentiel du Sepher-ha-Zohar, traduction integrale par Paul Vulliaud, Emile Nourry, Paris, 1930.*

Alexandre Safran, La Cabale, *Payot, 1960, Paris.*

Papus, La Cabbale, *Éditions Dangles, 2nd edition, Paris.*

Georges Vajda, *Recherches sur la Philosophie et la Kabbale dans la pensée juive de Mayen Age, Mouton & Cie, 1962, Paris.*

Gershom G. Scholem, Les Origines de la Kabbale, *Montaigne, 1966, Paris.*

Gershom G. Scholem, La Kabbale et sa symbolisme, *Payot, 1966, Paris.*

Georges Vajda, Introduction a la pensée juive du Mayen Age, *J. Vrin, 1947, Paris.*

Knorr von Rosenroth, Kabbala denudata.

Robert Ambelain, La Kabbale pratique.

In order to expound such a delicate thesis as the Christian interpretation of the Kabbalah, he wished to give the floor to the learned rabbi turned Drach, whose work Harmonie entre l'Église et la Synagogue *(Paris, 1844) is of incalculable value.*

On the other hand, on the major problem of the "cabalisation" of German idealism, and especially of Hegel, he has been inspired by the writings of Claude Tresmontant, who, in turn, has been able to avail himself of the authoritative work of F. Ch. Baur, Die christliche Gnosis oder die christliche Religions Philosophie in ihrer gestchichtlichen Entwiklung, *Tubigen, 1835.*

It goes without saying that this thesis of Hegel's cabalisation is of fundamental importance in the present book. Hegel is the maturity of modern culture. And to prove that Hegelian thought is a transposition of the Kabbalah is tantamount to proving that the whole of modern culture is Kabbalistic.

Finally, I must say a word with regard to the different spelling of the Hebrew words. Care has only been taken to use the correct spelling in Drach's work, which is reproduced in the second chapter under the title of "Christian Interpretation of the Kabbalah" and which runs from page 49 to 71. There it was necessary to reproduce Hebrew words written in Hebrew characters. In the rest, which fills all the chapters of the present work, no uniform criterion has been maintained, but the different spelling has been used according to the different author, from whom, as the case may be, the Hebrew words have been taken.

The present book expands and systematises, in an outline of a Theology of History, my previous works, especially The Church and the Modern World. *This Theology of History revolves around the problem-axis which moves History in the present providence and which is the problem of the Synagogue-Church dialectic. The Kabbalah is the most significant thing about the Synagogue, and therefore its projection into History constitutes the strongest and most dynamic thing that gives meaning to the whole life of the Church. It goes without saying that the polemical character that the thesis of the present book may take on must be placed at the summit where the whole of History unfolds, which, in the end, as the genius of St. Augustine has marvellously seen, is a polemic between the City of God and the City of Man.*

It only remains for me to thank the editors of Gershom Scholem, Claude Tresmontant, A. Koiré and F. Secret, who have authorised me to make extensive use of the books cited in this work. My thanks also go to my dear friend Father Cornelio Fabro, from whose Introduzione all'atheismo moderno *I transcribe important paragraphs.*

CHAPTER I

THE JUDEO-CATHOLIC TRADITION AND THE GNOSTIC-KABBALISTIC TRADITION THROUGHOUT HUMAN HISTORY

The two oral traditions

The natural-supernatural truths stem from a tradition communicated by God directly to man from the first day of human existence. This tradition is partly recorded in writing in the books of the Old and New Testament. We call this the Judaeo-Catholic tradition. For it is the tradition which is faithfully preserved first among the people of Israel, as long as they accept the rule of Yahweh, and then in the Roman Catholic Church, especially in its public magisterium. Strictly speaking, this tradition predates the existence of the Jewish people, which begins with Abraham and Moses. The Judeo-Catholic tradition to which we refer is that of the great patriarchs of humanity, that of Adam, Seth, Noah, Abraham, Isaac and Jacob. We call it Judeo-Catholic and not Judeo-Christian in order to avoid the misunderstanding to which the name "Christian" is subjected in modern language[1].

We also say that this Judaeo-Catholic tradition contains natural and supernatural truths. We call natural truths those which can be arrived at by the rational nature of man by making good use of his reason. These truths have been expounded in detail by Claude Tresmontant in a series of valuable works[2] and are the existence of a transcendent, personal, intelligent and free God, who has created the world, not out of its

---

[1] See my work *De Lamennais a Maritain*, Ed. Theoria, 2nd ed. p. 278.
[2] *Estudios de la metafísica bíblica*, Editorial Gredos, Madrid, *1961*; *Les idées maitresses de la métaphysique chrétienne*, Aux Éditions du Seuil, Paris, *1962*; *La métaphysique du christianisme*, Aux Éditions du Seuil, Paris, 1961; *La métaphysique du christianisme et la crise du treizième siècle*, Aux Éditions du Seuil, Paris, *1964*.

substance but out of nothing, and the existence of a strictly spiritual soul, created at the moment of the animation of the human composite and which, at death, separates from the body to render an account to God for its earthly actions. Strictly speaking, these truths are part of the metaphysical heritage of humanity. We argue, then, that the Judeo-Catholic oral tradition contains a metaphysics, i.e. the natural metaphysics of human intelligence.

In addition to natural and rational truths, the Judaeo-Catholic tradition contains supernatural truths, that is, truths to which man can only attain by a revelation from God. These truths consist especially in the two great mysteries of Christianity, that of the Unity and Trinity of God and that of the Incarnation, Passion and Death and Resurrection of Our Lord Jesus Christ. These two mysteries include, in turn, that of the destiny of man, who is ultimately called to be united with God in this life by faith, hope and charity, and, in the next, by the intuitive vision of the divine Essence.

This oral tradition communicated by God to man on the first day of his existence in the earthly paradise was immediately distorted and falsified by man's rebellion. The Judeo-Catholic oral tradition gave rise, under the instigation of the evil spirit, to a gnostic-cabalistic tradition. We use these terms, as we will explain later, in a pejorative sense. There can be a good gnosis and a good cabala. The Judaeo-Catholic oral tradition is the good gnosis and the good cabala. But the prevailing usage of gnosis and Kabbalah attributes a pejorative meaning to them. As we will determine later, gnosis and kabbalah are called any conception of God, the world and man which assigns a single, homogeneous substance to these three realities. It starts from an indeterminate God - from Chaos, Silence, the Abyss - a God who contains the yes and the no, the evil and the good, the masculine and the feminine, and who becomes the world and man. Man would be, in the Gnostic-Kabbalist conception, the culmination of the emanative process of the universe. It is clear that such a conception alters and perverts the natural and supernatural truths of the Judaeo-Catholic oral tradition.

The characterisation of these two oral traditions, the good and the bad, the Judaeo-Catholic and the Gnostic-Cabalistic, is linked to the problem of human knowledge; the Judaeo-Catholic oral tradition assumes the value of reason and metaphysical reason and, in addition, the value of the assent of faith. The value of reason is based on the teaching of St Thomas, who maintains that "our understanding naturally knows being and the things that are of being as such; and on this knowledge is based the knowledge of first principles, such as, for example, that one cannot simultaneously affirm and deny a thing, and so others"[3]. In other words, human reason, when it proceeds rightly, is determined by reality and especially by extramental reality. The subject is determined by the object which is connected with reality and depends on it. The intellectual subject, when it proceeds properly, attains objective and real truths. It attains first of all the knowledge of the material essences[4] and, from these, also the knowledge of the human spiritual soul and of God. This knowledge, though very extensive, is, however, limited. It cannot know the divine essence and the truths contained therein[5]. Only if God deigns to reveal these truths to him can man have access to them. The Judaeo-Catholic oral tradition teaches that God has deigned to transmit the revelation of the great divine mysteries to man, and that man can know them by the act of faith, that is, by an act of firm and certain assent to God's teaching. Thus, by reason and faith, man can come to know the Judaeo-Catholic tradition. In this tradition man *receives* through reason and faith the natural and supernatural truths, the acceptance and fulfilment of which assure him of the eternal destiny of his existence.

In the gnostic-cabbalistic tradition, on the other hand, man, far from *receiving*, elaborates and constructs a whole system of fictions that refer to God, the world and man. These fictions are not based on reality, but on the *subjective* construction of the human understanding and imagination. Therefore, in the Gnostic-Kabbalistic tradition, the subjective and the immanentist predominate over the objective and the transcendent.

The Judeo-Catholic tradition

Having made these preliminary clarifications, we are going to enter into our subject and expose the two oral traditions of humanity, the good and the bad, the Judeo-Catholic and the Gnostic-Kabbalistic.

At the dawn of humanity the first man receives the revelation of the mysteries of God. The traditional theology of St. Thomas Aquinas considered the first man to be in a state of the highest perfection, so that

---

[3] *Contra Gentes*, Book II, ch. 83.
[4] *Sum*, 1, 79, 3.
[5] Ibid., all of question 12 of part one.

he could be the beginning of the others not only by bodily generation[6], but also by instruction and government[7]. That is why St. Augustine says:

> "Perhaps in the beginning God spoke to the first men in the same way as He speaks to the angels, enlightening their intelligence with immutable truth, although without granting them as much participation in the divine essence as the angels are capable of receiving"[8].

In addition to a very high knowledge, God had placed Adam in a state of innocence[9]. This consisted in the rightness by which reason was subject to God, the lower faculties to reason, and the body to the soul. The first subjection was the cause of the other two, for, inasmuch as reason remained subject to God, the lower faculties were subject to Him. The gift of the first subjection of all nature to God was secured by the supernatural gift of grace, which was the root of the other subjections. The subjections by which the lower powers were subject to reason and the body to the soul were secured by the gift of integrity and impassibility.

This state of innocence assured man perfect dominion over all visible things, both animate and inanimate. Commenting on these passages of

---

[6] According to this theology, the evolutionary hypothesis, according to which man came by transformation from lower animal species, becomes very difficult if not impossible. Evolutionism, although not an impossible hypothesis, is not proved by the facts and is rather repudiated by them. Indeed, biology, especially genetics, proves the impossibility of a species coming from a different species. And palaeontology is, so far, an arbitrary construction that is not based on properly verified facts. A typical case is provided by Professor Hurzeler, who in an interview states: "My discovery of the oreopithecus differs the origins of man by 60 million years". And there are pictures of the Oreopithecus (12,000,000 years old), the Australopithecus (less than a million years old), the Pithecanthropus (less than 300,000 years old), Neanderthal man (less than 80,000 years old) and Cro-Magnon man (less than 30,000 years old). But the article ends with this confession: "To be sure, there is no lack of authors in palaeontology who accept macromutations; it is the easiest way to solve the problem (of the evolution of species). But so far there is no proof at all" (*Realités*, March 1964). See for this question my book *Teilhard de Chardin o la religión de la evolución*", Ed. Theoria, Buenos Aires, 1965.
[7] I, 94, 3.
[8] I, 94, 1.
[9] I, 95, 1.

Scripture in which man is given *dominion* over creation, St. John Chrysostom says:

> "It is manifest here that man had at first a full and perfect dominion over the beasts. That we now fear them, and that they frighten us, and that we do not have this dominion over them, I do not deny either. But this does not claim falsehood in the divine promise, for at the beginning it was not so, but on the contrary, the beasts trembled and reverenced their lord. But we lost this principality since we broke our obedience to God".

In addition to these gifts of perfect innocence, Adam was given the privilege of immortality, that is, the power of not dying.

In the theological tradition of the Church, Adam's communication, before sin, was habitual with God. There was, therefore, a revelation of God to man. In this revelation, God had made known the great mysteries of the Trinity and the Incarnation. God had made known his infinite transcendence above creation. He would have revealed to man the supernatural mystery of grace and glory fixed to man. Man can enter into the divine life of the Trinity, but not by merit or by his own strength, but by the free gift of grace. St. Thomas[10] clearly teaches that "before sin man had explicit faith in the incarnation of Christ, in so far as it was ordered to the consummation of glory, but not in so far as it was ordered to liberation from sin by the passion and resurrection, since man was not aware of future sin".

The knowledge of the mystery of the Incarnation was given to man in the natural sacrament of marriage. "For this reason a man shall leave his father and mother and cleave to his wife", as *Genesis* says (2:24) and the Apostle makes clear *(Ephesians* 5:32): "A great sacrament in Christ and in the Church". Which sacrament, teaches St. Thomas,[11] it is not credible that the first man was ignorant of it.

Hence it must be affirmed, as a certain and certain truth, that in Adam begins a tradition or good cabal which brought to man's knowledge natural and supernatural truths necessary for his salvation. These truths are: the existence of a personal creator God endowed with intelligence and will. This God creates the world out of nothing by a free act of his will. He creates it as he wills, according to the ideas or exemplary forms

---

[10] 2-2, 2, 7.
[11] 2-2 2 7.

existing in the divine mind[12]. The human soul is a strictly spiritual reality, also created by God, at the moment of the production of each human being.

In addition to these natural truths, God communicates to man the mystery of the Trinity and the mystery of the Incarnation and of man's destiny to share in the life of grace and glory.

Man can attain a *divine* state, not by nature but by adoption, not by his own merits, but by a generous and gratuitous gift of divine goodness.

These natural and supernatural truths of divine Revelation have been systematised in an incomparable and in a certain way definitive way by the genius of St. Thomas Aquinas. St. Thomas has reached the true pinnacle of metaphysics, namely, that of determining as the proper form of God that of subsistent being - *esse subsistens* - and as the ultimate truth of theology the contemplation in an act of intellectual vision of the divine Trinitarian essence. He has also succeeded in harmonising in a perfect and balanced system the relations of nature and grace, of natural and supernatural order, of world and Church, of metaphysics and theology.

The three economies of the Judaeo-Catholic tradition.

This good tradition or cabala is communicated to man in three economies. An *oral* or natural law economy; a *written* or Mosaic law economy; and a third *evangelical* or law of love economy.

The first revelation, at the origin of the human race, is all oral and is therefore transmitted from generation to generation for a thousand years before it is translated into writing and *inserted into the natural law* in Adam himself, continuing through various strands of the peoples; the other is that which begins with Abraham, taking shape with the covenant of the Covenant, which only under Moses will be expressed in the written law, and after Moses in the prophets and other writers[13].

In the line of the Gentiles, which is that of Adam, Revelation is explicit as to the Incarnation and, consequently, as to the Trinity,[14] according to

---

[12] 1, 44, 4.
[13] *J. Scaltriti O. P.*, Rivelazione e Magistero, *in* Renovatio, 2-67, *p. 205.*
[14] 2-2, 2, 8.

the reason of good and evil and is *justified in the Christ who is to come;* In this line there were authentic sacraments, according to divine inspiration in conformity with the rule of human acts, which is the natural law, whence are such sacraments "according to the bread and wine" of Melchisedech, clearly inspired by God, as Abraham shows, who pays the tithe to that priest of the most high God[15].

In the line of Abraham, which is that of the chosen people, Revelation takes the way by which redemption will in fact come, involving "a more express knowledge of Christ according to the intensity and remission of sin"[16]. In addition to the line of natural law, but not contrary to it, Revelation after Abraham will teach, always in the form of symbols, that the Christ will be the ruler of the nations, Son of God, victim of the burnt offering, Author of a new creature; which will be His Church, the true people, His Mystical Body, in which the burnt offering of Christ will be renewed collectively and one by one in its members, in order that the merit of the one mediator, Jesus Christ, may be applied to the whole human race. All this in the form of figures and in an almost implicit way. [17]

The Second Vatican Council recognises the three economies of the Judeo-Catholic tradition

These three economies of the Judaeo-Catholic tradition, i.e. of the Church, have been recognised in the recent Second Vatican Council. There, the Church becomes aware of her own depth and latitude and in the document "Lumen Gentium" appears as *the secret hidden in the centuries,* whose dissemination and illustration among the peoples was entrusted to St. Paul as his Gospel[18]. There the mystery of the Church appears as the key to the whole successive tradition and as the motif of the progressive Revelation, transmitted orally in the vast stage of the history of the human race before Christ.

---

[15] *Genesis,* 14, 18.
[16] 3, 61, 3, ad. 2.
[17] Scaltriti O. P., Jacinto, *Rivelazione e Magisterio,* Ibid.
[18] Ibid.

> "The Church is in Christ as a sacrament or sign and instrument of the intimate union with God and of the unity of the whole human race..."[19].

Such a concept is then developed by the same constitution in chapter II, the People of God [20], and is taken up in chapter VII [21] in the eschatological prospective of the whole redemptive plan, when the two strands of tradition - in the line of nature and therefore of the Gentiles, in the line of the Law (Old and New) and therefore of the Chosen People in figure (Israel) and no longer in figure (the Church of the baptised) will have finalised God's design through the infinite dialectical combinations of the reversibility of merits, and Jesus Christ will return the second time in the glory of universal judgement[22].

> "The Church to which we are all called in Christ Jesus and in which, through the grace of God, we acquire holiness, will have its fulfilment only in the glory of heaven, when it will see the time of the restoration of all things[23], and when, with the human race also the whole world, which is intimately united with man and through him comes to its end, will be perfectly restored in Christ"[24].

This concept is taken up again by all the other documents of Vatican II; in the Constitution on the Liturgy[25] ; in the Constitution on Divine Revelation[26] ; in the Constitution Pastoral "Gaudium et Spes"[27] ; in the Decree on the Missions[28] ; in the Decree on Ecumenism[29] ; in the Decree on the Apostolate of the Laity[30] ; in the Declaration on Christian Education[31] ; in the Declaration on the relations of the Church with other non-Christian religions[32].

---

[19] Lumen Gentium.
[20] Ibid., nos. 8 to 11.
[21] Ibid., no. 48.
[22] Scaltriti, O. P., ibid. p. 207.
[23] Acts, 3, 21.
[24] *Col.* 1. 10; 2 *Pet.* 3, 10-13; *Lumen Gentium*, no. 48.
[25] Nos. 1 and 5.
[26] N. 8.
[27] N. 42.
[28] N. 1.
[29] N. 2.
[30] N. 2 and 3.
[31] N. 2.
[32] N. 1.

The "Logos" of Plato and the beauty of Athens, the law of Rome and the poetry of Virgil, before being written things, are the continuing genius of the "Humanitas" which suffers the pains of generation, in the expectation of the revelation of the Sons of God: "And the man who, knowing his own sickness, cries out to the physician and claims the help of grace"[33].

And even in the line of Israel, when the Scriptures are about to be fulfilled, there is still a "voice"[34] that establishes contact with the word of God made man: a "voice" that cries out in the wilderness, the voice that for the first time will point the disciples to the Expected One of all peoples: "Behold the Lamb of God, behold the One who cries out the sin of the world"[35]. Only John will record these words in writing seventy years after they were spoken[36].

And in John the Baptist himself, the word of God was together with the "voice" of tradition when he was still growing in his mother's womb before the Visit of the One who carried in her virginal and immaculate womb the promised one from the first days of Adam and Eve[37].

In Mary, Tradition was together with the voice of the Angel on the day of the Annunciation, about the things concerning the Christ as Son of the Most High, in the light of the Most Holy Trinity. In the greeting of Mary of Nazareth to Elizabeth, mother of John, it is the voice of Revelation that sanctifies the Forerunner.

And to Elizabeth's recognition, Mary responds with the gift of the *Magnificat* which is the "voice" of Tradition, in the line of Abraham, as she herself says, before all nations, who will call her blessed[38].

It is the word which, born of the Lady, as "seed from Her", crushes the head of the ancient adversary, whose seed is the lie, whose alteration of the Word will be constantly documented as a falsification of the Scriptures[39].

---

[33] St. Thomas, *Summa*, 3, 1, 5.
[34] John, 1, 19.
[35] Ibid.
[36] Scaltriti, O. P., ibid. p. 207.
[37] Luke 1, 41.
[38] Scaltriti, O. P., ibid. p. 208.
[39] Matthew, 4, 6.

The Ancient Kabbalah of the Jews

Kabbalah[40] is written by the most responsible authors in various ways. Diez Macho's "The Encyclopaedia of the Bible" writes Qabbalah; Cecil Roth's "The Standard Jewish Encyclopedia", Kabbalah; Gershom Scholem, Kabbala; Henry Serouya, Kabbale; G. Vajda and Paul Vulliaud in the same form as above; The Jewish Encyclopedia, Kabbala. We, without going into the reasons for the one or the other transcription, will simply write it Kabbala.

The Synagogue possessed, prior to the books of Moses, an *oral* tradition which served in some way as *"soul to the body of the letter";* without which the text ran the risk of being obscure or incomplete, or of lending itself to the vagaries of individual *interpretation.* Never *to this day* would the Synagogue have tolerated this excess of insanity.

Now, while the civil law rested in Israel under the guardianship of the whole nation, the *oral* teaching was entrusted to a special body of doctors placed under the supreme authority of Moses and his successors. "The scribes and Pharisees," said Christ, "sit in the Seat of Moses; therefore observe and do all that they say unto you, but do not do as they do."[41].

And this tradition of the ancient Synagogue was divided into two branches: the one patent was the Talmudic tradition; it was preserved in writing later, and formed a Talmud pure and distinct from those after Christ, and fixed the meaning of the written law. It dealt with the Mosaic prescriptions; one knew from it what was permitted, what was obligatory, what was unlawful; it constituted also the material and practical degree of tradition.

The second branch was its mysterious and sublime part. It formed the Kabalistic tradition, or *Kabbalah,* i.e., according to the etymological sense of this word, the teaching received by the word.

---

[40] On the development of all that is to be read about the two Cabals we take advantage of the valuable appendix entitled: "The two Cabals or the science of traditions", from the book "Le juif, le judaisme et la judaisation des Peuples chrétiens" by le Chevalier Gougenot des Mousseaux, Henri Plon, Paris, 1869. This author has astonishing information on the whole question mainly because of his links with the famous Jewish convert Drach, who wrote: "Harmonie entre l'Église et Synagogue", Paris, 1844.
[41] Mt. 23, 2.

This cabala dealt with the nature of God, his attributes, the spirits and the invisible world. It was based on the symbolic and mystical meaning of the Old Testament, *"which was equally traditional"; it* was, in a word, the speculative theology of the synagogue. *What was essential* in the mysteries *of the Holy Trinity and the Incarnation* was not omitted, *and several rabbis converted to the Kabbalah reading alone*[42]. The doctors of the Synagogue trace the ancient Qabalah back to Moses, while admitting that the early patriarchs of the world had known its principal truths by revelation.

The doctors of the ancient synagogue teach by common voice that the hidden meaning of Scripture was revealed on Sinai to Moses, and that this prophet transmitted this knowledge by initiation to Joshua and his other close disciples. This teaching itself descended at once orally from generation to generation, without being allowed to be put in writing.

Perversion of the Jewish Kabbalah

However, the Egyptian captivity first (1300 B.C.) and then the Babylonian captivity (6th century B.C.) created an immense upheaval within Israel, and the orthodox Kabbalistic tradition was forgotten. Moreover, on the return of the faithful to Jerusalem, it was ordered by God to be written down. But the sixty volumes of which it is composed were not made public, and the prophet was ordered not to entrust them to any hands other than those of the sages[43]. Later, when the times were fulfilled, the guilt of the doctors of the synagogue consisted, not in the indiscreet revelations of the depositaries, but, far from this, in the jealous care they took, and which the Saviour reproaches them with, of hiding from the people the *key of knowledge, the* traditional exposition of the holy books, in whose clarities Israel would have recognised in His sacred person the Messiah[44].

Towards the later days of Jerusalem and when Judea suffered the terrible ravages of idolatry, the cult was miserably invaded by Pharisaism, whose abundant vegetation seriously threatened the whole synagogue. The attention of the doctors was then directed to Talmudic

---

[42] Drach, *Harm*, Vol. I, p. X-XI, 1844.
[43] Drach, vol. II, p. XXI.
[44] *Gougenot des Mousseaux*, Le juif, le judaisme et la judaisation des peubles chrétiens, p. 512.

theology, which existed in the state of oral teaching and regulated the practical and *material* side of religious prescriptions, while mystical and speculative theology fell into disrepute since its Christian tendency was of palpable evidence. This movement was especially accentuated when the crisis aroused by the opposition of the Pharisees to the doctrine preached by the Saviour and His Apostles.

The Talmudic tradition then became what the Talmud calls *the vinegar, son of wine;* and, denatured in its essential part, it received the impure mixture of the fantastic dreams of the rabbis, of their vain subtleties, of their absurd, grotesque, unimaginable tales. A little later, after the dispersion of the Jews, the Rabbis took a taste for the speculations of metaphysics, and, returning to their mystical cabala, introduced an amalgam of Greek and Oriental philosophy whose systems were loudly opposed to the Mosaic revelation. *Such is the modern Kabbalah or Left Kabbalah, or Pharisaic Kabbalah, or magical Kabbalah.*

The rabbis have admitted, almost without understanding them, formulas whose equivocalness lends itself to Greek materialism and Jewish pantheism, or, let us say better, to the sacrilegious vanities of the magic of the Sabæan peoples, given over to the idolatrous doctrines of the descendants of Ham. It was, moreover, in the midst of these peoples that their fathers had lived before Abraham, during the Babylonian and Egyptian captivity, accustomed to mingle unceasingly the worship of the holy God with the cults of demons[45].

If, therefore, by consulting its doctors, the second Kabbalah is of Jewish origin and relatively modern, it goes back to the most ancient times by the magical traditions and superstitions to which it is linked. The Jews, by appropriating them and combining them with their traditions, have stamped them with their own seal.

The Pharisaic cabal indulged in star worship or Sabeism. Strictly speaking, this cult predates Judaism. They are cults from Chaldea, Egypt and neighbouring countries. The Kabbalah, infected with these cults, then penetrates and infects the patriarchal traditions, infiltrates their doctrinal books, settles in their medicine, insinuates itself into their social science, undergoing successive modifications, and finally takes root in their customs. Thus, the Jew, under the eye of whom the Christ

---

[45] Dii gentium, daemonia, Psalm 96, 5. Sabeism is the religion of the ancient Chaldeans and consisted in the worship of the stars.

is born, becomes, in spite of this focus of light and according to the fathers of magic and the Fathers of the Church, the prince of heresy, which magical spiritism impregnates with its poisons, the missionary of evil, the great master of Christian occultism. For "the Cabala, the oracle of the secret societies tells us, is the mother of the occult sciences; and the Gnostics, these heretics who have pushed the errors of intelligence and the perversion of customs to the point of abomination, were born of the cabalists"[46].

Content of the perverted Kabbalah

The world, say the doctors of the Qabalah, has been formed on a mystical plan of the Hebrew alphabet, and the harmony of the creatures is similar to that of the letters which God has used to compose the book of life. It is a certain arrangement of the letters that makes the beauty and excellence of the universe; and since the world has been made according to the dictates of the alphabet, there are necessarily certain things attached to each letter, of which each is the symbol and emblem. This is easily discovered by the initiates of the cabala, but it is necessary for them to distinguish the letters into single and double.

Let us say it by repeating his doctrine: God makes advantageous use of the letters and combinations of his name to work upon the angels; these angels influence the twelve signs of the zodiac; they pour their influence upon the earth and preside over the various generations that succeed one another there. Thus letters ordinarily have an admirable power, not only because they help to discover the analogies of the world and certain harmonies of the universe, that is, of things terrestrial and celestial, which the ignorant would not know how to see, but above all because they are so many other channels through which the action of God works upon the intelligences.

If such is the virtue of letters, what may not be the virtue of their compounds? Thus the Qabalists are strong in obtaining by the arrangement of certain words, in a certain order, miraculous effects; and these words give birth to certain effects, according to the greater or lesser sanctity of the language to which they belong. For this reason, the Hebrew language has an infinite advantage over other languages.

---

[46] Ragon, *Maçonnerie occulte*, p. 78, Paris, 1853, quoted by Gougenot des Moussenaux, ibid. p. 516.

The miracles are in proportion to the value of the words which express the name of God or His perfections or His emanations. Hence, the use of preferring for this purpose the names of God or the ten sefirot.

The sefirot are the names, the attributes of God or God Himself in His attributes and the angels who represent these attributes. Of the ten sefirot, seven are the angels of God's presence and three are the splendours of the Holy Trinity. These are the sefirot of the divine Kabbalah.

When the words, and particularly the seventy-two names of God, are arranged in a certain way, they acquire an irresistible force. But if it happens that the words do not contain the meaning in which their power lies, they must be changed, and there are prescribed rules for bringing about this change. Thus speak the cabalists, and for the present we will be content to say that to pronounce on what the Pharisaic cabal contains or does not contain would be an arduous task. But what is not to be wondered at is that its bosom is open to sublime truths; and since we have taken it for a caricature of the true cabala, we express for this very reason, that in deforming itself, it should recall the traces of the august. If the divine mysticism contains in a certain number an incomprehensible virtue, the magic cabala also accumulates innumerable follies on this dogma, on this adulterated belief of which Pythagoras took possession in his peregrinations and of which he remembers the unfathomable antiquity[47].

The initiates of the Kabbalah claim to grasp a fatal linkage between second causes and spirits or higher intelligences. Every creature, they say, partakes of the qualities of a super-eminent being; they devote themselves to find out from which planet that which they have in view depends. They seek at once by what channels the planet and the intelligence shed their influences on this object, and endeavour to separate the secret rings of the chain which binds heaven and earth.

One of their beliefs is that souls are pre-existent to bodies; that, passing through the Sephiroth, they pass through certain spheres, and upon the play of circumstances their fate in this world depends. God, they say, when man is born, dispatches to him a guardian, an angel who directs him according to the inclinations he has received from the planet under

---

[47] Gougenot des Mousseaux, ibid. p. *521*.

which he is born; the Kabalist must devote himself to find out what this genius is.

It is enough for us to see that thanks to these detestable and invincible beliefs, thanks to their innumerable variants, the Jewish cabalists, heirs of the *sidereal* or *Sabbatean* Cabala, whose antiquity goes back to *Babylon, to the sons of Ham,* spread magical doctrines from one end of the earth to the other. With the help of this sidereal magic, the Chaldeans and the men of Judaic Muslim astrology took over pagan Rome and the spirit of its terrible emperors, infested the palaces of kings and filled the castles of the feudal nobility and the mansions of the opulent bourgeois with crimes until times bordering on our own. The Cabala was, therefore, the main root of magic[48].

All truly dogmatic religions, says the professor of magic, Eliphas Levi, in 1861, have come out of the Cabala and return to it. All that is scientific and grandiose in the religious dreams of the enlightened - Jacob Boehme, Swedenborg, Saint Martin - has been taken from the Cabala. All Masonic associations owe their secrets and symbols to it. The Kabbalah alone consecrates the hallelujah of universal reason and of the divine Word, it holds the keys to the present, the past and the future"[49].

In the ceremonies of reception practised by all mysterious societies we find the traces of a doctrine everywhere the same and carefully hidden. And this sacred doctrine, which is found in that of theurgy or of the high magical initiations, is at the same time that of the Cabala which the Jews teach us, after having received the deposit of the Chaldean Sabaeans, who came out of Ham, and who, according to a very authoritative opinion in science, were the heirs of the doctrine of the sons of Cain.

Familiar with Jewish artifices and superstitions, another Father of the Church, St. Epiphanius, teaches us that the Jews mix with their science the demonic arts, that they often do not shrink from murder, and that they put into practice the cabalistic article of faith which Thomas of Catimpré once recalled in these terms: "A very wise Jew, converted a short time towards the faith, affirmed to me that one of his co-religionists, on the point of death, had made this prediction to the Jews: 'You cannot cure yourselves of the shameful disease which afflicts you

---

[48] Ibid., p. 525.
[49] Dogma and Ritual of High Magic, *vol. 1, p. 95.*

except by the use of Christian blood... for human blood is at the bottom of the practices of magic"[50].

Magic needs blood, human blood and human fats to fulfil its rites and to perfect its sacred chrisms, its maleficent ointments, *its sacramentals*, to reach its sacrilegious goal. Here, there and everywhere, according to the times, according to the genius and the degree of civilisation of the peoples, this blood and flesh, the brew and means of mystical regeneration, is needed. And, from the origin of historical times, the Bible itself gives us, on the soil of Canaan, the spectacle of these odious practices, of this sacred anthropophagy, of this flesh and this human blood which the Jews ate and drank with the cabalists of Canaan and whose incantations they demanded to use.

Kabbalah and magic, that is to say, demoniacal means, but employed as *religious or scientific* means, are two things which are constantly reproduced by the Jew in the exercise of the art of curing or predicting the ills of the body. And, in the close examination of the crimes of children committed by Jews, what will most vividly attract the attention of an astute investigator will not always and only be a fierce feeling of religious hatred; it will often be the intention of making human blood and torn flesh serve for magical operations endowed with the virtue of curing evils of body and spirit.

But what is important, and what must be sufficiently emphasised, is that the dream of the cabal conspirators has always been to seize power skilfully and to retain it disguisedly for their own advantage. They were to create a society devoted to self-denial by solemn vows, protected by severe regulations, to be recruited by initiation, and which, alone *the repository of the great religious and social secrets,* would make kings and pontiffs without exposure to the corruptions of power".

This idea was, in turn, according to the Kabbalist Éliphas, "the dream of the dissident sects of the Gnostics or of the enlightened who claimed to refer their faith *to the primitive tradition of the Christianity of St. John.* It finally became a threat to Church and society when a wealthy and dissolute order, *initiated into the mysterious doctrines of the cabala,* seemed ready to turn the conservative principles of the hierarchy against legitimate authority and threatened the world with an immense revolution. Forerunners of the subsequent occult societies, the

---

[50] Gougenot des Mousseaux, *Le juif...*, p. 535.

Templars, whose history is so poorly known, were these terrible conspirators.

The cabalistic doctrine, says Éliphas Levi - who professed it with enthusiasm - is the dogma of high magic and the occult philosophy of magic, concealed under the name of kabbalah, and indicated by all the hieroglyphs of the ancient shrines and of the still little known rites of ancient and modern Freemasonry[51].

The great cabalistic association known in Europe under the name of Freemasonry suddenly appears in the world at a time when the protest against the Church has just dismembered Christian unity. Now, the Masons have the Templars as their models, the Rosicrucians as their fathers, the Johannites as their ancestors. Their dogma is that of Zoroaster and Hermes, their rule is progressive initiation, their principle is equality and universal brotherhood.

The primordial tradition

Humanity has been instructed in the divine mysteries in its very cradle. There is therefore a *primordial tradition*, or Kabbalah, which teaches man the fundamental truths of nature and grace that can save him. However, although the tradition goes back to the cradle of humanity, this does not mean that it is complete and perfected there. Tradition is progressive and is perfected by the three economies mentioned above. Christ Himself is the Perfection of Tradition. Hence the great error of René Guénon's traditionalism[52], which we will consider in due course. Suffice it to say here that the authentic Tradition, the Judeo-Catholic Tradition, does not look properly to the *Past*, but looks *to Christ*. Therefore, all the truths, all the symbols and figures with which these truths are proposed refer definitively to their Divine Exemplar, to Christ, to the Logos made Man. St. Paul teaches this magnificently in *Col.* I, 15:

---

[51] Histoire de la Magie, *pp. 23-24*.
[52] René Guénon's main works are: *Introduction générale a l'étude des doctrines hindoues*, Marcel Riviere, Paris, 1921; *L'Homme et son devenir selon le Vedanta*, Chacornac, Paris, 1941; *Le Roí du Monde*, Edit. Traditionnels, 1939; *La crise du monde moderne*, Bossard, Paris, 1927; *Le Symbolisme de la Croix*, Vega, 1931; *Les etats multiples de l'être*, Véga, Paris, 1932; *Le regne de la Quantité et le signe des temps*, Gallimard, 1945.

> "The image of the invisible God, the firstborn of every creature, for in Him were created all things in heaven and on earth, things visible and invisible, thrones, dominations, principalities, powers, all things were created by Him and for Him. He is before all things and all things subsist in Him. He is the head of the body of the Church; He is the beginning, the firstborn from the dead, that He might have the primacy of all things. It pleased the Father that in Him all the fullness should dwell, and through Him to reconcile to Himself, making peace through the blood of His cross, all things, whether things on earth or things in heaven".

But this Christ-oriented tradition is immediately altered and perverted by the instigation of the serpent, as referred to in Genesis. The serpent, the most cunning of all the beasts of the field that Yahweh God made, said to the woman:

> "God has commanded you that you should not eat of all the trees of paradise? And the woman answered the serpent: Of the fruit of the trees of paradise we eat, but of the fruit of the one in the midst of paradise God has said to us, 'Do not eat of it, nor even touch it, lest you die.'" And the serpent said to the woman, "No, you will not die; God knows that in the day you eat of it your eyes will be opened, and you will be like God, knowing good and evil.

Adam's sin consisted then in the claim to "be like God, knowing good and evil". It did not consist in wanting to be like God by an "all-embracing equality". This did not fit our first fathers; it was an impossible pretension. They wanted to imitate God by copying an attribute that was not theirs to copy. They lusted for "some spiritual good above their measure" and "consequently lusted inordinately after the divine likeness"[53]. "The first man sinned chiefly by lusting after the likeness of God as to the knowledge of good and evil, as the serpent suggested to him: namely, that by virtue of his own nature he should determine for himself what was good and what was evil". He therefore desired a "sufficiency and autonomy" proper to God, who, with his eternal law, sets creatures their limits and, on the other hand, does not allow them to set their own limits. Adam's sin implied the constitution of the order of morality and happiness. Man would be the rule for man. The supernatural order would then depend on man himself. Here the Pelagian heresy, naturalism and humanism of the modern age were

---

[53] 2-2, 163, 2.

involved. Man, arrogating to himself divine attributes of supreme legislator. Therefore, Adam's sin was one of *pride*. And pride is opposed to the humility and obedience of Christ who humbles Himself to the lowliness of the cross *(Phil., 2, 8)*.

Adam's sin was a sin of *gnosis,* of knowledge. Wanting to know in a disorderly way what only God can know. The sin lay within the will, but with respect to an act of knowledge. And this knowledge was an act *that was exclusive to* God. Man wanted to enjoy a *divine prerogative* in knowing, that is, to constitute the order of morality and law. Such an act of *gnosis,* by giving man a divine attribute, made man God. Man rejected all transcendence and remained in the absolute immanence of the human.

> "Angelus in primo suo peccato inordinate diligens bonum spirituale, nempe suum proprium esse, suamque propiam perfectionem, sive beatitudinenm naturalem... ita voluit, ut simul ex parte modi volendi, quamvis non ex parte rei volitae, per se voluerit aversionem a Deo, et non subjici ejus regulae in prosecutione suae celsitudinis" [54]

The angel, as well as man, in his first sin, in disorderly loving the spiritual good, that is to say, his own being and his own perfection to natural happiness, in such a way that, if not in the part of the thing willed, then certainly in the manner of willing it, he willed at the same time separation from God and not to submit to the rule which God had imposed on him in the pursuit of his greatness.

In Adam's sin, then, we have first of all an act of pride, referring to a knowledge or gnosis of his own excellence or sufficiency by which he constituted himself a supreme regulator of good and evil and the source of his own happiness. Sin consisted then in an act of will and intelligence by which man constituted himself omnisufficient and in need of no other, and especially of the Word to fulfil him. He committed this sin under the suggestion of the serpent and at the invitation of the woman. Hence God says to Adam: "Because you listened to your wife...". And God says to the serpent: "Because you have done this, you will be cursed among all the cattle...". Man's gnosis is then regularly mixed with the influence of the devil and sexuality.

---

[54] *Curs. Theol. Salmanticienses,* I. XI d. 10, dub. 1, p. 559.

The result of the first sin was that man became a knower of good and evil, that is, a being of malice. That is why God said: "Behold the man as one of us, knowing good and evil"[55].

This deviation in the very heart of man, which affected *his meaning and his destiny*, could not fail to influence the *tradition* or cabal which God had communicated to man. If man was transformed from an innocent being into a being of malice, the cabala, likewise, was to be changed from good into evil, especially after the crime of Cain.

Fundamental content of the two Kabbalahs or traditions

Hence, two fundamental conceptions of God-world-man have developed throughout history, the one which, in the final analysis, places the source of all good in a personal and transcendent God (*James 1, 17*), and in the face of which man and the world are not in themselves but creators of disorder and ruin, and therefore, in order to be good and obtain salvation, need to subordinate themselves to a Church-Institution which is the law of the people *(Constitution on the Church in Vatican II)*. The other, which, in short, makes man and the world, at the ultimate and deepest root of their being, into something divine, of which God would be nothing but an emanation and epiphenomenon. In this second conception, the Church has no raison d'être, and if for historical reasons it were to exist, it would be nothing but an epiphenomenon or emanation of the world.

In these perspectives, two systems of thought emerge that are well characterised in the following truths or errors respectively.

a) Existence of a personal, intelligent and free God, transcendent to the world.	a') The immanence of God in the heart of man and the world. Atheism or pantheism, which divinises the world or makes the world appear divine.
b) God, the efficient cause of man and the world, whose reality he brings out of nothing.	b') The world and man made of the substance of divinity.

---

[55] *Gen.*, 3, 22.

c) God destines man for divinisation, giving him by grace a destiny that surpasses all the demands of his being.	c') Man is divinised in his nature. Man is God.
d) Man, having lost his primitive divinisation, can recover it by adhering to Jesus Christ, God made man, who, by virtue of his passion and death, restores this divinisation to him.	d') Man draws his divinisation from himself, but Jesus Christ can show him the way how to draw it from himself. Man is in himself a *Gnostic*. Jesus Christ, the first Gnostic, is a paradigm of the divinisation of man.
e) Jesus Christ has instituted in the Church, his mystical body, a means of salvation for man, who of himself and of himself comes in a state of creatureliness and sin. Man, of himself, goes to sin and ruin.	e') Man saves himself and in himself by surrendering himself to the autonomy and freedom of his inner reality, which is divine. He does not need the Church. At least of a Church opposed to the world.
f) There are necessarily, by virtue of the order established by God, two realities, one that does not save man and one that saves him. Man has in the present providence two dimensions, one profane and natural and the other sacramental and supernatural.	f') Since the Church is not necessary for man's salvation, there is no other reality and no other dimension than the purely human and worldly.
g) The Church exists as an institution outside and above the world, by virtue of the merits of Jesus Christ, as of necessity to save the world.	g') There is no society transcendent to man himself and to the world.

Hence, by virtue of these two irreducible conceptions which, like St. Augustine's two cities, extend through history, it is easy to discern truth from error.

The denial of the Church as a health society transcendent to the world implies the affirmation of the other errors. Whoever denies the Church must deny Christ and therefore deny God. This sometimes does not happen immediately, but arises in the dynamics of the centuries, which gradually operate and realise the logic of the city of evil. This is what happened in the Reformation, which, by denying the Church, prepared and opened the way for the denial of Christ and God, and for the current process of secularisation.

The word Church means, in a general sense, the community of the faithful of the New and Old Testaments, who are united in the same substantial faith in a provident God of the supernatural order and in Jesus Christ who has come or is to come, and who share in the same supernatural life originating in the merits of the redemption already accomplished or soon to be accomplished.

In this sense, St. Augustine includes in the universal Church all the just who, from Abel to the end of the world, belong to the Mystical Body of Jesus Christ[56]. Likewise, St Thomas says that the Church *secundum statum viae* for all times of trial, *est congregatio fidelium*[57]. He explains how the faith of the faithful of all times is substantially one, by reason of the explicit faith in these two truths which contain all the others, God provident and Jesus Christ redeemer[58] ; and how the same supernatural life before as after the redemption, comes from the merits of Jesus Christ and is manifested, in both periods, by the same faith and by the same love in Jesus Christ expected and due to redeem us or already come and immolated for us[59].

This Church or Tradition unfolds in three economies: one, of natural law; the second, of Mosaic law; the third, of evangelical or Christian law. St Thomas deals expressly with this in the Treatise on the Law 1-2, 90-108.

Stages of the Jewish perverted Kabbalah

The second cabala, or perverted cabala, begins with sinful Adam and is perpetuated in the Cainite Cabala, before the Flood, and with the Camite Cabala, after the Flood. This Kabbalah develops over three major dates: the first in the 6th century B.C., which coincides with the exile of the Jews in Babylon; the second, around the appearance of Christianity, culminating with Simon ben Jochai, in the 2nd century CE; and the third brings together the fabulous lucubrations of medieval Judaism, German Chassidism and ends with the elaboration of the Sefer-ha-Zohar by Moses of Leon.

---

[56] *Serm.*, CCCXLI, c. IX, n° 11. P. L. XXXIX, col. 1499.
[57] *Sum.*, 3, 8. 4, ad. 2.
[58] 2-2, 1, 7.
[59] 2-2, 1, 7.

Already the Hebrews, taken out of the land of Canaan by Abraham, had the opportunity to infest themselves during the first exile in Egypt in the 14th century BC.

But this defilement was not decisive because of the strong personality of Moses, who fought a tremendous war against it. Hence the Babylonian captivity of the sixth century B.C. must be regarded as more dangerous, for it operated upon a spiritually weakened people, and no strong personality was able to stop the evil influence of Babylonian practices and cults. Thus, the centre and spiritual home of the *Pharisaic Kabbalah* is Babylon, circa 586 B.C., and from there until 1040 A.D., when the last of the Talmudic academies passed from Babylon to Europe, Asia and Africa.

From the Academies of Sura, Nehardea, Nisibis, Pambeditha, Talmudic and Kabbalistic ideas were accepted by the Jews of the world. The Jewish Encyclopaedia devotes an article to the general influence of Babylonia on European Judaism. Luzzato ("Hebrew Letters", p. 865) describes it as follows: "The West received both the written and the oral Law from Babylon. Punctuation and accentuation also began in Babylonia; likewise piyyut, rhyme and metre. Even philosophy had its origin here, for the often mentioned but little known David ha-Babli or Al-Makammez, who lived in Saadia, is the oldest known Jewish philosopher. The greatest if not the oldest payyetan, Eleazar Kalir, of the ninth century, was apparently a Babylonian. It is also true, Luzzato adds, that heresy is a Babylonian product[60].

The mixing of traditions and peoples in the 6th century BC

The Babylonian captivity of the Jews must be seen in the context of the general uprooting of peoples and traditions that took place in the 6th century BC. Of course, contrary to Jaspers[61], we do not accept to make the 6th century B.C. the pivotal time of history. The pivot of history is Christ and Christ alone. However, the exceptional significance of the 6th century in history must be acknowledged. "At that time a multitude of extraordinary events converge and coincide. In China, Confucius and Lao-Tse lived, all the directions of Chinese philosophy appeared, Mo-ti, Chuang-Tse, Lie-Tse and many others meditated. In India the

---

[60] The Jewish Jan., *295-296*.
[61] Karl Jaspers, *Origen y Meta de la Historia*, Rev. de Occidente, Madrid, 1950.

Upanishads appear, Buddha lives, all possible philosophical trends develop, from scepticism to materialism, sophistry and nihilism, as in China. In Iran Zarathustra teaches the exciting doctrine that presents the world as a battle between good and evil. In Palestine the prophets appear, from Elijah, through Isaiah and Jeremiah, to Deutero-Isaiah. In Greece we find Homer, the philosophers Parmenides, Heraclitus, the tragedians, Thucydides, Archimedes. All that these names only indicate originates in these few centuries almost at the same time in China, in India, in the West, without any knowledge of each other[62].

The Jews, who were deported to Babylon in the 6th century, had the opportunity to interact with all the religions and traditions of the world, and therefore with all the pagan gnosis of humanity, the content of which is the same in all of them. We are going to verify this by going through the most ancient gnosis.

Brahamanic gnosis

In the Rigveda, one of the oldest books of Hinduism, the origin of all things is described:

> "Neither non-being existed then, nor being; there was no airspace, no firmament beyond". There was at this time neither death nor non-death; there was no distinguishing mark for night or day. The One breathed of its own impulse, without breath. Apart from this, there was nothing else. Its desire was the original development (desire) which has been the first seed of consciousness"[63].

Here are these texts from the Brihad-Upanishad, 4, 8, 17: "Verily, in the origin, *Bráhman* alone existed. He knew only Himself: I am *Bráhman*. He was All. Then each of the gods was, as they awakened, the thought. So were the rsis, so were men. This is what the seer rsi Vamadeva has declared: "I have been Manu and Surya". The same today, he who says thus:

> "I am *Bráhman*, he who is the All, and the gods themselves cannot prevent it because they are *atman*"[64].

---

[62] Ibid., p. 8.
[63] Émile Gathier, *La Pensée Hindoue*, Éditions du Seuil, Paris, 1958, p. 125.
[64] Ibid., p. 145.

India, in addition to the notion of Brahman, a neutral, impersonal, indeterminate god, to which the *Ein sof* of the Kabbalah must be related, accepted the idea of the transmigration of the individual soul. Here is a text translated by Olivier Lacombe in *L'Absolu selon le Vedanta:*

> "We affirm that the Supreme Lord does not experience the pain of transmigration as does the individual soul. For the soul possessed by Insciousness is constrained by it to enter into a state in which the body, etc., becomes more or less 'its own self', and abusively imagines that it experiences that produced by this Insciousness, saying to itself: 'I undergo the suffering engendered by the body'. But for the Supreme Lord there is no state in which the body appears to him as "his self", no abusive imagination of pain."

The Iranian gnosis

In order to summarise the *Iranian gnosis,* about which so much has been written, we have found it most convenient to translate a few pages of the great modern Iranianist J. Duchesne Guillemin, "Ormazd et Ahriman", Presses Universitaires de France, 1953, Paris, p. 32.

Is this system, first of all, a dualism or a monotheism? From a certain point of view it is a monotheism: Ahura Mazdâh is superior to the two confronting spirits. He is the creator of everything:

> *Who is the first father of righteousness in the beginning? Who hath assigned his ways to the sun and to the stars? Who is he, if not thou, by whom the moon waxes and wanes? Who hath fixed the earth below, and the sky of clouds, which falls not? Who hath fixed the waters and the plants? Who hath joined to the wind and to the clouds their steeds? Who is, O Wise One, the creator of the Good Thought? What artist hath made light and darkness? What artist, sleep and waking? Who hath made the morning, the noon, the evening, to indicate to the intelligent his task?*

From another point of view, the system appears as a dualism: Ahura Mazdâh is declared to be identical with his Beneficent Spirit, and it is indeed he who creates (see the whole Yasma, p. 47); but he creates only a good order, a possible happiness which has thwarted the rebellion of the wicked.

It is men who are responsible for their misfortune, for they are free in their choice; it is also the Evil Spirit, for having set the example of evil action; hence evil has spread through the daivas to man: *You have frustrated man of happiness and immortality.* The evil spirit has inspired you demons with evil thoughts.

In any case, the Beneficent Spirit has nothing to do in this, whether man alone or man corrupted by the evil spirit and the demons, who are the cause of this disaster; therefore, neither has Ahura Mazdâh, since he is identical with him. Thus, then, the world has two masters, two creators...

But, rather than discussing Zarathustra's monotheism or dualism, it is worth noting the ambiguity of his system and remembering that he had other concerns than the theoretical one. His mission was to act and to do work: to reform the rites, to proclaim the new myths"[65].

The Sumerian-Acadic Gnosis

This is an astrological gnosis, Sabeism or the cult of the stars, as we have already noted above. Edward Dhorme in "Les religions de Babylonie et D'Assyrie"[66] explains the character of this cult in this way. What idea, he asks, does one have of the divine personality that is venerated under the most diverse names and that is found under the most varied forms? Scripture teaches us. A determinative sign precedes the ideograms to the words representing men, gods, superhuman beings, genies, demons, heroes. This sign, in the origin, represents a star. When the star is used as a divine determinative, it is given the value of "god", *dingir* in Numidian, *ilum* in Akkadian. But according to the vocabularies, the proper meaning of the sign is the sky, *an* in Sumerian, *shamu* in Akkadian. Whatever the physiognomy of the god or goddess, he or she is assimilated to a celestial being. This is why we find the sky-god An (Sumerian), Anum (Akkadian) at the head of the Pantheon in our study of the gods of the world.

We have seen that the ideogram representing the sky, *an* in Sumerian, *shamu* in Akkadian, also came to mean "god", *dingir* in Sumerian, *ilum* in Akkadian, and that it could be used as a determinative before divine names. The same sign - star - was used to designate the personified sky, *An* in Sumerian, semiitised by the Akkadians in the form of Anum or,

---

[65] See also *La Religion de l'Iran Ancien*, by J. Duchesne Guillemin, Presses Universitaires de France Paris, 1962.
[66] *Les religions de Babylonie et d'Assyrie,* by Edouard Dhorme, Presses Universitaires, 1949, p. 11.

without miming, Anu. In classical cosmogony *Enuma Elish* is the god Anum who first appears as a distinct personality after the principles of being have been dissociated into Ar-shar and Ki-shar, celestial Universe and terrestrial Universe. He emanates from Anshar, becomes first his equal and can rival his parents. He is first in time and space[67].

Egyptian gnosis

Ancient Egyptian religions depict the genesis of created things as if they had not come out of *nothing* by the action of a timeless divinity. The texts allow us to guess the preliminary existence of a chaos, of a "previous world", one could say, which already contained within itself, but in a latent state or under a different disposition, all the "first matter" that was going to be put to work in creation. Better still, the demiurge in potency is as it were drowned in chaos; it must therefore first of all become aware of itself before it can awaken to existence and set to work.

What would this chaotic world look like? Chaos cannot be explained, it resembles nothing, it is, in a way, the negative of the present. Thus speaks a formula in the *Pyramid Text,* when it seeks to deify the deceased king by assimilating him to the demiurge: "(this king was born) when heaven had not taken birth, when the earth had not taken birth, when men "had not taken birth, when the gods had not been begotten, when death itself had not taken birth".

Egyptian texts depict genesis as a placing of the universe we are in - as we see it - but not as a pure coming out of nothing: water already existed[68].

The old Heliopolitan cosmogony is revealed to us by the *Pyramid Text* (2500-2300 B.C.), by the *Sarcophagus Texts* (2300-2000 B.C.), and by the *Book of the Dead* (from 1500 B.C.).

Extracts from the Pyramid Texts

1. *Before Creation:* "This (king) has been placed in the world in the Num, when the sky did not exist, when the earth did not exist, when

---

[67] Ibid., pp. 22-23.
[68] *La Naissance du monde,* Aux Éditions du Seuil, p. 24, Paris, 1959.

nothing (yet) existed that was established, when disorder (itself) did not exist, when this terror that was to be born from the eye of Horus had not (yet) been produced".

2. *Appearance of the demiurge:* "Greetings to you, Atum. I salute thee, Krepi, who hast come from thyself into existence. Thou culminate in this thy name of "hill"! Thou comest into existence in this thy name of Khepri!".

* * *

4. *The solitary creator:* Atum has manifested himself in the form of a masturbator in Heliopolis.

He took his member in his fist; the twins were put into the world, Shu with Tefnut[69].

Hermetic gnosis

The Hermetic Gnosis has been studied especially by A. J. Festugiere[70] and consists of a collection of writings that circulated from the 1st century BC to the 2nd century AD; they deal with astrology, occultism, philosophy, religious revelation, giving an accurate reflection of the syncretistic situation and the philosophical-religious anxiety that pervaded the Roman Empire in the early Christian centuries.

We extract from the "Poimandres", one of the most remarkable hermetic books, the following: 2. "And I said: "But who are you?" "I, I say, I am Poimandres, the Nous of absolute sovereignty. I know what thou wilt, and I am with thee everywhere". And I said: "I want to be instructed about beings, to understand their nature, to know God...". At these words, it changed its aspect and suddenly everything opened up before me in a moment, and I saw a vision without limits, all made light, serene and joyful, and, having seen it, I fell in love with it. And a little later there was a darkness moving downwards, in its turn, hideous and gloomy, which had coiled itself in tortuous spirals, like a serpent, which seemed to me... 5. Yet out of the light... a holy Word came to cover

---

[69] Ibid., p. 46.
[70] *La Révélation de Hermes Trismegiste,* four volumes, Gabalda, Paris, 1950-1954; also, *Hermétisme et Mystique Paienne,* Aubier, Paris, 1967; and also, *Hermes Trismegiste,* ed.

nature, and an unmixed fire darted out of the dank nature in worship into the sublime region...

6. Then Poimandres: "Have you understood what this vision means?" - And I: "Shall I know?" said I. - "This light, he says, is I, Nous, your God, he who exists before the moist nature that has appeared out of the darkness. As for the luminous verb coming out of the Nous, it is the son of God." - "What then?" said I. - "Do you know what I mean by this means: that which in you looks and understands is the Word of the Lord, and your Nous is God the Father: they are not separate from each other, for their union is life." "I thank thee, I said." - "And well, then, fix thy spirit upon the light and learn to know this."

9. Now the Nous God, being male-and-female, existing as life and light, begot by his word a second Nous demiurge, who, being god of fire and wind, fashioned the governors, seven in number, who envelop the sensible world in two circles, and their government is called the Fate.

12. Now the Nous, the Father of all beings, being life and light, begot a Man like himself, whom he loved as his own son. For Man was very beautiful, reproducing the image of his father: for it is truly of his own form that God became loving, and gave him all his works.

14. Then Man... showed Nature below the beautiful form of God. Nature smiled with love, for she had seen the features of this marvellously beautiful form reflected in the water and its shadow upon the earth. But he, having perceived this form like himself present in nature, reflected in the water, loved it and wished to dwell there. From the instant he did so, he fulfilled it and came to dwell in the form without reason. Then Nature, having received her beloved into her, embraced all, and they were united, for they burned with love.

15. For this reason, alone of all beings living on earth, man is twofold, mortal through the body, immortal through the essential Man.

The Hebraic gnosis

In the first centuries of the Christian era, when the Hermetic Gnosis circulated, it was a sort of Greek-Egyptian mixture that brought together all the philosophical-religious syncretism of the time. The Greek thought and sentiment that came from the philosophers and religious men, such as Orpheus, Pythagoras, Plato, the Stoics, to mention a few great examples; the Egyptian mysteries that in one way or another wanted to put us in communication with the divinity, brought a load of all the myths and mysteries of the East, those of Chaldea, Persia, Babylon, and even of India. It is in this milieu that we must place the Kabbalah and the Jew in order to understand its universality and how it, in a certain sense, will be an *expression* of all the religious-philosophical aberrations of all peoples and traditions.

The Hebraic gnosis is slowly being elaborated in this environment, but it remains a secret undercurrent for several centuries. The new discoveries at the Dead Sea will undoubtedly reveal important writings of the *Hebraic Gnosis*.[71] What Gershom Scholem writes in his great book *The Great Currents of Hebraic Mysticism* [72], especially in chapter 2, "The Mysticism of the Merkaba and Hebraic Gnosis", is still relevant today.

"Hebraic mysticism began in Palestine. We know the names of the most important representatives of mystical and theosophical speculation among the teachers of the Mishna belonging to the circle of Jocham ben Zakkày; towards the end of the first century after Christ.

We have good reason to maintain that the greater part, and even the most essential part of their spiritual heritage, was collected in the esoteric conventuals and later in the circles which at the end of the Talmudic period attempted, in a whole literature, to achieve a synthesis of their new religious vision of the world. The authors of these writings do not appear under their own names but under those of Yochanan ben Zakkày, Eliezer ben Hircanos, Aquib ben Yosef Ismael, the High Priest: they are presented as characters of their work, "heroes" of mystical action, representatives and custodians of the secret wisdom[73].

"We know that during the existence of the Second Temple, an esoteric discipline was being followed in Pharisaic circles, in which especially the first chapter of Genesis - the story of Creation, *Ma'aseh Bereshith* -

---

[71] There is no need to stress here the significance of the excavations and discoveries at Qumran for the illustration of Hebraic gnosis. Robert Grant warns in *"La Gnose et les origines chrétiennes,* p. 13, that "the data supplied by Qumran as well as by Nag-Hammadi will bring about a profound revision of the history of Christian origins... The Essenes of the Qumran seem in a certain way linked to the later development of Judeo-Christianity... It must be admitted that in the past, the Jewish element, or more precisely the heterodox Jewish element of Gnostic thought has been neglected and deserves to be valued with too much insistence".
[72] Le grandi correnti..., p. 65.
[73] Ibid., p. 66.

and the first chapter of Ezekiel, the vision of the chariot with the divine throne, the *Merkaba*[74] were the subject of discussion (which in any case was discouraged to be made public).

> "What is the true and proper subject of those very ancient mystical ideas in the Hebraic sphere? There can be no doubt about it: the most ancient Hebraic mysticism is the mysticism of the throne. Here it is not a matter of immersing oneself in meditation on the true nature of God, but in the vision of His appearance on the throne, of which Ezekiel speaks, and in the knowledge of the mystery of this heavenly throne world. The world of the throne means, for the Hebrew mystic, what for the Hellenistic and proto-Christian mystics designated as Gnostics and Hermetics is the *pleroma*, the luminous world of the divinity, with its power, aeon and domination (...) The pre-existent throne of God - which contains within itself in exemplary form all the forms of creation - is the goal and object of ecstasy and mystical vision"[75].

The Hebraic gnosis, which, as Gershom Scholem teaches, was transmitted in the esoteric circles of the Pharisees, will later be recorded in writing. And so writes Gershom Scholem himself: "The most important documents of this movement - in which its original vitality is still affirmed - date back, at the latest, to the 5th and 6th centuries. It is rather difficult to establish an exact chronology, but many indications seem to point to a time before the spread of Islam... Of all this fine material, much has not yet been published.

Some of them are called "books of the Hekhaloth", descriptions of visionary experiences, in the last of which stands the throne of divine glory. One of these writings was published in 1928 under the later period title "Book of Enoch" by the Swedish scholar Rugo Odeberg. More important, however, are the treatises that have been handed down under the name of "Great Hekhaloth" and "Little Hekhaloth", whose Hebrew text is found in current editions and which received a critical reworking, commentary and translation like those of Odeberg... If a history of religions were to consider these works, one of the great contributions to the history of ancient gnosis would have been made[76].

---

[74] Ibid., p. 66.
[75] Ibid., p. 68.
[76] Ibid., p. 69.

For the communication of the mysticism of the Merkaba there were still severe restrictions and it was not to be permitted except by the presidents of the courts or by some category of men designated in Isaiah, 3, 3. Likewise, chapter XIII of the "Great Hekhaloth" lists eight moral conditions for being worthy of initiation: but the novelty lies in the fact that along with these conditions were added criteria, of a somatic type, which had nothing to do with the moral or social conditions of the adept. The dignity of the novice was judged according to physiognomic and chiromantic criteria, to which the revival of Hellenistic physiognomics in the 2nd century BC must have contributed[77].

... "Those who, according to the above criteria, were deemed worthy, could prepare themselves for the "descent" to the Merkaba, which after a perilous journey through the seven heavenly palaces... led them to the throne of God. This pilgrimage through heaven, its preparation, its technique and the description of what is seen in its course, all this constitutes the content of the writings on the mysticism of the Merkaba[78].

"Originally we had a Hebraic variation of the ascension of the soul, which was one of the aims of the mysticism of the Gnostics and Hermeticists of the second and third centuries; the soul of the earth - through the spheres of the angels of the hostile planets and lords of the cosmos - reaches its divine abode in the calm of the world of God's light. This idea of ascension has been considered by some scholars to be the central idea of gnosis. The description of this pilgrimage, which appears throughout the "Great Hekhaloth" part two, chapters XV to XXIII, has in general and in particular a gnostic character[79].

"*In* addition to this visionary mysticism of the Merkava, another of a speculative nature is found in the writings compiled under the title of *Ma'aseh Bereshit*. These texts comprise the attempt at a mystical cosmology and cosmogony: the aforementioned *Sefer Yetzira* or 'Book of Creation' which, judging from its style and terminology, is closely related to the Merkava mystique. A short volume, it is difficult to

---

[77] Ibid., p. 73.
[78] Ibid., p. 74.
[79] Ibid., p. 74.

establish when it was written, although it was probably written between the 3rd and 4th centuries.

It represents the first speculative attempt at writing in Hebrew. Its solemn, and often very vague and obscure, style is characteristic of a text of mystical meditation: it is therefore not surprising, being sometimes pompously ambiguous, sometimes lapidary and divinatory, that so many medieval philosophers and kabbalists have taken it into consideration[80].

"This little book deals with the elements of the world. As such it indicates the ten primordial numbers - called *Sephiroth* - and the twenty-two letters of the Hebrew alphabet. These represent the secret forces from whose encounters are born the various combinations which then gave rise to creation; they are "the thirty-two secret ways of wisdom" by which God has produced that which exists. The *sephiroth* do not represent ten stages: the thing is not so simple; on the contrary, "their end is in their beginning, and their beginning is in their end, as the flame belongs to the coal - shut thy mouth that it speak not, and thy heart that it judge not. After the author has distinguished the functions of the *sefirot* in the cosmogony, or rather, after he has surreptitiously alluded to them, he elaborates on the secret functions of all the letters in particular: "(God) devised them, fashioned them, combined them, weighed them, and blended them, and by means of them brought about the whole creation and all that was destined to be created"[81].

"But Hebraic gnosis was not speculative. Between the book of Yetzira and magic and liturgy there was a close relationship. In esoteric circles, beyond the static asceticism before the throne, there is another practice, very close to magic; for example, "putting on the name", a complicated ceremonial rite in which the magician, so to speak, imbues himself with the great name of God as soon as he symbolically wears a cloth on which a name has been written. The invocation of the prince or ruler of the Torah, *Sar Tora*, also belongs to this category. Such rites procure a knowledge that is fundamentally acquired through the vision of the Merkava, which in some cases is revealed by a voice coming from the fire of the throne, while in others it is revealed by the "Prince of the Torah": the secret of heaven and earth, the measure of the dimensions of the demiurge and the secret names whose knowledge gives power

---

[80] Ibid., p. 103.
[81] Ibid., p. 104.

over all things. Incidentally, these magical rites also promise a greater understanding of the Torah, the main feature of which is that the addict can no longer forget it and other such things which for the mystics of the Hekhaloth were evidently important but not in such a vital way, since they sought to conform to rabbinic Hebraism, and thus in the "Great Hekhaloth" clearly accentuated the links with the halakhic tradition. In this theurgic doctrine one finds, to a large extent, magic and ecstasy. The theurgic element is elaborated in a series of writings which have various points of contact with the treatises of the Hekhaloth, such as, to cite one example, *Moshe's Charbah*, the Sword of Moses, Rabbi Aqiva's *Havdala*, and the prescriptions prescribed in the book *Shimmushé Tehillím*, whose title means "The Magical Use of Psalms". These have made a long career in Hebrew folk life and belief"[82].

The Sefer-ha-Zohar

When, in the 13th century, Moses Leo was to record in writing, for the first time, in the Sefer-ha-Zohar, the fullness of the Hebrew gnosis, it was already perfectly mature.

---

[82] Ibid., p. 105.

CHAPTER II

THE VARIOUS INTERPRETATIONS OF THE KABBALAH

The current book of the Kabbalah, especially the Zohar, updated by Moses Leo, brings together in one and the same volume ancient oral traditions, good and bad, those of God and those of the devil, inextricably mixed. It is not possible to discern what corresponds to one and what corresponds to the other. Hence, different interpretations of the Kabbalah are possible, as history in all times, especially after Raymond Lullaby and the Christian Kabbalists of the Renaissance, unequivocally demonstrates. We will therefore give four interpretations of the Kabbalah: one, the Christian one, following the famous converted rabbi, the Chevalier Drach, who has expounded this subject at length in *Harmonie entre et l'Église et la Synagogue;* the second, what we call the naturalistic interpretation, given by the Jewish scholar Gershom Scholem[83]. A third, the occultist, typical of esoteric and occult authors, such as Papus and Éliphas Levi; and a fourth, the Judaic and demonic, as expounded by the Jesuit scholar Monsignor Leon Meurin in *Filosofía de la Masonería,* Editorial Nos, Madrid, 1957.

l. *THE CHRISTIAN INTERPRETATION OF THE KABBALAH*

Of the importance of the Christian interpretation of the Kabbalah, F. Secret's well-documented book, *Les kabbalistes chrétiens de la Renaissance (The Christian Kabbalists of the Renaissance),* [84], gives an account of its importance. It is an impressive work because of the

---

[83] *Le grandi correnti della mística ebraica,* Il Saggiatore, Milan, 1965. In French, Payot, Paris, 1968.
[84] Dunot, Paris, 1964.

number of Christian kabbalists who are reviewed. However, it is worth bearing in mind what the author Paul Vulliaud says about Drach's Christian Kabbalah[85] : "Now, Drach is not a revelator. We mean that he does not reveal to Christians an ignored category of documents: the rabbinical texts. Even if he had not revealed it, Christian science would not have ceased to know what he repeated with his authority as a profound kabbalist. The converted rabbi has made the contribution of all the documentation of the Christian Hebraists. He quotes them at least. But to what degree the homage is deserved is not known. And he regrets, his racial knowledge being a fact, that he has not accomplished the revelatory work that we would have wished. This attitude stems from the traditionalist character of the author and the intellectual trends of the time in which he lived. He considered the Kabbalah only from an apologetic and confessional point of view.

He does not expound it under the theosophical aspect. He does not study the Kabbalah except in relation to Christianity, i.e., with this author, as at the time of the Renaissance, esoteric Hebraism supplies a material of traditional proofs, as this or that religion would supply, and does not itself examine it as a whole. Nevertheless, his book is interesting under more than one heading. Its author had not foreseen the service he rendered against the Christian and especially Catholic opponents of the Kabbalah. How could he dare, after Drach's works, to sustain the heterodoxy of essential points of the esoteric tradition of the Jews?

There were writers who did so, no doubt. They raise the question of whether their complete ignorance is in bad faith". So much for Paul Vulliaud.

And now what Knight Drach says, according to what appeared as an appendix to the book by Papus, Docteur Gérard Encausse, *La Cabbale* sixième edit. Dangles, Paris.

> *"What the Hebrews teach concerning their Kabalah and its antiquity. Principal Doctors of this esoteric science. The Qabalah, first transmitted orally, put in writing in later times. Remaining books of this writing. Unbelievers have tried to distort its meaning".*

---

[85] La Kabbale juive, *p. 246*.

1. The written law and the two oral laws: one legal, the other mystical or cabalistic [86]

The term kabbalah, which in Hebrew means received tradition, qabala, from the verb qbl, indicates that this science is regarded by the rabbis as a traditional teaching. It consists, according to these doctors, of traditions going back to the most ancient times, to Moses and even to Adam. The lawgiver of the Hebrew people, they maintain, has received from God not only the written law, but also the oral law, i.e. its interpretation, both legal, i.e. Talmudic, mystical and Kabbalistic. Indeed, it was never permitted to the Hebrews to explain the word of God differently from the tradition taught by the ancients; ultimately, in doubtful cases, from the decision of the supreme pontiff of each age.

These two parts of the oral law are therefore composed of nothing but traditions and the logical deductions to which they have given rise in order to determine their meaning. No doubt many apocryphal or distorted traditions have crept in, so to speak, by which the Pharisees falsified the meaning of the holy law, and which Our Lord condemned in the severest manner.

But this is the place to recall the rule which I have given in several passages of my works. Here it is: every tradition which bears the stamp of true religion, which, as St. Augustine expresses it, goes back to the cradle of the human race, is undoubtedly authentic. Certainly, the traditions which represent in the Godhead *three supreme splendours* distinct and yet inseparably united in an essence of the most absolute unity; those which established that the Redeemer of Israel would be at once true God and true man; those which taught that the Messiah would offer Himself *to take* upon Himself the atonement for all the sins of men; those which teach us that the Holy One, promised by the patriarch Jacob (Gen. 49:10), is really the Messiah; all things which the doctors of the modern Synagogue obstinately deny. It is certainly not a Rabbi who attempts to give the Zohar the following explanation, which confirms that of the Gospel, Matt. XXI, 4, 5: *the poor man riding on an ass*, prophesied by the prophet Zechariah, IX, 9, is the Messiah son of David.

---

[86] Papus, *La Cabbale, tradition secrète del'Occident*. Éditions Dangles, Paris, 6th Ed., p. 328.

2. Main doctors of the Kabbalah. The Zohar [87]

It was the famous Simeon ben Yohhai, a rabbi of the early second century A.D., who taught the Kabbalah with the greatest impact and trained the largest number of distinguished disciples. The dialect in which he expressed himself is the one used by the Jews of that time, Syro-Syriac-Syriolimitan, to which Latin and Greek terms had already been mixed.

He taught the tradition and doctrine of teachers older than himself, and attributed a great number of them to the prophet Elijah, to Moses, called in the Zohar *the faithful shepherd*, and to the angel Metatron. His disciples and their disciples then busied themselves with putting his lessons in writing, gathering them together in a single body which received the name Zohar, i.e., clarity. This writing evidently lasted for several centuries, or at least for a long period of time it received further additions, for there is mention in it of the two much later parts of the Talmud, the mishna and the ghemara, and also of the false prophet Mohammed. Jewish historians claim that only a small part of this writing has come down to us. Rabbi Ghedalia, in his chronicle entitled Salšelet haqqabala, *Chain of Tradition*, writes: "I know from an oral tradition that this compilation is so voluminous that if it were found in its entirety, it would form the load of a camel...".

3. Treatises and supplementary books to the Zohar [88]

The text of the Zohar, as we have it today, contains numerous treatises which have been successively inserted at different times. Among these treatises is the Seper habbahir, the *Illustrious Book*. It dates from before the birth of Simeon ben Yohhai, for its author is Nehhunia ben Haqqaneh, who flourished between thirty and forty years before the Incarnation. They were published separately afterwards, to complete the Kabbalistic compilation: 1st the Complements of the Zohar; 2nd the New Zohar; 3rd the Zohar of the Song of Songs, the Zohar of Ruth, the Zohar of Lamentations. Among the Kabbalistic books we must not neglect the Seper Yesīra *Book of Creation*, and many other ancient books, a part of which is no longer to be found, hidden among the manuscripts of libraries. The Kabbalistic commentary on the Pentateuch offers extracts from several of these now lost Kabbalistic

---

[87] Ibid., p. 330.
[88] Ibid., p. 331.

books. Also mentioned among the most important books is the Seper Raziēl, *Book Raziel*, which is more of a treatise on theurgy.

True idea of the Kabbalah. Its use in the Synagogue [89]

I am going to set forth what the Jewish Cabala really is, while fearlessly submitting my evidence to the appreciation of every man of good faith and sound judgement. It will be seen that, according to the fundamental doctrine of the Kabbalah, the universe is a creation *ex nihilo* of the infinite power of God.

In fact, every science must have a practical aim. What, then, is that of the Kabalah? The Zohar, the chief code of the Qabalah, part 2, col. 362, and after him all the Qabalists, answers that its object is to teach how one should direct his intentions in supplication to God; to what *splendour* and what *attribute* of God one should have recourse especially in this or that necessity; what angels it is possible to invoke to obtain their intercession in certain circumstances; by what means to save himself from the ferocity of the evil spirits, of whom the air is full.

It is precisely in order to indicate precisely these intentions, these prayers and these formulas, that Rabbi Isaiah Hurwitz, one of the most learned kabbalists of the 17th century, has composed a voluminous kabbalistic commentary on the customary prayers of the synagogue under the title Sa'ar haššamayīm, *The Gate of Heaven*. The consequence follows naturally. The Kabbalah teaches that there is a personal God to whom we should address our prayers, while the pantheistic consider themselves to be God. They assert, with a crowned philosopher of Egypt: *Meus est fluvius meus, et ego feci memetipsum*[90] (Ezek. XXIX, 3).

I have known rabbis who heard for the first time how the Kabbalah was claimed to contain the principles of atheism, and who were astonished. It sometimes happens that, suddenly attacked by a strange, ridiculous proposition, we are stupefied. A mountain of confused answers appears, each one in such a hurry to manifest itself that one does not know where to begin. These rabbis could only exclaim: "But it is not possible, it is madness, folly! What! Our pious kabbalists of all centuries denying the existence of God!

---

[89] Ibid., p. 333.
[90] My river is mine and I made myself.

The doctors of the modern synagogue fear a danger of the opposite nature from the spread of Kabbalistic science. Several of them pronounce anathema against those who publish the books of the Kabbalah. Rabbi Jehuda Arie, known as the *Lion of Modena*, writes in one of his works entitled The Roaring Lion: "And I doubt whether God will ever forgive those who have caused such books to be printed... Indeed, some Israelites, distinguished both for their science and social position, have been led to embrace the Catholic faith because of the mere reading of the books of the Cabala. I have mentioned several of them in my *Harmony*... A disciple of the same Rabbi Arié, *Samuel ben Nahhmias*, of a wealthy Jewish family of Venice, was baptised in his native city on 22 November 1649 under the name of Julius Morosini. This Morosini is the author of a book in Italian, voluminous and learned, whose title is: *The Way of Faith Shown to the Hebrews*, Rome Propaganda Press, 1683, 2 vol. inc. 4°.

1. The emanation of the Kabbalah and the ten sephiroth or splendours. The three supreme splendours [91]

The authors of pantheism have thought to use the cabala to their advantage because it often speaks of *emanation*. By abusing this word, they have made a mockery of a great number of people who are incapable of verifying the pieces of the process. Well, it is precisely this doctrine of emanation that gives the Cabala its eminently Christian character, which no man of good will can fail to recognise. Nothing could be easier than its demonstration.

The Kabbalah distinguishes *all that exists* into four worlds, subordinate to each other. The *atzilutic* (emanative) world. 2. The *bryatic* (creative) world. 3rd The *ietziratic* (formative) world. 4° The *akiatic* world (factitious, factivus). The last three, starting from the creative world, are, as their name already announces, creations of the Essence of God. The texts I transcribe below are explicit.

The emanation stops in the first world, which is the uncreated one and which remains concentrated. It is important to describe this first world according to the Kabbalah. The atzilutic world comprises ten *sefiroth*, i.e. splendours. The first is the supreme crown, Keter'Elyon, also called

---

[91] Ibid., p. 334.

the *Infinite*, 'En sof. From this emanates the second splendour, called Wisdom, Hakema.

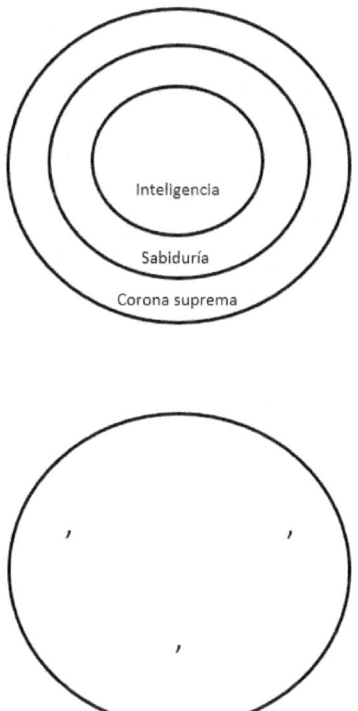

She is the *primitive Adam*, 'Adam Qadmon, so called to distinguish him from the first man.

Let us note that St. Paul calls this incarnate splendour *the new Adam* (1 Cor. XV, 45).

From here, with the concurrence of the supreme splendour, emanates the third splendour, called *the Intelligence* (Bīna).

Such, the Qabalists teach, are the three higher or supreme splendours, the only so-called intellectual ones. Though distinct, they form a single crown, they are *one, an absolute, unum absolutum*. This is why they are represented by these three concentric circles, and why they are called *holy, holy, holy* (Qadoš, Qadoš, Qadoš), by three *yods*, arranged in an equilateral triangle enclosed in a circle.

One would have to be blind not to perceive, or very obstinate not to declare, that these three splendours are the most holy and indivisible

Trinity of Persons in the Divine Essence, *one of the most absolute unity*. The Kabbalah enunciates this truth in identical terms with those of Catholic theology, as will be seen from the fragments I transcribe below. But I will quote a curious text. I do not call it that of a Jewish cabalist, for it belongs to Cicero's treatise *De natura Deorum (*book I, paragraph 21): "Parmenides has imagined something that has the form of a crown. He calls it "stepháne" (in Greek, crown), a continuous, shining circle, enclosing the *sky;* likewise, he calls it God". Do we not see here the three supreme splendours forming a single crown? Let us emphasise that the first splendour encloses the whole sky in its continuous circle without solution. Cicero, not understanding anything of the sublime lesson repeated by the metaphysician of Elea, adds with the sufficiency worthy of a philosopher: "It could not come into anyone's mind that a circle is the figure of the Divinity, nor that it has feelings". Cicero, however, must not have forgotten that the Egyptians and other ancient peoples renowned for their wisdom represented by means of a serpent *coiled in a circle,* with its tail in its mouth, the supreme, eternal, infinite God; in kabbalistic terms, *absque fine,* 'In Soph. The other seven splendours, each emanating from the one preceding it, are: The fourth, *Greatness* (Gedulla), also called *Benignity* (Hesed).

The fifth, *Strength* (Gebura), also called *Rigour, strict justice* (Medet haddīn).

The sixth, *Beauty* (Tif'eret).

The seventh, *Victory* or *Eternity.*

The eighth, the *Glory* (Hod).

The ninth, the *Foundation,* or the *Base* (Yesod).

The tenth, *Beauty* (Malkuth).

These seven splendours form a classification under the generic denomination of *Knowledge* (Da'at). *Knowledge* says Joseph Qicatilla, in his treatise *The Gates of Light,* ša'arê Hora, is the mode of being of the divine representations that come according to the splendour *Intelligence* (Bīna), without forming by itself a special splendour.

2. The seven splendours comprised under the denomination of Knowledge or the divine attributes [92]

It is evident to every accurate spirit that if the first three *Splendours* are God in three persons in the order taught by the Catholic faith, the seven Splendours which follow are, as the Qabalists expressly declare, the *attributes* of God, and, more exactly, God *in His attributes*. Indeed, they comprise all the divine perfections. These splendours are also *emanations*, for the divine attributes are inseparable from the Divinity and constitute a *perfect unity* between them and in God.

That the ten splendours, in Hebrew sepirot, are but the whole; if this expression is lawful, it is also proved by the divine name given to each of them, viz:

The first one is called 'Ehye, *I am the one who is.*

The second, YH, is short for Yahweh.

The third, Yehowī, the tetragram with the vowel punctuation of the divine name 'Elohīm.

The fourth, 'Elo, and according to others, 'El, God.

The fifth, 'Elohīm, God.

The sixth, Yahweh, Yahweh.

The seventh, Yahweh Seba'ot, Yahweh of Hosts.

The eighth, 'Elohīm Seba'ot, God of Hosts.

The ninth, 'El Hay; the living God.

The tenth, 'Adonay, Lord.

I have already affirmed that the divine attributes are inherent in God, as Christian philosophy and theology teach. This is how the coryphaeus of modern theologians, R. P. Perrone, expresses himself: "No distinction can be admitted between God and his attributes, whether absolute or relative, nor between the absolute attributes themselves. For if such a distinction were to be made, real composition would have to be admitted in God, and this composition cannot be made in God, who is completely simple; all real distinction, whether between the Divinity and its absolute or relative attributes, or between the absolute attributes

---

[92] Ibid., p. 337.

themselves, must be excluded from God". *Praelect. theol.*, De Dei simplicitate, Prop. IV.

And lest it should be said that this philosophy of a religious man creeps into the ways of theology, I will quote what is said by a philosopher by no means suspected of excessive zeal for Christian ideas: "First of all, says Bayle, that there is nothing in God which is not God, and therefore his divine attributes are not qualities or perfections distinct from the divine Essence, except as regards our mode of conceiving". *Systema totius philosophiae*, Metaphysica specialis, chap. III, art. 3.

The Evangelist lacks but one word to express this truth, namely, to know that the attributes of God are essentially in God. *Deus charitas est*, says John (I, *Ep.* IV, 16).

3. The Seven Spirits of the Apocalypse, I, 4[93]

The beloved disciple, who has been happy enough to rest his head on the sacred heart of Jesus - recumbens in sinu Jesu - has exhausted in this divine fountain the knowledge of the deepest and most fearful mysteries. I do not hesitate to affirm that I see the ten *splendours* clearly, enunciated in the famous verse I, 4, of his Apocalypse: Gratia vobis et pax ab eo qui est et qui venturus est, a *septem Spíritus qui in pectu throni ejus sunt*. I will not repeat that these three tenses of the verb to *be*, venturus est, are equivalent according to the Hebrew to *erit* and are, if one may say so, like the coinage of the divine name Yahweh, which by its elements admirably expresses the mystery of the Holy Trinity. Serious commentaries have shown that the Apostle designates by these three tenses of the verb par excellence the three adorable Persons of the *one* God; I myself, in my *Harmony*, have developed at length this meaning of the Tetragram. Here, in the first place, are the three *supreme Splendours*. But what I propose to establish here is that the *septem Spiritus* of this verse are really the seven ultimate splendours, that is to say, God in His absolute attributes.

The opinion of those who consider these seven spirits to be angels seems to many to be inadmissible.

For God alone, to the exclusion of every creature, however high it may still be in the heavenly hierarchy, has the right and the power to attain this state of spiritual grace, called *gratia et pax*, *a* verbal translation of

---

[93] Ibid., p. 339.

the Hebrew hen wšalom. These two biblical terms clearly express the happy union of the soul with God; grace: a precious and fragile vessel in the hands of weak men!

The fifth chapter distinguishes the *seven spirits* from the angels in such a way that it would not be possible to confuse them. See verses 6 and 11. In no paragraph of Revelation are the angels called *spirits*. This salutation *gratia et pax* is repeated by St. Paul at the head of almost all his epistles (except the one addressed to the Hebrews), a treasure of Christian theology. The great Apostle attributes this heavenly gift only to God: *Gratia et pax a Deo patre nostro et domino nostro Jesu Christo*. It may be concluded, then, that in our verse of the Apocalypse St. John asks for *grace and peace of soul* for the seven Churches of Asia from all that is in God, his hypostases and attributes.

The preposition *et*, before *Septem Spiritus*, does not distinguish these spirits from what precedes.

Grotius, with his powers of observation, observed that the figure so common among the Hebrews and Greeks of expressing one thing in two ways was given here. In his commentary he explains that the *seven spirits* are the divine Providence which expresses itself in various ways called later (ch. V, 6), *the eyes of God:*...seven eyes, which are the seven spirits of God sent into all the earth", says St. John. Grotius adds: *"And so it was...; vows are made that peace may come from God and from the seven spirits, that is, that it may come from God operating by these seven modes"*. The Apostle of the Word simultaneously declares in his Apocalypse that the Word is God and that consequently the seven spirits are inherent in him as well as in his Father. He expresses himself in this sense when he says in the fifth Letter which he wrote by order of our Lord: *"This is what he says who has the seven spirits of God.* A wise Jesuit, Father Alcasar, author of a voluminous commentary on the Apocalypse, has perfectly recognised that these seven spirits are nothing else, in the literal sense, than the absolute divine attributes. Here is how Cornelius a Lapidus sums up his exposition: "By these seven spirits he understood seven virtues or attributes in which consists the complete perfection of Providence. For these endowments are in God and are in reality *God himself:* whence John *of them* asks for peace and grace for his own. For these virtues are in God immense, they have no end and no limit: for this reason they are called spirits, since John calls angels in the Apocalypse angels and not spirits.

4. The seven dazzling lights in the Apocalypse, IV, 5, and the seven eyes of Jehovah in Zechariah IV, 10 [94]

That these seven spirits are precisely the seven last splendours of the kabalists is something which the text of chapter IV, verse 5, makes incontestable. It is positively stated there that the seven spirits are the *dazzling* and resounding *lights* of the fires that shine before the heavenly throne. *Et de trono procedebant fulgura et voces et tonitrua, et septem lampades ardentes, ante thronum, qui sunt septem spiritus Dei.* This whole verse is about one thing, as stated above. These lights, attributes, modes, of the Providence of God are called in Zechariah IV, 10, the seven eyes of Jehovah which walk over the whole earth. St. John the Apostle declares in his turn that *eyes* are the *spirits* of God. *Et oculos septem (scil Agni tamquam occisi) qui sunt septem spiritus Dei, missi in omnem terram.* The kabbalists maintain that according to the text of Zechariah, the seven splendours were represented by the seven luminaries of the candlestick of the Temple; Finally, what confirms that this is the meaning of the seven spirits of St. John is that the Apostle, in Chapter V of the Apocalypse, after having attributed to the lamb to repeat the *Deus erat Verbum* of his Gospel, gives in verse 12 the exact numbering of the seven splendours: 1, Virtus; 2, Divinitas; 3, Sapientia; 4, Fortitudo; 5, Honor; 6, Gloria; 7, Benedictio.

It is seen from the above that commentators of great authority have thoroughly recognised in these spirits divine attributes. Eichorn, who in the eighteenth century became famous for his great works on the Bible, took the last step with his Introduction to the New Testament. In volume one, page 347, he does not hesitate to declare that the seven spirits of the Apocalypse belong to a *sephirotic* system of the Cabbala. "Cabbalististischid sind, he says, die sieben Geister Gottes".

Such, therefore, is the atzilutic world of the kabbalists, the *uncreated* world alone, i.e. God with his relative attributes and his absolute attributes (his perfections, as *one* God).

These first ten sefirot are therefore an indivisible whole. "Mystery of mysteries from the first of days, says the Zohar, which has not been revealed even to the angels". It is the *Deum nema vidit unquam* of St. John, chap. IV, 18. Neither have the angels, say the Fathers of the

---

[94] Ibid., p. 340.

Church, for we are dealing here with what theologians call *comprehensive vision*.

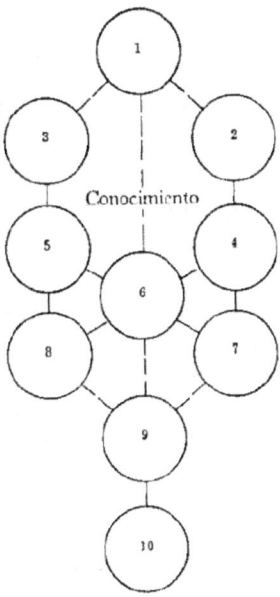

5. The cabalistic tree. Et nolite tangere [95]

The most common figure by which the ten Sephiroth are represented is known as the *Kabalistic tree*, and is reproduced on the following page. The various worlds, the categories of angels, both good and evil, are equally distinguished into ten *Sephiroth*. Each Sephiroth, in turn, has an even ten Sephiroth. This results in an unlimited number of kabalistic trees. This is called the *orchard* (Pardes). This is why the Qabalists teach that whoever seeks to draw from this system erroneous doctrines, *destroys the plants,* and that to attempt to scrutinise these sublime mysteries is to *enter the orchard.*

The Talmud, treatise Ilhaghiga, fol. 14, mentions four individuals who have dared to *enter the orchard*. The first suffered a sudden death. The second, mental alienation. The third *destroyed the plants* and, despite

---

[95] Ibid., p. 342.

his profound knowledge of the holy doctrine, became impious and died impenitent. The fourth retired in time and suffered no accident.

I will gladly quote here these words from the admirable book The Imitation: "If you do not understand and comprehend what is below you, how can you understand what is above you?

The Kabalistic rabbis of the Middle Ages did not turn away from these exemplary punishments, and agitated questions as curious as they were dangerous. Among other things, they asked themselves: God filling all space, where could the supreme Crown, the cause of causes, have caused some other sefira, for example the first, to emanate from Himself? It is like asking: where could the immensity, the ubiquity of the Father have begotten the Son? They answer that *the Infinite* has effected a kind of contraction upon itself, that it has withdrawn into itself, without space being deprived of its light. It must be agreed that *to enter the garden in the* most reckless manner, and to raise such questions, comes very near to *destroying the plants.*

Moreover, the kabbalists were too *rabbinical* to understand that in the divine atzilutic essence the existence of the *Cause of causes* and the generation or procession of *causes, causatorum,* are coeternal, without beginning or end, *nihil prius aut posterius.*

> "Gloria santissimae et individuae Trinitati, Patri et Filio et Spiritui Sancto; sicut erat in principio et nunc et semper, et in saecula saeculorum. Amen".

6. *Extracts from Kabbalistic books*[96]

Warning to the reader

I take these extracts only from books which enjoy unquestioned authority. I could have multiplied their number to the point of making up a large volume; but I limit myself to those which are sufficient to provide evidence for my subject. The texts of the cabalists of the Middle Ages sometimes contain obscurities which I have not always been able to remedy in this translation, which I want to be scrupulously accurate. In certain passages, however, I have taken the liberty of adding one or two words to clarify the meaning. The rabbis themselves often express themselves in a way that will displease Catholic theologians: it must be

---

[96] Ibid., p. 344. Here we continue quoting the converted Rabbi Drach.

remembered that if the substance belongs to the verbal tradition, the style belongs to the rabbis who put it in writing.

The first volume of my "Harmony" contains a good number of texts which have a bearing on our subject. As this work is, thank God, very widely distributed, I shall confine myself to referring to it.

I. Zohar, part 3, column 307: There are *two* to whom *one* is joined, and they form *three;* and being *three* they are but *one*. These *two* are the two *Jehovahs* of the verse, *Hear, O Israel*, etc. *(Deut.* VI, 4).

'Elohênu *(our God)* is united. And it is the seal of the Seal of God: TRUTH. And being united together they are *one in* the *one unity*.

It is the *Unissime* de San Bernardo.

II. Idem, part 2, col. 236, on the text of Deut. quoted: Yahwê 'Elohênu Yahwê 'ehad (Yahweh, our God, is the one Yahweh). "Of a single unity, of a single will, without any division".

III. Idem, on the same text: "The first Yahweh is the supreme point, the beginning of all things. Elohênu, mystery of the coming of the Messiah. The second Yahweh joins the one on the left in a single whole".

IV. Idem, col. 116: "Come and consider the mystery of the name of Yahweh. There are three degrees, and each of these degrees is distinct, and yet it is a single whole, interwoven in unity, degrees inseparable one from the other".

The Kabbalah often uses the expression *degrees* by *hypostasis*, according to our theology. The same is found in the Fathers of the Church. Tertullian, for example, writes: "Tres autem, non statu sed *gradu;* quia unus Deus, ex quo et gradus isti, et formae et species, in nomine Patris et Filii et Spiritus Sancti", adv. praxam, chap.

V. Idem, part 3, col. 131. "The hidden ways, the unfathomable *lights*, the ten *words*, all emanate from the lower point below the aleph. The *Sephiroth* emanate from the free will of God. The *Sephiroth* are not creatures, but *notions* and *rays* of the *Infinite*, consequently, eternal as the Infinite itself".

It is little more than superfluous to underline that *ways, lights* and *words* in these and other places in the Kabalah signify *Sephiroth*. The letter aleph is especially the symbol of the *Infinite* itself. The Zohar insists on the point.

VI. Idem, 3rd part, col. 302: "The Most Holy, praised be He, possesses three worlds in which He keeps Himself hidden. The first is the supreme world (the atzilutic), the most mysterious which could not be seen or known except by Him who hides Himself there. The second is the one that approaches the supreme world (the brythic). The third is below the first two, separated from them by some distance. This is the world where the angels of the heights are (the ietziratic).

Somewhat further, the Zohar, dealing with the fourth world (the asiatic) says: "Come and consider that if man had not sinned he would not taste of death in this lower world when he must rise to the other (higher) worlds; but because he has sinned he must taste death before he rises to those worlds. The spirit is separated from the body which remains in this lower world, and the spirit is at once purified according to its guilt; this done, it enters the earthly paradise. It is fitted with another garment, luminous, but in form and appearance entirely similar to that which it had in this world.

Something similar to *purgatory* is observed. In Part 3 the Zohar teaches the *eternity* of the sorrows suffered by the wicked dead in impenitence. "Those who descend into *horror*, it says, *will never enjoy God;* for those who descend into *horror* remain forever in infinity, *in gehenna permanebunt*".

VII. Complements of the Zohar. "The admirable and hidden craftsman, who is *no, not being* ('yn, 'en), comprehends in himself the *Three Sefirot* (supreme). The 'alep (of this name) is the *Crown;* the yod, *Wisdom;* the nun, *Intelligence*".

The Kabbalist Rabbi Schabbati develops these words as follows: "From the explanations we have given in the preceding chapters, it is possible to form an idea of the mystery taught by the teachers of the Kabbalah; to know that the first three (Sefirot) are considered as one. And it is possible to ask: Why *are they considered as one* and not absolutely one, since all the *Sephiroth together* are one unity? Answer. Because the first three, Crown, Wisdom and Intelligence are three *brains*, and although they manifest in a single point, single simple ones, they do not want to be confused, for any one of these brains is distinct from the other two. That which is in the other seven *Sephiroth* is found in the first three, and that which is in the three brains is found in the unity of the point, and that which is in the unity of the point is found in the Infinite, praised be it; so that there is no difference between the *Sephiroth*".

VIII. Here the Rabbi, in imitation of the Zohar, part 1 col. 27; part 3 col. 376 and *alibi pluries*, compares the mystery of the *sefirot* to the component parts of a tree, which in its entirety is a single individual. He continues: "The same is true of all that lies before us. The crown, the mystery of the point, is the hidden root; the three brains are the trunk: they are attached to the *point* which is the root. The other seven sefirot, which are the branches, are united to the trunk, which is the three brains, and the whole is united in the *point*, which is the root. For this reason, all together, the *point* and the three brains and the seven Sefirot are called an *absolute unity*, a *single unity*, 'Ehdut 'ehad. For this very reason the doctors of the Kabalah have represented the ten sefirot with a tree, since they resemble a tree, as we have explained and will continue to do. And if someone were to separate the sefirot from one another, *quod absit*, and split them *quod absit*, the same doctors have pronounced that this man *would destroy the plants:* for it would be as if someone were to cut our tree in pieces, or to tear from its place the roots, by which it receives its sap...".

IX. Supplements to the Zohar, fol. 17 of Livorna's edition, with the commentary accompanying the same text in the book ietzira.

What is reproduced in capitals is from the speech attributed to the prophet; the rest belongs to the commentary.

"Speech of the prophet Elijah. IT IS THOU, O LORD OF THE WORLD, WHO HAST PRODUCED THE TEN PERFECTIONS. That is to say, the *Infinite*, praised be He, has caused to emanate, by drawing them from His own essence, the ten perfections, which are the ten Sephiroth, instruments of His perfections for the perfection of the worlds. For by them he creates, forms and makes all that he creates. The biratic (creative) world forms the formative *ietziratic* world, and makes the akyatic (factitious) world.

It means that these ten sefirot are in the *Infinite*, may He be praised, as an instrument in the hands of a craftsman, to perfect through them all works.

"AND WE CALL THEM SEFIROT. That is to say, these *Perfections*, which He, praised be He, has caused to emanate, has produced from His own essence, we call them *Sefirot*. The intention of Elijah, of blessed memory, is to make us understand that it is not necessary to deceive ourselves by thinking and saying that the ten perfections are as separate from him as the tool is from the craftsman. When the craftsman needs to work, he takes his tool, and when he has finished his work, he puts it away and leaves it in the place where he keeps it, in order to take it up again when he needs it: for the tool is not inseparably united to the craftsman's hand by a continuous, eternal union. You too might fall into the error of thinking the same of the *Sephiroth*, assimilating them to tools left at will, and of saying that they are one thing apart from the *Infinite*, praised be He. Here is why Elijah, of blessed memory, warns us that this is not so. The ten perfections with which we are concerned are designated as *Sephiroth, a* term which in Hebrew means *lights that shine.* They do so from the very Essence of the Infinite, praised be He; they persist, and are inherent as fire to the burning ember. This fire is in the ember, and could not subsist without it. So it is with the Sephiroth: they are sacred flames, lights that make a hidden hearth glow, holy treasures of the Essence, of the Infinite, praise be to Him. They are all bound, united, to the Infinite, may He be praised, by a union, a connection, an unceasing, eternal bond; and they are also united to each other, inseparable throughout eternity. He (Elijah) designates them *Sephiroth,* which means *lights, splendours.* The root of this name means to *illuminate, to shine with a burst of light,* as the sacred text says in Exodus, XXIV, 10, and in Job, IV, 7. This is what Elijah makes us understand with these words: TO SHINE THROUGH THEM THE HIDDEN WORLDS THAT DID NOT APPEAR AND THE WORLDS THAT APPEAR. The meaning is: to illuminate by the *Sefirot* themselves and by means of them to illuminate, I mean, the hidden and concealed worlds, which are:

The worlds of the Bria (2nd world) called the throne of glory, in number of ten thrones, ten Briatic worlds. Their quiddat and their mode of being are beyond our comprehension, so I will develop it in the section on the mystery of the four worlds *Atzila, Bria, Ietzira* and *Acia.*

The worlds of the Ietzira (3rd world), which form ten worlds of angels. These are hidden worlds, hidden from the material eye.

These two worlds, the *Bria* and the *Letzira,* are called *worlds that do not appear.* These, in turn, serve to enlighten and create, not only by their intermediary, but also by their own substance, by the intelligence of the material beings that compose the worlds of the *Acia* (4th world), for the *Acia* comprises ten worlds, ten spheres which are ten heavens. And our doctors teach that these ten heavens are at a distance of five hundred years' march from each other, that each of them is a separate world, and that they envelop the whole work of the six days of creation, that is to say, the spheres and all that they enclose down to the bottom of the earth, the stars, the planets, the *crusts*, the powers of impurity, the demon of evil thoughts. This is what is called the *apparent worlds*.

But let us return to the words of Elijah. And BY THEM [the *Sephiroth*] THOU HIDEST THYSELF FROM THE SONS OF MEN. He means that since the *infinite*, praised be He, has done all His deeds through the sefirot, praised be they, and not by Himself, He *hides and conceals Himself behind them*, just as a man who hides himself from the sight of others covers his whole person with a garment which is thus the only thing visible. God makes Himself known only by His deeds, and these are operated by His Sefirot, which are His garments.

He then adds: AND IT IS YOU WHO JOIN AND GATHER THEM TOGETHER. This means that, even when the sephiroth manifest themselves by acting upon all the worlds, their action is not, however, independent of the Infinite. It must not be thought that the sefirot alone act, while the Infinite remains extraneous to what they do. That would be impiety, for they act only by virtue of the almighty influence, which draws and binds them together in perfect, absolute unity. The Sephiroth are linked to the Infinite as fire to the ember. He is thus the source and spring of all their activity.

AND SINCE THOU ART THE NUCLEUS AND THE HOME, WHOSOEVER SHALL SEPARATE THESE TEN SEPHIROTH ONE FROM THE OTHER, SHALL BE GUILTY AS THOUGH HE WERE TEARING AND CUTTING ASUNDER THYSELF, O MASTER OF THE WORLD. This means that, since the Infinite is within the flames in which the Sephiroth shine, for they shine only from the great clarity which has no limit, and since he himself is clothed with the potency of the lights which come forth from himself, to work by them all his actions, whoever separates the one from the other, saying: the potency of light which is in such a Sephiroth is not in another Sephiroth, which possesses a different potency of light, by dividing, separating and dispersing the Sephiroth, would commit the enormous sin of cutting, dividing, splitting, splitting the one Essence of the Infinite, praised be He. For He is the simplest unity, and the Sephiroth emanate from this simple unity. He is the pit, perdition, death and hellfire of the deepest abyss for him who dares to become guilty.

X. The Qabalistic system of the Book of Yitzirah, which the Rabbis attribute to the Patriarch Abraham, is based entirely upon the dogma of the Divine Trinity. It distinguishes in God *Three Splendours*, Sephiroth, which are merged in the *Supreme Splendour*, and which together constitute but *one essence,* viz:

1. The Infinite, also called *the crown, supreme.*

2. Wisdom.

3. Prudence.

These three supreme Splendours are also called, in the books of the Qabalists, *the three ways, the three degrees, the three higher branches* (of the Qabalistic tree), the *three columns*. What we shall transcribe in capital letters belongs to the text of the book ietzira.

THE FIRST WAY IS CALLED IMPENETRABLE INTELLIGENCE, SUPREME CROWN. IT IS THE PRIMORDIAL, INTELLECTUAL LIGHT; THE PRIMEM GLORY, INCOMPREHENSIBLE TO ALL CREATED MEN.

Commentary by R. Abraham-ben-David, commonly called Raabad:

"The mystery of this *Way* is indicated by the letter aleph. The letters of which the name of this character is composed, pe, lamed, 'aleph, also form the name pele, which signifies *the Admirable One*. This name is appropriate to the first Way, for it is written: '*And He shall be called the Wonderful, the Counsellor, the Mighty God*' (Isaiah, IX, 6).

This passage from Raabad is remarkable. It recognises that the ninth chapter of Isaiah refers to the Messiah, and that the Messiah is indeed God, God made man. Parvulus enim natus est nobis, et filius datus est nobis; et vocabitur nomen ejus *admirabilis*.

THE SECOND WAY IS ILLUMINATIVE INTELLIGENCE. IT IS THE CROWN OF CREATION, THE SPLENDOUR OF UNITY. IT IS ABOVE ALL THINGS. THE MASTERS OF THE TRADITION CALLED IT THE SECOND GLORY.

Rabbi Saul, speaking of this second way, expresses himself in analogous terms. Novissime diebus istis locutus est nobis in Filio, per quem fecit et saecula; qui cum sit splendor gloriae et figura substantiae eius, sedet ad dexteram majestatis in excelsis (*Rom.* I, 1).

THE THIRD WAY IS CALLED THE HOLY INTELLIGENCE. IT IS THE FOUNDATION OF THE PRIMORDIAL WISDOM CALLED UNSHAKEABLE FAITH. AMEN IS THE ROOT OF THE QUALITY OF THIS FAITH. THIS WAY IS THE MOTHER OF FAITH, FOR FAITH EMANATES FROM VIRTUE, THAT IS, FROM THE STRENGTH THAT IS IN IT.

Our Holy Mother Church teaches us that faith is one of the fruits of God's third way, the Holy Spirit.

It has been seen earlier that the term *degree* does not belong exclusively to the kabbalistic rabbis. The Kabalistic term *via* goes back to a high antiquity. It is altogether Christian, and I prostrate myself before the Divine Redeemer when He makes Himself known as the *Way*. When St. Thomas asked him: -

Lord, what way should we follow, he replies: "I am the *Way*". Six centuries earlier, Isaiah, the Gospel prophet, in chapter XXXV where he announces the coming of the Messiah, announced that the *holy way* would then be on earth. Et erit ibi semita et via, et *via sancta* vocabitur.

XI. Moses Nahhmenides, commentary on the first verse of Genesis: The doctrine of our teachers is that the word bere'šīt (meaning *at the beginning*) indicates that the universe has been created through the ten sefirot. And (this word) designates especially the sefira called Wisdom (the second Person of the Supreme Trinity). It is the foundation of the whole theme of our text, for it is written: *Yahweh has founded the earth by wisdom* (Prov. III, 19). The word *bereschit* thus refers to Wisdom. It is certainly the second in the order of the sefirot, but it is the first to manifest itself. It is indeed the beginning of beginnings. This is why the Targum of Jonathan and the Jerusalem Targum translate in Chaldee: *By Wisdom Jahweh created*.

XII. Commentary by Moses Nahmenides himself on the beginning of Genesis, developed by the kabbalist Isaiah Hurwitz in his book Schelah, fol. 271: "The Most Holy, praised be He, has created all creatures, bringing them out of absolute nothingness. And we have in the holy tongue no other term than bara'(created) to express *bringing being out of nothingness*. And there is nothing of all that has been made under the sun or above it whose existence has not had a beginning. He (God) has brought out of the most absolute nothingness a subtle, impalpable element, a productive power capable of receiving sensible forms. The Greeks called this primitive element hýle.

After him nothing else has been created; but from this element he has drawn, formed and fashioned all things, clothing them in forms that were appropriate to the use to which each thing was to be put. And know that the heavens with all that they contain are matter; also the earth and all the things it contains are one matter. The Most Holy, praised be He, has created the one and the other out of nothing. And they have been created separately, and then all the things that accompany them have been created. And this hýle matter is called in Hebrew tohu, and the form with which this matter is clothed is called in Hebrew bohu. Such is what our doctors mean in the book ietzira: *He has formed everything out of* tohu *itself, and has made essence out of that which did not exist.* Thus, the text is naturally explained according to the letter. *In the beginning God created the heavens.* He has brought forth from nothingness its matter. *And the earth.* He has brought out of nothing its matter. And in this creation all the creatures of heaven and earth were created".

XIII. Menahhem of Recanati: "The first three Sefirot are called śekalot, *intellectual, notions,* and not da'at, *knowledge, attributes* (like the remaining seven).

XIV. Meir, son of Todros of Toledo: "The three supreme Sefirot, which are the *superior Crown, Wisdom and Intelligence,* are the intellectual Sefirot, the notions: and the other seven Sefirot are those named in the book ietsira *Attributive Splendours.*

XV. Abraham Irira, in his book *The Gate of Heaven:* "God in his ten Sefirot does not communicate his nature to the three worlds bhiratic, ietziratic and akyatic... The Sefirot are but the *determinate Divinity.* The Bhiyatic, Yitziratic and Akiatic worlds are creations *ex nihilo.* The same is not true of the Sephiroth. They have not come out of nothing, but emanate eternally from the substance of the *first Infinite;* and this, their immediate cause, undergoes no diminution, just as one light communicates its brightness to another light. The Sephiroth are of the same nature as the first Infinite, with the only difference that the Infinite exists by itself, *est a se ipso, causa sine causa,* and the Sephiroth emanate from it; in a word, they are caused by the first cause. From the Infinite, the most absolute unity, is produced, is engendered, the *celestial world,* that is, what in Kabbalah is called the *primeval man, primeval Adam,* 'Adam Qadmon, a divine being not to be confused, the Kabbalists warn, with the first man, first Adam, 'Adam hari'šon, terrestrial. The primeval Adam is one and manifold, for all things are of him and in him".

XVI. In the same book, Dissertation III, chapter IX, Irira develops more fully what he has just pointed out, and explains in detail the nature of the angels of the various hierarchies, a subject which I will not deal with in this article.

The greatest teachers of the cabala of the Hebrews have been heard, and I could considerably increase the number of my quotations. Let it now be judged whether the unbelieving philosophers have grounds for invoking this cabala in favour of pantheism".

II. NATURALISTIC INTERPRETATION OF THE KABBALAH

The Kabbalah also admits of a naturalistic or pantheistic interpretation. This interpretation was first modernised by the orthodox Jew Adolph Franck in 1843, who consequently adhered to Mosaism. After Franck, this was the current interpretation of the Kabbalah, modernised in our times by the Jewish scholar and specialist in Hebraic mysticism, Gershom Scholem.

Gershom Scholem studies the subject at length in "Le grandi correnti della mística ebraica"[97], where he devotes two long chapters to the Zohar. In the first he studies the antiquity of the Kabbalah, especially the Zohar, and is inclined to attribute the book to Moses of Leon in the 13th century. Gershom Scholem takes a categorical and decisive position: "In the same way, he says, certain theories which trace the Kabbalistic doctrines, without any other form of process, back to antiquity, are also eliminated. These theories, as defended in the frequently consulted work of Adolph Franck, can no longer be scientifically disputed". [98]

"All the testimonies[99] agree in saying that the Zohar was disseminated around the years between 1280 and 1290 by the kabbalist Moisés de León, who until 1290 lived in the small community of Guadalajara, in the heart of Castile, He then lived in various localities and spent the last years of his life in Ávila, where he may have been attracted by the appearance in 1295 of a Hebrew "prophet" who in his time caused cries and finally died in 1305 in the town of Arévalo, while returning to Ávila from Valladolid, the seat of the Royal Court.

But apart from these few details concerning his life, we know that Moses de Leon published a considerable number of writings in Hebrew,

---

[97] The original text appeared in German in Rhein-Verlag A. G., Zurich, 1957, under the title "Die jüdische Mystik in ihrem Hauptstr6mungen". In Italian, Casa Editrice Saggiatore, Milan, 1965.
[98] *Les origines de la Kabbale,* Aubier-Montaigne, Paris, 1966, p. 14.
[99] Le grandi correnti, *p. 251, and in French:* Les grands courants de la Mystique Juire, *Payot, Paris, 1968.*

most of which are known to us, of which only two were later given to the press; we also know that he had intimate relations with the family of Todras Abulafia, belonging to the aforementioned circle of Gnostic cabalists, and that he took part in the circle of a man of eminent position in the Hebraic milieu of Castile between 1270 and 1280. Moses de Leon expressly states that the first book written by him (and of which he is formally recognised) was the *Sefer Shusham Eduth*, "Rose of the Testimony"; this book - of which about half remains - was written in 1286, and in 1287 was followed by a work of considerable importance on the meaning of the commandments, the *Sefer ha Rimmon*:

> "These two works, but especially the second, contain, throughout their length, more or less explicit allusions to mystical sources. If the author does not expressly quote from the Zohar, a close examination of his quotations proves that he uses the main parts of the *Midrash ha-ne-elam* up to the section on Leviticus and Numbers.
>
> Now, since none of the various fantasies about the writing of the Zohar at different times, about its origin in the East, about the antiquity of its sources, and since it is not possible to raise any doubt that the work was born in Castile, and that the intense dynamics that determined its writing and diffusion must be clearly recognised", and that it is not possible to raise any doubt that the work was born in Castile, and that the intense dynamics that determined its writing and diffusion must be clearly recognised".[100]

The Zohar

As is well known, the book of the Zohar is the first book of the Kabbalah in importance. *The Zohar, in turn, comprises several works*:

1. *Sifra di Tseniutha* or "Book of the Arcane".

2. *Idra Rabba* or "Great Assembly".

3. *Idra Zutta* or "Small Assembly".

4. *Idra di-be-Mashka,na* or "Assembly on the occasion of a lesson on the Tabernacle".

5. *Hekhaloth* or "Description of the Seven Palaces".

6. *Razin's Race* or "The Mystery of the Mysteries".

---

[100] Ibid. p. 251; French ed. p. 203.

7. *Sava* or "The Old Man".

8. *Yenuka* or "The Child".

9. *Rav Methivtha* or "The Head of the Academy".

10. *Sithre Tora* or "The Mysteries of the Torah".

11. *Mithnithin.*

12. *Zohar of the Song of Songs.*

13. *Kav Ha-Midda* or "The Mystical Measure".

14. *Sithre Othioth* or "The Mystery of Letters".

15. An untitled commentary on the vision of the Merkaba.

16. *Midrach Ha-Neelam* or "Mystic Midrach".

17. *Midrach Ha-Neelam* or the Book of Ruth.

18. *Raya Mehemna* or "The Faithful Shepherd".

19. *Tikkune Zohar* or Commentaries on the first chapter of the Torah.

20. *Tikkune Zohar* or "other texts of the same style.

We shall immediately set forth what we shall call the naturalistic interpretation, which arises from the obvious sense of the writings of the Zohar. We believe there is no more undisputed authority for such an interpretation than that of Gershon Scholem in "The Great Streams of Hebraic Mysticism" and therefore we use it here.

The doctrine of the Zohar revolves around two great themes: The new God, who is none other than the old God of Creation and Revelation, and in his relation to this God, Man; but all this explained in a rationalised theosophy, which attempts to delve into the very secrets of divinity[101].

The En-sof

The hidden God - to say almost the innermost subjectivity of divinity - has no quality or attributes. This, his innermost essence, is called *En-sof*, that is, infinite. The world of the *En-sof*, deeply hidden, is neither shown nor known to anyone outside of God himself.

---

[101] Ibid. p. 284; French ed. p. 221.

The world of the Sephiroth

There is a second world known by the divine attributes. However, the two worlds actually constitute a dynamic unity, like coal and flame, to use a likeness from the Zohar (III, 70a), and although the coal subsists without the flame, its secret life manifests itself only when it is externalised in the flame.

This world is constituted by the ten Sefirot which are emanations of the *En-sof*. The emanation of the Sefirot is a process that takes place *in* God Himself, but at the same time gives man the possibility of reaching God. In the emanation of the Sephiroth something springs from God Himself and breaks through the closed shell of His hidden being: this thing is the creative power of God, which therefore does not live only in the earthly creation, although it naturally also lives in it and is immanent to it and recognisable from it. This creative power appears to the kabalist as a pure and proper theosophical world, which naturally precedes the world and is subordinate to it. The hidden God, *En Sophis*, thus appears to the intuition of the kabalist under ten different aspects or manifestations, which, however, have within themselves infinite shades and gradations. All the Sephiroth form a complex edifice of mystical symbolism.

The names of the Sephiroth are as follows:

Kether Elyon, the supreme Crown.

Hochma, Wisdom.

Bina, the Intelligence.

Hesed, mercy.

Gevurah or Din, the Severity.

Rahamin, a Sephiroth who acts as a mediator between precedents.

Netsa, God's constant patience.

Hod, the Majesty of God.

Yesod, the foundation of all forces active in God.

Malkuth, the "kingship" of God. It is also called *Chekina*, this Sefirot.

The sefirot of the "mystic crown of the holy King" (*Zohar*, III, 30 b)... are the garments of divinity, are the ten degrees of the All, by which God descends from the innermost recesses to the revelation of the Chekinah. They are the archetype of man, the "Makro-Anthropos", and also the primordial days of all creation from which the time of the real creation springs ". [102]

The Tree of God. The ten sefirot form the mystical tree of God, whose hidden root is the *Ensof*, from which the lymph is communicated to all its branches. This tree of God is, at the same time, the structure of the universe; it grows through all creation and spreads its branches everywhere. Thus everything in the lower world, in the earthly world, exists because something of the potency of the sephiroth lives and operates in it[103].

The Adam Kadmon. Next to the image of the tree is the image of man. Man, created in the image of God, has as a counterpart to consider God as man, as the *Adam Kadmon*.

The conception of the Sephiroth as members of the mystical Anthropos in the Zohar leads to an exceptionally tight anatomical symbolism[104].

Language, a divine symbol

Other symbols, such as language, also apply to the names of God. The Sephiroth are the creative names which God evoked in the world, the names by which He called Himself. The world of the divine emanations is thus a world of the Sephiroth which, one after the other, represent the abyssal will, thought, the inner word, which cannot be heard, the perceptible voice, and, finally, speech, that is, articulate and differentiated expression[105].

The divine self and the Chekina

God, in the deepest of His manifestations, where He gives impulse to creation, is called "He"; God, in the full unfolding of His essence, of grace and love, which make Him accessible to the meditation of our hearts, and thus also make Him an expressed being, is called "Thou"; but God, in His supreme manifestations, where all the fullness of His being comes at last to realisation in the last and most comprehensive of His attributes, is called "I". This is the degree of true individuation, in which God as a person says to Himself "I". This "I" of God, according to the kabalists of the theosophical school, and this is one of their most

---

[102] Ibid. p. 292; French ed. p. 230.
[103] Ibid. p. 292; French ed. p. 230.
[104] Ibid. p. 292; French ed. p. 230.
[105] Ibid. p. 294; French ed. p. 231.

important and profound doctrines, is the *Chekina*, the presence and immanence of God in all creation. It is the point at which man attains the deepest knowledge of his own self, finds himself in God, in the divine Self, and only from that encounter - which opens the door to the world of God - can he advance into the deepest degrees of the divine being, into his "Thou", and into his "Him", and finally into the depth of the "Nothingness". "It seems to me," says Gershom Scholem here, "that the paradox implicit in such a significant and pregnant thought is this: when the mystics speak of the immanence of God in creation, they are easily inclined to deprive him of his personality. An immanent God quite easily becomes an impersonal divinity. And this is, as is well known, one of the main difficulties of pantheism. But not so for the kabbalists: the degree of divine activity which is closest to man, as well as the immanent foundation in each of us, is at the same time that in which the personality of God, in the sense of the Zohar, is also most fully developed[106].

God and nothingness

Another symbol, very frequent in the Zohar and its school, used to represent the unfolding of the Divine in its revelation is that which derives from the concept of the mystical "Nothingness". The fundamental creation, according to the kabbalist, is that which takes place in God Himself; and, especially for the Zohar, there is no other essential act of creation unfolding outside of the Sephiroth. The creation of the world, that is, the production of something out of nothing, is nothing other than the outward aspect of an inner knowledge, and in that which appears eternal, which takes place in God Himself. The most profound of all theosophical processes, which itself comprises the problem of creation and revelation, is represented by the conversion of the hidden *En-sof* into creation. This conversion can be conceived under the image of the sudden emergence of the primordial will; but the kabalists of the theosophical school also like to write it using the bolder image of "Nothingness". That sudden intimate movement which causes the divinity, withdrawn into itself, to burst forth and externalise itself, before it radiates its light only internally, this prolectic revolution transforms the *En-sof, the* ineffable fullness into the "Nothingness". And from this mystical Nothingness come all the other moments of the unfolding of God's yes in the Sephiroth. This mysterious Nothingness

---

[106] Ibid. p. 295; French ed. p. 232.

- which the kabbalists designate as the first Sefirot, and also as the "supreme crown" of divinity - represents, if I may so express myself, the abyss that is visible in the deprivation of all being[107].

Gershom Scholem has subsequently written on this subject, [108], explaining what Azriel, of the school of Gerona, in particular, teaches on this subject. We do not share Scholem's opinion that this teaching is due to Neoplatonic influences, particularly those of Scotus Eriugena. We believe, on the contrary, that the truth lies in an influence of the Cabala on Scotus Eriugena which would have come from a cultural circle of the Palatine School. We shall refer to this in particular when we deal with Eriugena's thought. The background of the Kabbalistic "Nothingness" that Scholem brings would corroborate this statement.

Indeed, Gershom Scholem notes that Nahmenides, in his commentary on the Yesira, I, 7, speaks of Nothingness, and not of the Nothingness of the philosophers, but of divinity itself, or at least of the first *Sefirot*. "If anyone asks you how he has brought his being out of nothingness, answer: he who has brought his being out of nothingness lacks nothing by this fact, because being is in nothingness in the manner of nothingness and nothingness is being in the manner (i.e. according to the mode) of being"[109].

Gerschom Scholem points out here that "Reuchlin, the admirer of Nicholas of Cusa, had quoted these decisive phrases from the Kabbalah[110] "there is a nothingness of God which gives birth to being and there is a being of God which represents nothingness..."; "nothingness is not nothingness, independent of God, but *his* nothingness. The transformation of nothingness into being is an event that is placed in God himself"[111].

Gershom Scholem had already expounded this aspect of the Kabbalah in "La Kabbale et sa symbolique", when he says[112] : "God comes out of his secret retreat to appear in his power, in the trunk and branches of the theogonic, cosmogonic "tree", and his power works in ever more distant spheres. Everywhere we have a continuous movement, and if a break,

---

[107] Ibid. p. 296; French ed. p. 233.
[108] *Les Origines de la Kabbale*, p. 445, Montaigne, Paris, 1966.
[109] Ibid., p. 447.
[110] Ibid., p. 447.
[111] Ibid., p. 448.
[112] Payot, Paris, 1966, p. 120.

an original nothingness appears, this could only come from the essence of God. *This is precisely the consequence that the Jewish mystics have drawn through the maintenance of the ancient formulas.* The chaos that had been eliminated in the category of Creation from nothingness, reappears in a new metamorphosis. This nothingness is present all the time in God himself, and not outside him, nor provoked by him. Coexistent with the infinite fullness of God, it is the abyss in God that is mastered in the creature, and the word of the kabbalists about God dwelling in "the depths of nothingness", in vogue since the 13th century, expresses this sentiment in an image all the stranger because it has been reconstituted from an unobvious concept.

And there Gershom Scholem insists that the root of all roots from which the tree of creation and, with it, God himself is nourished is this nothingness which is together the highest and the first of all Sephiroth[113].

Note that Scholem acknowledges that this conception of God comes from the *ancient formulas,* i.e. it is essentially Kabbalistic and not Neo-Platonic or Erigerian.

By introducing nothingness into God, the Kabbalists must have invented the Hegelian dialectic long before Hegel.

Mysticism and dialectics

Remarkable in this respect is a mystical play on words, which corresponds entirely to the ideas of the Zohar, and which was already used by Gigatilla. The Hebrew word for "Nada" (*ayin*) has the same consonants as "ani", "I". But the "I" of God is, as we have seen before, that last degree in the sefirot in which the personality of God - itself comprising all the other degrees - is revealed to His very creation. As soon as *ayin* therefore becomes *ani*, the Nothingness of the act of the progressive manifestation of its content suddenly transcends the sefirot, and from the latter is transformed into the "I", in a mystical dialectic of which thesis and antithesis are thus synthesised in God Himself. This dialectic seems rather bold, but it is the easy consequence of a mystical thought which - as we have seen - seeks to express the religious

---

[113] Ibid., p. 121.

paradox; and furthermore the kabbalists are not entirely alone in testifying to such an affinity between mysticism and dialectic[114].

This dialectic had already been noted by Gershom Scholem in the *En-Sof* proposed by Asriel of the Kabbalistic Centre of Gerona. In the *En-Sof*, opposites are abolished because the infinite is reached. And here Gershom Scholem notes how "already in 1516 Johann Reuchlin, referring expressly to the treatise on Faith and Heresy which we have recognised as belonging to Azriel, defines well the notion of the indifferent *En-Sof*: It is called *En-Sof*, that is, infinitude, which is a certain great thing in itself incompressible and ineffable, which withdraws and conceals itself in the very far backwardness of its divinity and in the inaccessible fontal abyss of light, so that nothing is understood to proceed from it, as if it were an absolute divinity, immanent in its total enclosure, naked, unclothed and without any shelter of circumstances, without any profusion of itself, and without the goodness of its splendour, being indiscriminately being and non-being and appearing all contrary and contradictory to our reason, as a separate and free unity in all simplicity". And then Reuchlin refers the reader to the *coincidentia oppositorum,* coincidence of opposites, in God, as bequeathed to posterity, as representing his decided opinion, about fifty-two years ago, by an eminently philosophical archpriest of the Germans"[115].

The "primordial point", the centre of theogony and cosmogony. *In many passages of the Zohar* - not unlike in other Hebrew writings of Moses of Leon - the sudden passage from Nothingness to Being is represented by the sign of the primordial point. Already in the school of Gerona the principle of the emanation of the "hidden cause" is compared to the mathematical point, which with its movement generates the line and the surface; to this is added in Moses of Leon the symbolism of the point as the centre of the circumference. The primordial point - which shines out of the Nothing - is the mystical centre around which the processes of theogony and cosmogony are concentrated. The point which itself is dimensionless, standing between Nothingness and Being, thus serves to represent "the source of being", *hatchalath ha-yeshuth,* that "beginning" which is the first word of the Bible. The very first words with which the Zohar introduces its

---

[114] Le grandi correnti della mística ebraica, *p. 297; French ed. p. 233.*
[115] Les origines de la Kabbale, *p. 463.*

interpretation of the creation story describe, rather lavishly, that shining forth of the originating point, in this case truly not of the reason of Nothingness, but of that ethereal breeze of God[116].

The wisdom of God and the bottom line

This primordial point is also identified - both in the Zohar and in the other kabbalistic authors - with the wisdom of God, with the *Hokhma*. This represents the ideal thought of creation, conceived as the ideal point which also springs from the impulse of the abyssal will. But this point is the mystical seed, sown in creation, since the core of the similarity, in what appears, is not only in the subtlety of the two things, but in the fact that in one and in the other - plant and seed - the potentiality of an ulterior being is still enclosed, not acted upon[117].

This point unfolds in the successive Sephiroth of the "Palace", or of the "Building", alluding to the fact that preceding this sphere when it produces its effects outwardly, the "building" of the cosmos is built to the point. That which was first complicated at the point is unfolded and separated. The name of this Sefirot, Bina, does not mean intelligence alone, but can be interpreted as "that which separates things", that is, as differentiation. In the bosom of the *Binah*, "the mystical mother" of all things, whatever was undifferentiated in the divine wisdom now exists as the "pure totality of all individuations. In it all forms are already preformed, but always preserved in the unity of the divine understanding, which contemplates it in itself[118].

God, subject of the cosmic process

The truth is that this supreme being that springs from Nothingness, this entity that is in God Himself, this essence of the divine sophia, is beyond all human appearance. It cannot be known by enquiry, it is not a being whose knowledge can be attained in analysis, without which knowledge appears impossible. This process of the splitting of divine knowledge is interpreted in the Zohar as one of its most profound symbols, as a moment of the progressive unfolding of the living God Himself. Among the divine manifestations there is one - the kabbalists call it, for various reasons, *Bina,* the divine intelligence - in which He

---

[116] *Le grandi corren ti...*, p. 297; French ed., p. 234.
[117] Ibid. p. 298; French ed. p. 235.
[118] Ibid. p. 299; French ed. p. 236.

appears as the eternal subject, as the great *Who*, in whom all demand and all response finally ends. You will say that here we are confronted with an apotheosis of the well-known Hebraic tendency to raise questions... But in the end, at any rate, meditation on God reaches a point where one can still ask "who", but without receiving an answer; and so the question is, in such a case, the answer. If this is the sphere of *"My"*, of the *Great Who*, in which God appears as the subject of the cosmic process, conceivable at least in the question, the supreme sphere of divine wisdom is instead something positive to which no further question can be addressed, and which is indefinable in abstract thought[119].

God, subject and object of the cosmic process

This idea has found expression in a play on words of profound significance. The Zohar asks what is meant by the first verse of the Torah, *Bereshit bara Elohim*, and answers that *Bereshit* means, by the beginning, namely by the essence which we have known by the name of "divine sophia," *bara*, created, that that hidden Nothing, which is the grammatical subject of the word *bara*, evolved or emanated; *Elohim*, that is, the emanation is *Elohim*. Thus, this last word is the object and not the subject of the whole proposition. But what is *Elohim*? It is the name which guarantees the stability of creation inasmuch as in it, the hidden subject *Mi*, and the hidden subject *Eleh*, are united in a perennial unity. The Hebrew words *Mi* and *Eleh* have the same consonants as the name Elohim. Elohim is thus the name given to God after the subject and object have separated, but in which the abyss of this separation is continually bridged and overcome. The mystical Nothingness which precedes the fracture of the primordial idea in the thinker and the thought, is not for the kabbalists a real subject. Human contemplation can dwell perpetually on the lower degrees of divine manifestations: but the highest degree that meditation can attain, that of the vision of God as mystical *My* (Who), as the subject of the cosmic process, can be none other than a sudden ray of intuitive light shining in the heart of man, "like the play of the sun's rays on a mirror of water," as Moses of Leon says, with an oft-repeated image,[120].

---

[119] Ibid. p. 300; French ed. p. 236.
[120] Ibid., p. 301.

The pantheism of the Zohar

"In the history of the Kabbalah, theistic and pantheistic tendencies are frequently contrasted: the latter are very difficult to recognise, since their representatives have always been concerned to use the language of theism, and the authors who have clearly expressed their pantheistic convictions are very rare". Thus Gershom Scholem[121].

The work of Creation in the Zohar, as described in the first chapter of Genesis, has a dual character. Understood mystically, it represents the story of the divine self-revelation and unfolding of the world of the divinity of the sephiroth, it is a theogony (it is difficult to find a more precise term, even if it derives from the world of mythology); insofar as it gives rise to the "lower" world - that is, the one which, in the more precise sense of a *processio ad extra, is* a cosmogony. The two are distinguished by the fact that in the upper world the dynamic unity of God reigns, while in the lower world differentiation and separation take place. The Zohar likes to speak of this lower world as the world of separation, *Olam ha-perud*. The Zohar often says, "if one contemplates in mystical meditation, everything becomes one". Already Gigatilla uses the formula: "He is in all and is all".

Indeed, theogony and cosmogony do not represent two different acts of creation, but are, in the final analysis, only two sides of the same process. Creation always looks at the intimate movement of the divine life, in every degree, whether in the world of the Merkaba and the angels, the place below the Sephiroth, or in the various cycles of the world of the four elements. Creation is but an external development of those forces which work and live in God Himself.

Moses de Leon says in turn: "Everything is linked to everything, to the last of the rings of the chain; and the true being of God is equally high and low, in heaven and on earth, and nothing exists apart from Him. And this the sages understand when they say: "When God saw the Torah in Israel, He opened its seven heavens and they saw that it was really none other than His glory; He opened its seven earths and they saw that it was none other than His glory; He opened its seven depths and they saw that it was none other than His glory". Meditate on these facts and you will understand that the true existence of God is bound and chained to all the worlds, and that all the forms of existence are

---

[121] Ibid. p. 301; French ed. p. 237.

bound to one another, and implied one in the other, for everything proceeds from His real existence" (From a long quotation from the *Sefer harimon*, by Moses de Leon, quoted by Gershom Sholem)[122].

Creation before Adam's sin

The Zohar teaches that originally everything was conceived as a great unity and the life of the creator flowed freely and simply into the life of the creatures. Everything was in a direct mystical relationship with the whole and could have been known in its unity immediately without the need for symbols: only Adam's guilt has made God transcendent and by its cosmic repercussions things have lost their immediate connection and have taken on the appearance of an isolated and independent existence. All creation was of a supersensible nature and would not have taken on a material form without the intervention of evil. No wonder, therefore, if in a messianic world and, by the blessed knowledge of the devout, in a world redeemed from the stain of sin, this original relationship of all things to each other would again be restored[123].

The sexual in the Zohar

It is well known that in the history of mysticism those deeper layers of human nature which are related to the sexual life have played an important part; erotic images are found in abundance in the writings of many mystics, and many of these mystics describe the very relationship with God as a loving relationship of the soul.

There is exceptionally only one instance in which the Zohar uses sexual symbolism to characterise a mortal's relationship with the Divine or, to be more precise, with the *Chekinah*.

The exception is represented by Moses, the man of God; of him and of him alone it is said with a bold image that he had a relationship with the *Chekinah*. In this case, the permanent relationship with the image of a mystical betrothal of Moses to the *Chekinah*. Some passages of the *Midrach* - which speak of a cessation of Moses' sexual relations with his wife after he has been favoured with relations with God "face to

---

[122] Ibid. p. 303; French ed. p. 239.
[123] Ibid. p. 304; French ed. p. 240.

face" - have given the variant to Moses de Leon to argue that the nuptials with the *Chekinah* have supplanted the earthly marriage[124].

The language of sex dominates instead the description of God's intimate relationship with Himself, as in the world of the Sephiroth. Its insurgence into the life of man is for the kabbalists a symbol of the loving relationship between the divine "I" and "Thou", the "Holy One, praised be He, and His *Chekinah*". The *hierogamos, the* sacred union of King and Queen, of husband and celestial wife, or whatever name is used for these symbols, among all the ultimate processes of the world of divine manifestations is that which occupies the most central place. In God Himself there is a union of the active and passive forces, of the element that generates and the element that conceives, from which all life and all bliss in the earthly world springs[125]. One of the images depicting the unfolding of the Sephiroth describes it as the point of a mystical procreation, in which the first ray emerging from the Nothingness was sown in the divine understanding, that is, in the "heavenly mother", from whose womb the Sephiroth will be born, as King and Queen, son and daughter. In this mystical and archetypal image can be recognised the traces of the male and female divinity of antiquity, even if it arouses a sense of dread in devout kabbalists[126].

The ninth Sefira *Yesod*, from which all the highest Sefirot - gathered in the image of the King - flow into the *Chekinah*, is conceived as the generative force of creation, the secret life of the universe. The phallic symbolism, always connected with the speculations of the *Yesod*, finds great expression in the Zohar. M. D. George Langer has drawn from this for his psychoanalytical speculations on the Zohar in *Die Erotik der Kabbala*, Prague, 1923[127].

The Chekina as a female aeon

In the Gnostic speculations on the male and female eons that constitute the world of the *Pleroma*, of the Fullness of God, these ideas later take on a new form, in which they become known to the early Kabbalists through fragmentary sources. The similarity used in the book *Bahir* when speaking of the *Chekinah* reveals this Gnostic character even

---

[124] Ibid. p. 307; French ed. p. 242.
[125] Ibid. p. 307; French ed. p. 243.
[126] Ibid. p. 307; French ed. p. 243.
[127] Ibid. p. 307; French ed. p. 243.

more clearly. For some Gnostics the "inner Sophia represented the last aeon, on the fringe of the *Pleroma*, "the daughter of light", who falls into the abyss of matter. Many reasons have contributed to this image of the *Chekina* as it appears in the Zohar. First of all, it is identified with the community of Israel, a kind of invisible Church, which represents a mystical idea that Israel, in its connection with God, and in its happiness, but also in its sufferings in exile... In the world of Zohar symbols this new idea of the *Chekinah* as a symbol of the eternal feminine has a prominent place, presented in various names and images[128].

Original sin

In his original paradisiacal nature, man had an immediate relationship with God. As Moses de Leon often repeats, man was a synthesis of all the spiritual forces that have built up creation; in his organism and in his structure is reflected the secret organism of God's own life. The original man was a purely spiritual being. Only after sin did he have a corporeal existence, out of the confusion of all matter with the poison of sin. Only original sin destroyed this immediate contact between God and man, and in some way also influenced the life of God in His creation.

This interpretation says that the Sephiroth were revealed to Adam in the form of the tree of life and the tree of knowledge, and this in symbolic representations of the penultimate and the last Sephiroth; instead of guarding their original unity, and thus uniting the spheres of life and knowledge, and by this union bringing about the redemption of the world, he separated them and resolved to honour the *Chekinah* exclusively without regard to their unity with the other Sephiroth. Thus Adam broke the vital current that runs from sphere to sphere, and brought about the separation and isolation that reigns in the world[129].

The origin of evil

In the Zohar sometimes, evil is really a metaphysical world of darkness, of the tempter and temptation, and has an existence independent of human sin and man's actions; and sometimes it seems that only with man's sin does it really become free and independent, when sin has broken its union with the divine world. Thus it would have become

---

[128] Ibid. p. 310; French ed. p. 245.
[129] Ibid. p. 313; French ed. p. 248.

isolated and actualised by man alone. Indeed, according to the Zohar, moral evil always represents that which has been separated from a union, and thus isolated, or that which enters into a relationship that is not appropriate to it. Sin separates that which is union; such a ruinous separation was also at the basis of the first sin in that the fruit was separated from the tree, or - as another kabbalist significantly puts it - the tree of life was separated from that knowledge in which it originally had a single root. When man thus falls into isolation, when he wants to assert himself, instead of remaining in that original unity of all created things, then another consequence of such a fall cannot be lacking, namely, the demiurgic presence of magic, in which man seeks to put himself in the place of God, and to unite what God has separated. Evil thus creates a fictitious world of false bonds after it has destroyed the world of authentic bonds[130].

But there is a deeper cause of evil, according to the Zohar. The divine forces form a harmonious whole, and none of these forces or qualities is holy and good unless it is united with the others in a living relationship of being. This applies especially to the quality of justice in the strict sense, to judgement and to severity - in God and of God - which is the deepest cause of evil. God's anger is like his sinister hand in intimate relationship with the quality of grace and love, his right hand. The one cannot manifest itself by making less of the other. This Sephira of Severity is thus the great "focus of wrath" which burns in God, but which is continually sweetened and restrained by grace. If, however, in an enormous, hypertrophic development, it bursts forth and breaks the union with grace, then it flees with violence from the world of divinity and becomes the radical evil, the world of Satan opposed to that divine one[131]. These ideas have also been expounded by Jacob Boehme, where he reveals "the closest affinity with the Kabbalah[132].

There is in the Qabalah the idea that it was not Adam's action that was the first cause of evil, but that the existence of evil would be independent of man, and that its cause must be sought in the structure of the world, or rather in the very process of the life of God. The Zohar tends to the latter conception and regards evil as a residue or detritus of the organic process of the hidden life. Thus, the demonic element

---

[130] Ibid. p. 317; French ed. p. 252.
[131] Ibid. p. 318; French ed. p. 253.
[132] Ibid. p. 320; French ed. p. 253.

springs from divinity itself. The Zohar shows evil as the bark, *Kelipa,* of the cosmic tree or as the husk of the nut[133].

The doctrine of the soul

In a mystical hymn Moses ben Nachman has described the birth of the soul from the depths of the divine spheres, from which life flows. For the soul too is a spark of divine life and carries within it the life of the various divine stages through which it has passed[134].

The Zohar preserves the distinction between the three souls of man *Nefesh,* or life, *Ruach* or spirit, *Neshama* or soul. But these three souls are no longer three diverse faculties, for they are present in the first soul, *Nefesh;* and the higher degrees of the soul are instead new and deeper powers which the soul of the worshipper gains through Torah study and good deeds[135].

Especially *Neshama,* the holy soul, is obtained through meditation on the divine mysteries, and consists of the deepest intuitive force, a kind of spark of *Bina,* the divine understanding itself. The Zohar holds that only *Nefesh* - that is, the natural soul with which everyone is endowed - is capable of sin. *Neshama,* the most intense divine spark, is beyond any sin[136].

The Zohar maintains the pre-existence of all souls from the beginning of creation, and thus goes so far as to say that all souls were pre-formed in their full individuality when they were hidden in the bosom of eternity[137].

After death, souls who have fulfilled their mission return to their original home, while sinful souls are brought before a tribunal and purified in the "wave of fire" of Gehenna, or, in the case of serious enough sins, burned.

Nor should it be denied that the idea of metempsychosis as a form of punishment is not unknown in the most ancient Kabbalistic tradition[138]. Gershom Scholem notes in *Les Origines de la Kabbale*[139] that the

---

[133] Ibid. p. 320; French ed. p. 253.
[134] Ibid. p. 321; French ed. p. 256.
[135] Ibid. p. 322; French ed. p. 257.
[136] Ibid. p. 323; French ed. p. 257.
[137] Ibid. p. 323; French ed. p. 258.
[138] Ibid. p. 325; French ed. p. 259.
[139] Ibid., p. 493.

doctrine of the transit of souls in animal bodies denotes a direct contact with the conceptions of the Cathars.

Conclusion on the Zohar

The conclusion about the Zohar is given by Gershom Scholem himself in laconic but definitive words. "Considered complexly, he says, the spiritual world of the Zohar can be defined as a mixture of theosophical theology, mythical cosmogony and mystical psychology and anthropology. God, the world and the soul do not, each on its own plane, have separate lives. The original creative act absolutely ignores such a separation, which, as we have seen, is determined in the cosmos only by man's sin".

The Zohar merely makes explicit and carries to its ultimate consequences the intimate and essential conception of the Kabalah, at any time of its existence. This Kabbalistic conception contains as its own distinctive character the idea that God - the world - man move on one and only one plane. As will be explained below, this conception can be translated into a monism, or an emanatism, or an immanetism, or an intrinsicism in which Creator and creature, yes and no, truth and error, nature and grace, good and evil unfold in a unitary world of a single dimension.

Kabbalah after the Zohar

The Kabbalah undergoes a change after 1492 with the expulsion of the Jews from Spain. "Death, conversion and recognition are the greatest events, the real breaking points, from which the new Kabbalah takes the movement for the rebuilding of human life towards a happy union with God. Humanity is not only threatened by its own corruption but by that of the whole world, which comes from the first fracture of creation, the fracture of the organs, in which the subject and the object of the world have separated". The kabbalists of this time would write a series of texts, more or less voluminous, many of which represented finished systems of mystical theory. The most famous are those of Moses ben Jacob Cordovero (1522-1570) and Isaac Luria (1534-1572).

The doctrine of Tzimtzum

At the apex of Luria's conception is the doctrine of *Tzimtzum*. *Tzimtzum* means concentration or contraction. How can there be a world when God's being is everywhere? How can there be anything concrete in this place, anything other than God, since God is "all in all"? God - Luria answers - must make a zone vacant in His being, from which He withdraws; a kind of mystical primordial space, in which He can return to the act of creation and revelation: The first movement of the *En-sof* ni was therefore a movement outwards, but inwards, a movement within itself. The Tzimtzum could be seen as a banishment at the point of the divine being itself. Thus the cosmic process consists of a continuous concealment and revelation of God, a withdrawing or concentrating into oneself and then a manifesting in creation.[140] This process of *Tzimtzum* is like a purification of the divine organism from the elements of evil[141].

This conception of a successive process in the *Tzimtzum* as a process taking place in God Himself was all the easier for Luria as he admitted that a trace or a remnant of the divine light - for him, called *Reshimu* - remained after retracting from the substance of the *En-sof* in the primordial space produced in the *Tzimtzum*[142].

The rupture of the vessels

Along with the original conception of *Tzimtzum* there are two other fundamental theosophical ideas. These are the breaking of the vessels and the *Tiqqum* or doctrine of separation. The doctrine of the vessels affirms that the divine light burst into primordial space, unfolded in various stages and appeared in a variety of guises. The important point is that, according to this doctrine, before all other beings, the Adam Kadmon or primordial man originated in primordial space. The *Adam Kadmon* is therefore the first and highest form in which the divinity, after the *Tzimtzum*, begins to manifest itself. From his eyes, from his mouth, from his ears and from his nose will burst forth the lights of the Sefirot. At first, all together in a single whole and without any separation between each of the vessels that contain them, but then the lights from the eyes emanate in an "atomised" form, in which each sefirot will constitute an isolated point. This world of "dotted lights" is called by Luria "the world of confusion, of disorder". From the moment that, on the plane of creation, the existence of finite entities, in a given order, was considered, "vessels" were created - or rather emanated - to collect each of those lights, to contain and preserve them. The vessels corresponding to the three highest Sephiroth gathered their light from here also, while the light of the other six lower Sephiroth burst forth,

---

[140] Gershom Scholem, *Le grandi correnti della mistica ebraica*, p. 355; French ed. p. 278.
[141] Gershom Scholem, *La Kabbale et sa symbolique*, p. 129.
[142] Gershom Scholem, *Le grandi correnti...*, p. 359; French ed. p. 281.

because it was too strong and the vessels too weak. The same thing happened, though in more moderate proportion, to the vessel of the last Sefira.

This idea of the breaking of the vessels derives from a mythical Zohar that the Kings of Edom, of worlds past, died because of the reign of rigour, or that the world was not tempered by compassion. For the world subsists only by the harmony of grace and rigour, of the masculine and feminine element, of a harmony which the Zohar indicates as the balance.

From the residues of the broken vessels, in which some sparks of the holy light from the essence of God remained, the demonic worlds of evil derived, which thus nested in all possible states of the cosmic process[143].

Partzufim. According to the theory of the Tiqqum, after the breaking of the vessels caused by the original ray of the En-sof, a new ray of light burst forth from the forehead of *Adam Kadmon* and reunited the disordered elements. The lights of the Sephira from the *Adam Kadmon* were thus arranged in new configurations, and in each was reflected the *Adam Kadmon* according to certain definite forms; and hence each Sephiroth was transformed into a general attribute of God, which the Qabalists call *Partzùf, the* face of divinity. And Gershom Scholem adds: The God who now manifests Himself is the living God of religion, the goal of the Qabalists, who represents much more than the hidden *En-sof: He* is the God who realises Himself as the fulfilled person of the process of *Tiqqum.* In all the attempts of the Lurianic Kabbalah to describe the theogonic process in inspired symbols of human existence an effort is evident, to attain a personal God; but such an effort culminates in a new form of Gnostic mythology, and it would be vain to entertain any illusions about it. In the process of *Tiqqum,* of the restoration of the divine lights to their rightful place, Luria tries to explain how the various aspects by which the Divinity manifests itself can emanate from each other as so many *Partzufim,* contained in a personalistic manner. In reading his description, one tends to forget that he means to refer to purely spiritual processes. And as if one were reading one of those myths in which Basilides, Valentinus or Mani seek

---

[143] Ibid. p. 361; French ed. p. 283.

to represent the cosmic drama, only in this case it is a more complex myth than in those of the Gnostic systems"[144].

God shapes himself

Luria goes so far as to describe a myth of God giving birth to himself. For this," writes Gershom Scholem, "seems to me the salient point of all these expositions, which give the impression of being impenetrable: the development of man through the various stages - conception, pregnancy, birth, infancy - to the formation of the complete personality, which can be master of the free and full use of its moral and intellectual faculties, is boldly regarded as a symbol of *Tiqqum, of* the Process in which God shapes Himself[145].

And Gershom Scholem adds: "There is a latent conflict here: either the *En-sof* is the personal God, the God of Israel, and all the *Partzufim* are only his manifestations, under different aspects; or the *En-sof* is the impersonal substance, the *deus absconditus,* which only in the *Partzufim* becomes a person".

This, to which an answer could easily be given, while dealing only with the theosophical interpretation of the doctrine of the Zohar which brought the *En-sof* and the sephiroth into immediate relationship, becomes a pressing problem in this most complicated process of the *Tzimtzum* and the Shevira, and in the long series of events leading up to the formation of the *Zeir Anpin.* The more dramatic the processes taking place in God become, the more inevitable is the question: in all this, where is God[146].

The process of restitution in God and in mankind

All this leads us to consider another aspect of the doctrine of *Tiqqum,* even more important for the subject of practical theosophy. The process by which God conceives, begets and develops Himself is not completed in Himself alone; in part, the process of restitution is fulfilled in man. Not all the lights fallen into the prison of the powers of evil are resolved there; in other words, it is man who gives the final touch to the divine countenance, and it is for him to install God, as King and mystical Author of all things, in the heavenly Kingdom. It is man who gives the

---

[144] Ibid. p. 364; French ed. p. 287.
[145] Ibid. p. 366; French ed. p. 289.
[146] Ibid. p. 366; French ed. p. 287.

final form to his creator himself. The divine being and the human being at a certain point in the cosmic process are interdependent; thus, in the intimate process of *Tiqqum*, which is outside of time - symbolically represented by the birth of the personality of God - corresponds the temporal process of the history of this world. The historical process and its more secret soul which is the religious action of the Hebrew, which operates the final restitution of all the separated and scattered lights and sparks in the banishment of matter. Therefore, it depends on the free action of the Hebrew - who, thanks to the Torah, to the observance of the law and to prayer, is in intimate relationship with the divine life - to accelerate this process and to propel it. Every action of man is related to this final task that God has attributed to the creatures.

The coming of the Messiah is, according to Luria, nothing other than the final seal of this process of restoration of the *Tiqqum*. The redemption of Israel comprises in itself the redemption of all things.

Man must, in every action, renew his innermost purpose to restore the original unity, that unity destroyed because of the original stain - the breaking of the vessels - and the forces of evil and sin brought into the world because of it. To reunite the name of God in which JH has been separated from the letters WH.

The Chekinah falls, like the last Sefira when the vessels were broken. When *Tiqqum* began, the union of the Chekinah and the *Zeir Anpin* would have been realised. But because of Adam's sin, the harmony of the worlds was destroyed and caused the Chekinah to fall plummeting into the darkness of the demonic world and evil, which were to be separated, again with the resumption of the elements of light and the return to the preceding position. Adam was a spiritual being on the verge of the spiritual world, *Asiya*. It was only immediately after his sin that this world too was precipitated from its sphere and mingled with the lower domain of the *Qelipoth*. Thus was constituted not only the material world in which we live, but also man as a being composed of matter and spirit[147].

And Gershom Scholem adds:

---

[147] Gershom Scholem, *Le grandi correnti...*, p. 377; French ed. p. 298.

"It reveals a strange affinity with the fundamental religious ideas of the Manicheans..." [148]

Metempsychosis

The Kabbalah of the school of Luria also upholds metempsychosis. But the ancient Kabbalists believed in *Gilgul* - a Hebraic term used to indicate the transmigration of souls only in relation to certain faults, and mainly of a sexual nature. They ignored metempsychosis as a universal law, regulated according to the moral causality of human actions, what the Hindus call by the Sanskrit term *Karma*.

The transmigration of souls is thus in Luria a part of the restitution process of *Tiqqum*. But because of the forces of evil in man, transmigration is immensely prolonged and makes redemption more distant. But Luria maintained that through appropriate religious acts, such as rites, penitential exercises and meditation, this process could be considerably shortened. Every man carries with him the secret traces of his soul's pilgrimage in the line of his forehead and hands and in the air that radiates from his body. And only he who can decipher the writing of the soul of which the great mystics are capable can penetrate into the destiny of the soul and succour it. [149]

The Lurianic Kabbalah accentuated all the gnostic features of the Zohar of Moses Leo. Hence its great significance in later kabbalistic currents.

III. OCCULT INTERPRETATION OF THE KABBALAH

What we call the naturalistic interpretation of the Kabbalah is the university interpretation, initiated by Franck and today renewed by Gershom Scholem. But there is also that of the occultists or esoteric, supported in all times by a number of authors, including Éliphas Levy, *Dogme rituel de la haute magie*, Paris, 1854, *Le clef des grandes mystères, Histoire de la Magie;* Fabre d'Olivet, *La langue hebraique restituée*, Paris, 1825, 2 vols.; Stanislas de Guaita, *Au seuil du mystère*, Paris 1890; *Le Temple de Satan*, Paris 1891; H. P.

Agrippa, *Philosophie occulte*, 2 vols., The Hague, 1727; Lenain, *La sciencie cabalistique*, Amiens, 1823; Papus, *Traité elementaire de*

---

[148] Ibid. p. 377; French ed. p. 298.
[149] Ibid. p. 380; French ed. p. 301.

sciencie occulte, Paris, 1887; *Le Tarot des bohemiens,* Paris 1889; *Traité méthodique de science occulte,* Paris 1887; Josephin Peladan, *La decadence latine,* 11 vols, Paris, 1884; Abbé Roca, *Nouveaux Cieux, nouvelle terre,* Paris 1889; L. C. de Saint Martin, *Le Crocodile,* Paris; Ed. Schuré, *Les grands initiés,* Paris, 1889; Saint Yves d'Alveydre, *Mission des Juifs,* Paris, 1884; Hoené Wronsky, Raymond Lulio, Pico de la Mirandola, Reuchlin, N. C. Agrippa, Pastel, Kircher, Knorr de Rosenroth, Joseph Voysin, Paracelsus, Henry Morus, Van Helmont, Mercure Van Helmont, Robert Fludd, Buxtorf.

Antiquity of the Kabbalah according to occultists

Occultists maintain that university criticism cannot deviate in its work from certain established rules, the main one of which consists in basing the origin of the doctrines it studies only on authentic documents, without dealing with the more or less interested assertions of the advocates of the doctrine under study. This is the method followed by Franck and Gershom Scholem[150].

The occultist need not take these limitations into consideration. An ancient symbol is to him as authentic and as precious a monument as a book, and the oral tradition can only transmit the dogmatic formulas which reason and science must subsequently control and verify.

Several great civilisations have succeeded each other on our planet in the following order[151].

1° The colossal civilisation of Atlantis, a civilisation created by the *red race* and the evolution of a continent that has now disappeared, which stretched across the Atlantic Ocean.

2° At the time when the red race was in full civilisation, a new continent was born, which constitutes the *Africa of today,* generating as the ultimate term of evolution, the *black race.*

At the time of the cataclysm that engulfed Atlantis, a cataclysm known to all religions as the *Great Flood,* civilisation quickly passed into the hands of the black race, to whom some survivors of the red race passed on their main secrets.

---

[150] Papus, *Le Cabbale,* Dangles, Paris, 5th edition, p. 139.
[151] Ibid., p. 140.

3° Finally, when the blacks reached the apogee of their civilisation, the *white race* was born with a new continent (Europe-Asia), to which the supremacy over the planet was subsequently to pass.

The facts just summarised are not new. For occultists, those who know how to read the *Sepher* of Moses esoterically will find the key in the first words of the book, as Saint Yves d'Alveydre has shown; but without going so far, Fabre d'Olivet, from 1820 onwards, discovered this doctrine in the *Histoire philosophique du Genre Humain*. Moreover, the author of *Ivlission des Juifs* has the explanation of this doctrine in the *Ramayana* itself[152].

"All traditions, those of the *Bohemians*, the *Freemasons*, the *Egyptians*, the *Kabbalists*, corroborated by official science itself, agree in considering India as the origin of our philosophical and religious knowledge[153].

The Kabbalah is nothing other than this tradition adopted by the Western spirit.

Every religious or philosophical reformer of antiquity divided his doctrine into two parts: one veiled, for the use of the multitude or *exotericism, the* other clear, for the use of the initiated or *esotericism*.

Without wishing to speak of the oriental Buddha, Confucius, Zoroaster, history shows us *Orpheus,* describing esotericism to the initiates by the creation of the *mysteries;* Moses selecting a tribe of priests or initiates, that of Levi, from among whom he chose those to whom the *tradition* could be entrusted. But the esoteric transmission of this tradition becomes indisputable until 550 B.C., with Pythagoras, initiated in the same sources as Orpheus and Moses, namely Egypt.

Pythagoras had a secret teaching based mainly on numbers, and some quotations from this teaching which have been handed down to us by the alchemists show their absolute identity with the Kabbalah, of which they are but a translation.

Lastly, let us note the existence of this oral tradition in Christianity, in which Jesus reveals to his disciples the true meaning of the parables in

---

[152] Ibid., p. 141.
[153] Ibid., p. 142.

the discourses on the mountain, and entrusts the whole secret of the esoteric tradition to his favourite disciple, St. John.

Revelation is entirely Kabbalistic, and represents true Christian esotericism[154].

Kabbalah's teachings on mankind[155]

The Kabbalah teaches first of all that man represents exactly the constitution of the entire universe. Hence the name microcosm. A small world given to man as opposed to the macrocosm, or great world, given to the universe.

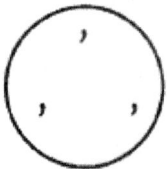

The Kabbalah regards matter as an adjunct created subsequently to all beings because of the Adamic fall.

Man, according to the Kabbalists, is composed of three essential elements: 1st A lower element, which is not the material body, since matter essentially did not exist, but which is the principle that determines the material form: *Nephesh*.

2. A higher element, a divine spark, the soul of all idealists, the spirit of the occultists: *Neschmah*.

These two elements are to each other like oil and water. They are of such disputed essence that they could never enter into relation with each other without a *third term*, which partakes of the two natures and unites them.

3° This third mediating element between the two previous ones is the life of the sages, the spirit of the philosophers, the soul of the occultists: *Ruach*.

These three elements are synthesised in the unity of being, so well that man can be represented schematically by three dots encircled in a circle:

---

[154] Ibid., p. 143.
[155] Ibid., p. 144.

Man comes from God and returns to Him. There are three points to consider in this evolution[156] :

1. The starting point.

2° The point of arrival.

3° What happens between departure and arrival.

1. *The Departure.* The Qabalah always teaches the doctrine of emanation. Man has therefore *emanated* primitively from God in the state of pure Spirit. In the image of God he is constituted in force and intelligence (chomah and bina), i.e. in positive and negative. It is constituted in male and female, Adam and Eve, forming in origin a *single being.* Under the influence of the fall two phenomena occur:

a) the division of the one being into a series of androgynous Adam-Eve beings.

b) the materialisation and subdivision of each of these androgynous beings into two material beings of separate sexes, a male and a female. This is the terrestrial state.

It should be noted, however, as the Tarot teaches us, that each man and each woman contains within himself or herself an image of the primal unity. The brain is Adam, the heart Eve in each of us.

2nd *Transition from departure to arrival.* The materialised man, subject to the influence of the passions, must *voluntarily and freely* find his primitive state, must recreate his primitive immortality. For this purpose *he will reincarnate* as many times as necessary in order to be rescued by the universal and all-powerful force of all: Love.

3rd *Arrival.* Man must therefore first constitute a primitive androgynous being in order to synthetically reform the primitive being from the division of the great Adam-Eve.

These reconstituted androgynous beings must, in their turn, synthesise with each other until they are identified in their origin first God. The Kabbalah teaches, therefore, the same as India, the theory of involution and evolution and the final return to *Nirvana* [157].

---

[156] Ibid., p. 146.
[157] Ibid., p. 148.

Kabbalah's teachings on the universe[158]

In the universe, life is maintained by the streams of light which bathe all the planets, and which spread the principles of generation there in torrents. It is the same of the streams of light and such is the origin of the angels, the personified forces of the Kabalah, and thus of a whole part of the tradition which M. Franck has not dealt with in his book The Practical Kabalah.

Practical Kabbalah comprises the study of these invisible beings, receivers and transmitters of the life of the universe, contained in the streams of light. The Qabalists endeavour to act upon these beings and to know their respective powers; hence all the data of astrology, demonology, and magic contained in the Qabalah[159].

It is the same in the universe, according to the Kabbalah. Above, or rather within these streams of light there is a mysterious fluid, independent of the created beings of nature as the nerve force is independent of the blood corpuscles. This fluid, directly emanating from God, is the very body of God. *It is the spirit of the universe*[160].

The universe appears to us thus constituted as man, 1) of a body, the stars and what they contain; 2) of a life, the streams of light, bathing the stars and containing the *active forces* of nature, the angels; 3) of a directing *will* transmitting itself everywhere by the fluid invisible to the material senses, called by the occultists universal magnetism and by the Qabalists *Aour;* it is the *gold of the* alchemists, the cause of the universal attraction or *Love of the stars.*

Let us further say that the universe, like man, is subject to periodic involution and evolution, and that it must finally be reintegrated into its origin: God.

Kabbalah's teachings on God[161]

Man is made in the image of the universe, but man and the universe are made in the image of God.

God in Himself is unknowable to man, as the Kabalists proclaim by their *Ain-Soph* and the Hindus by their *Parabrahm.* But he is capable

---

[158] Ibid., p. 149.
[159] Ibid., p. 149.
[160] Ibid., p. 150.
[161] Ibid., p. 151.

of being understood in his manifestations. The first divine manifestation, the one by which God, creating the principle of reality, thereby eternally creates His own immortality, is the Trinity.

This first Trinity, prototype of all natural laws, absolute scientific formula, as well as fundamental religious principle, is found in all cults more or less altered.

Whether *Sun, Moon and Earth; Brahma, Vishnu, Siva; Osiris-Isis, Horus or Osiris, Amman, Phta; Jupiter, Juno, Vulcan; the Father, the Son, the Holy Spirit, it* always appears identically constituted. The Qabalah designates it by the following three names: *Kether, Chocmah, Binah.*

These three names form the first trinity of the ten *Sefirot* or numerations. These ten Sefirot express the attributes of God. Let us look at their constitution. If we remember that the universe and man are essentially composed of one body each, of one soul or mediator, and of one spirit, we shall be led to seek the source of these principles in God Himself. Now, the three elements enunciated above, *Kether, Chokmah, Binah,* represent God, but as consciousness represents the whole of man, in a word, these three principles constitute the analysis of the Spirit of God.

What, then, is the life of God? The life of God is the ternary that we have first studied, the constituent ternary of humanity in its two poles Adam and Eve. Finally, the body of God is constituted by this universe of triple manifestation. In short, if we put all these elements together, we obtain the following definition of God: God is *unknowable in his essence* but knowable in his manifestations. The universe constitutes his body, Adam and Eve constitute his soul, and God himself in his double polarisation constitutes his spirit.

The ten Sefirot of the Kabbalah can be taken in various senses:

1° They can be considered as representing God, man, the universe, i.e. the spirit, soul and body of God.

2° They can be considered, as, expressing the development of any one of these three principles[162].

---

[162] Ibid., p. 151.

Influence of the Kabbalah on philosophy

If, as we have said about tradition, the Kabbalah is but the Hebraic translation of these truths taught in all the temples and especially in Egypt, what is impossible in Plato being strongly inspired, not by the Kabbalah itself, as we know it today, but by the primordial philosophy which gives rise to the Kabbalah? What were these Greek philosophers going to do in Egypt and what were they teaching in the initiation into the mysteries of Isis?

Let us just recall the influence of the esoteric tradition on Orpheus, Pythagoras, Plato, Aristotle and all Greek philosophy on the one hand, and on Moses, Ezekiel and all the Hebrew prophets, not to mention the school of Alexandria, the Gnostic sects and the esoteric Christianity revealed in the Apocalypse of St. John; let us quickly say a few words about the influence that tradition may have exerted on modern philosophy.

The alchemists, the Rosicrucians, the Templars, are too well known as kabbalists to mention them. Suffice it to point out the great philosophical reform brought about by *Raymond Lullaby*'s *Ars Magna*.

Spinoza has studied the Kabbalah, and the influence of the Kabbalah is felt at the highest level of this study.

A lesser known point of history is that *Leibnitz* was initiated into the esoteric traditions by Mercury Van Helmont, son of the celebrated occultist and noted sage himself. The author of the Monadology was in frequent contact with the Rosicrucians. German philosophy touches on many points with occult science. Finally, let us mention Freemasonry, which has various cabalistic elements[163].

The world of "quliphah" or demons

To conclude this question on the occult Kabbalah, I find it convenient to add this point on "the world of the Quliphah or demons". We take it from Robert Arnbelain's work, "La Kabbale Pratique[164].

A passage from Jamblichus[165] gives us the full scope of Arnbelain's book. "There is, says Jamblichus, in the Soul a Principle superior to the

---

[163] Ibid., p. 156.
[164] Robert Ambelain, *Le Kabbale pratique*, Niclaus, Paris, 1951.
[165] Ibid., p. 13.

outer nature. By this Principle we can overcome the Cosmos and the systems of this universe. When the *Soul* rises to essences higher than its own, it leaves this cosmos to which it is temporarily bound. And by a mysterious magnetism, it is attracted to a higher plane with which it blends and identifies itself...".

> "Theurgy unites us so closely with the divine Power engendered by itself, unites us so closely with all the creative actions of the gods according to the capacities of each, that the Soul, after having fulfilled the sacred rites, affirms itself in its actions and its intelligences, and finds itself at last placed in the Creator God Himself..." (The Mysteries, V, VI, VII).

This passage from Lamblichus, which brings together all the mysteries of the pagan cults, reveals to us the essence of the Jewish Kabbalah, both theoretical and practical, namely, man's communication with the underworld of demons.

As Ambelain[166] says, the Kabbalah is the

> The traditional "Initiatic Way" of the Christian West. As Swami Sideswarananda recommended, the purely Asian method is not made for the man of Europe. And, in spite of its seductive appearances, and with rare exceptions, it can only lead to a quagmire".

Ambelain continues:

> "The Kabbalah is based on the Judaeo-Christian esoteric tradition. It constitutes a metaphysics and a philosophy, from which a mysticism is derived, the latter actuated and regulated by a particular asceticism, constituting Theurgy or practical Kabbalah; the latter is divided into two sections. The first constitutes a kind of Western yoga; it is of a ritual, ceremonial form; it is the external aspect"[167].

For this reason, Ambelain himself recommends that, before confronting the terrible operations of the practical Cabala, the student of High Science should have familiarised his spirit with the works of Philip of Aquinas, of the Reuchlin, of the Pico della Mirandola, of the Rosenroth, of the Molitor, and then, as Dr. Marc Haven says, he should have familiarised his spirit with the works of Philip of Aquinas, of the Reuchlin, of the Pico della Mirandola, of the Rosenroth, of the Molitor,

---

[166] Ibid., p. 16.
[167] Ibid., p. 16.

and then, as Dr. Marc Haven says, he should have familiarised his spirit with the works of Philip of Aquinas:

> "If he is called to the spiritual life, these pages will be luminous for him. But he will face these studies in vain if he has not tempered his brain in the Hebraic forms, read and assimilated the preparatory works that we have quoted and habituated his soul to the mystical life..." [168]

The aim of the Art is thus, *practically speaking, to* bring the adept into psychic connection with the higher planes and with the intelligences which reside there. It is also to work altruistically and occultly upon his fellow men, in the best interests of the human community[169].

Ambelain goes on to describe "this *syncretistic* religion, *which* spread throughout Western Asia in the centuries before the Christian era and which gave rise to numerous particular groups. This syncretistic religion is given by an esoteric *revelation,* a gnosis... All peoples, Ophites, Naassenes, Cainites, Essenes, Perateans, Sethians, Heliognostics, and all the Pregnostic sects before our era, await the mysterious being who will descend from heaven and incarnate in human form to scatter the demons, purify the earth and mankind, and lead "them to the abodes of the blessed souls in the "mansion" of the Father"[170].

The Sephiroth in the Five Worlds

The Kabbalah starts from the existence of the *Ain Sof;* the absolute nothingness, *Ain,* which evolves into the *Ain Sof* proper, a mixture of nothingness and being, of limitless light, the indeterminate God, i.e. Nothingness. God reveals Himself through the ten Sephiroth that form the kabbalistic tree or Man.

This kabalistic tree or Man can have existence in five worlds. In the world of the *Aziluth* or wholly divine world. In the world of the *Beriath* or world of the angels. In the world of the *Jesirath* or world of the collectivities. In the world of *Asiah* or the world of plants, animals and men, and finally, in the world of demons or "quliphah"[171].

---

[168] Ibid., p. 17.
[169] Ibid., p. 17.
[170] Ibid., p. 22.
[171] Ibid., p. 67.

The world of the Quliphah. Malkuth, the last of the sephiroth, is the nadir of evolution, the lowest point, in Asiah, which must ascend towards Kether. But which, situated on the last step of the *Tree of Life*, in Malkuth, is in osmotic contact with the *Tree of Death*, the inverted tree. Just as Malkhuth was called the "Queen", the "Bride", the "Virgin", the "Wife of the microposop", so, on the contrary, she is called *Quliphah*, the *Prostitute*[172].

Ambelain adds:

> "Everything in life that is corrupt, contrary to the eternal designs of the *Absolute*, eternally rejected by Him, must be expelled and this kind of metaphysical "execration" takes place in the inverted Tree, the *Tree of Death*, as opposed to the *Tree of Life*, outside the Wife, in the Prostitute"[173].

> *"For we are not unaware that God, in whom all "possibles", good and bad, reside, by the fact of his absolute omniscience operates from all eternity an eternal discrimination between what he retains, chooses, adopts and realises by means of his "Emanations" and what he refuses, rejects and reproves"*[174].

What He rejects has constituted the evil Powers, these sinister "Kings of Edom" who existed before all that now is had been brought out of nothing: they are the broken vessels spoken of in the Zohar[175].

To the sephirotic tree that manifests itself in *Malkhuth* corresponds an inverted tree that is but its dark reflection. There the Kabbalistic tradition classifies the "evil beings" into categories corresponding to the blessed choirs[176].

Opposite enlightened Sephiroth	Dark Sephiroth or "Quliphoth".	Names of evil beings	Demons
Malkhuth/Kether	The "Valley of Death	"False gods	Beelzebub

---

[172] Ibid., p. 95.
[173] Ibid., p. 97.
[174] Ibid., p. 97.
[175] Ibid., p. 97.
[176] Ibid., pp. 98-99.

Malkhuth/Hokmath	The "Valley of Oblivion"	"Spirits of lies".	Python
Malkhuth/Binah	The "Valley of Sleep"	"Vessels of iniquity"	Belial
Malkhuth/Chesed	The "Gates of Death"	"Crime Avengers"	Asmodeo
Malkhuth/Geburah	The "Shadow of Death"	"Prestidigitators"	Satan
Malkhuth/Tiphereth	The "Pit of the Abyss"	"Powers of the air"	Merimim
Malkhuth/Netzah	The "Uncleanness"	"Evil-sowing furies".	Abbadom
Malkhuth/Hod	The "Doom"	"Accuser-executors".	Astaroth
Malkhuth/Yesod	The "Trench"	"Tempting and lurking".	Mammon
Malkhuth/Malkhuth	The "World"	"Damaged souls"	The Antichrists

And in the table reproduced below, the respective correspondences between the Quliphah, the demons that rule them and the magical and symbolic image that corresponds to each of the Quliphah are established.

Name of the Quliphah	*Name of the ruling demon*	*Magical image of the Quliphah*
Aretz (the world)	Behemot (the beast)	A woman dressed in purple and scarlet, adorned with gold, jewels and pearls, holding a cup, seated on a scarlet hydra with seven heads and ten horns.
Sheol	Mammon	A woman with horns, mounted on a bull, dressed in white and green, holding an arrow in her right hand and a mirror in her

(the pit)	(greed)	other hand. Two snakes are coiled around her horns, and one on each of her hands and feet.
Open (the doom)	Astaroth (the spy)	Man mounted on a peacock, with eagle's feet, crest on his head, holding fire in his left hand.
Tit aisoun (the filth)	Abbadon (the exterminator)	Woman with a bird's head and eagle's feet, holding an arrow in her left hand.
Bershaat (the pit of the abyss)	Merimim (the midday demon)	Crowned king, seated on a throne, with a raven in his bosom, a globe at his feet, dressed in yellow.
Irasthoum (the shadow of death)	Shatan (the adversary)	An armed man, mounted on a lion, holding a thick cloud in his right hand and a man's head in his left.
Ozlomoth (the gates of death)	Asmodeo (the executor)	Man with the head of a ram, feet of an eagle, dressed in yellow.
Gehenna (the valley of sleep)	Belial (the rebel)	A man with a deer's head, seated on the magnet stone, in turn on a dragon, with camel's feet, holding a sickle on his right and an arrow on his left.
Gehenoum (the valley of oblivion)	Python	A leopard with seven heads and ten horns, the feet of a bear and the paws of a lion.
Gehenomoth (the valley of death)	Beelzebub (the old God)	Red dragon with seven heads and ten horns.

IV. THE JUDEO-MASONIC-DIABOLIC KABBALAH

In his encyclical "Humanum Genus" against Freemasonry, Leo XIII pointed out the grandiose plan in which the two cities of St. Augustine are developed. "The human race, says the wise Pontiff, after having been, through the envy of the devil, miserably separated from God, creator and giver of heavenly goods, has been divided into two different and adverse camps, of which the one fights assiduously for truth and virtue, and the other for what is contrary to virtue and truth. The one is the kingdom of God on earth, that is to say, the true Church of Jesus Christ, to which whoever wishes to be attached from the heart and as is fitting for salvation, must serve God and His only begotten Son with all his understanding and all his will; the other is the kingdom of Satan, under whose rule and power are all those who, following the fatal example of their leader and of our first fathers, refuse to obey the divine and eternal law, and undertake undertakings against God or apart from God Himself.

> "The Roman Pontiffs, our predecessors, being solicitous for the salvation of the Christian people, soon knew who this capital enemy was and what he wanted as soon as he appeared in the darkness of his hidden conspiracy, and, as if declaring his watchword, they warned princes and peoples with foresight not to be hunted in the evil arts and lurks prepared to deceive him. The first warning of the danger was given in 1738 by Pope Clement XII, whose constitution was confirmed and renewed by Benedict XIV. Pius VII followed in the footsteps of both, and Leo XII, including in the Apostolic Constitution *Quo graviora* what had been decreed in this matter by the former, ratified and confirmed it for ever. Pius VIII, Gregory XVI and Pius IX, by the way, repeatedly spoke in the same sense.

> "And, in fact, the nature and intent of the Masonic sect having been made clear by manifest indications, by proceedings, by the publication of laws, rites and annals. And indeed, the nature and intent of the Masonic sect having been made clear by manifest indications, by instructed processes, by the publication of laws, rites and annals, and often by the declarations of the accomplices themselves, this Apostolic See openly denounced and proclaimed that the Masonic sect, constituted against all right and convenience, was no less pernicious to the State than to the Christian Religion, and threatening with the most serious penalties which the Church usually employs against criminals, it strictly prohibited all from enrolling in this society".

> "There are various sects which, though different in name, rites, form and origin, united together by a certain communion of purpose and

affinity in their fundamental opinions, agree in fact with the Masonic sect, a sort of centre from which they all go out and to which they all return.

"And it is precisely this change and upheaval that many societies of *communists and socialists*, to whose designs the right-wing Freemasons cannot be said to be alien to, as it greatly favours their aims and agrees with them in the principal *dogmas*". So much for Leo XIII in "Humanum Genus".

Meurin's book

Freemasonry is the great enemy of the Church and of Civilisation, of the supernatural and the natural order. An enemy worse than communism, since communism is instrumented by Freemasonry. Who is behind Freemasonry? To clarify this, nothing better than the book by the Jesuit Mgr Leon Meurin, former bishop of Port-Louis. It is an extraordinary book, undoubtedly the best ever written on Freemasonry[177].

What does Archbishop Meurín say in summary?

He says in brief that Freemasonry is a Jewish invention to destroy the Church, a Jewish invention built on the basis of the Kabbalah. What are the Jews and why do they want to destroy the Church? What is the Kabbalah and why is it an instrument of the Jews?

The Jews

The Jews are a messianic people. God took Abraham out of his land to make him the father of a great people from whom the Messiah, Jesus Christ, the Saviour of the world, was to be born. This people, whose raison d'être consisted in their lineage so that from them, from their blood, would come the Saviour, defected in part. Not only did they not receive the Messiah, they condemned him to death. Their raison d'être has since been changed to that of being the natural enemy of Christ, of the Church and of the work of the Church, Christian civilisation.

The raison d'être of the Jewish people is the destruction of the Church. This, which naturally arises, has been stated by St. Paul in definitive words: "The Jews are those who put to death the Lord Jesus and the prophets, and persecute us, who do not please God and are against all

---

[177] León Meurin, S. J., *Filosofía de la Masonería*, Ed. Nos, Madrid, 1957.

men; who prevent the Gentiles from being spoken to and their salvation from being procured". This sums up the task of the Jews throughout Christian history. Enemies of Christ and of the peoples so that the peoples will not be converted. And for this they have to carry out a task of *domination* of the peoples in order to close them to the Gospel. A task of degradation, because they can easily exercise their domination over degraded peoples.

The Jewish trajectory in relation to the Christian people is easy to follow. The story is driven by two poles. The pole of God and the pole of the devil. That of the Church and that of the Counter Church. That of the spirit and that of the flesh. That of the Church and that of the Jews. Since the departure of Christ, the Church rises and the Jewish power falls. The Jews are confined to the ghettos. The Church reaches its splendour in the Christian world, in Christian civilisation. There are still the monuments that testify to the splendour of the Church up to the 16th century. The Jews gradually penetrated Christian society. They always plotted and lurked with it. But to no avail as long as the Church remained faithful to Christ. But at the end of the Middle Ages, the Church gave in to its love for Christ and tried to make contact with the Jews. This was the time of the Christian Kabbalah. Raymond Lull, no doubt in good faith, had prepared the way. Pico della Mirándola and the Renaissance embraced the Jewish Kabbalah. The Jews penetrate Christian society. They penetrate and destroy it. And the world begins to Judaise, to Kabbalise. The Jews invent Freemasonry to recruit Christians to destroy the Church[178].

The instruments of destruction

It would be a mistake to think today that the Bible is the book of the Jews. Their book is the Talmud, and the soul of the Talmud is the Kabbalah. The Kabbalah is the great *secret* instrument of the Jews against the Church and against the Christian world. The Kabbalah may have been the authentic tradition of the Jews, but today it is distorted and is an instrument of perdition. Kabbalah informs Freemasonry, which is a Kabbalistic institution. This is the great demonstration of

---

[178] We present here, objectively and for the purpose of giving a complete idea of how the problem of the Kabbalah is posed, the interpretation which we call Judeo-Masonic-Diabolic, as it emerges from Bishop Meurin's book, without entering into a value judgement.

Mgr Meurin's book. There is therefore a Judeo-Masonic-demonic interpretation of the Kabbalah. This is what remains to be seen.

The Judeo-Masonic-Demonic Kabbalah

Archbishop Meurin shows that Freemasonry takes up the errors of the old pagan cults of Zoroaster, Brahmanism, Buddhism, the Syrians and Babylonians, the Chaldeans, Hermes Trismegistro, Gnosticism, Manichaeism. He gathers them because he finds them in the Kabbalah. *The Kabbalah is a mixture of all the old pagan religions.* Freemasonry is also a mixture of all the pagan cults. But the Kabbalah is above all the divinisation of man; the divinisation of Jewish man and the enthronement of Satan.

The Kabbalah is a mixture of all pagan cults. First of all, Mgr *Meurin studies the dogmatics of Freemasonry. "The dogmas of Freemasonry are those of the Jewish Kabbalah, and in particular those of its book, the Zohar".*

The Kabbalah teaches that the *En-sof* comes first. Before it produced the Universe, or whatever we want to call what is outside itself, the *En-sof* was absolutely ignorant of itself, let alone of other beings that did not yet exist; it had neither wisdom, nor power, nor goodness, nor any other attribute, for an attribute implies a distinction and therefore a limit... The *En-sof* thus begins to think. The *En-sof, in order to reveal itself,* begins by forming an imperceptible point like the Hebrew "iod". This is the first Sephira, the Crown.

From the first Sefira emanate the other nine Sefirot, and with them, the world of God and man, on all planes, from angels to demons. All is from God and all is God unfolding[179].

It is clear that all this is *pantheism* and repugnant and gross pantheism. The world has not come out of the divine substance by emanation[180].

The enthronement of the Jew

Where does the *Crown* that we have seen sandwiched between the *En-sof* and wisdom, between the eternal substance and the three divine persons, come from? We have consulted the Hebrew Bible to delve into this important question. And, in the book of Esther, we have found the

---

[179] Ibid., p. 54.
[180] Ibid., p. 57.

Kheter malkhuth. King Ahasuerus asked that she be brought before him and the princes of the kingdom, Queen Vasthi, with her royal diadem. The queen refused. She was then dethroned for her disobedience. Esther, the beautiful Jewess, was chosen in her place and crowned by Ahasuerus himself with the *royal diadem*, of which Vashthi was divested. Mordecai, Esther's uncle, was likewise honoured and awarded the *royal diadem*, which Haman lost because he wanted to exterminate the entire Jewish race. In these passages, the royal diadem is called *Kether-Malkhuth*[181].

After the fall of Queen Vasthi and of the prime minister Haman, and after the exaltation to the throne of the beautiful Esther and of the Jew Mordecai to the first place in the reign of Ahasuerus, the Jews exterminated their enemies on the thirteenth and fourteenth days of the month Adar; they then instituted a perpetual feast to be celebrated on the fourteenth and fifteenth days of the same month. And so we find ourselves in the footsteps of the first and tenth of the sefirot: Kether and Malkhuth: *The archetypal man is the Jew, with the crown upon his head and the kingdom at his feet*[182].

Political application of the Kether-Malkhuth

In Drumont's "Testament of an Anti-Semite", we have found the following confirmation of our exposition[183].

"In the *Israelite archives* of October 16, 1890, the Jew Singer appealed directly to Bismarck and said without further ado: "I beg you to read the magnificent book of Esther, where you will find the *typical story* of Haman and Mordecai. Haman, the omnipotent minister, is you, Sir; William is Ahasuerus, and Mordecai, German socialism, advocated by the Jews Lassalle and Marx, and continued by my namesake and co-religionist Singer. You have wished to annihilate Mordecai, and it is you, the Great Chancellor, who have become his victim".

Such recklessness on the part of the Jew Singer drew the attention of the world to the book of Esther, which featured his co-religionist Mordecai crowned with the Kether-Malkhuth, the image of which is borne by the Rose-Cross, the dutiful knights of the Jews.

---

[181] Ibid., p. 87.
[182] Ibid., p. 87.
[183] Ibid., p. 88.

The fear of the Jewish power," says Holy Scripture, "had overwhelmed all peoples. The Jews then made a great slaughter among their enemies, and by slitting their throats they did them the evil which they intended to do to them. In Susa itself, they killed five hundred men, not counting the ten sons of Haman. The king was soon informed of the number of those who had been killed in Shushan. The king said to Queen Esther, "How great do you think the slaughter of the Jews is in all the provinces? And the queen answered, 'I beg the king to command that the Jews be allowed to do tomorrow what they have done in Shushan, and that the ten sons of Haman be hanged. And the king commanded it to be done, and the decree was soon published in the city of Shushan, and the ten sons of Haman were hanged, and the next day three hundred other men were slain in the city of Shushan. And in all the provinces the Jews killed their enemies in such great numbers that the death toll was at least seventy-five thousand.

The holiday the Jews call Purim, February 14, is celebrated in memory of their liberation from the tyranny of Haman, through the courage of Esther and Mordecai[184].

"The Jews give their own children, when they reach the age of thirteen, a *crown* as a sign of strength".

The *Crown* on the head and the *Kingdom* at the feet: here is the Jewish ideal, patiently pursued ever since Jehovah chose Abraham's posterity as His chosen people.

Adam Kadmon, the primordial man, is the archetype of the Jew. The Jew is man par excellence. All the well-known phraseology about man and humanity, his liberation and freedom, his rights, etc., must be understood as applying first of all to the Jews, and then, by communication, to their affiliates, the Masons, for only in Masonry is man, already *perfect* in the 11th degree, so that to the question, "Are you a sublime Chosen Knight?", he can answer, "My name is *Emmarek*, *a* man true in every respect.

Emmarek means in Hebrew: "I am purified".

Apart from the Jewish people and the individuals Judaised by the Masonic mysteries, there are no *real men*, for the other nations are but a variety of animals". The goim", the non-Jews, "cannot be called men".

---

[184] Ibid., p. 88.

This is the doctrine of the Talmud, which is to the Jew moral theology, as the Kabbalah is dogmatic theology. But, as we have already said, if the Jews deceive the Masons, they are deceived in their turn by the enemy of the human race. Do we not see the Tempter concealed in the form of the "royal diadem" as he once concealed himself in the form of the serpent? The apple of Paradise has been changed into the *Crown*, with which he promises to satiate the appetite for power of *man*, the one man, the Jew. Do we not hear the words of the Tempter, later repeated to Jesus, showing him all the kingdoms of the world and their glory: "All these things will I give thee, if thou wilt worship me, bowing down and worshipping me"? But the Jew has not answered as Jesus did: "Begone, Satan, for it is written, 'You shall worship the Lord your God and serve Him only'".

As we shall see, Lucifer is worshipped in Masonic lodges. By the Jews worshipping the royal diadem, as their golden calf, Satan, with the name of Kether, has taken a place above the Holy Trinity[185].

Conclusion of this second chapter

The Qabalah, in its origin received from the hand of God, contains the divine and catholic interpretation of the highest mysteries entrusted by God to humanity. In the first three Sephiroth it refers to the august mystery of the Unity and Trinity of God, and in the Adam Kadmon to the no less august mystery of the incarnate Word, Our Lord Jesus Christ. But, man having sinned, this divine and catholic Kabalah, in the course of the centuries became more and more perverted and even carnalised as the Israelite people, chosen by God, fell into ever more abject degradation. Hence the grossest errors, such as pantheism and the worship of Man, have crept into it until it has become the sinister forces of the devil himself.

Hence it is no wonder that the Kabbalah, which admits of an authentic interpretation of Christianity, has become the receptacle of the most gross and clean aberrations which inspire and nourish all the present anti-Christianity of the modern world.

---

[185] Ibid., p. 90.

CHAPTER III

THE EXISTENCE OF A JEWISH GNOSIS SINCE THE 16TH CENTURY B.C.

The word gnosis is misleading. There can be catholic and healthy gnosis. Dupont demonstrates it in *St. Paul*[186]. But when we speak of gnosis, we commonly understand bad gnosis, theosophical and pantheistic gnosis. It is in this sense that we will speak here. Gnosticism is an esoteric system of philosophy and theology that became famous in the first centuries of Christianity and was fought against by the Fathers of the Church.

But the important thing to note here is what the Jewish Encyclopedia[187] clearly states:

> "There is no doubt that Jewish Gnosticism existed before Christian Gnosticism. As can be seen in the apocalypses, from the second century B.C., Gnostic thought is linked with Judaism, which has accepted Babylonian and Syrian *doctrines*".

The problem that arises here is the antiquity and origin of gnosis. Adolph Franck[188] traces the Jewish gnosis back to the 6th century B.C. through the influence of Iranian and Persian Zoroastrian ideas in Jewish circles.

Gershom Scholem traces Kabbalistic speculation back to Adam [189] "All this," he says, "is to signify that, in the intent of the Kabbalists themselves, mystical knowledge is not altogether of a private nature,

---

[186] *"Gnosis"*, La conaissance religieuse dans les Épitres de Saint Paul, *Louvain, Paris, 19-1-9.*
[187] New York and London. Funk and Wagnalls Company, 1905, art. "Jewish Gnosticism".
[188] *La Cabbale,* Paris, 1883.
[189] Le grandi correnti della mistica ebraica, *p. 40, French ed. p. 34.*

such that it can be acquired only through one's own personal experience; rather, it is all the closer to the original wisdom of mankind in general, the purer and more complete. Or, to put it in the words of the Qabalists themselves, the knowledge that Adam, the first man, had of things human and divine, is the knowledge of the mystic at any time. Hebraic mysticism therefore presented itself with the requirement and the hypothesis of transmitting and reviving in its followers this original revelation of God to Adam, this absolutely original knowledge". However, for Gershom Scholem, the most important book of Hebraic mysticism would have been written, as we have seen, by Moses of Leon in the 13th century AD.

We will follow the important work of Mauricio Carlavilla in which he shows that the origin of the Kabbalah is to be found in the 16th century B.C., when the prolonged contact of the Jews with the Egyptians took place[190].

Carlavilla starts from the research of A. Franck, who in his book draws this conclusion: "The shocking similarities which we have found between this doctrine - the Cabala and the beliefs of many sects of Persia, the numerous and strange relations which it shows us with the *Zend Avesta*, the traces which the religion of Zoroaster has left in so many parts of Judaism, and the foreign relations which, since the Babylonian captivity, have not ceased to exist between the Hebrews and their ancient overlords, have led us to conclude that the materials of the Cabala have been borrowed from the theology of the ancient Persians".

Maurice Carlavilla accepts the similarities between Zoroastrianism and the Kabbalah found by Franck, but he does not believe that the influence of Zoroastrianism on the Kabbalah can be deduced from this, but on the contrary, he proposes an influence the other way round, that is, of Jewish Kabbalah on Zoroastrianism. Certainly," says Carlavilla, "the tradition of the Kabbalah is not confirmed by authentic monuments such as the *Yzeschné or Yachá*, the *Vispered*, the *Vendidad*, the *Yeschtsadé, Sirozi, BundDehlsch*, contained in their compilation known under the name of *Zend-Avesta*, whose contemporaneity with Zoroaster is not disputed. But this difficulty, in no way external, loses its value when we know the proven reality that Zoroastrianism is not an esoteric doctrine, but quite the contrary: having become a religion, it is the

---

[190] This work by Carlavilla is an introduction to Franck's *La Cabbale*, which is in print.

official religion of the Persian empire; on the other hand, the Cabala, even accepting the original existence of an orthodox, Mosaic Cabala, and of perversion, the one known to us, both are obviously achromatic doctrines, secret by design of those who have professed them from the beginning. A secret faithfully kept, it is said, since Sinai by the College of the doctors of Israel, whose *reception* - Kabbalah - is oral by strict prescription scrupulously observed, except for exceptional and fragmentary transfers which, without canonical character, begin to appear very spaced out in the last century of the first Age and in the first century of our own, and with the same character, others continue to appear, although scarce, given the great lapse of time, until the end of the 13th century, when the so-called "Bible of the Kabbalah" appears in writing, a copious collection of treatises whose editors call *Sefer-ha-Zohar, the* Book of Splendour.

The existence of this secret tradition is reported in the 1st century AD by Philo, the famous Jewish philosopher[191]. He says: "They - the therapists - study the Holy Scriptures and apply the allegorical method to the *philosophy of our ancestors*. They believe in effect that the literal sense covers a mysterious meaning which interpretation unveils. *They also possess writings composed at a very ancient time* by the founders of the sect. These founders have left many commentaries containing models of allegories which their successors have used to compose others, imitating them.

Flavius Josephus, the famous Jewish historian, gives an account of the sworn commitment of those who were to be admitted into the sects of the Essenes.

> "They solemnly promise... to conceal nothing from their confreres of the most secret mysteries of their religion, which they will not reveal to others, even when threatened with death; that they will teach nothing but the doctrine they have been taught, and will carefully preserve the books, as well as the names of those from whom they have received them... There are among them some who pretend to know the things of the future, both by the study they make of the holy books and of the ancient prophecies, and by the care taken in it to

---

[191] *Philon,* De vita contemplativa.

sanctify themselves, and so it happens that they are seldom mistaken in their predictions."[192]

A magic formula very popular between 150 B.C. and 200 B.C. in Egypt says: "I am Moses, your prophet, to whom you have entrusted the mysteries, the ceremonies of Israel.... listen to me: I am an angel Phapo Osoronuphis: this is your true name, handed down to the prophets of Israel"[193].

Of this secret tradition or gnosis of the Jews, we have quite expressive allusions in the writings of the New Testament:

> "Woe to you doctors of the law, who have seized the key of knowledge, and neither will you enter in, nor let you enter in"[194].

> "You set aside the precept of God and hold to human tradition". And he said to them: "Indeed, you set aside the precept of God in order to establish your tradition... you set aside the word of God by your tradition which has been handed down to you, and you do many other such things"[195].

The existence of the *Jewish gnosis* is sufficiently documented in the famous Dead Sea Scrolls, which began to be discovered in 1947. Mauricio Carlavilla follows the exposition of Millar Burrows, professor of biblical theology at Yale University[196] :

> "All the results of the various investigations therefore converge on a historical period during which all the manuscripts were written and which extends approximately from 300 B.C. to 70 A.D. The relative age of the various manuscripts is also amply resolved and their relative position within this period. The relative age of the different manuscripts is also well settled and their relative position within this period.

> "Therefore," says Carlavilla, "the lesson to be drawn is that for about three centuries before Jesus Christ certain doctrines professed by a society which various historians call 'Essene' were already known; but if it is shown that the doctrines and the 'Essene' society cannot have been younger, it does not argue that they must have been worked

---

[192] Josephus, *De bello Judaico*, II, 8.
[193] Cf. E. A. Wallis Budge: *Egyptian Magie*, pp. 176-177, London.
[194] *Lk.*, 11, 52.
[195] *Mk.*, 7, 8.
[196] *Les manuscrits de la Mer Mars*, p. 126, Ed. Robert Lafont, Paris.

out and formed at that same period; that is, it does not prove that doctrines and society are only three centuries old when our era begins. Evidently, it may have been older".

Now," Carlavilla continues, "we are going to examine the main data extracted from the documents in order to find in them their possible relation to the Cabala. We insist again that we have recourse to Professor Burrows, because there is not in his extensive and meticulous book even the slightest trace that he knows anything of the Cabala, and therefore his appreciations take on great value, since there is nothing intentional, and nothing accidental, in the many things he points out that can and must be identified with Cabalism"[197].

Let's see:

> "The interpretation of Scripture plays an essential part in the literature of the sect. It is hardly an exaggeration to say with Brownlee: 'The sect finds its origin in the interpretation of the Bible'"....

> "The indispensable authority for interpreting Scripture has its source in a new revelation made to the head of the sect, the Teacher of Righteousness (textual), "the priest in whose heart God has put the necessary wisdom to explain the words of his servants the prophets, by whom God has announced what is to come to his people and to his Congregation".

This new revelation surpasses even the visions that were conceived to the prophets; thus:

> "God commands Habakkuk to write what would befall the last generation, but does not reveal to him when this period would be consummated. What the prophet himself is ignorant of, was, however, revealed to the Teacher of Righteousness, to whom God made known all the mysteries contained in the word of his servants the prophets"...[198]

It would seem that the portrait of Simon ben Jochai, the alleged author and hero of the *Zohar*, already known to us, is a replica, two centuries later, of the portrait of the Teacher of Righteousness in the Qumram documents.

Burrows says:

---

[197] M. Burrows, *Les manuscrits de la Mer Morte*, p. 126, Ed. Robert Lafont, Paris.
[198] Ibid., p. 284.

> "Apart from the devotion of the "sectarians" to the Hebrew writings, one discovers in their thought elements which may lead one to believe in certain Gentile influences. In particular, many scholars perceive in the Dead Sea Scrolls a reflection of the religious movement known as Gnosticism; others discover no trace of Gnosticism...
>
> "Strictly speaking, the word *Gnosticism* designates a heresy of Christianity which developed in the second century after Jesus Christ. This heresy was certainly not an entirely new or truly unique phenomenon; it represented a unique amalgam of new and old ideas, some of which dated back to the old Babylonian religion... Some scholars recognise a pre-Christian type of Jewish Gnosticism; others deny this interpretation.

Those who admit it find in the Dead Sea Scrolls further evidence in support of their claim.

> "When we speak of Gnosticism in connection with the Dead Sea Scrolls, the question is *not* whether the sectarians were Gnostics in the proper sense of the term, defined as a Christian heresy, but whether they were linked to a tendency, to a general movement which, in a broad sense, is called Gnosticism.
>
> "The primary feature of Gnosticism is the conception of health by knowledge; this knowledge is arrived at by instruction; it is received by a mystical illumination obtained by solitary contemplation or by participation in sacramental rites; but there is always an intellectual element mixed in. The fundamental idea is indicated by the very name Gnosticism, which is derived from the Greek word *gnosis*, knowledge.
>
> "Undoubtedly, the Dead Sea Scrolls and the *Damascus Document* insist strongly on knowledge. To illustrate this idea we can quote very typical passages: "God loves the knowledge of wisdom; He has set wisdom before Himself; prudence and knowledge pay homage to Him". Dupont-Sommer recognises here a characteristic inspiration of the gnosis... Commenting on Habakkuk, 2, 14: "For the knowledge of the glory of JHWH will fill the earth as the waters fill the sea", the *commentary* says: "And later knowledge will be revealed to them as abundant as the waters of the sea". Dupont Somer sees here the revelation of *divine gnosis*. The *Manual of the Discipline* prescribes to the members of the sect to bring their knowledge to the community... The *Sons of Truth* are those who "walk humbly, full of prudence in their conduct and love towards the truth of the mysteries of knowledge".

From the same Manual:

> "By prudence I will conceal knowledge,
> and with a reasonable prudence I will erect a fence
> around wisdom...
> My eye has beheld the deep wisdom
> Which is hidden from the wise man
> And prudent discretion to the sons of men
> Blessed art Thou, my God
> Who hast opened the heart of thy servant to knowledge
> Thou hast taught all knowledge.
>
> We are sorry," says Carlavilla, "that we cannot continue copying all the texts contributed by Burrows on the subject. As we can see, those quoted here fall squarely within the scope of gnosis, even according to the definition of gnosticism given by him, which is of course exact, but very general".

Now, if he recognises the historical existence of a general or universal Gnostic current, he does not even dream of its presence in the Jewish world. And how easy it would have been for him, right there, at the University of Jerusalem, which he had to visit during his long research work on Qumram, to learn about *Jewish gnosis*. A professor there was Gershom Scholem, who, ten years earlier, in 1938, had given a series of lectures in the Strook Chair at the *Jewish Institute of Religion* in New York, publishing them in 1941 under the title *The Great Currents of Jewish Mysticism: Merkaba, Gnosis, Kabbalah, Zohar, Sabbatianism, Hassidism*. The author or his book would have informed Burrows and his group of sages that the Kabbalah is the *Hebrew gnosis*.

Carlavilla continues: "In it we have arrived at approximately three centuries before the beginning of our era, with which, naturally, we still lack more than three others to find a greater antiquity than Zoroastrianism, with which, if it were found, Franck's thesis would be invalidated; because if the Cabala were earlier, it could not emanate from the doctrine of Zoroaster, since it is elementary reasoning to find it impossible for the earlier to proceed from the later.

But, in our opinion, if there are no Kabalistic documents prior to our Era for more than three centuries, which is explained and explicable, as we have just seen, there are, however, abundant reports of the existence of doctrines professed in Judaism, the characteristics of which enable us to identify them with the Kabalists. And those who point them out and denounce them are, no less, many distinguished prophets of Israel.

Carlavilla quotes Isaiah, Micah, Jeremiah, Zephaniah, Habakkuk, Ezekiel.

Of this last prophet we read:

> "Son of man, do you see what these do, do you see the great abominations that the house of Israel do right here to keep me from my sanctuary? But turn around and you will see even greater abominations. And he brought me to the entrance of the court, and I looked and saw a hole in the wall. And he said to me, Son of man, break through the wall. And there appeared a door. Go in, he said to me, and see what abominable abominations these do. And I went in, and looked, and saw all manner of images of creeping things and abominable beasts, and all the idols of the house of Israel painted on the wall round about.
>
> And seventy men of the elders of the house of Israel, among them Jozoniah the son of Shaphen, stood before them, every man with his censer in his hand, from which went up a cloud of incense, and said unto me, Son of man, hast thou seen what the elders of Israel do in secret, every man in his chamber, full of images? For they say to themselves, 'The LORD does not see us; he is far from the land. And he said to me, 'You shall see greater abominations than these.

The allegorical language of the chapter is clear here, and we believe we can easily interpret its meaning. The images engraved on the walls of the great room,

> "creeping things, beasts, abominations, and all the idols of the house of Israel" which also adorn the respective chamber of each of the seventy, seem to indicate hieroglyphic matters, reminiscent of the Egyptians. Also compatible with such a meaning, the allegorical language may mean that, on the walls, on their shelves, is a series of "abominable" writings, the doctrines of which the seventy elders of Israel profess, symbolising their profession, that incense which they offer to him, incense that can only be offered to God. This interpretation of the allegory is supported by the fact that, if the chamber in which the seventy elders are found could contain within its walls "all manner of images of creeping things and beasts and abominations and all the idols of the house of Israel, which is too much to grant, they could not fit within the walls of the particular chambers of each of the seventy elders. Undoubtedly this was the Council of Israel, later called the *Sanhedrin*, in which the supreme juridical, economic, moral and dogmatic authority resided. The full Sanhedrin is accused by Ezekiel of crypto-idolatry, in vulgar language, in allegorical language, of professing heretical written

doctrines. Even though, as we shall see, the one accusation implies the other. For the idolatrous religions of all cultured peoples since long before the eleventh century B.C. have their "Cabala", what are called "mysteries", doctrines and practices forbidden to the vulgar, professed and performed by the priestly and cultured *elite* of each people. And this is what we find through the prophet concerning the seventy elders of Israel, a kind of "mysteries" professed by them.

The practice of the mysteries in Israel

It is a fact abundantly attested by the history of Israel that from the earliest times false cults, "mysteries", were practised. The "god" made in the desert must have been the ox, identified in Egyptian mythology with Osiris; the young ox-calf must have come from the small size of the image cast by Aaron[199].

"But what we are interested in extracting from the event is the proof that the Hebrew people, until after their miraculous deliverance, after knowing experimentally, mystically, the existence of their true God through a long series of prodigies, for the most part, continue to profess the Egyptian religion, as their apostasy, which is to be so harshly and bloodily punished, so eloquently betrays.

Now, one wonders whether that majority of the Hebrew people would only profess Egyptian idolatry in its exoteric, popular, crude aspect. If so, logically it would not have lasted and the religion of Yahweh would have prevailed. But since the opposite is true, idolatry dominates and is in the majority, with very few exceptions, for short periods, from the end of Solomon's reign onwards. Logically, the existence of a minority among the Jewish *elite*, initiated in esotericism, in the mysteries, in Egyptian theology and theurgy, whose existence would explain, as in all the idolatries of those and many subsequent centuries, the popular reign of such absurd and crude religious mythologies, of which the "mysteries" were their spirit, their soul, animation, infusing them with vitality, life, thanks in truth to an unworthy resource, must logically be induced. For to all those initiated into the "mysteries," the popular beliefs were false, or, at best, mere reminiscences or symbolisms of their hidden truths; in short, a means of securing the obedience of the uneducated masses by means of those myths and practical superstitions.

---

[199] *Exodus*, 31, 18.

The episode of the "calf" took place in the 15th century B.C., according to the long chronologies; according to the short chronologies, in the 13th century. In any case, nine or seven centuries before the Babylonian captivity, the period in which the birth of the Kabbalah, the esotericism, the Jewish gnosis, engendered by a contagion of Zoroastrianism which perverts the law, is supposed to have taken place. When, as the Sinai episode shows, not the perversion of the law but the perversion of the vast majority of the Jewish people dates back centuries before the 16th or 13th century, as one wishes.

After the episode of the Calf, the unity of God's people in idolatry is constant, in the time of the judges and in the time of Solomon.

> "King Solomon, besides Pharaoh's daughter, loved many foreign women.... He had seven hundred wives of royal blood and three hundred concubines, and the women twisted his heart. When Solomon grew old, his wives dragged his heart to other gods, and his heart was not wholly of Yahweh, his God, as David's had been. So Solomon went after Astarte, goddess of the Sidonians, and after Nilcom, abomination of the sons of Ammon"[200].

Let us retain: "Solomon worshipped Astarte, Milcom, Kemos, and Molech... The worship of Molech was the immolation of human victims; sometimes the victim was the son of the immolator.

"Now, and this is where we should have come to, Solomon is the archetype of wisdom. Without being deprived of it by God, he falls at the end of his days into a manifold idolatry, he professes an idolatrous syncretism, in which is included the hideous worship of Molok. And one wonders whether, given Solomon's wisdom and knowledge, it is possible to explain his falling into such idolatrous aberrations, defying the wrath of the true God, by the mere seduction of his foreign wives. It is neither logical, nor plausible, nor probable. What is inducible must be that he is seduced precisely through his own wisdom, given his inherent and insatiable thirst for knowledge. Such a yearning, so typical of a wise man, would naturally lead him to want to know the "mysteries" of all those idolatries by being initiated into their most hidden esotericisms. His marriage to the daughter of the Egyptian Pharaoh, to a daughter of the god Ra incarnate, must have entitled him to be initiated by the Egyptian priests into their *egotism, the* ultimate

---

[200] *I Kings*, 11, 4.

secret of their mysteries, which they exported to Phoenicia, Greece and Syria... Israel would be no exception, having a king who was the political son of the "god incarnate". That *egotheism* of the Egyptian mysteries, that deification of the initiate in them, a true diabolical possession for us Christians, was the hidden and indomitable impulse to evil, whose most satanic expression was the human sacrifices perpetrated with greater or lesser publicity and in greater or lesser numbers by the immense majority of idolaters.

We ratify it, Solomon's fall into idolatries can only be explained by a previous doctrinal perversion with simultaneous magical experience, in the initiation of which he becomes aware of his self-divinity: the Kabbalah.

Readers will have seen that, from Solomon onwards, including himself, the kings who remain faithful to the God of Israel can be counted on one's fingers and fingers to spare, More, even when these reign, except in the case of Josiah, the worship of Yahweh, which should be the worship of a minority, is officiated simultaneously with idolatrous cults; doubtless because the kings do not dare, or lack the strength, to forbid them and destroy the temples and places of abomination.

At the beginning of this biblical synthesis of Israel's idolatry, we hinted at the existence in all idolatries of "mysteries", of esoteric doctrines professed by the intellectual and political *elite*, constituting the hidden ideological-magical (for the prophet, demonic) support of the gross and bloody idolatrous cults of the masses.

Egyptian mysteries

Egypt had the mysteries of Isis, and certainly many more, perhaps kept in greater secrecy. Many authors make more or less extensive allusions to them[201] :

"No religion of antiquity has left a greater and more colossal testimony than the Egyptian.

Its religious architecture, in terms of quantity and size, is unparalleled. Likewise, none of such remote antiquity has bequeathed us anywhere near such a quantity of texts: many indestructible by time, as they were engraved in stone; others painted on walls, many of them were hidden

---

[201] Sorames, *Life of Hippocrates,* preface.

in unknown and practically inaccessible burial dens. And there were so many writings on papyri that, despite the fatal destruction caused by the centuries and the violent vicissitudes, a large number of them have come down to us almost intact, in a state of being studied... However, all this immense documentation, which makes known to us ritual and priestly ceremonies, chants, cult formulas, names, attributes, symbols, biographies, etc., of their copious theogony, it must be confessed, does not reveal theological secrets nor the spirit, that is to say, the deep and transcendent aspect of that religion, which dominated the Egyptian people like very few others. In a word, its mysteries are perfectly unknown to us. Only its existence is known, not its essence or transcendence.

This lack of theological, metaphysical texts in a people so given, not only to bequeathing to posterity as much and as much as they have bequeathed, must only be due to a rigorous esotericism, imposed with severity and rigour on the depositaries of the doctrines, the monarch and the priests.

For the existence of a theology in ancient Egypt is evident from a study of its theogony as bequeathed to us; even, it seems certain, with allegorical symbolism and names, and not as it was known in the secrecy of the temples.

Herodotus states: "In Sais is the tomb of him whom I scruple to name... over the lake (of the temple) the Egyptians celebrate, at night, the representation of the sufferings endured by him: they call them Mysteries... On these mysteries, all of which are known to me without exception, my mouth keeps a religious silence"[202].

Exporting Egyptian mysteries

The first testimony about Orpheus is by Herodotus.

No other could be older. No prose works earlier than his have survived.

In them, he referred to the Egyptian custom according to which one could not enter a temple wearing a woollen dress, and he says: "In this the Egyptians agree with the customs called Orphic and Bacchic, but which are Egyptian and Pythagorean"[203].

---

[202] Heredotus, II, 70.
[203] Herodotus, II, 81.

Let us remember that Herodotus was born in 484 and died in 425; in other words, he lived from the second decade of the fifth century. Therefore, if the first liberation of the Hebrews from Babylon took place in the years 530 or 536, as we already know, Herodotus wrote only a century later. Consequently, he is not far removed from what was current and happening in the 6th century, and he must have had at his disposal the books then extant which, unfortunately, have not reached us, and he was even able to listen to old and not very old men living in that century; not only from Greece, but from many other countries which he is known to have visited besides Athens, where he resided for a long time, in contact with its most learned men, Cyprus, Egypt, Cyrenaica, Tyre, Libya, Phoenicia, Persia, etc.

The poet intimately associates and identifies the Mysteries of Eleusis, Phrygia, Cyprus and Egypt.

We consider that, within the limits imposed, sufficient evidence has been provided to demonstrate the existence of Mysteries in Egypt, from the most remote times and their exportation to other countries, having them more abundant in Greece; undoubtedly because their great culture, without any solution of continuity, thanks to Rome, is the same as ours.

However, some texts speak of the Assyrian and Phoenician mysteries also coming from Egypt. The vast majority of Egyptologists and Hellenists have come to the same conclusion.

We believe we have demonstrated with the possible proofs the existence of secret doctrines under the mythological theogonies long before the 6th century... we will already study in Egypt, not in the 6th century but before the 15th century, long before the most distant date calculated to mark the Exodus, the departure of the Israelites from the Pharaonic kingdom.

If Egypt exported its theogony and esoteric theosophy along with its culture, science and art, first to the East and then to the West of the Mediterranean, bridging geographical distances and racial and political boundaries, it is logical and we might even say fatal, that its religious esotericism should infect a family that became a people in its own bosom, Israel.

Let us note the seventy arrivals (of Jacob and his sons) who became numerous and powerful to an extraordinary degree, filling the land with them... becoming more numerous and stronger than the Egyptians. "To be mighty and to fill the land" must necessarily mean that the Israelites have access to the highest - culture, science, religion, etc. - how could they not have access to the mysteries?

In support of our deduction there is some documentary and archaeological evidence despite the meticulous destruction carried out by the Egyptians after their liberation from all things Hyksos. Even so, we find other Israelites in very high positions, as is shown by the sarcophagus of Nehmen, found at Saggara, a high official of a Hyksos pharaoh, precisely in an Aphopi. This is not the only case, for in later times we also find the Israelite vizier Jonhamu, in charge of Palestinian affairs, of doubtful loyalty, but who was omnipotent in the Pharaonic court.

"If we add to the confessed pre-eminence, power and numbers of the Israelites in Egypt the centuries of their permanence and their undeniable intelligence, what could be hidden from them?

It is not scientifically rigorous to attribute to the Chaldeans and Persians a religious, philosophical and cultural influence on the Hebrews by their coexistence with part of them of all their higher classes for seventy years, and to ignore that of the Egyptians on the Israelites themselves when *all of them*, in their religious, philosophical and cultural infancy, lived for 200 or 400 years with the people of the Pharaohs, whose cultural and religious monuments are the astonishment of the universe.

Moreover, if, as has been demonstrated by countless testimonies, Egypt exported its mysteries and its theogony, overcoming geographical, political and racial obstacles, to Greece, Syria, Phoenicia, etc., it would be a historical and even psychological consequence if a family that had become a people on Egyptian soil, intimately mixed with its people, part of its aristocracy and bureaucracy over a long period, had not been impressed, infected day after day by that imposing religion, whose monuments still astonish the world, and had refused to profess those famous mysteries and doctrines, reinforced by a theurgy, by such a prodigious image. It is historically absurd that the Egyptian religion, with its theurgic mysteries, magnified by an astonishing culture and degree of civilisation, should have transcended and proliferated throughout the length and breadth of all the Mediterranean peoples, but that the Hebrew people, dwelling for long centuries in the bosom of the Egyptians, should have been the only one immune to religious contagion.

And what, in the end, were the mysteries - a play on physical, psychological and fraudulent phenomena?

But no, readers, magic was a very serious thing, the most serious thing in the religious and political life of the States... In Egyptian initiations, human sacrifices were practised. In Phoenicia, the Fey, followed by his aristocracy, immolated his first-born son. The existence of a mystical experience is a purely dialectical necessity: an experiential knowledge of the believed God.

And this was the mysteries, an experimental knowledge of the "God", let us say, of the "inverse god": Satan, substituting for the Lord in the most varied deistic, aesthetic or anti-aesthetic, monstrous or ridiculous forms; but above all, under the dialectical forms most suited to the state of those rationalist intelligences of the *elite* - let us say it again - in their deific and ghostly *real* appearances; yes, real appearances many times, without prejudice of hypnotic, spiritist, necrophiliac superstitions... and also, yes also, of the frauds and theatrical tricks of theurgy.

The unheard of monstrosity of worshipping the Fautor of evil, going so far as to offer him human sacrifices, even that of one's own children, a monstrosity committed by the kings, the aristocracy and the majority of the Jewish people, the chosen ones, those who, like no other, have been favoured with the most eloquent and authentic *cognitio Dei experimentalis, in* spite of the constant anathemas endorsed by such frequent prodigies of their prophets; this monstrosity can only be explained by a supernatural intervention of Satan, provoking that high, mystical state of moral and rational perversion absolutely necessary to reach the monstrosity of human sacrifices; even those of one's own children. A subhuman state, which, without the prior and full satanic *possession* of the soul in all its powers, is impossible for humans to reach.

The Kabbalah which, in turn, emanates from the Theosophy and magic of Egypt, as the fundamental religious doctrines emanate from the religions of other peoples, perfectly demonstrated with respect to Greek theological doctrines.

"That the Hebrew Kabbalah is perpetuated to this day and reaches a higher degree of perversion than its progenitor, the Egyptian Kabbalah, has a twofold explanation. It is a mystery of Israel. As to the Hebrew Qabalah surpassing in perversity its progenitor and the doctrines engendered by it - Zoroastrianism, Buddhism, Taoism, Pythagoreanism and their offshoots - we must remember that the Qabalah comes from the Egyptian mysteries and has developed in the very bosom of those mysteries.

CHAPTER IV

CHRISTIAN GNOSTICISM OR A CHRISTIANITY ALTERED BY KABBALAH

The errors of the Kabbalah can be summed up in two fundamental points: God has an indeterminate existence, between being and non-being, between yes and no, between good and evil, and is only truly realised in the universe and in man, who, being an emanation of God, complete and terminate Him. Everything, then, by a homogeneous process, comes out of God: the world and man, the whole of history, with error and truth, with good and evil, and also everything returns to God. Man in the depths of his being is a divine spark on the way to his divinisation. For the complete and finished God is man realised in the history of mankind.

The Kabbalah is a Jewish invention originating in the corruption by pagan mysteries of the revelation given by God to the Jewish people. It is the divine tradition perverted by man. As soon as Christianity appears, the Jews try to destroy it. To destroy it on the outside by persecuting Christ and the Christians, to destroy it on the inside by corrupting it with the cabal. And this second destruction produces the phenomenon of Christian Gnosticism.

Why do the Jews, and precisely the Jews, want to destroy Christianity? Because the Jews are the natural enemies of Christianity. And just as they destroyed the Mosaic message of divine revelation, so they will try to destroy Christianity. The great sin of the Jews has been to wrap the gospel message in the traditions of men. Jesus said this to their face: "You set aside the commandment of God and cling to human tradition".

And he said to them: "Truly you do away with the commandment of God in order to establish your tradition"[204]. And the tradition of the Jews

---

[204] *Mk.*, 7, 9.

also involved an *earthly and human messianic kingdom* in place of the kingdom of God, of the Church over the peoples. An earthly kingdom run by the Jews. An earthly kingdom of power. Money power, political power, religious power over the souls of men. Totalitarian power of the same quality and dimension as the power of the devil over the peoples. The power of the three temptations. The power of pleasures. The power of pride. The power of the possession of goods.

Jewish origin of Christian Gnosticism

But to destroy Christianity it had to be emptied from within, leaving all its outward appearance behind. And this is the work of the Gnostics. Gnosis is an attempt to Judaise or cabalise Christianity. The heterodox Jewish filiation of the Christian gnosis has been well affirmed in modern times. "This filiation is attested to us by numerous data that make Jewish heterodoxy the original medium of Christian Gnosticism. The most ancient testimony is that of Hegesippus, which Eusebius refers to [205]. Eusebius' own testimony is of exceptional interest: Hegesippus "came to the faith from Judaism" [206]. He knows the unwritten Jewish tradition. On the other hand, he has precious sources concerning the Church of Jerusalem. It is from him that we have certain details about James and a list of his successors to the head of the Jewish-Christian Church [207]. No better qualified witness concerning Judeo-Christianity in Palestine.

> "Now Hegesippus writes that, under the episcopate of Simeon, the successor of James, the church "was not yet corrupted by hollow opinions. The initiator of this was Theboutis, because he had not been made a bishop. He himself came from an environment in which there were seven heresies that existed among the (Jewish) people. From this milieu also came Simon, the ancestor of the Simonians; Cleobios, that of the Cleobians; Dositheus, that of the Dositheans; Georthaios that of the Georteos and the Masbotheans. And from these have come the Marcionites, the Carpocratians, the Valentinians, the Basilidians, the Satornilians""[208].

---

[205] Ecclesiastical History, *IV*, 22, 4, 7.
[206] IV, 22, 18.
[207] IV, 22, 4.
[208] IV, 22, 5.

"The importance of this news of Hegesippus does not seem to me to have been generally recognised", says Daniélou[209]. Let us note first of all that the author affirms that Theboutis on the one hand, Simon and others on the other, come from seven Jewish sects. It is fortunate, however, that Eusebius has preserved for us another fragment of Hegesippus which lists the seven Jewish sects:

> "There were different opinions about circumcision among the children of Israel, against the tribe of Judah and against Christ. Here they were: Essenes, Galileans, Hemerobaptists, Masbothites, Samaritans, Sadducees, Pharisees"[210].

Having said that, let us come to the question that interests us, that of the origins of Gnosticism. Two names are known to us: those of Dositheus and Simon. Epiphanius links Dositheus with the heresies of the Samaritans[211]. On the other hand, the *Réconnaissances Clémentines* make him a Sadducee, which means that he was undoubtedly a son of Sadog, an Essene[212]. The prophecy *of Deut.* 18, 18, applied to the Essenes,[213] according to Origen[214].

He observed the Sabbath[215]. He was an ascetic. One thinks of a kind of Samaritan essenism. There are no properly Christian traces in him. Epiphanius places him among the founders of Jewish sects. The only trait that links him with the Christian milieu seems to be that he began to preach his doctrine after the death of John the Baptist, concurrently with the preaching of Jesus.

With Simon, on the other hand, we find ourselves for the first time in the presence of a specifically Gnostic speculation. He is related to Dositheus, according to the testimony of the elementary writings. This points to both Essene affinities and a Samaritan milieu. But on the one hand, dualistic speculations are involved in him, which indicate influences foreign to Judaism, Iranian, as the name magician indicates. On the other hand, he was acquainted with Christianity, as a passage in the *Acts of the Apostles* attests. Therefore, Epiphanius, with a just title,

---

[209] Théologie du Judeo-Christianisme, *Desclée, 1957, p. 93.*
[210] IV, 22, 7.
[211] *Bread,* XIII, 1-2.
[212] I, 54.
[213] *U* Q-Testimony.
[214] Cont. Cels.
[215] *Princ. IV,* 3, 2.

following Hegesippus, makes him a Christian heretic. Perhaps the title of Hellenes, which Origen[216] gives to Simon's disciples, should be compared with the Hellenists, with whom the *Acts of the Apostles* brings them into contact and in whom Cullman sees Essenes converted to Christianity. Simon would have been one of them for some time before forming their sect. It will be noted that the name Hellenes, in a passage of Justin, is that of a Jewish sect which could very well be that of the Essenes[217]. Justin was from Samaria. The Hellenes could have been the Samaritan branch of the Essenes, and the name would have remained for the Christian Essenes or Hellenists and for the Gnostic Essenes or Hellenes[218].

It is difficult to know whether the other Christian sects mentioned by Hippolytus refer to the same current. It is plausible for Cleobius, placed between Simon and Dositheus. On the other hand, Epiphanius links the Gorotenians with the Dositheans. Theobutis remains enigmatic. But it is clear that the first Christian heterodoxy is situated on the border of heterodox Judaism and Christianity. Therefore, this milieu appears as the original focus of Gnosticism. And when Hegesippus relates Basilides, Satornil, Menander, Carpocrates and Valentinus to it, he traces the genealogy which, in the pre-Christian Judaeo-Samaritan gnosis, leads through Simon to Christian Gnosticism.

> "The study of the news that has been preserved under these archaic forms of Christian Gnosticism confirms this genealogy by showing that we are dealing with the development of a Jewish, pre-Christian Gnosticism"[219].

So much for Daniélou.

Jewish Gnosticism

Hence we think it important to reproduce what *The Jewish Encyclopedia* writes about the word "Gnosticism": "Jewish Gnosticism unquestionably predates Christianity; for biblical exegesis it is five hundred years older than the first century. Judaism has been in close contact with Babylonian and Persian ideas for a long time, and for a not less long time with Hellenistic ideas.

---

[216] Contra Celsum, V, 62.
[217] Dial, LXXX, 4.
[218] Danielou, *Thèologie du Judeo-Christianisme,* Desclée, p. 85, 1957, Paris.
[219] Ibid.

The magical, too, which, as will be shown below, constituted a no less important part of the doctrines and manifestations of Gnosticism, occupied Jewish thinkers extensively. There is not in general a circle of ideas with which the elements of Gnosticism can be configured and in which the Jews did not have some connection. It is noteworthy that the heads of the Gnostic schools and the founders of the Gnostic systems were designated as Jews by the Fathers of the Church. Some derive all heresies, including those of Gnosticism, from Judaism[220]. It should also be noted that the Hebrew words and names of God provide the skeleton of some Gnostic systems. Christians and Jewish converts from paganism have used as the foundation of their systems terms taken from the Greek or Syriac versions of the Bible. This fact at least proves that the main elements of Gnosticism are derived from Jewish speculations.

Cosmogonico-theological speculations and philosophies about God and the world constitute the substance of Gnosticism. They are based on the first sections of Genesis and Ezekiel, for which there are in Jewish speculation two well-established and therefore two old terms: *Maaseh Bereshit* and *Maase Merkaba*.

"There is no doubt that Jewish Gnosticism existed before Christian Gnosticism or Jewish-Christian Gnosticism"... The great age of Jewish Gnosticism is further indicated by the authentic statement of Johanam ben Zakkai, who was born probably in the century before the common era, and who was, according to Sakkar 28c, versed in this science, and who refers to a prohibition of discussing creation before two pupils and of the Chariot of the Throne, before one".

"In second century Gnosticism, three elements can be observed: the speculative and philosophical, the ritualistic and mystical, and the practical and ascetic [221]. These three elements derive from Jewish sources. Gnosis is neither pure philosophy nor pure religion, but a combination of the two with the magical, the latter being the dominant element.

> "Therefore, it can be stated as a firm conclusion that *there can be no doubt that Christian Gnosticism is a mixture of Christian elements with the Jewish Gnosis or Kabbalah*".

---

[220] Hegesippus in. Eusebius, *Hist. Eccl.*, IV, 22; comp. Harnack, *Dogmen Geschichte*, 3rd ed. p. 232, note 1.
[221] Harnack, L. C., p. 219.

What is Christian Gnosticism?

Let us come to the *question of what Gnosticism is*. Strictly speaking, this is a question that will be fully clarified in the course of this book. A Gnostic fragment defines gnosis as follows:

> "The knowledge of what we are and what we have become; of where we have come from and where we have fallen; of the goal towards which we are rushing and from which we have been rescued; of the nature of our birth, and of our rebirth"[222].

But all this is said with elements taken from Christianity, Judaism, the Greeks, the Egyptians, the Babylonians, the Chaldeans, the Persians and the Hindus. Gnosticism is a syncretism. The Gnostic systems we know do not translate the spirit of a particular religion; on the contrary, they contain in unequal proportion Jewish, Christian, Persian, Babylonian, Egyptian and Greek elements in such a way as to form a kind of mosaic, made up of innumerable little cubes of different nature and origin. But this question must be elucidated more fully.

Christian gnosis

First of all, a clear distinction must be made between Christian Gnosis and Gnosticism, even Christian Gnosticism.

When we speak of Christian gnosis, we refer to that *knowledge* of God and His mysteries which the ancient authors describe as the highest ideal of the perfect Christian and which distinguishes it from simple faith. Christianity and the Jewish religion which preceded it is a *knowledge;* knowledge of a *secret* or *revelation* which is God's design to save man through Jesus Christ. This is a truth clearly contained in the Gospels and in St. Paul[223]. It is also contained in the Christian writers of the first centuries, especially in the Apostolic Fathers[224]. In a

---

[222] Clem. de Alej. *Excerpta ex Theodoro,* 78, 2.
[223] *Mt.,* 13, 11; *Le.,* 8, 10; *Mt.,* 11, 27; *Lk.,* 10, 22; *John, 6,* 69; 10, 38; 17, 8; 1 *John,* 4, 16; *John,* 10, 15; 14, 17; 16, 3; 17, 3; 8, 28; 17, 3; 2 *Cor.,* 4, 6; *Phil.,* 3, 10; 1 *Cor.,* 8, 1; 4, 19; 1 *Tim.,* 6, 20; *Gal.* 4, 9; 1 *Cor., 8* 2; 1 *Cor.,* 12, 7; *Eph.* 3, 19; *Phil.,* 3, 8; 1 *Cor.,* 8, 12; 13, 12; 1 Cor., 2, 10; *Rom.,* 11, 33.
[224] *Didache, 9,* 3; 10, 2; 11, 2; Clement Romanus (+100), *Letter,* 40, 1, 3; St. Ignatius of Antioch (+107); *To the Ephesians,* 17, 2; *To the Magnesians, 6,* 2; 19, 1; 21, 5; St. Justin (ca. 166); *Dialogue with Trypho,* 14, 1; 28, 4; 39,5; *69,* 4; *Epistle to Barnabas,* speaks of knowledge, gnosis, 5, 4; 1, 5; 2, 2; 2-3; 18, 1; 88, *6; St. Irenaeus* (+h. 200), *Adversus haereses,* I, 11, 1; IV, 33, 8; IV, 36, 4; I, 10, 3.

particular way, this Christian gnosis was to be fully and systematically elaborated, and to a great extent, against the Gnostic heresy, by Clement of Alexandria and Origen[225]. The Origenist tradition remains alive in Gregory of Nyssa (+ 395) and Evagrius the Pontic (+ 399).

We can conclude with Pierre Thomas Camelot[226] that Christian gnosis during the first four centuries has demonstrated the persistence of certain fundamental characteristics that have been present since its origins. A desire to "know" the mysteries of God which is always based on faith and the spiritual tradition of the Scriptures: the true gnosis is the doctrine of the apostles, the spiritual intelligence of the Scriptures.

But it will be noted, on the other hand, that the "Gnostic" is always in danger of straying from the true meaning of Scripture in order to elaborate a personal system under the veil of allegory.

For the same reason, gnosis will no longer be a deepening of the faith of baptism, but an overcoming of this faith, which will tend to leave to the simple faithful the literal sense of Scripture. This progress of gnosis supposes an ascetic effort to reach the purity of the heart and also the overcoming of all that is sensible, and even of all intelligible "form": gnosis is oriented towards a mysticism of the nakedness of the spirit and in the darkness.

But is there not still a danger of overcoming the humanity of Christ and the Sacraments of the Church? This desire to "know" is also from the beginning a desire to be united to God in charity, and this essential feature is always present: "gnosis" is affective "knowledge", and therefore also experience of God. It is both theology and mysticism. Having clarified the notion of Christian gnosis, let us now come to the notion of Christian gnosticism.

Christian Gnosticism. Christian Gnosticism, like all Gnosticism and especially Judaic Gnosticism, is characterised by certain features which we shall now point out.

1. *Monism and dualism at the same time in Christian Gnosticism.* In Christian Gnosticism, as in the Kabbalah, there is a *fundamental ontological monism*. All material and spiritual substance, good and evil, emanates from a single principle, the *Ein Soph* in the Kabbalah, and the

---

[225] See Clement of Alexandria's *Stromata* and Origen's works in general.
[226] Dictionnaire de Spiritualité, *Gnose et gnosticisme*.

Pleroma in the Gnostics. This feature of Christian Gnosticism must be regarded as the true and fundamental one, so that there is a continuity of substance in God and in the creature and in the material and evil world. The Catholic doctrine, on the other hand, rejects this *fundamental ontological monism* insofar as it places an ontological rupture between the being of God and the being of the creature.

The one is *Subsistens Being* and the other is *participated being*. The second comes from the first, but not by identity of substance or emanation, but by efficiency or participation. Creation, a free act of God, separates one, the Being of God, and the other, the being of the creature. The Thomistic theory of analogy clarifies this continuity and discontinuity against any *univocist* theory.

But along with this fundamental ontological monism there is in the Kabbalah and in Christian Gnosticism an ontological dualism as well, in that both systems regard matter and material beings as evil. This consideration of the evil of matter may derive from the constitution at the beginning of beings of two radical principles, one good and the other evil, as in the Iranian and Manichaean conception, or from a single principle, as in the Kabbalah, which would enclose within itself the kingdom of good and evil.

2. *The divine reality, the only reality in Christian Gnosticism.* This double monism and dualism, which all Gnosticism suffers from, is related to the monistic pantheism which characterises it. In fact, the various gnosticisms ascribe reality only to spiritual beings and, on the other hand, to material beings they assign a *semblance* of reality.

In India this conception has found its most enlightened exponents in the *Upanishads*. The only reality is the "within" of things, the Absolute *(brahman)*, present beneath the changing becoming of the appearances of man and things. Man must be liberated *(moksa)* and placed outside the vicissitudes of the world of generation and corruption *(samsâra)*[227].

In Gnostic thought the absolute is viewed in the mode of absence, and it is not by chance that Basilides in the second century catches up with Buddhist speculation by giving this Absolute the name of "nothingness". We have seen how in the Kabbalah everything comes

---

[227] See *Dictionnaire de Spiritualité*, phase. 39-40, p. 526. These points are a free development of the article by Etienne Cornelis, in the *Dict. de Spiritualité*.

from *"Ein Sof"*, which also means "nothing". There is a process from *Ain*, nothingness, to *Ein Sof*, darkness, and to *Ein Sof Aur*[228].

Apart from this absolute *(brahman)* which constitutes the background of things and which is identified with "nothingness", all other things are appearance and *maya*. Husserlian phenomenology, and phenomenology in general in all its variants, as we shall see below, resembles this *maic* conception of things.

3. *Evil, a positive reality in Christian Gnosticism*. Gnosticism makes evil a positive reality and, in one way or another, whether in the Iranian or Manichaean version, or in the Brahmanic version, makes it derive from the Absolute itself. The Absolute is not the pure act of St. Thomas, i.e. a transcendent reality that contains only Act, Perfection, but also the Negative, the Evil, the Tragic, which is precisely its dynamic element. This is why, in Gnosticism, God becomes a theogony. In the Gnostic Pleroma there is the war of the Aeons, or the unsatisfied Aeons, who have evil desires. It is evident that this comes from the Kabbalah, which picks it up from the ancient pagan mysteries, whether Chaldean, Egyptian, Iranic or even Brahmanic.

> "Gnosis can multiply the prodigies of speculative subtlety, willingly complicate the vicissitudes of its myth of creation, of emanation, distance its first principle, the Pro-Father, as far as possible from the empirical world where evil reigns, but it does not succeed, as soon as it seeks to constrain itself logically, even and especially when it strives to establish its perfects in peace, beyond the disturbing choice between good and evil, it fails, I repeat, to prevent its natural ambiguity from being reflected in the bosom of the abyss whose immaculate transcendence it would like to preserve"[229].

The problem of evil has but one solution, which was given by St. Augustine and St. Thomas, namely, that of being a purely negative reality, a deficiency, a deprivation of something due, whose guilt originates in the free condition of the rational creature.

By making evil a positive reality, gnosis was obliged to make sin an ignorance. Here, too, the resemblance to the Eastern theosophies *(avidyâ)* is striking.

---

[228] See Roger Ambelain, *La Cabale pratique*, p. 96.
[229] Dict. de Spiritualité, p. 527.

Let us underline, however, that on this point the gnoses are divided into two great families, according to whether they have suffered more or less the influence of the Hellenic or the Iranian environment. In the first case, ignorance serves as a stop to the first principle and to the evil world in the process of emanation, while, in the second case, the "darkness" coming out of the co-eternal evil principle, assaults the luminous world"[230].

4. *The time of the world in Christian Gnosticism.* One of the characteristics of gnosticism is the refusal to grant a positive value to the "time of the world", that is to say, to the intermediate period that separates the origin of the visible world (or the coming of the Saviour) from the apocatastasis of the elect that will put an end to the times. One of the strongest arguments in favour of the existence of a pre-Pauline gnosis is provided by the expression of the Epistle to the Ephesians (5, 16): "for the days are evil". A disciple of Valentinus, Ptolemy (ca. 180), visibly seeking to cover himself with the authority of the Apostle, while at the same time avoiding the immoral consequences drawn from him by certain doctors, admits with Paul that it is possible to make use even of these evil days; but he sees in the unnatural union of the *pneuma* and the *sarx* the necessary sequel to the spiritual to become fully conscious of their nature foreign to the flesh. In the course of this evil aeon, nothing positive is built up because the work of salvation consists in fleeing out of time[231].

5. *The persistence of the pneuma in the Pleroma and outside the Pleroma in Christian Gnosticism.* Gnosticism is distinguished by the teaching that pneumatic men descend and ascend in the cosmic period, in a certain automatic and necessary way. These men have a pneumatic seed derived from the Pleroma and fallen into matter, and must necessarily re-ascend to the same Pleroma. This recalls the Kabalistic teaching above of the *neshama*, necessarily subtracted from the world of sin and evil.

6. *The celestial man or Adam Kadmon in Christian Gnosticism.* Etienne Cornelis points out[232] that the place accorded by several gnosticisms to speculations on the *Archanthropos* should warn us that gnosticism is only interested in the world through man. Well aware of the mysterious

---

[230] Ibid., p. 528.
[231] Etienne Cornelis, ibid. p. 528.
[232] Ibid., p. 531.

significance of human existence, it strives to discover the ideal essence. The myth of the First Man allows him, precisely, to build a bridge between the first chapters of *Genesis* and religious Platonism, through a Platonising exegesis of the word *eikon*[233].

But this idea of the *Primordial Man, Heavenly Man*, is clearly expressed in the Kabbalah in the famous *Adam Kadmon*, one of the most typical symbols of the ten *Sephiroth*.

7. *Liberation through self-revelation in Christian Gnosticism.* In gnosis, man carries within himself the divine germ of health. This germ has to be actualised and can be dormant in more or less deep layers. Hence, the division of men into *pneumaticoi, psychicoi* and *hilicoi* should not be taken too strictly, as if there were only one kind of pneumaticoi and all men could not become pneumaticoi. Basilides compares the radical capacity to acquire gnosis to that of learning mathematics: it exists in everyone but may very well remain latent[234]. The necessity of the *message* or *revelation* in gnosis is also relative, because it would not be necessary to bring something new from outside, but to awaken an existing reality in every man. Gnosis presents an obvious affinity of structure with certain theosophies - Neopythagoreanism, Hermeticism, Vedanta - which define it better by the term *self-liberation*.

8. *Grace and freedom in Christian Gnosticism.* First of all, it should be noted that in Christian Gnosticism both the descent and the return of the spiritual sparks is a necessary process and that the latter consists in the illumination by gnosis which dissipates the veils of ignorance and forgetfulness and which introduces into the world of the ultimate realities signified by the pleromatic entities. The acceptance of the call makes the pneumatic aware of his "foreign" nature to this world. From this point of view, gnosis is an awareness of oneself.

The aim of gnosis is the *knowledge of salvation by which man recognises that he is God*. Of course, this can be formulated in different ways, according to the individual conception of each Gnostic and the school to which he belongs[235]. If man acknowledges himself to be god, it is clear that his divinity is not a free gift but his very nature.

---

[233] Cf. J. Jervell, *Image Dei, Gottingen*, 1960, pp. 122-170.
[234] *Cornelis in* Dictionnaire de Spiritualité, *p. 533.*
[235] *Schlier, in the article* "Gnosis", in Fundamental Concepts of Theology, *t. II, p. 173.*

This gnosis, by which man returns to himself and to his origin, includes another element that is given with man himself, which is his cosmic situation and his destiny. Every gnosis contains, then, even if only in germ, a conception of the totality of the universe. And in this totality everything necessarily moves, so that there is no room for a true freedom of man.

9. *Eschatology in Christian Gnosticism.* Etienne Cornelis in the magnificent article he devotes to Gnosticism in the *Dictionnaire de Spiritualité*[236] points out that the ultimate end or Gnostic happiness is considered as a state of rest or cessation. The parallel with *nirvana* is obvious. The introduction into the Pleroma is compared to the entrance into the bridal chamber, which evokes the vocabulary of the mysteries. In the Pleroma, man attains his eternal idea. The syzygy is a mystery in which the male pneumatic element gives the female element the stability it was lacking. According to the law of inverted exemplarism which dominates the whole structure of Gnostic thought, the nuptial mystery is presented as both the inversion and the sublimation of epithymia - desire - the cause of the fall, and implies the decantation of the passions of Sophia, the origin and substance of the sensible world. This union in the *Pastos* would have spared Adam and Eve the original fall if they had known it. The Gnostic is definitively liberated.

Essence of Christian Gnosticism. In conclusion, we will say that the essential structure of all Christian Gnosticism, once stripped of all the mythical lushness, which varies in each particular Gnosis, can be synthesised in the following points which reflect its similarity to the Kabbalah.

In all Gnostic systems there is a *first principle,* a *Super Principle,* which appears as transcendental to every value, to every idea, to every determination, to every distinction. It is called Abyss, Father, Propater, Silence, Theosagnotos, the "Nothingness"; it is the Ensof of the Kabalah.

From the Abyss of divinity appear eons or emanations, the Thought, Ennoia, the Intelligence, the Nous, the primordial Man. The divinity is thus conceived as a Plenitude of virtualities, a Pleroma of potencies or

---

[236] P. 537.

eons. Here again we have, in another version, the famous Sephiroth which form the Adam Kadmon.

The self of the Gnostic is but an ultimate emanation, a spark of this pure light, a seed of Spirit, a Pneuma of the Higher Man. The Gnostic becomes conscious of being this spark.

This too is kabbalistic. It is the *Neshama* of the Zohar.

This "gnosis", this "knowledge", is at the same time his salvation. Knowing himself, he knows at the same time his true nature, his origin, his destiny, which is realised by his knowledge. The Gnostic calls this knowledge "awakening"; illumination out of darkness, resurrection or vivification from the state of death, remembrance after the long silences of oblivion.

The myth of the fall and ascension is used to explain the presence of this living and luminous divine "I" in the midst of a world that is totally foreign to her. *Sophia* unfolds and finds her "double" involved in this world. Evil has slipped into the divine world and hardened in matter. It is in this matter and in this evil that wisdom is debated.

This too is kabbalistic in the world of *Asiah* and the Quliphah.

The Pleroma gathers all its forces and concentrates in the Saviour all its powers which come to regenerate *Sophia* and to separate all the confused elements which are foreign to her. With *Sophia* will be regenerated all the Gnostics, of whom she is both mother and exemplar. Thus the great Restoration will take place. The parcels of the divine which are the Gnostics will escape the evil powers of this world, the rulers of the seven spheres and their demiurge, attaining the Ogdoada, and joining with *Sophia* will enter the Pleroma with Wisdom in the company of the Saviour. We have seen in the Lurianic Qabalah the significance of the process of restitution or *tiqqum*.

In any case, the evil, the demons, the souls given to evil, the whole of the hellic substance will be annihilated in a general burning.

Development of Gnostic systems

Christian Gnosticism undoubtedly originates in Jewish Gnosticism. It is a Jewish infiltration into Christianity to corrupt Christianity. Perhaps it was a calculated and deliberate infiltration practised by the Jewish Pharisees once they failed to prevent the spread of Christianity. This was magnificently seen by the Fathers of the Church, who clearly denounced the Jewish character of the Gnostic errors. This is eloquently stated by Simon, the Jewish magician, the first Christian Gnostic. It is also said by Valentinus, Mani, all Jews. It is not surprising that Gnosticism can be reduced to Eastern or Greek errors, because it was precisely a mixture of the Judeo-Christian revelation with Eastern and Greek errors.

> "When St. John and St. Ignatius reproved Judaising gnosis, and above all docetism, Antioch, the capital of Syria, had long since become a centre of gnosticism; he owed it to Menander, a disciple of Simon Magus"[237].

The Simon Magician system

The system of Simon Magus can be reconstituted according to several versions. A first, that of the *Acts of the Apostles*, 8, 4-25; another, that of Justin, *Apol.*, I, 26; 56; and that of Irenaeus, *Adv. Haer.*, 16, 2; another, that of the *Homilies* and of the Pseudo-Clementine; a fourth, that of St. Epiphanius, *Pan.*, XXI, 3, 1-3; a fifth, that of Hippolytus, *Ref.* VI, 19, 2, 3. Whether these versions refer to a single system is still a matter of dispute.

The gnosis of Simon Magus can be summarised as follows: Simon teaches the existence of a Power, Dynamis, infinite, which he calls the Principle of All. Here are his terms: *This writing of the revelation of a Voice and a Name comes from the Thought of the great Power, the infinite Power. Therefore it will be sealed, hidden, veiled in the mansion where the Root of All has its foundations*"[238].

"Almost all the Samaritans," says Justin, "and some of other nations acknowledge and worship Simon as the First God, and say that a certain Helen who then accompanied him (but who had first been a prostitute) was the First Thought whom he had brought into existence *(Apol.* 1, 26, 3). We know that Simon was worshipped as Zeus and Helen as Athena.

In its semi-poetic structure, the story of Helen's origins is reminiscent of the prologue to the Gospel of John.

For her in the beginning, God decided to create the angels and the archangels
and their thought sprang forth out of him, knowing the will of his

---

[237] Dict. de Theologie, *"Gnosticisme"*, column 1.440.
[238] Leisegang, *La Gnose*, p. 55, Payot, Paris, 1951.

father's will;
She descended to the lower regions.
She begot the angels and the Dominations by which this world has been made.
has been made.
But when she had begotten them she was held captive by them, out of jealousy;
because they did not want to be thought of as begotten.
For the Father Himself was totally unknown to them:
But their thought was held captive by them.
-The powers issued by her and the angels-,
and from her he suffered all kinds of outrages
so that she could not soar to her father.
But she remained a prisoner in a human body,
and through the ages, as from vessel to vessel.
she incarnated herself in successive female bodies.
She passed from body to body
suffering ever new torments;
and at the end (or, to put it better, "at the end of time") [239]
she became a prostitute;
she is the lost sheep [240]
for her He has come,
to set her free
and to offer men salvation
by making Himself known to them[241].
As the angels mismanaged the world
because each of them wanted the primacy,
he came to restore all things
and came down metamorphosed.
He became like the principalities and dominations and angels.
and the Angels
with men he seemed to be man
though he was not man
and in Judea He seemed to suffer the Passion
although in fact He did not suffer it".

---

[239] *Hebrews*, 1, 2.
[240] *Lk.*, 15, 6.
[241] *Lk.*, 1, 71-77.

Simon, the Power of God, begets Sophia and through Sophia, the universe. Sophia is lost in the universe and becomes a prisoner of the lower forces. Simon, like Jesus, comes to rescue the lost sheep and restore all things.

We see here the scheme of the Kabbalah. God, the Ensof, manifests and becomes visible through the *Sephiroth*, good and evil, male and female, and so the universe unfolds. The *En-sof* descends to the lowest strata of matter, down to the demonic. And then begins the redemption, the return from the lowest to the highest.

The Christian Gnostic schema, like that of the Kabbalah, is presented first as a *theogony*, an unfolding of God, from the indeterminate to the determinate, from the one to the multiple, from the tragic to peace, from good and evil, from masculine and feminine to universal restoration. As a *cosmogony*, a continuous unfolding in creation, where cosmogony is already theogony. As an *anthropogony*, where divinity reaches the lower degrees of man and man reaches divinity. And a *return* or *restoration* of the primitive unity.

> The itinerary of the Gnostic does not go from the cosmic mechanism to the "I", but from the living "I" to the world. If we want a parallel with modern thought, writes Leisegang, one of the most acute connoisseurs of gnosis, we would compare it with the path opened by Schopenhauer: Schopenhauer, after having discovered in his own body the metaphysical principle of the will, immediately recognised it in the external world as being the heart of nature. What the will is for Schopenhauer, the spirit is for Simon. Spirit is for him the centre of force from which all life springs. As such, it has first of all no kind of extension; it is a point in which everything is given in potency. A problem arises for the spirit: how does this point become a figure, how does the spirit become a body, how does the potency become a graspable act? To solve this problem, the Gnostic does not turn to the external world. He descends into his own self, he scrutinises his own spirit. He first discovers the distinction between the spirit as a function, the product of this spirit: thought. Everyone possesses an aptitude for logical and mathematical thinking, but it is only when the aptitude is exercised that the subjective disposition becomes the object, logic or mathematics. The intelligence becomes the thought, the subject becomes the object, the thinking becomes the thought, the active becomes the passive? But the spirit does not exist, it is only a point without extension as long as it has not objectified itself and has not produced thought".

"Intelligence and thought are, therefore, in the first place, in the same relation as father and son, the one cannot exist without the other, because intelligence is nothing without the thought which produces it, and thought does not exist without its author. But in order for the thought to end in an act or in a work, a power is again needed which realises the real action on the basis of the pure thought. It could be said that to the thought must be added the will. But this will, in the Gnostic conception, is not a power distinct from that which produced the thought. Thought must receive in it, so to speak, a new influx of spiritual power in order to be transformed into action. The child is then transformed into a woman, who receives the flow of the potency of the paternal semen, engenders the act and brings forth from it an entity; this in all things responds to thought, or rather, encloses and manifests it in itself. At the same time, the entity produced contains at the same time the spirit which began by engendering this thought; one has thus three inseparable greatnesses, one from the other: the generating spirit, the engendered thought, the being engendered by the Spirit and by the Thought. They are all one: one and the same power, as Hegel shows us, one and the same Spirit *in itself*, Spirit *for itself*, Spirit *in itself and for itself*"[242].

The Valentinian gnosis

When St. John and St. Ignatius reproved the Judaising gnosis and especially docetism, Antioch, the capital of Syria, had long since become a hotbed of gnosticism. This was due to Menander, a disciple of Simon Magus. Like him, his disciples used magic, resorted to the use of filters, interpreted dreams, and had statues of Simon and Helen, whom they worshipped. Menander counted Saturninus and Basilides among his disciples.

Basilides, a fellow disciple of Saturninus and a disciple of Menander, moved from Antioch to Alexandria, and was the first known Egyptian Gnostic. Without departing from the teaching of his masters, he wished to do new work and devised a system that was more complicated, more abstract and more metaphysical, and at the same time less easy to understand. Basilides had his son Isidore as his disciple.

Another great Gnostic - from Alexandria - was Carpocrates, who distinguished himself by his immoral practices.

---

[242] Leisegang, *La gnose*, Payot, Paris, 1951, pp. 67-68.

Gnosis reached its peak with *Valentinus*, one of the most famous leaders of Gnosticism, whose system deserves a more detailed exposition[243].

Theogony

In the upper world of the Pleroma there is an infinite Being, the perfect aeon which bears the names of Propater, Abyss, and which is incomprehensible, invisible, eternal, unbegotten. From this first principle, which some, like Hippolytus, place alone, and which others, like Irenaeus, place together with a companion "Thought", "Silence", "Grace", there are couplets of "Aeons", according to syzygy

Father	Thinking
Intelligence	Truth
Logos	Life
Man	Church[244]

After the Ogdoado, the emissions continue until the number of thirty is completed. Only the intelligence alone beholds the Father and feels great joy. The other aeons wish to behold the Father peacefully. But Sophia, the last and thirtieth of the aeons, does not feel peaceful, but experiences a great *passion*, a suffering, which makes her want to know God Propater. This suffering led her to "dissolve into the essence of the whole".

But Sophia was saved by a special Aeon, by Oros, Limit, that is, by a force that consolidates the whole of the Aeons and keeps her out of the "Inexpressible Greatness". Sophia is saved by Limit.

The Monogen issues a new couplet. *Christ* and the *Holy Spirit,* and the Christ gives the aeons the gnosis of the Father, that is, he lets them know that the Father is incomprehensible and that no one can see or hear him except through the Son; and the Holy Spirit has among the aeons a curious mission of equalisation, of unity, of harmony, of rest and joy[245].

---

[243] In this exhibition we will follow in particular François M. M. Sagnard, *La gnose valentinienne,* J. Vrin, Paris, 1947.
[244] Ibid., p. 146.
[245] Ibid., p. 155.

All the Aeons with Christ and the Holy Spirit bear perfect fruit in Jesus the Saviour, who is like the quintessence of the Pleroma and who will fulfil an essential function outside the Pleroma[246].

Soteriology. We see that there are three substances, a spiritual substance, the pneumatic, coming out of Wisdom by a direct birth, which characterises the disciples of gnosis; below, a material substance, hylic, evil, coming out of the passions; and between the two, a passible substance, psychic. The demiurge separates the hylic substance from the psychic substance. The demiurge comes from conversion. There are three races of men, according to the substance of which they are made. To these three substances correspond three places:

1° The Mother, whose spiritual part supplies the pneumatic substance, resides in the *Intermediate* place, above the Demiurge, but below and outside the Pleroma.

2° The Demiurge has his place in the "upper heaven" of our universe and commands the seven heavens.

3° The Cosmocrator is in our sublunar world[247].

From this come three corresponding names: because of the seven heavens, the Demiurge will have the name of Hebdomad. It is also the name of the "heavenly place" where he resides. Its number is *Seven*.

The Mother, who is in the degree immediately below, has the figure *Eight*, and is therefore called Ogdoada. It is, as we have seen, "the name of the fundamental and primitive Ogdoada" - that of the Pleroma - which points well to the equally fundamental role of Wisdom in relation to our world. And finally Cosmocrator, by its very position, must have the digit *Six*. In any case, this digit will be that of *matter*[248].

The demiurge made himself Father and God of all that is outside the Pleroma, creator of all psychic and material (hylic) beings. He separated the one from the other, these two mixed substances; from incorporeal he made them corporeal. He made celestial and terrestrial beings and became Demiurge of the hylic and psychic, of the right and left, of the light and the heavy, of the rising and the falling bodies. He ordained

---

[246] Ibid., p. 157.
[247] Ibid., p. 174.
[248] Ibid., p. 175.

seven heavens, over which the Demiurge rules. These seven heavens are of an intelligent nature. They are, it is said, angels.

These creations, the Demiurge believed that he made them by himself, but he only realised the productions of Wisdom[249].

Formation of the Spiritual Man

The birth that his Mother, i.e. Wisdom (Achamoth), had produced by beholding the angels surrounding the Saviour - this birth is *consubstantial* with his Mother, therefore pneumatic - and the Demiurge, they say, ignored it. He was secretly deposited in the Demiurge, without knowing it, in order to be sown by him in the soul that would come from him, although in the hyllic body. So that in this gestation, growing, this seed would become ready to receive the *perfect logos*[250].

This makes the pneumatic man to have been seeded by Sophia in the very breath of the Demiurge, with an inexpressible virtue and providence, this fact escaped, as they say, the Demiurge.

This seed, they say, is the Church of the Spirituals, the replica of the Church above. There, they claim, is the Man in them.

So he receives: his soul from the Demiurge; his body of clay; his fleshly sheath of matter; his Spiritual (pneumatic) Man, from Mother Wisdom (Achamot).

The Christ of the Gospel has received from Wisdom the pneumatic element. The demiurge has clothed it with the psychic Christ. As for the hylic substance, he has not taken it in any way, because matter is not capable of salvation. Through the economy of the Encarnation he has seen himself surrounded by a body of psychic substance, organised with an unspeakable art so as to become visible, palpable and passible. As for the hylic matter, he has not taken it in any way, because it is not capable of salvation[251].

The final consummation

When the whole pneumatic seed has received its perfection, wisdom, its mother, will leave the Intermediate place to enter the Pleroma, where

---

[249] Ibid., p. 176.
[250] Ibid., p. 183.
[251] Ibid., p. 188.

it will receive as husband the Saviour out of all the Aeons; so that there will be syzygy of Saviour and Sophia.

The tyres will shed their psychic souls and, converted into spirits of pure intelligence, will enter the Pleroma to be the *spouses* of the Saviour's angels.

The Demiurge will also pass into the *Intermediary*. The souls of the righteous will have their rest in the Intermediary.

Once this is done, the latent fire, hidden from the world, will ignite, will burn and, destroying all matter, will be consumed with it and will be reduced to nothing[252].

The essence of the Valentinian gnosis. What does the Valentinian gnosis consist of? First of all, it consists in the *fundamental perception* of the *seed of gnosis*, or *seed of pneuma*, which comes from the "Father of all things, infinite transcendent, good, perfect". This seed constitutes the very *essence* of the Valentinian, the rest being nothing but a *psychic sheath;* the body, a garment, hylic or clay. The Valentinian is a parcel of the divine fallen into this world, being the old doctrine of the *soma-sema* complicated with all the syncretisms[253].

Consequently, after this seed has grown and perfected itself here below, the *return of* this parcel to its divine origin will take place. The Valentinian, by the mere fact of adhering to gnosis, proves that he has this parcel in him, that he has recognised by instinct, by natural kinship, the elements of gnosis that were proposed to him; thus the Samaritan woman recognised the Saviour, finding in him her true complement, which was unknown to her.

The Valentinian, who is a divine seed, Pneuma or Logos, is therefore *assured of his salvation*. Valentinian gnosis is a *gnosis of salvation*.

Since there is a radical *distinction* between the infinite Father, from whom he has received a parcel, and the God of Jews and Christians, represented in the Bible as the Creator and author of the Old Law, the latter becomes an inferior Demiurge to whom only Jews and Christians who are saved "by faith and works" attain, while the Valentinian attains to the infinite Father, of whom he is a parcel.

---

[252] Ibid., pp. 192 ff.
[253] Ibid., p. 567.

The three substances, of which they are constituted, explain the fate of the heathen who will perish in corruptible matter. That of the Christians and Jews who practise their religion, who will be saved in the Demiurge in a half-supraterrestrial, but who remain psychic, outside the sphere of the pneumatics and of the Valentinians, who, divine, will be united with the perfect Father. The detail of the return of the pneumatic to his Father is but an accessory. The picture is the ascent through the seven spheres (the nonal scheme of 2nd century astrology), escaping the psychic Demiurge and his angels[254].

Corresponding to the three substances, there are three worlds[255]. The Pleroma or divine world of the Father, a manifestation of God by successive emanations. The world of the Intermediate, in which the Wisdom outside the Pleroma or Enthymesis is realised. Here in the Intermediate Wisdom is purified and formed by the successive action of Christ and the Saviour. Here the residue of the purification will produce the psychic and hylic substances, the origin of our universe.

Inversely, this intermediary has its function in the ascent because there the pneumatic seeds are grouped around Wisdom, Enthimesis, with Mother and model, and there they unite with the angels of the Saviour Logos as Wisdom herself unites in this Saviour to make in common their entry into the Pleroma[256]. The Intermediate will have a function which will be final, for it will become the final habitation of the Demiurge and the psychics while the universe of the hellics will be destroyed[257].

The Valentinian gnosis consists in substance in that the Valentinian candidate must become aware of the Gnostic call and, in the image of wisdom, be instructed by the Gnostic master. Already formed by the Christ and the Spirit "in substance" (by the fact of his parcel of the pneuma) he must receive from the Saviour the "formation of the gnosis". Thus he will find rest and joy in the certainty of salvation. His seed will develop to a point of perfection that will allow him to enter the Pleroma[258].

---

[254] Ibid., p. 568.
[255] Ibid., p. 569.
[256] Ibid., p. 570.
[257] Ibid., p. 570.
[258] Ibid., p. 572.

And we move on to a second question: what is the origin of the Valentinian gnosis?

Sagnard studies this question in his book and comes to the conclusion that the elements of which this gnosis is composed are taken some from paganism, others from Judaism and others, finally, from Christianity. First of all, from the philosophy of the time, which is syncretistic, Stoic in the first place, but fused with elements of the Platonic and Pythagorean Renaissance.

The Plato, from whom Valentinus draws his elements, is a Plato stereotyped in the manuals of the 2nd century. Secondly, from the pagan mysteries which, in the 2nd century, are above all the so-called "oriental" mysteries: the mysteries of Isis, the Egyptian, the mysteries of Cybele, the Phrygian, and Astarte, the Syrian. Hermeticism also provides important elements.

Sagnard studies the contribution of Judaism to Valentinian gnosis, focusing on the biblical contribution of Wisdom to explain Gnostic wisdom and the contribution of Philo with his Logos. Wisdom, Divine Pneuma and Man. It should not be forgotten that Philo was active in Alexandria and echoed Kabbalistic ideas and influences.

Finally, it must be remembered that the Valentinians had come out of the Christians and were full of the language of Pauline mysticism.

Sagnard is keen to stress that "gnosis would thus have primitive pre-Christian, pagan or Jewish forms".

A great connoisseur of Gnostic problems in our days, Robert M. Grant, has written a book of great erudition and depth. The book is called *La Gnose et les origines chrétiennes*[259] and in it Grant argues that gnosis was born in the heterodox environments of Judaism, after the ruin of the eschatological hope that followed the fall and destruction of Jerusalem[260].

The author does not deny the presence in the Gnostic systems of Hellenistic, Iranian and Oriental elements in general, but he maintains that their first root is Judaic and precisely a sectarian and heterodox Judaism. Such an assertion by the author presupposes a vast knowledge of the Gnostic movements; indeed, Grant is not unaware of what the

---

[259] Aux Éditions en Seuil, Paris, 1959.
[260] Ibid., pp. 41 and 83.

Fathers have taught in this respect and which recent discoveries have confirmed.

First of all, Grant tries to define gnosis, a rather complex problem because of the variety of myths that veil the doctrine of the various gnostic systems. One thing the author can affirm with certainty: that for these systems it is always a problem of initiatory wisdom, in short, of knowledge, that is to say, of gnosis. Gnostics know: "What we are and what we have become; where we were and where the fall has dragged us; where we are tending to; from where we have been rescued; what it is to be born and reborn". The Gnostics affirm that, at root, individuals are purely spiritual, belonging to the world of spirit, precipitated in the world of flesh and sin; and that, thanks to the gnosis of their true nature, they are able to ascend to the world of spirit. The definition that the author proposes for gnosis is this: a religion that saves through knowledge; according to the Gnostic, to know is to know oneself, to recognise the divine absolute element, which constitutes the self; the self-knowledge of salvation and freedom[261].

In modern terms, Grant, following Puech, proposes as the essence of gnosis the return from an alienated existence to our ontological condition, to the authentic and permanent reality of our "I"; we pass, as the texts say, from the domain of the "cosmos" - the world of time and phenomena - to the "aeon", eternal and timeless[262].

Secondly, Grant accumulates powerful reasons to prove the thesis that gnosis comes from the Jewish apocalypse[263]. These reasons show that gnosis comes from the Jews, although not precisely from the apocalypses, since Jewish gnosticism, of Kabbalistic origin, is much earlier than Christian gnosticism.

Significance of Alexandria in the Gnostic polemic

In order to assess the significance of Christian Gnosticism vis-à-vis Judaism and paganism, on the one hand, and Catholic doctrine, on the other, it is useful to outline briefly the significance of Alexandria in the early Christian centuries. Three great schools of thought coexisted

---

[261] Ibid., pp. 17, 18 and 19.
[262] Ibid., p. 21.
[263] Ibid., pp. 41 and 133.

there, the pagan school of Plotinus, the Jewish school of Philo and the Christian school of Origen and Clement of Alexandria. The *Jewish Encyclopedia* shows that Alexandria, in the first century B.C., with its strange mixture of Egyptian, Chaldean, Jewish and Greek cultures, provided the soil for mystical philosophy[264].

The pagan school of Plotinus. Emile Bréhier[265] has written in *La Philosophie de Plotin* a chapter on Plotin's orientalism, where he studies the oriental influences registered by the philosopher. At the time when Plotinus frequented Ammonius, he tells us, "he had progressed so far in philosophy that he wished to take direct knowledge of the philosophy practised among the Persians and of that in vogue among the Indians". It was with this intention that he accompanied the army of the emperor Gordianus on his expedition against the Persians. The expedition failed and Plotinus was barely spared. For a Hellenised Egyptian like Plotinus, this "philosophy preached among the Persians" can only designate the set of theological ideas crystallised around the cult of Mithra.

And Bréhier adds: "I am thus obliged to look for the source of Plotinus' philosophy further away than in the Near East of Greece, even in the religious speculation of India which, at the time of Plotinus, had already been fixed for centuries in the Upanishads and had kept all its vitality[266].

And Bréhier notes that already Ritter[267] and, in 1857, Christian Lassen[268], had highlighted the great similarities between Hindu philosophy and that of Plotinus. Both in Plotinus and in the philosophy of the *Upanishad,* the central core is the identity of Brahman, the universal being, with Atman, which is this same universal being insofar as it resides in the human soul.

Plotinus is Greek science with the philosophy of India and Persia, as Porphyry pointed out in his time in chapter III of the *Vita Plotini.* Moreover, we must not forget that in Alexandria there was already an

---

[264] In the word *Kabala*. Also Matter in the same sense. *Histoire du Gnosticisme*, II, 58, 1844.
[265] Boivin et Cie, Paris, 1928.
[266] Ibid., p. 188.
[267] *History of philosophy*.
[268] Indischen Alterthumskunde, *III, pp. 415-439.*

Indian colony in the time of Ammonius Saccas and Plotinus and that both could have known and frequented it[269].

The great significance of Plotinus in the third century AD (204-270) is that he brought together Greek rationalism and Eastern mysticism in a coherent and rigorous system. His presence in Alexandria signifies all typically pagan science, both that of Greece and that of the Eastern world.

The Jewish school of Philo. The Jews were responsible for communication between the Greeks and the Eastern world. This has been emphasised in the *Historie Critique de l'Ecole d'Alexandrie*, by E. Vacherot[270], who points out that "the Jews became everywhere, and particularly in Alexandria, the intermediaries of the communications that were established between the East and Greece. Thus the Greeks know the Eastern ideas of Syria, Persia, Chaldea, Egypt, and thus also the Easterners receive the doctrines of the Greek philosophers". It will be seen with what shrewdness and plasticity Philo introduced Greek ideas into the heart of Judaism without corrupting or destroying it. Vacherot continues: "But Philo is not the only Jew who stands out in Alexandria. Eusebius, according to Alexander Polystor who was writing between 90 and 75 B.C., quotes Eupoleus, who was writing between 90 and 75 BC. B.C., quotes Eupolemus, Aristeus, Artapan and Demetrius. Philo is quoted by Polystor and Josephus".

For several historians (Ravaisson, Vacherot, Fouillée, etc.) a true fusion of Greek and Hebrew genius took place in Alexandria. Undoubtedly there is a great distance between the naturalism of early Greek philosophy and the transcendent God of the Jewish religion, but on both sides an evolution had taken place which by parallel and opposite movements would have erased the primitive differences between Jewish theology and Greek philosophy and would have prepared them to unite[271].

Philo was already imbued with kabbalistic and therefore Gnostic ideas. His God is a God without quality, *apoios*[272], which is close to the *Ein Sof* of the Kabbalah. Between God and the creature Philo places the

---

[269] Dict. de Theol. Cath., *Panthéisme*, col. 1862.
[270] Librairie Philosophique de Ladrange, Paris, 1846.
[271] L. Saltet, Dict. de Theol. Cath., *Ecole juive de Alexandrie*, I, p. 805.
[272] Bréhier, Les idées philosophiques et religieuses de Philon d'Alexandrie, *Paris, 1950, p. 72.*

Powers, which, like the Sephiroth of the Kabbalah, are intermediaries even in creative action. The indeterminacy surrounding these Powers in Philo is characteristic of the Sephiroth of the Qabalah. And above all, their dividing Logos, the origin of which has lent itself to so much discussion, has an undoubted origin in the Binah, the intelligence of the Qabalah, whose characteristic is division and dialectic, as we have seen[273].

Bréhier does not find it implausible that Philo in his *Questions on Genesis* (chapter III) echoed Pythagorean and Hermetic conceptions[274]. According to Bréhier himself, Philo would alter the concept of creation, since matter would not be the object of the same[275]. The Man of God in Philo is similar to the Adam Kadmon of the Kabbalah[276]; he would also be benevolent towards astrology and Chaldean cults[277]. Bréhier denounces the similar influence of Egyptian religious conceptions of the Hellenistic period on Philo[278]. Finally, the rapprochement that Bréhier establishes between Philo and the Therapeutae can be explained by a common influence of both by kabbalistic ideas[279].

Philo is a key man in Kabbalistic influence, not because he was an important figure in the transmission and elaboration of the Kabbalah, but because at a decisive moment, which was the emergence of Christianity, he had a prominent position that allowed him to be the centre of the currents of Greek rationalism, Eastern mysticism and Jewish theology, in the most influential cultural centre of the Empire. It is clear that Jewish theology, both Palestinian and Diaspora, was not the orthodox theology of Mosaism, but was already strongly influenced by Kabbalistic ideas.

The Christian school of Alexandria

Against the pagan school of Alexandria, represented by the great figure of Plotinus, and also against the Jewish school of Alexandria itself,

---

[273] G. Bardy, *Dict. de Theol. Cath.*, vol. 12, p. 1,450.
[274] Les idées philosophiques et religieuses de Philon d'Alexandrie, *pages 18 and 19.*
[275] Ibid., p. 81.
[276] Ibid., p. 121.
[277] Ibid., p. 165.
[278] Ibid., p. 237.
[279] Ibid., p. 321.

represented by Philo, there was the Christian school, represented by Panto, Clement and Origen.

This school played a prominent and leading part in the reaction against Gnosticism.

He was able to accomplish magnificently a philosophical and theological task which gave a powerful impetus to the development of ecclesiastical studies. At the beginning of the third century and in the universal movement of dissolution and reconstruction in which the fundamental questions of religion and natural morality were being agitated, Christian theology had precisely to affirm its primitive data and present them to the world under the aegis of revelation, with the authority of a supernatural tradition, not only as a philosophical teaching but also as a theological doctrine[280].

---

[280] See A. de la Barre, in *Dict. de Theol. Cath.*, t. 1, col. 810.

CHAPTER V

THE KABBALISTIC INFLUENCE IN THE ANCIENT AND MIDDLE AGES

In order to destroy Christianity from within, the Kabbalah inspires the Gnostic heresies, which are the great systems set up for the total and radical destruction of the purity of the Christian message. When the attempt to root out Christianity failed, the Jews confined themselves to a smaller task, which was to attack one dogma or another, while leaving the core of its fundamental truths intact to a certain extent. Hence the various Trinitarian and Christological heresies that followed on from Arianism.

Manichaeism

Among the Gnostic heresies, Manichaeism must be singled out. Manichaeism[281] is something of an enigma for the historian. It appeared abruptly around the middle of the 3rd century in Babylonia, i.e. in a country of intense religious syncretism, where the most diverse influences met and mingled: Christianity, Judaism, Mithraism, the old local religions of Chaldea; it spread rapidly to Spain and North Africa on the one hand, and on the other, to the extremities of Mongolia and China[282]. Such a universal and rapid spread cannot be explained without the cooperation of the Jews, a universalist people par excellence. There is also a version that Mani was of Jewish descent.

The similarity of Marcion's dualism is not doubtful; the Arab historians, who are not suspicious witnesses here, have not hesitated to pronounce the same names as the Christian heresiologists. According to Sharastani, Mani depends on Bordesane on all points, except for the

---

[281] G. Bardy, in *Dictionnaire de Théologie Catholique*, t. 9, col. 1.841-45.
[282] Ibid., col. 1869.

mediator[283]. Masoudi sees in Mani the disciple of Cerdon, of whom the early Christian polemicists often make Marcion's teacher. We know, on the other hand, that Mani himself knew the Gnostic writings and was interested in their speculations... "In short, Mani was a great reader. And his readings were directed to the recent works of the great representatives of the Gnosis, of which everyone around him spoke. There he found a more vast and comprehensive doctrine than what he had learnt in the mughtasilas. He was therefore led to abandon the latter in order to elaborate a new system which gave his teaching a broader and more systematic form"[284].

We know the tone of Mani's preaching from some fragments of his writings, such as, according to Biruni, the beginning of *Shapurakan*: "Wisdom and good works have been brought with a perfect constitution and from one age to another by the prophets of God. They came at one time by the prophet called Buddha in the religion of India, at another by Zoroaster in that of Persia, and at another by Jesus in the West. Accordingly, the present revelation has come and the present prophecy has been realised by me, Mani, the messenger of the true God in Babylon"[285].

What, then, were these ideas, first taught by Mani, and successfully propagated from Spain to the extremities of China? It seems that Mani himself in his works and in his letters has expounded a complete body of doctrine, and that the Manichaean preachers have endeavoured to transmit the teacher's teaching in its entirety without changing anything. In fact, a system as complicated as that of Mani must inevitably have received, according to the country and the usury of time, certain modifications: the Manichaeism of which St. Augustine speaks differs in a certain number of details from that of the treatises discovered in Chinese Turkestan.

The basis of the Manichean system is dualism. There are from all eternity two opposing principles: Good and Evil, Light and Darkness. "Each of them, declares Mani, is uncreated and without beginning, either Good, which is light, or Evil, which is both darkness and matter. The difference which separates the two principles is as great as that of

---

[283] Flügel, *Mani*, p. 165.
[284] P. Alfaric, *Les écritures manichéennes*, I, p. 22.
[285] *Chronologie*, trans. Sachan, p. 909.

a king and a pig. In its essence, primal Light is the same thing as God. There is no need to add that this realm of Light is purely spiritual.

At the opposite of the Light are the primitive Darknesses. They touch the light, they limit it. Between the two worlds there is no gulf; the one begins just where the other ends. They are juxtaposed without being confused. The opposition of their natures is enough to separate them. The principle of darkness is not a second God, for by essence it is the opposite of God. His proper name is matter, *Hylé;* he is also, according to the language of the multitude, the devil or the demon.

The peace that reigned between the two worlds was a precarious one: it stemmed mainly from the ignorance in which the dark world found itself with regard to its neighbour.

But when they saw the spectacle of the admirable and splendid light superior to their own, they gathered together and plotted against the light in view of mingling. Such was the origin of the struggle between the two worlds. Satan and his, having reached the confines of the kingdom of light, produced a great tumult. God sensed this and was frightened. He decided to send succour to those in distress. He evoked the Mother of Life and the Mother of Life in turn evoked primitive man.

But primitive man was powerless to triumph over the demon in high strife. He resorted to deception to weaken his enemy. He gave himself up to his enemies like a sheep in the midst of wolves. They rushed upon him and devoured him. The portions of his soul, suddenly submerged in matter, lost with intelligence the memory of their first condition.

But his defeat was only temporary. It was to prepare for the triumph of the Father of Enlightenment.

This, in effect, evoked a second creation, the Friend of Lights. The Friend of Lights evoked the Great Ban; the Great Ban evoked the Living Spirit. The Living Spirit was destined to liberate the spiritual elements devoured by demons. A first effort enabled him to liberate primitive Man. To finish separating the light that had swallowed the darkness, the Spirit became a demiurge; he began to organise matter in such a way as to separate the luminous elements from their dark refuse. The mixture at his disposal comprised the principles from which the world was to emerge. If in the created universe everything has a double aspect, good and bad, light and dark, it is in remembrance of its origin, and because the pure elements have not found their true place.

Made of spirit and matter, partaking of both God and the devil, Adam had to seek separation from the luminous elements he possessed within himself. Rebirth takes place when the fallen spirit finds the memory of its first state and realises its present misery.

Salvation has knowledge as its essential condition. It belongs to Jesus to communicate this knowledge to men. Jesus alone is the teacher and the saviour. The prophet presented himself as the one sent by Jesus. "Mani, apostle of Jesus Christ, by the Providence of God the Father", he wrote at the beginning of the *Epistle of the Foundation*. But perfect men, with gnosis, are but an exception. Most of them have followed the deplorable example of Eve and Cain, who transmit life through generation. Thus the mixture of good and evil is perpetuated; thus the liberation of the luminous elements and the return to the Father of Lights, which is the ultimate goal of creation, has been retarded.

But it is up to each individual to realise the providential plan as far as he is concerned. Born of the flesh, we have the power and the duty to live according to the spirit, to practise in full vigour the precepts of morality which the great reformers, Buddha, Zoroaster, Jesus, had taught, and which Mani has come to remind humanity of. Dark thought, dark feeling, dark reflection, which give rise to hatred, irritation, lust, anger and stupidity, are opposed in us by luminous thought, luminous feeling, luminous reflection, luminous intellect, luminous reasoning, which give rise to piety, good faith, contentment, patience and wisdom. It is only a matter of penetrating into the true nature of this dualism and of living according to the spirit, mortifying the passions and desires of the flesh.

Manichaean morality is very severe. First of all, everything that can defile the mouth, such as lying, blasphemy, apostasy, perjury, swearing, and food, such as meat and wine, is to be avoided. Whatever may defile the hand, such as killing, even animals, and waging war. And that which defiles the breast, such as sexual intercourse.

The Manichaeans divided their followers into two classes, the *elect*, who had to practise Manichaean morality severely, and the *hearers*, who had to listen to the word of life even if they did not practise it.

The elect will enter immediately after death into the paradise of light. The hearers will pass from body to body until they reach the body of a chosen one, and in the end the separation is to operate forever between the righteous and the sinners, and, more exactly, between the world of light and the world of darkness. And the kingdom spreads out brightly as in the beginning, no longer having to fear any invasion by the cohorts of the devil. The first order is entirely and forever re-established.

Manichaean dualism appears as a kind of gnosis, more complete, more logical and even, on the whole, simpler than most of those that have preceded it. Mani himself is the apostle of Jesus Christ. He is the last of the divine messengers and in him are realised all the promises made by Jesus Christ to his Apostles.

In this sense, Manichaeism is dependent on Christianity. It would not be what it is if Mani had taught before Jesus Christ and if he had not known Christian doctrines. But this dualism, as a system, has nothing Christian about it. It is, rather, in the East that the fullest expressions of it are to be sought. Manichaeism", writes K. Kessler[286], "is the most complete gnosis, on the one hand, because it took from the primitive source of all the gnoses of earlier Asia, from the Syro-Babylonian religion, the richest mythological material, without any intermediary; on the other hand, because its founder, Mani, has worked and systematised this material in a more consistent way than all the Gnostics, making of it a body of doctrine".

Manichaeism is nothing but a gnosis with an Iranian variant. Like all gnosis, it is a mythical or novelistic invention forged by the Jews with elements from the ancient mysteries, Judaism and Christianity.

In this respect, it is curious to note the similarities between Mani's childhood and St. Luke's accounts of Our Lord's childhood. The approximations show at least that the legend of Mani has been partly constructed according to the earlier accounts and that the formulas of An-Nadim[287] could not be taken literally.

Manichaeism was extraordinarily widespread in Europe, Egypt, Syria, Palestine, Persia and even in China and Mongolia.

The Arian heresy

No philosophy of history that dispenses with the struggle of the Jew against the Christian faith can be considered true. St. Paul testifies to the greatness of this struggle. Writing to the Christians of Thessalonica

---

[286] See G. Bardy, *Manichéisme,* in the *Dict. de Théologie Catholique,* col. 1841-1895.
[287] Ibid., col. 1.859.

he says those memorable words which have since remained the pivot of history: "Of the Jews, of those who put to death the Lord Jesus and the prophets, and persecute us, and who do not please God and are against all men; who prevent the Gentiles from being spoken to and their salvation from being procured"[288]. And St. John in the Apocalypse: "I will bring you quickly some of those who are of the synagogue of Satan, who call themselves Jews and are not, but are liars. I will make them come and bow down at your feet, and they will know that I love you"[289]. The first major persecution of Christians in the Gentile world, that of Nero, was probably unleashed at the behest of the Jews who surrounded his wife, Poppaea[290].

The great heresies that agitated the Church were raised and armed by the Jews. The Arian heresy in particular. The Jewish priest Arius, a former disciple of St. Lucian of Antioch, was in charge of the Church of Baucalis in Alexandria, when about 330 he began to teach a heretical and scandalous doctrine.

At the head of the profession of faith presented to St. Alexander by Arius, *De Synodis*, 10, Migne, P. G., vol. 26, c. 708, we find a fundamental notion, common to all the disciples of Lucian of Antioch: "We know only one God, only agenetos, only unbegotten, only eternal, only anarjos, only true God... the God of the law, of the prophets and of the ages". It is easy to suspect from this sentence alone that for Arius the Father, only true God, is opposed as agenetos to the Son, gennetos. In Arius' thought, agennetos and gennetos were necessarily opposed as uncreated and created because he held the terms *begotten* and *created* to be synonymous. Hence the idea familiar to the Arians: there are not two agenetos, that is, two uncreated and two principles, just as there are not two infinities or two gods.

Arius identifies the terms *begotten* and *created*, because for him all generation, and not only human generation, essentially entailed the idea of a contingent beginning or production. In this he denied the consubstantiality of the Son with the Father and therefore the divinity of the Son, Jesus Christ.

---

[288] I, 2, 14.
[289] IV, 9.
[290] William Thomas Walsh, *Philip II*, Espasa Calpe, p. 266.

In the genesis of the Arian heresy there was much influence of the Logos of the Alexandrian Jew Philo.

It is the conception of the Logosdemiurge, referred to Proverbs, VIII, 22, in which Wisdom says, following the version of the Seventy: *"The Lord has created me as the beginning of his works"*. More supposedly than expressed in Arius' profession of faith, this theory is, on the contrary, clearly formulated in *Thalia Orat. 1 contra Arius*[291] : "God was not always Father. He was first alone; the Logos and wisdom were not. God, wishing to create, first made a certain being whom He called Logos, Wisdom, Son, in order to create us through Him". The consequence of all this doctrine is that the Son is not equal or consubstantial with the Father.

This altered the Trinity and Christology. The person of Christ was not a truly divine person, since the Logos incarnate in the fullness of time was not true God.

In fact, there are Platonic infiltrations in the Arian doctrine, but through Philo, and in particular through the theory of the Logos-demiurge, under the Judaeo-Gnostic form of this Jewish philosopher. The Arian heresy is a syncretism in which one finds, under the guise of Aristotelian dialectics, elements of different origins, especially Philonic.

It is well known how widespread the Arian heresy became. It spread to the West and East, and then to the Germanic peoples: Visigoths, Burgundians, Vandals, Ostrogoths, Lombards. But then it disappeared without a trace in Europe. In the 16th century it was reborn with the Reformation, although in very different conditions from those that marked its first appearance. To tell the truth, no sect presented itself as specifically Arian. However, Servetus rejects the Trinity of consubstantial divine persons, treating it as God divided into three parts. Faustinus Socinus sees as contradictory the idea of a numerically one God and that of three persons, each of whom is God. In Christological matters, the relations between the Arians and the antitrinitarians of the Reformation are no less clear-cut.

---

[291] 5, *P. G.*, t. XXVII, col. 21.

From the Manichaeans to the Albigensians

The Jewish penetration, and therefore of the Talmud and the Kabbalah, was felt throughout the Middle Ages by Manichaean heresies such as Catharism, in the Novatian (3rd century onwards), Priscillian (around 370-375), Paulician (7th-10th centuries), Bogomila (927-14th century), Patarine (around 1179), Pasagian (around 1239) movements.

According to a tradition referred to by the chronicler Alberic de Trois Fontaines, the Manichean Fortunatus, after fleeing from Hippo, took refuge in Gaul, where he found other followers of Manes, especially in Champagne. This would be the origin of the dualist cult of Montwimer. Historical fact or legend? Nothing is known. In 563, the Council of Braga, in Spain, drew up several canons against Manichaeism. Around 800, an anathema written in Latin shows that the Manichaeans were persecuted in the West.

Catharos

Catharism has the fundamental dogmas of dualism and the evil of matter, and as theological corollaries, the doctrine of a fictitious Christ and the rejection of the Old Testament; as moral consequences, the interdiction of marriage and abstinence from animal flesh. It spread at the beginning of the 11th century to central France, Italy, Spain, Germany and England.

Far from being a Christian philosophy, the Cathar system is related to the metaphysical and religious speculations of Paganism... Although pagan in essence, Catharism wanted to adapt itself to Christianity, but at the cost of a thousand contradictions; it retained only an illusory form of it, and in spite of its Christian considerations it destroyed Christianity in its essential doctrines and in its historical reality.

Bogomilas

It seems that the Bogomils were a branch of Catharism and that the origins of both Western and Eastern Catharism, like those of Bogomilism, must be sought in Bulgaria.

Bogomilism acquired a certain importance in the 10th century. It soon split into two divergent churches. Its main centre was Philipolis in Thrace. From one and the other church it radiated in all directions and from the second half of the 10th century it had gained Constantinople.

Originally, Bogomila dualism was absolute: it admitted the perfect equality of two principles, the one and the other eternal. A tendency to mitigate them was soon noticed, for eternity was attributed to the one good principle, God supreme, and the evil principle was held to be a created spirit which was detached from the good principle by an act of free will. Hence two systems, or as Western documents express it, two orders, arose among the Bogomils, the Bulgarian, *ordo of Bulgaria*, which adopted the mitigated dualism, and the *ardo of Dngutria*, in Dalmatia.

Among the Bogomils, along with dualism, there are other doctrines which together constitute primitive Catharism: rejection of water baptism and infant baptism, communication of the Holy Spirit by the laying on of hands, condemnation of marriage, condemnation of animal food, denial of the real presence of the Eucharist, contempt for the cross and images, as well as for buildings used for worship.

Paulicians

Dualistic heretical sect that spread mainly in Upper Syria and Armenia, then to Phrygia, then Bulgaria, and spread to the West under various names.

The main personage who gave this sect its true form and particular existence seems to have been one Constantine, who called himself Silvanus, a native of Mananalis, near Samosata, in the 7th century.

The essential point of the Paulicians' doctrine was the distinction between the good God, the Lord of heaven, the Creator of souls, who alone is to be worshipped, and the evil God, the demiurge, the creator and lord of the sensible world. For them all matter is evil. This dualism is clearly Marcionist, but it is possible that it was not originally so and that Paulician dualism was Manichaean with an evolution towards Marcionism.

Albigensians

The main centre of Catharism was Albi and perhaps Toulouse. The Albigensians developed in the 11th, 12th and 13th centuries. To exterminate them, Innocent III had to mobilise the archbishops of Narbonne, Arles, Embrum, Aix, Vienne and the counts, barons and knights of France, King Philip Augustus, the archbishop of Tours, the abbot of the Cistercians and the archbishops of Paris and Nevers [292]. As

---

[292] Ferdinand Niel, *Albigeois et cathares*, Presses Univ., Paris, 1965, p. 76.

in the Cathars, dualism is at the heart of the system. There are two principles, they said. But only the good principle is eternal; it has created, in the spirits, the four elements, and from these elements the evil principle has formed the world. Of the Trinity they retained only the name, because they made the Son a creature. The Church would have been corrupted since Constantine's donation. In morals, the matter being evil, they preached absolute detachment and divided the organisation into two classes, that of the perfect and that of the believers. The perfect were, practically speaking, impeccable.

Armand de Lunel, referring to "The Golden Age of the Occitan Jews", cites among the ideological currents circulating at the time of the Cathar or Albigensian heresy "the most original, the most fertile, that which, underground and mystical, was to spread with the Cabala". "Due to a lack of usable documentation, the origins and development of Jewish mysticism in the Occitan Middle Ages have not been sufficiently studied until today... It would certainly be clearer in the related and no less exciting problem of the doctrinal relations between the Jews and the Cathars... It is no less certain that Jews and Cathars lived side by side under the benevolent authority of the counts of Toulouse... There was certainly a reason for the alliance between Cathars and Jews in the practical interest of confronting their common adversary: the Roman Church. The sign of the cross could be, for different reasons, equally odious to them"[293].

Gershom Scholem in *Les Origines de la Kabbale*[294] notes that "all that we know of the ancient Kabbalists and their groups comes from Languedoc. In towns such as Lunel, Narbonne, Posquieres and perhaps also in Toulouse, Marseilles, Arles, we find the first personalities known to us as Kabbalists. Their disciples immediately transplanted the Kabbalistic tradition to Spain, where it must have taken root in places such as Burgos, Gerona and Toledo, and from where it also spread to other Jewish communities...

"But the South is more than this, it is a region of high religious tension, a tension that has no equal in other countries of Christian culture. In many parts of Languedoc, it is no longer Christianity that reigns at this time, but the dualist religion of the Cathars or Albigensians, whose

---

[293] Armand de Lunel, *L'age d'or des juifs d'oc*, Aspectus du génie d'Israel, p. 161, quoted by Mauricio Carlavilla, *Judaism and the Catholic Church*, p. 58.
[294] Aubier, Paris, 1966, pp. 22-25.

fundamental character has been the subject, not without reason, of a long controversy... Today, another generally accepted opinion prevails: we have to deal with a religion which, by using certain Christian notions, undermines the very foundations of Christianity. A difficult problem which has not yet been solved is that of the survival of Gnostic influences and ideas, not Manichaean, in the religion of the Cathars.

> "The Judaism of Provence, which also experienced a period of great flowering in the 12th century, flourished at this time in an environment in which Catholic Christianity marked with the seal of orthodoxy was literally struggling for its existence, where it had effectively lost its influence in wide circles, both in the ruling class of feudal and chivalry and their cultural representatives and in the popular strata, among the peasants and shepherds".

And Gershom Scholem is forced to acknowledge the relations of Catharos with Kabbalistic Jews. Speaking of the former, he says, that "their metaphysical anti-Semitism did not prevent them necessarily from proceeding when the occasion arose to exchange views with Jewish adversaries like themselves of Catholicism".

The Templars

The Templar affair is one of the most resonant in history.

After seven centuries, we have not been able to determine with certainty what truth there is in the accusations made against this military order, what truth there is about the actions of Philip the Fair and Clement V, what truth there is about the trial and condemnation of the Order.

However, it must be recognised that the documentation that exists on this notorious affair should have been sufficient to make a calm and somewhat definitive judgement. M. Michelet[295] has brought together in two large volumes the most important documents of this great cause, such as the interrogations made in Paris in 1307 by the tribunal of the Inquisition and then the entire procedure of the seven pontifical commissaries from August 1309 to May 1311.

The result of these trials is such a vast and well-considered mass of testimonies and concordant confessions by the accused that it is impossible to doubt, at least in general, the truth of the accusations,

---

[295] M. Michelet, *Proces des Templiers*, Paris, Imprimerie Royale, 1844-1851.

most of them very serious, which were formulated[296]. And let it not be said that these accusations were extracted by torture, since both the Protestant Wilcke, in the *History of the Templars,* and Michelet himself, director of the *Proces des Templiers,* and his testimony is not suspect, testify that the interrogation held by the Grand Master and more than a hundred knights in Paris was conducted by the judges slowly and with care and gentleness. Moreover, it is certain that none of the one hundred and forty knights who were examined by the inquisitor Fra' lmbert in the first trial of 1307, none of the seventy-two knights investigated by the Pope and the cardinals in Poitiers, none of the two hundred and thirty-one knights who were examined by seven papal commissioners in Paris between August 1309 and May 1311, none of these were subjected to torture[297]. In the interrogations nothing was required of them but an oath to tell the truth, and on the faith of this oath their whole exposition was received: *"Having taken the oath that on all the things in question they would tell the pure and full truth, freely and spontaneously, without any coercion or terror, they deposed and confessed,* etc. Thus testifies the Pope in the Bull *Vox in excelso*[298].

And what were the crimes of which the Knights Templar were accused? The enormous crimes mentioned by the Pope in the *Bull Vox in excelso* and others are, for example, blaspheming and disavowing Jesus Christ, spitting on the cross, practising obscene rites in the act of their secret initiation, to worship an idol's head, the famous Bahomet[299], in their secret assemblies, to consider nefarious actions against nature as lawful and to abandon themselves freely to them, to confess and absolve each other, even if they are simple laymen, of their sins; These and other similar enormities were witnessed and confessed by more than a hundred Templars, and no longer by obscure servants of the Order, but by the most conspicuous knights, by the preceptors and senior officers, and by the Grand Master himself. They were confessed repeatedly

---

[296] *La Civilta Cattolica,* Rome, 1866, Anno 17, vol. VII, p. 699.
[297] Ibid., p. 702.
[298] Ibid., p. 702.
[299] The androgynous goat-goat of Mendes (goat demon), which according to the Roman Church was worshipped by the Templars. Despite the demonic nature assigned to it, H. P. Blavatsky maintains that it was a hermetic-cabalistic symbol derived from Anmon, the ram-headed god of Lower Egypt, which unfortunately served certain ecclesiastical designs (?) Zaniah, *Dice. Esoteric,* Kier, Buenos Aires, 1962.

before the inquisitors, bishops, cardinals and the Pope himself, often with the most sincere signs of repentance.

These confessions took place not only in France, which was still the seat and main nerve of the Order, but in England and Italy and elsewhere, where the Templars had houses and could be examined, so that the corruption of the Order was, if not universal, certainly quite widespread. And not only widespread, but also ancient, since Grand Master Molay confessed in *1307* that, having been received into the Order forty-two years before, he had also disowned Christ, according to the impious and obscene rite introduced, it is not known how long before[300].

The problem of the Templars raises a very delicate question, especially if we take into account that modern Freemasonry presents itself as continuing the aims of the same Order of the Temple. What these aims are is magnificently revealed in a work which, although written in a novelistic tone, nevertheless reflects an aspect worthy of serious consideration. We are referring to the book by the journalist Gérard de Sede, *The Templars are here*[301], in which the Order of the Templars is linked to the Cabalists, Gnostics and Assassins. In turn, the doctrine of the Assassins is situated, we read here, along the lines of Hermeticism, the Cabala and Gnosis, which he still takes pleasure in raising to a higher degree of abstraction[302]. It is also said that "the Christian Church was quick to recognise an enemy of order, maleficent and possessed of enigmas, in the Alexandrian Gnosis[303]... But we shall see that its existence is still strong and that its sisters, the Kabbalah and Hermeticism, along with it, will be content to walk the dark esoteric path, not conforming to their origins, transmitting from century to century their ritual and ideological heritage, of which certain Pythagorean rites still form a good part".

The Order of the Templars took up the whole movement of ideas and revolution that had been stirring in the underworld of the Middle Ages, and of which the Jews were the most powerful promoters. The

---

[300] La Civilita Cattolica, *ibid. p. 700.*
[301] Editorial Bruguera, Barcelona, 1963.
[302] Ibid., p. 110.
[303] Ibid., p. 108. See also Louis Charpentier, *Les mysteres templiers,* 1967, Robert Laffont, Paris.

subversion was not concentrated in one point, but in all the fabric of Christian society.

But, for the purposes of our work, we will focus on two authors who expressively reflect the Kabbalistic influence in the Middle Ages, an influence that was counterbalanced by the fidelity to the Church and to Christ that filled the saints, doctors and Christian people of that Age of Faith.

John Scotus Eriugena

In order to situate John Scotus Eriugena in his milieu, which was the Palatine School of the Carolingians, it is necessary to point out the framework in which the whole social-political and cultural life of the time unfolded.

The Jewish historians Max L. Margolis and Alexander Marx in *Histoire du Peuple Juif*[304] note that "Jews throughout the Frankish kingdom shared in the benefits of a firm regime. Under Charles the Great, or Charlemagne (768-814) and his son Louis the Pious (814-840), the Jews, thanks to their relations with their co-religionists abroad, concentrated in their hands all the trade of the country, and especially the export and import of merchandise. One Jew, Isaac, was part of the embassy sent by Charlemagne to Harun-al-Raschid, and was the only survivor. Christian merchants paid an eleventh of their profits to the Treasury, while Jews paid a tenth. Certain Jewish merchants dear to the ambassador enjoyed special protection, such as Donatus and his nephew Samuel David and Joseph in Lyon, Abraham in Saragossa. An imperial official called the "Lord of the Jews" ensured that each community maintained its privileges and the security of life and property[305].

The Jewish Encyclopaedia, under Kalonymous, reports that Joseph Hakohen, in his *Emek-ha-baiá*, relates that Charlemagne brought a Kalonymous family to Mainz from Lucca in 787, and Rapoport and Zunz report that it was Charles the Bald who authorised Moshe Kalónimo, the Elder, and his son Yekutiel to settle in Mainz.

---

[304] Payot, Paris, 1930, p. 323.
[305] See also Joseph Kastein, *Historia y destino de los judíos*, Claridad, p. 230, 1945, Buenos Aires.

Simon Dubnow tells us that "two legends symbolise in the figure of persons the process of national culture that moved from the old centres of the diaspora to the new centres.

According to one popular tradition, Charlemagne brought from Baghdad to Narbonne the Nabi scholar Majir who founded the first Jewish academy in the south of France and was the initiator of a dynasty of "nasi", the head of the Jewish community in Provence. Another account tells that Charles transferred the Nabi scholar Kalonymous from the Lombard city of Lucca to Mainz, where he and his descendants were for generations at the head of the Jewish community"[306].

The Palatine School, founded by the Carolingians, must be placed in the context of the commercial and cultural influence of the Jews, and John Scotus Eriugena must not have been unscathed by it, especially if one takes into account the cabalistic character of his doctrines.

The problems posed by the thought of John Scotus Eriugena are not sufficiently clarified, since his works are not yet in current editions. Moreover, Christian philosophy had not yet refined a number of concepts and notions that would later be elaborated, especially by the genius of St. Thomas, so that it is very difficult to appreciate whether there are real errors in Eriugena's thought or whether, on the other hand, they are the inaccuracies that characterise all earlier thinkers. There is some truth in Gilson's statement: "For those who love to shoot at heresy, Eriugena is an easy target. Every target is hit; but one is sometimes confused to find that by shooting at Eriugena one has hit Dionysius, Maximus the Confessor, St. Gregory of Nyssa, St. Gregory Nazianzus, St. Ambrose and St. Augustine"[307].

This is true to a certain extent, insofar as Christian philosophy and theology had not yet reached a level of maturity and precision at which the formulas of these authors could suffer from a somewhat malevolent interpretation. But in Eriugena there is something more, as we shall see immediately. "It has recently been considered that, rather than the pseudo-Dionysius, "the source of Eriugena's inspiration was the Cabala". Scotus sometimes says: *ut sapientes Hebraeorum tradiderunt*. Did the philosopher know this tradition himself? I doubt it, answers Vulliaud, for often, when Scotus quotes etymologies taken from

---

[306] The History of the Jewish People in Europe, *IV, p. 104.*
[307] La philosophie mediévale, *2nd Ed., p. 206.*

Hebrew, he does so according to St Jerome or simply by copying his master the Areopagite... However, although we do not know how he knew the Kabbalah, it is undeniable that he speaks its language and we often find in the *De divisione naturae* a symbolism identical to the Kabbalistic symbolism" (P. Vulliaud, "The Kabbalah and the Kabbalistic Symbolism in the *De divisione naturae*"). (P. Vulliaud, *Entretiens idéalistes*, 25, 3, 1910). There is a vein to be exploited here, especially as the esotericism of the Cabala was certainly widespread and more or less known to Christians in the 9th century. J. Brucker *(Historia critica philosophiae*, Leipzig, 1743) had already linked the doctrines of Eriugena with the Kabbalah, rather foolishly in fact,[308].

In any case, the comparison of Eriugena's fundamental doctrines with the Kabbalah does not fail to produce and arouse surprise.

1. *The concept of God:* The negative theology used by Eriugena is opposed to the infinite losing its supreme rank, which would happen if, wishing to designate it, to define it, it were enclosed in a determination; it denies that it can be determined; it denies that it is, that is to say, that it is accessible to the intelligence and expressible by the word. Affirmative theology is concerned above all with God as cause, and cause is expressed in what it produces and because it studies effects; this theology can affirm something about eternal being; it is concerned with God who is an infinite cause, whereas negative theology is concerned with God who is the infinite substance.

> "And despite appearances these two theologies do not contradict each other. In saying "God is truth", or God is wisdom, the second does not understand the divine substance to be properly truth or wisdom, but may be called truth or wisdom by the metaphorical application to the creator of a name suitable to creation. By saying "God is not truth" or "God is not wisdom", the first affirms that the divine nature, incomprehensible and ineffable, is not properly truth or wisdom, although it may metaphorically be so called"[309].

We must see, in expounding St. Thomas's opinion on the present question, that Eriugena reduces our knowledge of God too much to the point of agnosticism. The same must be true of *The Divine Nature:* "One cannot define God except by denying what He is not, and the more

---

[308] Dict. de Theol. Cath, *Erigène*, col. 409, art. by F. Vernet.
[309] *De Divisione naturae*, 1. I, chap. XIV, col. 461; F. Vernet, Dict. De Théol. Cath., *Erigène*, col. 413.

one thus denies, the more one affirms that God is nothing, that is, nothing of what He is for us, nothing determined; and this denial is the highest affirmation, all determination being a higher denial. God is nothing, and this is not only a form of our thinking, but God thus knows himself, knowing that he is nothing and that this nothingness is superior to everything"[310].

Here the *omnis determinatio est negatio* of Spinosa and Hegel and the Ein-Sof of the Kabbalah appear, which is to be made more sensitive in the concept of creation.

The concept of creation

"From the super-essence of his nature in which it is said not-to-be, *in qua dicitur non-esse*, by a first degree he creates himself, *a se ipso creatur*, in the primordial causes and becomes the principle of all essence, of all life, of all intelligence...

Then, descending from the primordial causes which constitute as an intermediary between God and the creature, it is realised in its effects, *in effectibus ipsarum fit*... Then, through the manifold forms of these effects, it comes and reaches the last order of eternal nature, which comprises the bodies. All things are therefore both created and eternal. Scotus claims to find this doctrine in Scripture, in St. Augustine, in pseudo-Dionysius. The other things which are said to be, are only theophanies, *ipsius theophaniae sunt*. "God, therefore, as St. Dionysius the Areopagite says, is all that he truly is because he *has made* all things and *is made* in all things, *facit et fit*". He himself summarises his doctrine by distinguishing four kinds of causes: a) *quae creat et non creatur;* b) *quae creatur et creat;* c) *quae creatur et non creat;* d) *quae nec creatur nec creat.* Apart from the pseudo-Dionysius and St. Augustine who had Christianised them, Scotus finds and reconstructs Proclus and Plotinus.

He retains the term creation, but like the modern monists, separating the term from its meaning. The Council of Valencia, which condemns his errors on predestination, warns against the rest of his doctrine. Express condemnations fulminated against his *De divisione naturae* when the Chartruese schools tried to revive it[311].

---

[310] *De Div. naturae*, 1. II, chap. XXVIII-XXX, col. 586-589; F. Vernet, ibid. col. 414.
[311] H. Pinard, Dict. de Théol. Cath., art. *Création*, t. III, col. 2080.

The concept of creation in Eriugena is very close to that of emanation and eternal emanation. Eriugena calls it diffusion. *Ineffabilis diffusio et facit omnia, et fit in omnibus, et Omnia est.* The ineffable diffusion and makes all things, and is made in all things, and is all things. But this conception is in contradiction with the doctrine of the Fathers, who agree in affirming that God created the world out of nothing. How can we call eternal that which has begun to be? How are things eternal at the same time as being made out of nothing, that is, existing before they were made? Eriugena's answer to this is that the eternity of creation must be maintained, that God only precedes it with a logical anteriority, for in God there are no accidents. That the world is eternal and created should not be surprising, since God is also eternal and created, remaining in himself perfect and more than perfect, separate from all things and involved in all things, making all things, becoming all things[312].

He then explains creation *ex nihilo* in the sense that God was when creatures did not exist and that, existing eternally in the first causes and, as such, known to God alone, creatures have in a certain sense begun when they appeared with accidents of quantity, quality, etc., which they receive in time and which manifest them. Let us be more precise. In creation *ex nihilo* the *nihilum* is God himself, *who is insinuated in the negation of all things that are properly, because he is exalted above all that is said and understood, which is nothing of the things that are and that are not, which are best known by not knowing*[313].

Indeed, how did God create the whole world in the Word? He sees things, and for Him to see is to create them. But He sees no other nature than His own; before creation there was nothing but Himself, He sees Himself and creates Himself; the creature is eternal in God, its necessary foundation, and God is created in the creature, for through it He becomes visible, intelligible.

Several times in the dialogue, the disciple uttered cries of outrage, and the master himself experienced the sensation of vertigo. He declares that, in order to soar to these heights, a spirit stripped of earthly

---

[312] F. Vernet, Dict. de Théol. Cath., art. *Erigène,* col. 416.
[313] *De Div. nat.,* l. III, cap. XXII, col. 686-687; F. Vernet, ibid., col. 416.

imaginations and the grace that Christ has given us by his Incarnation is necessary" [314].

Eriugena's thought cannot be more homogeneously assimilated with that of the Kabalah, which makes *Ein-Sof the* nothingness and a nothingness which is created and realised in the Sephiroth. This does not prevent, however, that, if the expressions are greatly refined, an interpretation compatible with the Catholic dogma of creation can be given to these expressions. But in any case, the Kabalistic influence would exist, since Eriugena's thought does not achieve a formulation that really overcomes the contradiction of Kabalistic thought with Catholic doctrine.

The lower creation and man

Between the intellectual world, which develops in the most sublime of angels, and the sensible world, which descends to the lowest of unreasoning creatures, is human nature, which has something of both. Man is not to be defined as "a reasonable animal", but as "an intellectual notion eternally made in the divine mind". This definition does not stop at accidents, but goes directly to the substance and is found in God. Centre of creation, summary of the universe, man is the mediator and saviour[315].

Its image is the image of the Trinity. The only difference is that the divine Trinity is uncreated and that it is God par excellence of its essence, whereas the trinity of the soul is created by that of which it is the image, and is not God except by the largesse of divine grace. All other differences result from sin. To the mortal body, the soul has been united after sin, as an instrument somehow made in its image. Before sin, man's body was spiritual and immortal, as it would be after the resurrection. All that remains immutable in the body corresponds to its primitive condition; all that is changeable and diverse has been added after the fall. The innumerable differences due to the manifold combinations of the four elements, susceptible of growth and diminution, form the material body, the garment of the spiritual, inner, primitive body, the identical, universal form, common to all. It follows that before sin human generation did not exist, for neither did it exist

---

[314] F. Vernet, ibid., col. 417.
[315] L. IX, C. VIII, col. 768; F. Vernet, ibid., col. 417.

among the angels. Nor was there any distinction of sexes, as there will not be in heaven"[316].

Also kabalistic is this idea that man before sin would be a purely spiritual being, manifesting himself in a material body only after sin. Equally kabalistic is the malice attributed to the organs of generation and sexuality.

Predestination of the wicked

If Eriugena has the merit of maintaining against Gotescalc, that God wills the salvation of all, that he does not predestine the reprobate to punishment, without there being any fault on their part, that sin comes from the freedom of man, he is not right in rejecting every virtual distinction between the divine attributes and in not recognising that sin can be foreseen by God and the punishment of sin foreseen and predestined, that punishment, although having a negative character as a deprivation of God, is formally the manifestation of divine justice. Here and there, in this treatise, the errors that will spread in lustful fronds in the *De divisione naturae*[317].

The reintegration of humanity into God

Should the whole of mankind return to God? asks Eriugena. He answers that, in effect, evil, which God does not do, and the punishment of evil, will be abolished and erased from creation whether it is the devil or guilty man[318]. If this is so, what of the tortures that Scripture says? To understand it, it is necessary to detach oneself from the coarse ideas of the people: there will be no material punishments, nor a place under the earth where these torments will be inflicted. The torment will be in the consciences. The whole of humanity will return to its primitive state. This is paradise. All gathered together in paradise, the elect will be in thought close to Christ through love, blessed, deified, yet unable to rise up to God and become one with God, for Christ, head of the Church, has reserved this for them; while the reprobates will feel far from Him by their perverse thinking. To realise that they are far from Christ, far from God, is their judgment.

---

[316] F. Vernet, ibid., col. 418.
[317] F. Vernet, ibid., col. 420.
[318] L. V, C. XXVII, col. 921 quoted by F. Vernet, ibid., col. 421.

To stay away from Him by the thought and direction of one's actions is hell. The descriptions of a material hell given by the Fathers are but modes of expression which they used before carnal hearers. For the tortures of the wicked will not stop the return of mankind to God. Humanity *tota in omnibus est et tota in singulis;* as the sun pierces the filth without obscuring its rays, it is not obscured by the darkness of sinners; the faults of the individual do not reach it, nor do the punishments inflicted for these faults; God will preserve nature in purity, which is His work and which cannot be an evil; He will let the punishment of the sinner's disordered will, that is, of that which is nothing, *quoniam in numero eorum quae a canditore omnium substituta sunt, non sunt,* be fulfilled. In short, evil will be destroyed in human nature, but the memory of evil will always remain, and hence the punishment in the soul of the wicked. It is not accurate to say, as has been done, that Eriugena finally abolishes the eternity of punishment. His opinion is expressed from chapter XXVII to chapter XXXIII; such an isolated text might provoke doubts, but the whole of the developments and the march of ideas do not permit indecision: nature, as he explains it, will escape evil and its consequences; the wicked will always be punished. This is very mysterious: but if in all these things not only the human but the angelic intelligence falters, be patient and give place to the divine and incomprehensible power and honour it with silence[319].

General appreciation of Eriugena:

1) Formulas of pantheistic appearance abound in the works of Scotus. He says and rephrases in a thousand ways that all things proceed from God, that they are in the divine ideas, that the ideas are in God, drawn from God himself, that they are in the Word and begotten in him, that God is the being of all things, that all things, proceeding from God, will return to him. Are they not the frank expression of the most rigorous pantheism? On closer inspection, doubts arise. And one perceives that these and similar formulas are taken from the orthodox writers.

2) However one may judge the orthodoxy of Scotus Eriugena himself, it must be admitted that the worst errors can be drawn from his works. Abelard took for the basis of his doctrine of God the agnostic symbolism of Scotus. Bernard of Chartres professes a kind of pantheism

---

[319] L. V, C. XXXIII, col. 950, quoted by F. Vernet, ibid., col. 4ZZ.

which is linked with the theories of Scotus. Amaury of Chartres, or de Bene, transported, by enlarging them, the ideas of Scotus from the field of metaphysics to that of morals. Documents reveal Amaury's relationship with Eriugena. Amaury was condemned at the Lateran Council (1215). It has been noted that the book of David of Dinandus which was condemned with that of Amaury, the *De Tomis*, or "Of Divisions", recalls the main writing of Eriugena. To a certain extent, all the heterodoxy of the Middle Ages comes, by deviant routes or directly, from John Scotus Eriugena. And in modern times, Catholics - not of a sure doctrine, like Frederick Schlegel or Baader - have lamented that scholasticism has not come closer to the Eriugenist teachings[320].

The conclusion reached by Gustavo A. Piemonte in *Sapientia*[321], in an article that focuses on the *creatio ex nihilo, the* key point of all Eriugenian thought, seems to us to be correct. This new interpretation of the nothingness out of which the world was made has, if we are not mistaken, weighty consequences with regard to the distinction between creatures and the Creator. The alternative clearly indicated by Augustine for the origin of created things: from nothingness and not from the divine nature, is blurred in a doctrine where *a Deo de nihilo* ultimately means *a Deo de Deo*. The passage from nothingness to being does not take place, let us say, below God, thanks to the intervention of causality *ad extra;* but neither does it imply the formation of entities outside God with the divine substance conceived as indeterminate matter; it is *within God himself* that the descent from super-essentiality to the multitude of essences takes place. The only true nothingness is the divine goodness which transcends all things; the only true creation is the *eternal conditio rerum in Verbo Dei, the* eternal condition of things in the Word of God.

Did Scotus Eriugena influence the Kabbalists or did they influence him? The question is justified in that there is a clear affinity between the two doctrines. This affinity has been recognised since ancient times and Brucker already admitted it in his *Historia critica philosophiae*[322]. Modern Gershom Scholem has studied it with singular prolixity. In *Le grandi correnti della mística ebraica*[323] he announces having examined

---

[320] F. Vernet, ibid., col. 130.
[321] Notes on the "Creatio ex nihilo" in Juan Scoto Eriugena, *no. 87, 1968, p. 57*.
[322] T. III, p. 621, Leipzig, 1743, quoted by F. Vernet, ibid, col. 409.
[323] p. 62 n; French ed. p. 370.

it in a contribution to "Eranos-Jahrbuch"[324] and in *Les Origines de la Kabbale* he deals with it at length when he studies the first kabbalists of Provence[325] and then those of Gerona[326], and above all Azriel[327]. Gustavo Piemonte faithfully follows Scholem, whose arguments he reproduces at length[328].

But Gershom Scholem speaks throughout of the probable influence of John Scotus on Jewish esotericism. And here is what he fails to prove. Gershom Scholem has to admit that Jewish esotericism existed long before it was written down. Hence he himself writes: "The first epoch of Jewish mysticism, before its crystallisation in the medieval Kabbalah, is at the same time the one that lasts the longest: the remaining important literary documents cover about a millennium, from the first to the tenth century AD... I do not understand how to hypothesise on the difficult problem, however seductive it may be, of the first beginnings of Hebraic mysticism and its links with the religious world of Hellenistic-Eastern syncretism... Hebraic mysticism began in Palestine. We know also the names of the most important representatives of mystical and theosophical speculation among the teachers of the Mishnah, belonging to the circle of the disciples of Jochanan ben Zaccai, towards the end of the first century after Christ. We have also good reason to maintain that the greater part and also the most essential part of their spiritual inheritance has been gathered in the esoteric conventuals and then in those circles which at the end of the Talmudic period attempted, in a whole literature, a synthesis of their new religious vision of the world"[329]. So much for Scholem.

Scholem traces esotericism back long before Scotus Eriugena. This is enough to exclude Eriugena's influence on the Kabbalah. All the more so, if, as we believe, the Jewish Gnostic current had been developing for a long time, until it was traced back to the captivity of the Hebrews in Egypt in the 16th century B.C., as we have argued in chapter III of the present work. And it is clear that the theme of creation was a favourite of the Jewish Gnostic tradition. It is therefore difficult, if not impossible, that a Christian philosopher, alone in the ninth century,

---

[324] 1956, vol. 25, pp. 87-119.
[325] Pp. 286-287; 331-332; 336; 363.
[326] Pp. 397; 412.
[327] Pp. 445-454; 464-465.
[328] *Sapientia*, no. 88, 1968.
[329] *Le grandi correnti...*, pp. 64-66; French ed., p. 53.

could have imagined and invented speculations that constituted the obligatory subject of kabbalistic speculations. It is right to imagine that, in one way or another, this philosopher fell into the orbit of a Jewish esoteric circle. This is why we have attached so much importance to the information given by Jewish historians about the intense Jewish commercial and cultural exchange in the Carolingian period, first with Charlemagne and then with Charles the Bald. The Palatine School, which became so significant under the Carolingians, must have been influenced by a Jewish circle. This is where research should be directed if it is to achieve positive results.

Mere Neoplatonic speculation does not provide sufficient foundation for Kabbalistic interpretation, as St. Thomas' commentaries on the pseudo-Dionysius demonstrate. On the other hand, Neoplatonism and the biblical exegesis of Genesis, in the hands of Kabbalistic theosophists, which operated before the advent of Christianity, amply explain the esoteric current which emerged in the Christian era and which could not manifest itself in writing before, not only because it was deliberately esoteric and most secret, but because it was severely repressed by orthodox Rabbinism and by the repression of it in the Christian world.

Precisely in *La Kabbale et sa symbolique*, Gershom Scholem himself, speaking of the identification of God with the original Nothingness, warns that it is nothing but the consequence that the Jewish mystics have drawn through the maintenance of *the old formulas*. He adds: "Chaos, which had been eliminated in the theology of "Creation from Nothing", reappears in new metamorphosed formulas". It is clear that *these old formulae* predate John Scotus Eriugena.

The same conclusion is reached by developing the principles that the distinguished teacher George Vajda gives about *the Kabbale*, who recognises that it is "legitimate to affirm that the Kabbalistic doctrine is very ancient. As old as the penetration of gnosis in Judaism, probably even preceding Christianity by two or three generations"[330]. And how this Jewish esotericism moved is shown precisely in the subject of creation, when he writes: "The solution in accordance with the faith consisted, by the confession of all, in showing that God has drawn out of nothing"... conceiving this nothingness as "Outside of God". On the

---

[330] Introduction à la pensée juive du mayen âge, J. Vrin, Paris, 1947, p. 198.

other hand, "the kabbalist, using the same terminology, completely inverts its meaning: Nothingness is the most intimate aspect, the most latent mode of being of God. Creation *ex nihilo* means, therefore, somehow one or more manifested modes of being of that which, in its innermost essence, is unmanifested"[331].

Georges Vajda expresses here clearly how the Jewish Gnostic and esoteric circles, which, according to him, were active two or three generations before Christ, had an esoteric and Gnostic interpretation of creation *ex nihilo,* by which they conceived of it as the innermost essence of the divinity, which, consequently, took the world out of its own substance. And Eriugena was merely repeating in Christian circles a doctrine current in Jewish esoteric circles.

Joaquín de Fiore

John Scotus Eriugena also seems to have influenced Joachim of Fiore. Joachim of Fiore, condemned at the Lateran Council, at the same time as Amaury and David, but for his Trinitarian errors and not for his theory of the three kingdoms - that of the Father in the Old Testament, that of the Son in the New Testament, that of the Holy Spirit in a new and definitive age, Joachim of Fiore would, like Amaury, depend on Scotus Eriugena in this conception of three ages, three revelations, according to E. Gebhart in his L'Italienne, and not by his theory of the three kingdoms - that of the Father in the Old Testament, that of the Son in the New Testament, that of the Holy Spirit in a new and definitive age, which was to begin and last until the end of time - by which he approaches the Almaricians, without ever having been in relationship with them. Gebhart in his *L'Italie mystique.* To tell the truth, the related texts do not establish this dependence; what can be conceded is that Scotus' ideas about the third revelation, that of the Paraclete, which will take place in the Church in heaven and which has been given in advance in the pure ones, *nunc ex parte inchoata in primitiis contemplationis,* worked, enlarged and transposed, could have become the dangerous dreams of Amaury of Chartres or of Joachim of Fiore[332].

---

[331] Ibid., p. 205.
[332] F. Vernet, *Erigene*, in Dict. de Théol. Cath., col, 430.

The doctrine of Joachim of Fiore boils down to two essential points: 1) A theology of the Trinity; 2) A theory of the great divisions in the history of mankind.

1st *Trinitarian Theology:* Here Joachim of Fiore attacks Peter Lombard because he had taught that the Father, the Son and the Holy Spirit is one great thing, which is neither begetting nor begotten nor proceeding. On the other hand, he taught that even if it were conceded that the Father, the Son and the Holy Spirit are one essence, one nature and one substance, this unity was not to be regarded as true and proper, but as collective and similar, as when many men are said to be one people and many faithful one Church. In short, Joachim compromised the divine unity and ended up in a kind of tritheism.

2. *A theory of human history:* To this theological tritheism corresponded in a way a historical tritheism. Here Joachim argued that if the Old Testament was a figure of the New Testament, the New Testament was in turn a figure of a third economy which would replace the second. And if the Old Testament was the age of the Father, and the New the age of the Son, a third, that of the Holy Spirit, was to be expected. There was a time, said Abbot Joachim, when men lived according to the flesh, and that is the age that began with Adam and lasted until Jesus Christ; there was a second, when they lived according to the flesh and the spirit, and there will be a third, which will be lived according to the spirit and which will last until the end of the world. The first of servitude, the second of filial submission, and the third of freedom. Each of these ages is as it were personified in different classes of people: the first in married people, the second in clerics and the third in monks.

In this third epoch, the visible Church, without being destroyed, will in some way be absorbed into the spiritual Church; the clerical order of the second age will be able to take its place in the spiritual order.

Abbot Joachim was not content with affirming the future advent of the third age, but announced a great persecution, in the short term; then a quiet period; at last "the revelation of the *everlasting Gospel,* that which the Angel of the Apocalypse carries through the heavens".

Abbot Joachim's doctrine of the Trinity was condemned at the Fourth Lateran Council. And his doctrine of the three ages was strongly censured by St. Thomas[333]. "In two ways, he teaches, the states of the world can vary: one, according to the diversity of the law. In this way, the state of the new law will not be succeeded by any other state. It succeeded the state of the law, the state of the new law, as a more perfect state to an imperfect one. But no state of the present life can be more perfect than the state of the new law, for nothing can be nearer to the end than that which immediately introduces the last end. And this is what the new law does. And St. Thomas adds: "Dionysius counts three states of men: the first, that of the old law; the second, that of the new law; a third will follow this, but not in the present life, but in the future, that is, in the homeland. And as the first was figurative and imperfect with respect to the state of the gospel, so this one is figurative and imperfect with respect to the state of the fatherland. When the latter arrives, the former will disappear, as it is said in the first Corinthians: Now we see through a glass and darkly, then we shall see face to face".

The exclusion of Abbot Joachim's thesis could not be made with a more peremptory argument.

The law of the Gospel cannot be succeeded in history by another age, since it is figurative of the state we are awaiting in heaven. But, moreover, St. Thomas would immediately demonstrate that it was the heretics who were awaiting a new age of the Holy Spirit. And so he adds:

"According to St. Augustine, Montano and Priscilla affirmed that the promise of the Lord concerning the Holy Spirit was not perfectly fulfilled in the apostles but in them. So did the Manichaeans affirm that this promise was fulfilled in Mani, whom they called the Paraclete, where it is manifestly stated that this promise was fulfilled in the apostles, as the Lord had repeatedly promised: "Ye shall be baptized with the Holy Ghost before many days. This was fulfilled on the day of Pentecost.

"All the vanities of the heretics are excluded by what St. John says: "The Holy Spirit had not yet been given because Jesus had not yet been glorified". From which it is understood that the Lord having been glorified by the Resurrection and Ascension, the Holy Spirit was given.

---

[333] *Summa Theologica*, 1-2, 106, 4; *Quol.* 7; 4 *Sent.*, d. 43.

This also excludes the vain illusion of some, who would like to say that another time of the Holy Spirit is to be expected".

The state inaugurated by the apostles brings history to a close. History measures its density, not by earthly events, but by the plans for the salvation of mankind which are fulfilled in them. Now these plans for the salvation of mankind have been fixed by the Father and remain reserved to the Father, who has only revealed to man what he needs to believe and practise in order to be saved, but not the course of future events. The Holy Spirit," says the Holy One, "taught the apostles all the truth necessary for salvation, whether of things to be believed or of things to be practised; but He did not teach them the future events; this was not for them to know, as it is said in the Acts: It is not for you to know the times and the moments which the Father has fixed by virtue of His sovereign power".

On the other hand, it is not appropriate to assign historical times to each of the three persons of the Trinity, since "the old law was not only of the Father, but also of the Son, for Christ was in it figuratively; therefore the Lord says: If you believed in Moses, you would believe in me, for he received from me". Likewise, the new law is not only of Christ, but also of the Holy Spirit, according to that sentence: The law of the spirit of life in Christ Jesus. "There is therefore no room to expect another law from the Holy Spirit".

St. Thomas could conclude that "it is a most serious folly to affirm that the Gospel of Christ is not the Gospel of the kingdom. But the preaching of Christ can be understood in two ways: one, as the spreading of the news of Christ, and in this way the Gospel was preached throughout the whole world, even in the time of the apostles, as St. John Chrysostom says. According to this, what is then added: "And then shall be the end"; the destruction of Jerusalem, of which he then spoke literally, is meant. Otherwise, the preaching of the Gospel throughout the whole world can be understood as fully effective, so that the Church is established in all nations. In this way, says St. Augustine, "the Gospel has not yet been preached in the whole world, but when it is preached, the end will come".

The teaching of St. Thomas, well founded on the word of God, is opposed to four theses of Joachim of Fiore. That history is fulfilled by history. That history is open to some truly new historical event. That the historical process must unfold in a Trinitarian chronology. That there is a Christian logic of history.

History is already, in principle, closed in its own sphere. Something new will come, but not historical, but metahistorical. To the state of the *road, the way*, history, will come the homeland.

No new event is to take place, then. Everything that concerns man's health has already fully taken place. It is useless to inquire into the times, as if anything were to come. Whatever happens, or has happened, or will happen, will add nothing to health. It will have a purely human value. It does not belong to the need for health. Even the speculations of St. Augustine and Bossuet about history will have a purely human and conjectural character.

History does not have to follow a Trinitarian chronology. Revelation teaches nothing about it and we can know nothing about it unless God reveals it to us. The course of history is not necessarily determined, but depends on the will of God, who has freely chosen a particular one out of an infinite number of possibilities.

Finally, history does not have a certain logical coherence, but depends on the free action of man under the free action of God. History has no meaning for us, but only for God.

Joachim of Fiore's thesis is typically cabalistic in that it is messianic. History, in the Gospel stage, is directed towards a superior and new event, as the whole Old Testament was directed towards, which refers as a figure to Christ, the Reality.

We have seen how in the Kabbalah, especially in that of Luria, the event of messianic restoration occupies a prominent place.

Godfrey of Auxerre assures us that Joachim was of Jewish origin and that he never fully renounced the Jewish mentality. "He was born of Jews, and in Judaism, which he does not seem to have thrown up entirely, he was educated for many years... Nor little authority is conferred on him by the barbarous name itself; for his name is Jehoiachin. For of none of our day have we heard that he has retained in baptism the name he first had in Judaism"[334].

B. Dupuy, O.P., who wrote the article "Joachim" in the Encyclopédie Catholicisme, tells us that "the problem of the sources of Joachim remains obscure. Origen (X. Rousselot), St. Augustine (H. Crocco),

---

[334] Quoted by Henri de Lubac, *Exégese mediévale*, Aubier, 1-2, partie, Paris, 1961, p. 510.

Rupert of Dentz (Y. Ratzinger), the Basilian monks (E. Anitehkof), the Jew Peter Alphonsus (B. Hirsch-Reich) have been invoked, without arriving at anything other than distant approximations.

However, the fact that he was a late Jewish convert and was influenced by Pedro Alfonso is all the more significant. Pedro Alfonso was the man who baptised the Jew Moses Sepharda, born in Huesca in Spain in 1062. He embraced the Christian religion in 1106 and had as his godfather Alfonso VI, King of Castile and Leon, who gave him the position of physician at his court. His former co-religionists accused him of having converted out of ambition. Undoubtedly, this learned Jew must have been initiated into the Kabbalah, which had been inspiring Jewish groups in the Iberian Peninsula for years[335].

The dialogue in which Peter Alphonsus answers Moseh was often reprinted with the "Booklet of the learned Rabbi Samuel to demonstrate the true Messiah", by Samuel Marrochianus or Israelite, converted in 1085. Peter says in particular: "If you examine more penetratingly this name of God which is explained in *The Secrets of Secrets*, you will notice that the name YHWH, which is a three-letter name although it is written with four characters, since one of the four is used twice, it will appear to you that this name is three and one. One, designates the unity of substance; three, the trinity of persons. This name is indeed composed of four letters, iod, he, va, he; if you join the second to the third you get a second name; likewise if you join the third to the fourth, that is, va and he, you will have a third name. And if you put them together again, there will be but one name". This was illustrated by the figure of a circle joining three others, cutting, according to the description, the tetragram.

The theme was taken up by Joachim of Fiore (1132-1203) in his *Exposition of the Apocalypse*, which does not fail to recall that it was Peter who revealed these mysteries by quoting from the *secreta secretorum*[336]. And the *secreta secretorum* was undoubtedly a cabalistic book.

Gershom Scholem has noted the parallels between the doctrines of Joachim of Fiore and the doctrine of Shemitoth codified in Gerona in

---

[335] Menéndez y Pelayo, *Historia de los heterodoxos españoles*, III, Emecé, Buenos Aires, pp. 112-122; *Le legs d'Israel*, Payot, Paris, 1931, p. 206.
[336] Les Kabbalistes chrétiens de la Renaissance, *Dunod, Paris, 1964, p. 8.*

the 13th century. Scholem does not believe in a direct historical influence of one on the other doctrine and hypothesises an inner dynamic and a common mystical structure of divinity that would have produced similar consequences in both cases[337]. Nor does he believe that the question recently raised by Herbert Grundmann[338] about the possibly Jewish origin of Jehoiachin has anything to do with the matter. However, the recognition of a typically Jewish doctrine similar to that of Jehoiachin and the Jewish contacts of Jehoiachin himself lead one to think that he drew from Jewish sources a doctrine so far removed from the Christian conception. The common element of the two conceptions, which remains striking, lies in the fact that in one case the Trinity, in the other seven of the ten Sephiroth - in which God manifests Himself - were regarded as forces which dominate and embody the aeon of the cosmic process.

General conclusion of this chapter

It is worth noting that the only two heterodox thinkers of note in the Catholic camp who were to have a decisive influence on posterity were influenced by the Kabbalah. This influence was to make its way, in a singularly eruptive way, with the penetration of the Kabbalah into the heart of Christianity with the Renaissance.

---

[337] *Le grandi correnti...*, p. 242; French ed., p. 195.
[338] *Deutsches Archiv für Erforschung des Mittealters*, vol. 16 (1960), pp. 519-528, quoted by Scholem, *Les origines...*, p. 489.

CHAPTER VI

CHRISTIAN METAPHYSICS AND THE PROBLEM OF GOD, THE WORLD AND MAN

Thus far we have insisted preferably on the exposition of the Qabalah or perverse tradition, exposing its content or projection, first in pre-Christian thought and then within Christianity itself. The anti-Christian errors of Gnosticism and Manichaeism were typically Kabalistic; likewise, the various heresies of Arianism and the others, such as Monophysitism and Monothelitism, were born as partial expressions in Christian dogmas of Kabalistic influences; the medieval heresies of Catharism and Albigensianism, which, under various names, infested the whole Christian world, and particularly the south of France, were also acclimatised under Kabalistic influence; and, finally, the typical errors of Eriugenism and Jehoiakinism in the philosophical conception of the Middle Ages arose under the influence of the Kabalah.

The Christian world reacted firmly and effectively against any cabalistic influence, mainly because of the great strength of the Christian faith itself. The Christian world understood perfectly well the value and meaning of fidelity to Christ; fidelity to doctrine, fidelity to grace and, ultimately, fidelity to the person of Christ. But this fidelity was translated on the natural plane of thought into fidelity to Christian metaphysics.

1. Is there such a thing as a Christian metaphysics?

Christianity is a religion and not a philosophy. Christ came to save us, that is, to bring us eternal life. This is a first truth that must be made clear. This religion contains truths to be believed and practised, sacraments and rites to be received. But all this is conditioned by the idea of salvation. However, not every mental structure can express the demands of the Christian religion. Claude Tresmontant has firmly reminded us of this against Emile Bréhier in a series of magnificent works he has been publishing since 1953, in which he has highlighted the metaphysics embedded in biblical thought and in Christianity[339].

Claude Tresmontant rightly says: "In the present work *(La métaphysique du christianisme et la naissance de la philosophie chrétienne)* we propose to discover and analyse the metaphysical structure of Christianity, its philosophical content, to seek the essence of Christianity from the metaphysical point of view... It is a question of knowing whether Christianity has no metaphysical content of its own, original, or, on the contrary, what is the metaphysics of Christianity, this metaphysics that Christianity *is*, because Christianity is not only a theology and a morality: theology and morality imply and presuppose a certain metaphysical structure".

2. What are the problems involved in Christian metaphysics?

A metaphysics necessarily involves an answer to the supreme questions of all philosophy: where does the world and man come from and where are they going? And this answer, in turn, involves one, the most fundamental of all, which is the question of the First Principle and End of things, the question of the Absolute.

a) *The Absolute:* Claude Tresmontant himself developed the great systems of a Christian metaphysics in "Les idées maîtresses de la métaphysique chrétienne". The doctrine of the Absolute, according to Christianity, is original when compared to the doctrine of the Absolute according to Brahmanism, Platonism, Aristotelianism, Neoplatonism, Spinozism, or other earlier philosophies, in particular German Idealism.

According to Christianity, the Absolute is not the world, or in other words, the world is not the Absolute. The world is not uncreated, eternal, ontologically sufficient. Nor is the world something of the Absolute; neither shadow of the Absolute, nor emanation, nor modality of the divine substance. No, the world is, radically, ontologically, something other than the Absolute.

---

[339] Essai sur la pensée hébraïque, *Ed. du Cerf, Paris, 1953;* Études de métaphysique biblique, *J. Gabalda et Cie, Paris, 1955;* La métaphysique du christianisme et la naissance de la philosophie chrétienne, *Ed. du Seuil, Paris, 1961;* La métaphysique du christianisme et la crise du XIII siècle, *Ed. du Seuil, Paris, 1964;* Les idées maîtresses de la métaphysique chrétienne, *Ed. du Seuil, Paris, 1962.*

It is not of divine essence, nor of divine nature. Nature is not the alienated, petrified, exiled Absolute Spirit.

According to Christianity, the Absolute is unique. Things can be conceived differently, and indeed, religions and philosophies have often conceived them differently.

According to Egyptian and Assyrian cosmogonies, for example, primal chaos is the uncreated and eternal absolute. The divine has emerged from this primeval chaos. The divine is not the absolute itself.

According to these religions, there is, as in Hesiod, a genealogy of gods and goddesses, and a battle of gods at the origins of history. In Manichean dualism there are two Absolutes: Matter, the evil principle, and Good, the good and luminous principle.

According to Christianity, the Absolute is of all eternity, happy, uncreated, ontologically sufficient, without birth, without becoming, repudiating everything that recalls, from far or near, the theogonic myth.

The relations between the Absolute and the world are not a relation of identity of substances, nor a relation of eternal procession or logical explicitness as theorems flow from a premise, but a relation of freedom or *creation*.

b) *Relations between the Absolute and the world:* Against Egyptian and Assyro-Babylonian mythologies, against Platonism, Aristotelianism, Stoicism, Neo-Platonism and Gnostic systems, Christian thought teaches:

1 Creation is the work of one God.

2° Creation is free. It is not a necessary and eternal process, nor is it imposed by an external or an internal need for development.

3° Creation is total without presupposing pre-existing matter.

4° Creation is not a generation, but is necessarily external to the Creator.

5° Creation implies an original doctrine of evil, which is neither substance nor nature.

6° Creation is the work of the gratuitous goodness of God, who does not create in order to be fulfilled and accomplished.

7° Creation has a beginning and the world must have an end.

c) *Christian anthropology:* In the Upanishad, in the Bhagavat-Gita, in Empedocles, the soul is eternal, uncreated. In Christian anthropology the soul is not a parcel, a fragment or a modality of the divine substance. It is created and creaturely, and does not pre-exist its body, nor does it pass from body to body, nor has it fallen into an evil body.

Against the Gnostic and Manichaean systems, against Platonism, Origenism and medieval dualism, Christianity defends the excellence of the corporeal man.

Against the metaphysics of India, against Orphism, Plato, Plotinus, the Gnostics, the Manichaeans, who consider sexuality evil and hold it responsible for ensomatosis, for the fall of souls, Christianity affirms in St. Thomas the laudability of sexuality[340].

d) *The supernatural destiny of man:* According to Brahmanic theosophy, Orphism, Platonism, Neo-Platonism and Gnosis, the soul is a divine particle that has forgotten its divine essence, has fallen into an evil body and is alienated in corporeality and individuality.

His health consists in freeing himself from the bonds of the body by asceticism and initiation and in returning to his beloved homeland from whence he came. Salvation does not consist in *receiving* something but in *taking it away*.

Christian thought rejects all this myth, this anthropogeny, and holds that the soul, *created* by God, is invited, *by grace*, to participate in the divine nature in Christ through the Holy Spirit.

3. Christian metaphysics in the face of anti-Gnostic polemic

The great Fathers of the Church who bore the brunt of the anti-Gnostic struggle, at the same time laid the first foundations of a Christian metaphysics. The great champions of this struggle were St. Justin, Tertullian, Hippolytus, Epiphanius, St. Irenaeus, Clement of Alexandria and later St. Augustine.

Rational arguments belonging, one might say, to a natural philosophy, played an important role in this struggle. They were not always appropriate arguments, but they responded to a clear Christian metaphysics, and they responded above all to a Christian decision

---

[340] *Summa Theologica,* I, 98, 2.

which did not always translate into happy formulas and concepts. The first thesis of this metaphysics consisted in the clear and definite affirmation of the creation of the world by one God, in contrast to the mythological speculations of the Gnostics, who made the world emanate from the substance of God.

The second thesis emphasised the work of creation as a direct and immediate operation of God Himself, radically excluding any action of a demiurge working on pre-existing matter.

The third thesis attributed the work of creation to one God, the creator, radically excluding any dualism that would make creation dependent on two principles - one good and one evil - or on a single divine principle, which would undergo a tragic process or fall within the very sphere of the divine.

The fourth thesis describes creation as a process, in which the Absolute works freely without being constrained to effect the creation of the universe.

The fifth thesis insists on the capital distinction to be made between generation, which is in God and is given in the only-begotten Son, begotten before all ages of the substance of the Father, and creation, which is an action of God that puts the effect outside God Himself and which takes place *ex nihilo*, out of nothing.

The sixth thesis maintains a beginning for the work of creation and excludes any metaphysics of eternal return. Preexistence of souls, eternity of the world and eternal return are intertwined themes. Christianity must, in contrast to these metaphysics, formulate its own principles: non-divinity of the soul, which is created and begins to be; non-divinity of the world, which is created and also begins to exist; irreversibility of time.

The seventh thesis excludes any fall of the souls, which, taking their origin from the Absolute, would undergo a more or less prolonged process of exile, until they would return to the Absolute, from whence they came.

Finally, the last thesis, which affirms that creation produces beings endowed with conscience, reflection and freedom, who are also invited to become participants in the divine life, through grace, in a communion of love, of *agape;* and who, being able to refuse this invitation, give rise to sin and moral evil. All these theses have been clearly formulated in the anti-Gnostic polemic by the various Fathers of the Church.

4. Development of Christian metaphysics

The Bible in general and the New Testament in particular presuppose a metaphysics. The Christian writers of the first centuries understood this perfectly and developed it in the fight against heresies. When they read the warnings of the Apostle Paul against the dangers of pagan philosophy and against inflated science[341]; against discussions, the result of which is to moralise the hearers[342]; against vain questions of words[343]; against the seduction of philosophies which explain everything by the elements of nature and ignore Christ[344], they did not understand them as excluding all philosophy; On the contrary, they understood the value of the Apostle's teaching, "because since the creation of the world, the invisible of God, his eternal power and his divinity, have been known through creatures"[345], which demanded the formulation of a metaphysics. There was, in short, the whole theory of the relations between reason and faith. The first apologists admitted, albeit implicitly, this theory in germ. But they were in the presence of philosophies already constituted, at least one of which seemed to provide the Gospel with peremptory demonstrations.

They are then content to juxtapose the doctrines of Plato and those of Jesus Christ, and thus fall into inextricable embarrassments, as in the case of Justin and Origen. St. Irenaeus, the first of the great theologians, drew a clear boundary between the natural knowledge of God and the supernatural. Two different scientific systems must correspond to these two kinds of knowledge. But Irenaeus is so fearful of the abuses to which profane philosophy gives rise that he has so little confidence in the often misguided efforts that he is rather inclined to proscribe all philosophy than to assign to it its proper object.

It was not until Augustine that the problem of the relationship between philosophy and theology was posed and resolved, and that the foundations of a Christian metaphysics were laid.

Augustine demonstrates by reason the existence of God, the destiny of the soul, the foundation of all knowledge in God, the legitimacy of faith,

---

[341] I *Tim.* 6, 20.
[342] II *Tim.* 2, 14.
[343] I *Tim.* 6, 4.
[344] *Col.*, 2, 18.
[345] *Rom.* 1, 20.

the fact of Revelation, the appropriateness of the mysteries. St. Augustine demonstrates by walking how reason is capable of constructing a philosophy. *Intellige ut credas, crede ut intelligas.* The natural intellectual activity precedes, accompanies and follows the act of faith; it only differs in everything according to whether it precedes or follows: *intellige ut credas verbum meum, crede ut intelligas verbum Dei.* Understand so that you may believe my word, believe so that you may understand the word of God. After St. Augustine, Boethius is undoubtedly the one who has exerted the preponderant influence on the destinies of philosophy and theology. In his *De consolatione philosophiae* he has set the example of a thought which, without using truths supplied by revelation, establishes a complete doctrine on the search for and nature of God, and the government of the world and of human life. Philosophy proves its autonomy by exercising itself autonomously.

In the Palatine school, John Scotus Eriugena uses philosophy with unbridled audacity. His intentions are Christian, the authority of God the revealer is supreme. But reason possesses, by right, a dignity which belief by authority certainly does not have.

However, the authority of St Augustine retained its preponderance; it continued to dominate until the end of the 13th century and produced two philosophical systematisations which are the glory of Christian thought: those of St Anselm and St Bonaventure.

The books of St. Anselm (1033-1109) will give an attentive reader the impression of a rationalism confident in its own strength: a doctrine of truth, a doctrine of the existence and nature of God, are established by dialectics; more seriously, the Trinity and the Incarnation are also demonstrated by dialectics, as if they belonged to the spring of natural philosophy. But this impression is soon dispelled; in fact, Anselm constantly quotes the Fathers, especially St. Augustine, from whom he has penetrated the living doctrine to its very depths[346].

It is fair to say with Bishop Grabmann that St. Anselm has rejuvenated St. Augustine in order to give a foundation to Thomas Aquinas. However, a certain ambiguity remained concerning the nature and meaning of philosophy. For Augustine and for Anselm, in fact, theology is aided by the data of faith and its function is to understand these data.

---

[346] Dict. de Théol. Cath., art. *Philosophie,* t. 12, col. 1484.

But, in fact, is an autonomous philosophy, which is constituted by its own forces, in order to obtain natural clarity, legitimate? The question will be resolved by St Thomas.

The other tendency, Augustinianism, finds its most perfect expression in St Bonaventure (1221-1274). The starting point is faith, which is much more certain than all the rest and whose data it is important to penetrate little by little in the measure of our strength and grace. The point of arrival must be God: philosophy is an *itinerary of the soul towards God*. The method itself is linked to faith. Let us not forget, in fact, in what conditions we have been placed by sin: prayer, grace, purification of the heart, are essential conditions for the search for the true. If this is so, a separate philosophy is a dangerous thing and will lead to error.

Bonaventure, who lived in Paris at the time when Averroism and Thomism were spreading, reproved Averroism and did not approve of Thomism, which for him meant autonomous philosophy.

5. *Culmination of Christian metaphysics in St. Thomas*

Christian philosophy is slowly being elaborated in a process that starts from the preaching of the Gospel and has as its great stages St. Irenaeus, Dionysius, the Areopagite, St. Augustine, Boethius, St. Anselm and St. Thomas Aquinas. Behind these names move the great currents of Platonism, Aristotelianism and Neoplatonism, more or less modified by the leaven of the Gospel. St Thomas was to produce an *unprecedented synthesis*, the culmination of all previous thought and the greatest realisation of Christian thought.

On the one hand, St Thomas, in opposition to the Averroists, posits the necessity of the agreement of truth with itself, of philosophy with theology; but he also considers that it is necessary to distinguish the domains of the one and the other, and here he takes on the appearance of a revolutionary in relation to certain Augustinians. Philosophy has its own domain, that of truths knowable by reason; theology has its own, that of revealed truths. What is the object of faith cannot at the same time and with the same title be the object of science; what is the object of science cannot at the same time and with the same title be the object of faith. Philosophy is therefore autonomous; it possesses in itself its principles, its method, its legitimacy, its certainty. Since truth cannot contradict truth, if a philosophical system were to manifest itself contrary to faith, this disagreement would be the sign of an error, and it would be necessary to find where the philosopher had committed an error of reasoning, having admitted a false proposition without examination. On the other hand, philosophy, if it can help by its methods to better understand dogma, must avoid demonstrating it. The objects of faith cannot, as such, be objects of science, because if they have been revealed they are beyond human intelligence[347].

6. The great theses of Thomistic metaphysics

We are going to indicate the great theses of Thomistic metaphysics, which are radically opposed to cabalistic and gnostic thought in all the forms and variants in which it has been expressed throughout history. Although these theses cannot be considered as a necessary expression of Catholic truth, they are the ones that best express it and for this reason they have deserved the warm approval of the Church, especially of the last pontiffs.

a) *Intelligible being and first principles.* St. Thomas teaches, following Aristotle, that the first object known to our intelligence is the intelligible being of sensible things; it is the object of the first intellectual apprehension which precedes judgment[348]. *The first thing that falls into the conception of the understanding is the being; for according to this, each thing is cognizable in so far as it is in act; whence being is the very object of the understanding, and so it is also the first intelligible, as sound is the first audible.*

In the intelligible being thus known, our intelligence first grasps its opposition to the noser, which is expressed in the principle of contradiction, being is not non-being[349] : *Our understanding naturally knows being and the things that are of themselves of being, as such, on which knowledge the knowledge of first principles is founded, as one cannot affirm and deny at the same time (or the opposition between being and non-being) and the like.*

Thus our understanding knows intelligible being and its opposition to nothingness before it explicitly knows the distinction of self and non-self. Then, by reflection on its act of knowledge, it judges the actual

---

[347] See the magnificent article that Gaston Rabeau devotes to philosophy in the *Dict. de Théol. Catholique*.
[348] *Summa Theol.* I, 5, 2.
[349] *Contra gentes*, l. 11, ch. 83.

existence of the latter and of the thinking subject, and then of such a singular sensible thing, grasped by the sense[350]. The intelligence first knows the universals, while the senses reach the sensible and the singular.

The first principle enunciates the opposition of being and nothingness; its negative formula is the *principle of contradiction*. Its positive formula is *the principle of identity:* what is, is; what is not, is not. The principle of contradiction or identity is subordinated to the principle of *reason of being,* taken in all its generality: everything that is, has its reason of being in itself, if it exists by itself; in another, if it does not exist by itself. "The question of *why-if* asks for the cause, but the question of *why-if* can only be answered by one of the four causes"[351].

The principle of sufficient reason is subordinated to the principle of *causality*, which is formulated as follows: everything that comes into existence has a sufficient cause, or again, every contingent being, even if it existed *ab eterno,* needs an efficient cause, and in the last analysis, an uncaused cause.

As Gilson points out, [352] Thomistic realism is not founded on a postulate, but on the intellectual apprehension of the intelligible being of things felt, on the evidence of this fundamental proposition: *that which is first conceived by the understanding as the most knowable and in which all conceptions are resolved, is the entity.*[353] Without this first principle, Descartes' principle *cogito, ergo sum* would not be true.

b) *Thomistic ways of the existence of God.* The classical proofs of God's existence rest on the principle of causality. If in the world there are beings who come into existence and who immediately disappear, if in it there are beings who have a temporary and perishable life, men of a very limited wisdom, of a very restricted goodness, of a holiness which always has its imperfections, it is necessary that there should be at the summit of all, the One who is of all eternity, Being itself, Life itself, Wisdom itself, Goodness itself, Holiness itself. Otherwise, the more would come out of the less. This general proof contains virtually all

---

[350] *Summa Theol.*, I. 86, 1.

[351] *In phys.*, l. II, l. 10. We will not examine here the reducibility or otherwise of the principle of causality. See on this, *Le prince de causalité*, by Raymond Laverdiere, J. Vrin, Paris, 1969.

[352] Réalisme thomiste et critique de la connaissance, *Paris, J. Vrin, 1947.*

[353] De veritate, *1, 1.*

other *a posteriori* proofs, which are founded on the principle of causality.

St Thomas demonstrates very well[354] that the summit of the proofs of the existence of God is none other than the *Esse subsistens, the subsistent being itself.* These five ways are but five arches ending in the same keystone. Each one, in fact, ends in a divine attribute: first mover of bodies and spirits, first efficient cause, first necessary, supreme being, supreme intelligence that directs everything. Now, each of these attributes can only belong to Him who is Subsistent Being itself and who alone can say: *Ego sum qui sum.*

c) The transcendence of esse, of the being of entities. By making *esse*, the very constituent of the divine essence, the question arises that *esse* cannot be identified with the created essence and, therefore, must be a new actuality added to the created essence and by which the latter exists. That is to say that every existing created essence is so by "an act of esse". This brings the transcendence of the "act of esse" or of *esse* over actual existence as a principle and as an act.

It is more important than the subject or the content on which it acts[355]. Consequently, while existence as a "fact" is a founded thing, *esse* is the act that founds it, and essence is a possibility (realised by *esse* in existence): man emerges only by referring, typically his own, to the *esse* of the things he encounters and not properly by referring to the world of essences, as formalist philosophers think, i.e., in the last analysis, essentialists.

The *being of entities* is then what is important and original in Thomistic and Christian metaphysics; it is what transcends the entire created universe, including man. *But* the being of entities is nothing but a participation, or an imitation, or an assimilation of the *Esse subsistens.* This being of created entities is communicated by God to creatures by way of efficient causality, by way of exemplary causality and by way of quasi-formal causality. What makes things to be is not the essences but *the "Esse"*, Being, which is communicated to them by God, by way

---

[354] *Sum*, 1, 3, 4.
[355] *See* Cornelio Fabro, La nozione metafisica di participazione; Participation et causalité selon Saint Thomas, *Paris, Louvain, 1960;* Fondation metation métaphysique de l'être, *in Revue Thomiste, April-June, 1966.*

of efficient causality, producing that *esse*, being of things, and through that *esse*, being and the thing itself.

If there is efficient causality, the one who causes, i.e. God, stands outside the caused effect. God stands outside the creature. The creature is ontologically something other than the Creator. The being of the creature is not the being of the Creator, although the Creator is intimately present in the creature sustaining its being, which would dissipate and be reduced to nothingness if God ceased to sustain it.

God communicates being by way of exemplarity, i.e. God, intelligent and free to create, first conceives in his divine mind and conceives it from eternity, the whole order of created things in their infinite relations. This whole order of what things are and of the relations of things to each other, which represents an *eidos*, an idea, an intelligent form, an essence and an essential order, also comes from God.

Finally, God communicates being by way of quasiformal causality, inasmuch as that being of the creatures, the infinite distance being bridged, is being that derives from and partakes of the Being of the creator. Just as fire comes from Fire itself, and light from Light, so the being of the creature comes from the *"Esse subsistens"*. The creature would not receive the *esse* if God were not *Esse* in his essence which communicates it to the created order. For this reason, the *esse* of creatures is, in a certain sense, the Esse of the Creator extended to creation. The same form of *esse* is extended to the creatures. This in a certain sense. That is why we say quasi-formal. For it is not the very same and identical Being of God that is communicated to the creature - it would be absurd pantheism to assert this - but another new, participatory being, distinct from the Creator and yet, in the most intimate and essential reality, *esse*, because it springs from the source of the *Esse subsistens*.

d) *The "esse" of creation.* We have said that it is proper to God, whose essence is the *Esse*, to communicate the first and most universal *esse* of creatures. "For it is necessary, says St. Thomas[356], that the most universal effects be reduced to more universal and higher causes; but, among all effects, the most universal is being itself: *Inter omnes autem effectus, universalissimum est ipsum esse*. Therefore, it must be the proper effect of the first and most universal cause, which is God. For

---

[356] I, 45, 5.

this very reason, it is said in the book *De causis* that neither the intelligence nor the soul gives being except in so far as they work through the divine operation. Now, to produce being absolutely, not in so far as it is this or that being, is what constitutes the action of creation. Therefore, it is clear that creation is the exclusive action of God.

The *esse* of creation must necessarily be multiple, distinct and unequal. St Thomas demonstrates against pagan philosophies that the distinction and multitude of unequal things come from the intention of the first agent, who is God. Indeed, God brought creatures into being in order to communicate his goodness to them and to represent it by them. And since this goodness could not be adequately represented by a single creature, he produced many and diverse ones, so that what was lacking in each one to represent the divine goodness might be supplied by the others.

For the goodness, which in God is simple and uniform, is manifold and divided in the creatures. Thus the goodness of God is more perfectly participated in and represented by the whole universe as a whole than it would be by a single creature, whatever that creature might be. And as the divine wisdom is the cause of the distinction of things with a view to the perfection of the universe, so it is also the cause of inequality, for the universe would not be perfect if there were only one degree of goodness in all things[357].

Along with the multiplicity and inequality of things, unity must also be taken into account, because "the very order existing in created things manifests the unity of the world established by God"[358]. The world is said to be one with a unity of order insofar as some things are ordered in relation to others. Hence it is necessary that everything belongs to one world. And those who proposed several worlds, like Democritus, did not put divine wisdom as the ordainer of the world, but chance.

e) *Creation is a free act of the intelligence and will of the Creator. The exemplary cause of Creation.* "God is the cause of things by his understanding and will, as is the artificer of his artefacts. The artificer works according to the conception of his understanding and by the love of his will towards some end"[359]. The knowledge of the craftsman is the

---

[357] *Summa Theol.*, l. 47, 1 and 2.
[358] Ibid., l. 47, 3.
[359] Ibid., l. 45, 6.

cause of what is made, because the craftsman works guided by his thought, so that the form which he has in his understanding is the principle of the operation, as heat is the principle of heating.

This highlights the importance of the exemplary cause in creation. Creation is not the effect of the pure and sole power of God, of the efficient cause, but of the efficient cause directed by the wisdom of the understanding, by the exemplary cause. The exemplary cause directs and shapes the divine omnipotent action.

This exemplary cause does not impose itself on God from without; He finds it in Himself by contemplating His essence. By the very fact that He is Being, He makes all finite beings *possible*.

These exemplary ideas are not really distinct moments of the divine intelligence, but have no other existence than the existence of God, and exist *ab aeterno* in the simplicity of their nature. The number of these exemplary ideas is infinite in the sense that the divine essence, being infinite, ensures the possibility of producing an infinity of infinite types or species and even an infinity of individuals of the same type. This intelligible world of ideas, not being separate from God as in Platonism, nor being distinct in God from the divine essence, has no independent causality.

7. *The creation of man and anthropological problems*

Man is a composite of a spiritual soul and a body[360]. The soul is not made of the substance of God, as the Cabala teaches along with the Gnostics, but is created by God[361]. The rational soul is a subsistent form, from which it properly belongs to exist and to be produced. And since it cannot be made of former matter, neither corporeal - nor spiritual - because, in this case, spiritual substances would be transmuted into one another, it must be said that it is produced only by creation[362]. If it is produced by creation, it is produced immediately and only by God[363].

---

[360] St. Thomas, *Summa Theol.*, I, 75, *introd.*
[361] Ibid., I, 90, 1.
[362] Ibid., 3.
[363] Ibid., 3, 4.

And it was not created, as Origen said[364], before the body, but at the moment of the production of the body.

8. Man, through the gift of grace, participates in the divine nature.

Man is not God by his nature, which is created and finite. The soul is not a divine spark, as the Kabbalah insists. But man can become God by adoption, through the divine gift of grace. By grace there is something supernatural in man that comes from God[365]. Something supernatural means a gift that lifts man above his natural forces and demands and places him in the divine order of God's friendship and communication, so that he can ultimately see God face to face and love Him as He loves Himself. Grace falls into the category of quality and is a permanent habit, infused by God, by which man can have movement and inclinations that move him to attain the eternal and divine good of glory. Grace raises man up, as St. Peter says: "He bestowed on us precious and rich promises in order to make us sharers in the divine nature"[366]. Through grace, man's soul participates, according to a certain likeness, in the divine nature by a kind of new generation or creation[367].

Conclusions

From the Christian conception of God, of the world and of man, some conclusions can be drawn which it is convenient to point out in order to show the irreducible character of the Catholic teaching in the face of the Kabbalah and all kinds of gnosis.

Being the constitutive *Being* of God, there is no room in Him but Being itself, and hence Truth and Goodness. There is therefore in God nothing of negation, nothing of falsehood, nothing of evil, as perversely imagined by Kabbalah and gnosis. On the other hand, as creature and man are taken out of *nothingness*, in the deepest and most radical depths

---

[364] Peri Archon, *l. I, Ch. 6.*
[365] *Sum,* 1-2, 110, 1.
[366] II Pet., 1, 4.
[367] 1-2, 110, art. 1-4.

of every creature there is nothingness[368], and in nothingness, lies and evil.

However, the creature and man, in what they are, are truth and goodness, derived from that of the Creator. The nothingness in them is a *deficiency* or rather a continuous and total dependence of their being on the Creator. If the creature, out of pride, wants to free itself from this dependence, it already incurs evil and sin.

Evil and sin come from the creature and from man, not *necessarily,* but *freely,* i.e. when the intelligent and free creature misuses the gifts received *independently of* the Creator. The "Non serviam"[369] must remain the sinner's cry of rebellion against the divine ordinances.

Human history is the development in time and space of all the good and bad manifestations in which man's life unfolds. The protagonists of history are man, the devil and God. Man as the visible protagonist, who is influenced by all the influences of divine goodness, which gently but strongly lead him to his temporal and eternal destiny. The devil, as the great insidious one, who tries to lose man and divert him from his true happiness. God, in His justice, but above all in His mercy, who tries to repair the evils of the devil and his followers and lead man to the higher goal for which He has destined him.

History has a supernatural development with reference to Christ, so that all the profane and religious manifestations of man in which his eternal destiny is ultimately resolved, in one way or another, speak to us of Christ, the One Saviour of mankind.

This reference to Christ unfolds in three equally supernatural and divine economies, the so-called natural, the Mosaic and the evangelical. The new law or Christianity is the intra-historical culmination of humanity and there is no longer any need to wait for another age, as Abbot Joachim and the millenarianists of all times wanted, because with the coming of Christ the age of the Salvation of the World has come to an end.

The health of man and of history are made *in* history and not *by* history. The only health is Christ, who took on the defects of humanity in order

---

[368] A. Bultot, Spirituels et Théologiens devant l'homme et le monde, *in Revue Thomiste,* Oct-Dec, 1964.
[369] *Jeremiah,* 2, 20.

to satisfy for it. If health is Christ and not the world, history or man, there are *two* radically irreducible *dimensions*: one, that of things that are intrinsically and directly ordered to Christ; the other, that of things that are not intrinsically and directly ordered to Christ. One, that of the things realised in Christ, the sacred, the Christian, those of the Church, which is the way of Christ; the other, the profane, the secular, those whose intrinsic and immediate ordination is to man's temporal destiny.

These two radically irreducible dimensions of things, which are the things of Christ and the things of the world, are nevertheless harmonisable, because the things of the world, the profane and secular, must also be, not by intrinsic and direct ordering, *fine operis*, but by a reference of the operative subject - *fine operantis* - to the service of Christ. "Whether you eat, or drink, or whatever you do, do all to the glory of God" [370]. Consequently, Christianity necessarily means Christianity. And this by virtue of the indirect subordination which profane and secular things *must have* to those of Christ and His Church. These relations *must* operate in a world that wants to harmonise itself with Christ. But since all things that depend on the will of man can be defected and cease to be realised, then anti-Christianity is produced and with it anti-Christianity.

If the Church does not sanctify and save the world, that is, if it does not Christianise it, the world will, in a certain sense, lose the Church, that is, it will make it worldly. This is typically the error of progressivism.

Progressivism, in short, reduces human reality to a single dimension; to a profane and secular dimension, in which the other dimension, that of Christ and the Church, is absorbed. Christ is secularising, Christianity is secularising, the Church is secularising.

This is a typical Gnostic error, for in all Gnosticism there is only one dimension, because one and the same life flows from the Ein Soph or Pleroma to the demonic world of the *Quelipoth*. Since there is only one dimension of the divine and the human, the human cannot be saved by the divine, the human cannot be saved by Christ and the Church, but the human is saved by itself. And this, which is the typical error of all gnosis - that is, *self-salvation* - can occur in a sacred or in a profane, secular

---

[370] I *Cor.*, 10, 31.

variant. The old gnoses had a sacred character, but the new gnoses are deliberately secular.

CHAPTER VII

PENETRATION OF THE KABBALAH INTO THE CHRISTIAN WORLD

The Kabbalah is completed and recorded in writing with the publication of the Zohar by Moses of Leon at the end of the 13th century. Other books appeared in writing many centuries earlier. But after the Zohar was finished, it was introduced into Christianity, first timidly, and then, in the Renaissance, in the form of an irruption.

Raymond Lull (1232-1315) was the first to introduce Kabbalistic doctrines into Christian circles. The historian Leon Poliakov[371] writes: "In the same period (that of Alfonso X, the Wise, 1252-1284) Christian theologians and rabbis maintained close relations in Barcelona. A pupil of the kabbalist Abraham Abulafia (1240-1257), the scholar Armand de Villeneuve[372] seems to have been so strongly influenced by him that he was accused of having secretly become a Jew. The famous Franciscan Raymond Lull was one of this group. One of his manuscripts has been found dedicated by him to the main rabbis of the city, "to Master Abraham Denane (ben Adret), Master Aron, Master Solomon, and to the other Jewish Sages who are in aljama. His *Dialogue of the three Sages* (Christian, Muslim and Jew), perhaps inspired by the *Kuzari*, remains as the unequalled summit of medieval humanism and tolerance".

We have already noted the influence of the converted Jew Pedro Alfonso (1062-1110) on the cabalistic ideas of Joaquín de Fiore[373]. He was also very influential later on, Arnaldo de Vilanova (died before

---

[371] *De Mahomet aux marranes*, Calman Lévy, Paris, 1961, p. 126.
[372] *Undoubtedly*, "Arnaldo de Vilanova", see Menéndez y Pelayo, Historia de los heterodoxos, *Emecé, Buenos Aires, 1945*.
[373] See Chapter V, at the end.

1312), to whom Menéndez y Pelayo devotes a whole chapter[374] and two appendices[375]. But the irruption of the Kabbalah in the Christian world took place in the Renaissance. This point has been exhaustively studied by F. Secret[376] and we will follow him in particular.

The beginnings of Christian Kabbalah in Spain

We have indicated that Spain was home to the most illustrious and cultured group of Jews in the whole community. Of these groups, many more or less secretly cultivated Kabbalistic doctrines and practices. The beginnings of the Christian Kabbalah must therefore also be sought in Spain. We have already spoken of Pedro Alfonso, Raimundo Lulio and Arnaldo de Vilanova. But the cabalistic themes were spread by the book of the Dominican Raymond Martin (+ 1282 *The Dagger of Faith.)* The *Pugio fidei adversus Mauros et Judaeos* was written in 1278 and edited in Paris in 1651 by Bosquet, bishop of Lodeve, with precious annotations by G. de Voisin. The *Pugio fidei* reveals the cabalistic significance of the divine name, YHWH, according to the teachings of Peter Alphonsus. Strictly speaking, the *Pugio fidei* did not use the Kabbalah per se, but the themes of Talmudic and Midrashic literature[377].

The first mention of the term Kabbalah appears in the works of Abner of Burgos, who took the name of Alfonso at his baptism, around 1320, and became a canon of Valladolid. In a voluminous treatise, of which the Spanish translation has been preserved, the *Mostrador de Justicia, a* dialogue between the author and a rebellious Jew, he relates how, as early as 1295, he was impressed by the miracle that took place in Avila. Following the announcement of the Messiah among the Jews, a shower of pieces of the cross fell and attached themselves to the garments of the Jews. The *Counter of Righteousness* testifies that its author had read, in addition to the book of creation, *the Sefer Yeshira,* works of the Kabbalah and that he also uses the term "Kabbalah" to designate the doctrine of those who, in Hebrew, are called "Mecubalim"[378]. There it is also said that in God there are ten numerations and there is the passage

---

[374] *Heterodox*, pp. 194-245.
[375] Ibid., pp. 519-612.
[376] Les Kabbalistes chrétiens de la Renaissance, *Dunot, Paris, 1964.*
[377] Ibid., p. 9.
[378] Ibid., p. 14.

of the soul of a man into another man, of the soul of a woman into another woman and of man into the beast, serpent or star.

This subject of metemsomatosis attracted the attention of Marsilio Ficino[379], who notes: "The Hebrew cabalist doctors approve a way of punishment and think that the souls of men come several times to this life under the human form only, for the purgation of their sins. There can be but three returns; they add, lest any one should be excused for his sin, that all souls were present when God gave the law to Moses[380].

In the *Zelus Christi written* by a convert, Pedro de la Caballería, around 1450, it is said that "the books which in Hebrew are called Cabala, a term which means the ancient traditions or writings which were written by those who received them. Two of these works have fallen into my hands: *The Gates of Justice* and *The Gates of Light,* where the celestial secrets of the divine names are treated[381].

This apologetic literature, says F. Secret[382], which was to take on the splendour of the Renaissance in the work of Pico della Mirandola, with the contribution of the Cabala, also experienced an exceptional flowering in Italy at the same time. Its examination will enable us to better understand the destiny of Christian Kabbalah.

Pico della Mirandola and the Italian atmosphere of Christian Kabbalah

With Pico della Mirandola, the Kabbalah officially entered Christianity. Behind Pico della Mirandola were two Jewish converts who played a leading role. They were the famous Mithridates and Paul of Heredia. The story of Mithridates is very confusing, as is the whole story of his role around Pico della Mirandola. Mithridates or William of Sicily seems to be the convert Juda Samuel ben Nissim Abul Faraz of Girgenti, who took the name of his godfather, William Raymond Moneada. This is at least the signature of the famous sermon he dedicated to Sixtus IV, in which he demonstrated all the mysteries of the Lord's passion with the authority and writings of the Hebrews and

---

[379] Ibid., p. 14.
[380] Ibid., p. 14.
[381] Ibid., p. 16.
[382] Ibid., p. 21.

Arabs. The seriousness of this Mithridates is evidenced by the fact that when he returned to Ireland he claimed to have seen birds born from the leaves of certain trees in the contact of water.

In 1486, Raymond William Moneada, who had become Flavius Mithridates, met Pico della Mirandola. Mithridates, in the Count's service, taught him Caldaic, after having obtained from him an oath not to communicate his science to anyone. Mithridates, who resembles this Master Alfonso, whom Dr. Torralbe, immortalised by Cervantes, met in Rome, and who prided himself on having renounced the faith of Moses for that of Mohammed, which he then abandoned for that of Christianity, before preferring natural religion or atheism, also played a great part in Pico da Mirandola's elaboration of the Kabbalah[383].

Pablo de Heredia played a more important role in the constitution of the Christian Kabbala of Pico della Mirandola. There remain two works by Heredia, incunabula, the date of which is difficult to ascertain.

The first is the *Epistle of Secrets,* dedicated to Don Iñigo López de Mendoza, who was Spain's ambassador in Rome from 1486 to 1488. The second, *The King's Crown,* which deals with the Immaculate Conception, is dedicated to Innocent VIII, who favoured this cult. These two works, which use the term "Cabala", pose a problem, since it was at the end of 1486 that the scandal of the *Conclusions,* by Pico della Mirandola, occurred, and that Innocent VIII refused until his death the brief of absolution demanded by the Count's friends.

Pico della Mirandola expounded the programme of the Christian Kabbalah and said: "These books which I have acquired at the price of gold, I have read them thoroughly, with sustained attention and unceasing labour, and there I have found - God is my witness - not so much the religion of Moses as the Christian religion: here the mystery of the Trinity, there the incarnation of the Word, there also the divinity of the Messiah; there I have read, concerning original sin, its expiation by Christ, concerning the heavenly Jerusalem, the fall of the demons, the angelic hierarchies, the punishments of purgatory and hell, the same things that we read every day in Paul and Dionysius, in Jerome and Augustine. But as far as philosophy is concerned, one would think to hear Pythagoras and Plato, whose principles are so close to the Christian

---

[383] Secret, ibid. p. 27.

faith that our Augustine gives infinite thanks to God that Plato's books have fallen into his hands[384].

From these teachings, Pico composed his conclusions on the Kabbalah. They are arranged in two series, according to the plan of his nine hundred theses; the first, *Kabbalistic Conclusions in number of forty-seven, according to the secret doctrine of the Hebrew Kabbalistic sages, whose memory must always be respected;* the second, *Kabbalistic Conclusions in number of seventy-one (seventy-two in fact), according to the author's own opinion, drawn from the principles of the Hebrew sages, which best confirm the Christian religion.* They were also found in different series, such as the famous thesis withheld by the censorship commission, the ninth of the magical conclusions, according to the author's own opinion.

We know what a scandal the examination of the thirteen suspicious theses caused in Rome, Pico's recantation on 31 March 1487 and the heresy trial. After his flight to France, Pico della Mirandola retired to Florence, where he wrote the *Hetaplus*, the *De ente et uno*, the *Disputationes adversus astrologos*. However, his curiosity and enthusiasm for the Kabbalah did not diminish[385].

In short, and this is Secret's conclusion, if Pico della Mirandola was only a link in the development of Christian Kabbalah in the Renaissance, the legend that is often right against history has rightly made him the father of Christian Kabbalah[386].

Jean Reuchlin

With Jean Reuchlin (1455-1522), the humanist from Pforzheim, the battle for the introduction of the Kabbalah into Christianity unfolded. Reuchlin had an innate inclination towards the subtleties of mysticism. And he soon made use of his knowledge of Hebrew as a kind of key that helped him to penetrate into the marvellous domain of Kabbalistic science[387]. He had two Jewish teachers: Jacobus Loans, physician to Emperor Frederick III, and Abdias Sforno, who died in Bologna in

---

[384] Ibid., p. 29.
[385] Ibid., p. 38.
[386] Ibid., p. 40.
[387] Jean Jassen, *L'Allemagne et la Réforme*, t. 11, p. 37, Librairie Plon, Paris, 1889.

1550[388]. He also had a great admiration for Pico della Mirandola. They were all under the influence of the great Jew Elias Lévita (1463-1549), who was the intermediary between the Jewish grammar of the Middle Ages and the Christian Hebraists of the Reformation[389].

Reuchlin held that the art of the Kabbalah lifts the spirit of man to God and leads him to perfect happiness. He who cultivates this science will taste the greatest possible sum of happiness in this world and will enjoy eternal happiness in the next. To defend his theories, Reuchlin published two works, *De verbo mirifico*, the miraculous word, and *De arte cabalistica*, on the art of the Kabbalah. The latter was dedicated to Pope Leo, son of Lorenzo the Magnificent, and in the dedication he recalls the brilliant period when he met Pico della Mirandola among the humanists of Florence.

But fearing, not without reason, a new invasion of Judaism, the Dominican James Hochstratten, professor of theology in Cologne, inquisitor of the faith in the provinces of Cologne, Mainz and Trier, undertook the task of refuting Reuchlin in his *Destruction of the Kabbalah*.

He showed there that this doctrine in no way strengthened the dogmas of Christianity, but rather denied them, and that Reuchlin's books swarmed with erroneous propositions[390].

Shortly before the appearance of Reuchlin's books on the Kabbalah and Hochstratten's refutation, a long dispute arose over the authority of the Hebrew books, and Reuchlin, at the beginning of the quarrel, took sides against the Jews. The one who took the strongest part against the Jews was a baptised Jew, Jean Pfefferkorn, who, in *The Mirror of the Jews* (1507-1509) and in other books, denounced the danger of Jewish writings and arts. Although at first Jean Pfefferkorn obtained the support of the Emperor Maximilian, he later issued an ordinance in which he entrusted the whole matter to Archbishop Ulrich of Mainz, commissioning him to examine the Jewish books, already confiscated in some places by Pfefferkorn, and calling for the opinion of the universities of Mainz, Cologne, Erfurt and Heidelberg, of the inquisitor

---

[388] Max Margolis and Alex Marx, *Histoire du peuple juif*, p. 447.
[389] Ibid., p. 446.
[390] J. Janssen, *op. cit.*, p. 39.

of the faith in Cologne, James Hochstratten, of the priest Victor Caben, and finally of Reuchlin.

In this dispute, Reuchlin sided with the Jews and furiously attacked Pfefferkorn. The fact is that the dispute divided German opinion into two major parties, with some in favour of Pfefferkorn and the Cologne theologians, and others in favour of Reuchlin and the poets[391].

The matter did not look favourable to Reuchlin, whose book was banned by the emperor.

But he appealed to the Pope, and to win him over he wrote to the Pope's ordinary physician, a Jew named Bonet de Lates, in the most humble terms. Leo X referred the matter to the young bishop of Spira, the Count Palatine George. The latter, unversed in the points in question, left the assessment to Canon George Truchsess, a pupil of Reuchlin, who was of the opinion that *The Mirror of the Eyes* contained no appreciable heresy, that it could not cause scandal, that it was guilty of no irreverence, and that it did not defend the Jews with exaggeration.

In the meantime, Hochstratten appealed to Leo X, but Reuchlin had many influential supporters, both lay and ecclesiastical, in Rome, and the Pope, not suspecting the danger, remained inactive[392].

The matter went to the streets and the party of Reuchlin and the poets started a public defamation campaign against the Dominicans by means of satires against the "ravens" and against the barbarians, and finally Reuchlin, somewhat supported by Erasmus, was able to celebrate a resounding triumph.

Leo X, who had long been in favour of Reuchlin, did not condemn *The Mirror of the Eyes* until after Luther's storm in 1520. But this condemnation came too late. The Kabbalah had officially entered the Christian world. Reuchlin, like the contemporary Italian Hebraists, was attracted to Hebrew and Jewish literature by his interest in the Kabbalah. But his progress enabled him to appreciate the weaknesses of the Church-accepted Vulgate version of the Scriptures. With Kimhi and Raschi as his guides, he turned to the original. *"Thus was forged*

---

[391] Ibid., pp. 43-44.
[392] Ibid., p. 50.

the weapon with which the Reformation, to the surprise of all, assaulted the authority of the Roman Church"[393].

The Golden Age of Christian Kabbalah in Italy

With Pico della Mirandola and Reuchlin, whom it is impossible to separate, the Kabbalah triumphantly entered Christianity. But with the *De arte cabalistica* we are already in 1517, when Italy knows the extraordinary generation of Galatino (1460-1540), Justinian (1470-1536), George of Venice (1460-1540), Paul Ricci (+ 1541), Cardinal G.P. of Viterbo (1465-1532), to mention only the most eminent representatives of the Christian Kabbalah.

It is there that the famous Hebrew presses of Gerson Socino and Bomberg flourished, and where fruitful relations between Jews and Christians were forged. Besides Elias of Medigo, Mithridates, Johanam Alemanus, it is the country where Leo Hebrew wrote, where Elias the Levite, Paul and Augustine Ricci, Abraham of Balmes, Calo Kalonymous, Felix of Prato worked, where Reuchlin met Obadia Sforno, Bonnet de Lates. Famous names, together with other witnesses of the curiosity of Christians for Hebraic literature: the mysterious Antonio Flaminio, unknown friend of Pico della Mirandola[394].

We have already met Marsilio Ficino (1433-1499), whom the company of Pico della Mirandola led to an even greater interest in Hebraic literature and the Kabbalah.

Another work that had great resonance was *Dialogues of Love*, which Leo Hebrew published in 1502.

Very little is known about this eldest son of Isaac Abarbanel, who was born in 1470 in Lisbon, and who, in 1492, passed with his family from Spain to Italy. Leo Hebrew was interested in the Kabbalah, as was his brother Samuel, of whom Widmanstetter testifies that in 1532 he heard lectures on the Kabbalah at his home in Naples. And it is not surprising that the Latin translation of the *Dialogues*, by Juan Carlos Saraceno, is inserted by Pistorio in his collection of the treatises of the Kabbalah[395].

---

[393] Max Margolis and Alexandre Marx, *Histoire du peuple juif*, p. 447. The underlining is ours (J. M.).
[394] *Secret,* Les Kabbalistes chrétiens..., *p. 73.*
[395] Ibid., p. 79.

As important as Leo the Hebrew is, he is an episodic figure alongside *Paul Ricci*, called Paul the Israelite. He was a pupil of Peter Pomponazzi (1462-1524) and Erasmus became acquainted with him when, in 1506, he professed philosophy in Pavia. He wrote *De caelesti agricultura*. Ricci died in 1541, after publishing his *De caelesti agricultura* and his work was inscribed in the *Index, in* spite of appearing with two pages in-folio of favourable testimonies of the theologians of Bologna and Pavia. Ricci said that there is no better way than the Cabala to confirm the faith, and this he said against Hochstratten, who claimed the opposite in his letters to Pope Leo.

While Paulo Ricci was conquering Germany with the Kabbalah, it was developing in Italy, where two works of great resonance were published in 1516 and 1518: *The Polyglot Psalter* by Augustine Justinian and *The Secrets of Catholic Truth* by Peter Galantin.

Pantaleon Justinian (1470-1536), after having professed in the Dominicans of Bologna, published in 1513 a *prayer full of piety to Almighty God, composed of 72 divine names in Latin and Hebrew*, dedicated to his nephew Cardinal Sauli. Justinian transcribes for the first time and translates into Latin texts from the *Zohar*, taken largely from the *Sifra of Tzniutra* or Book of the Arcanum. It is not without interest to note that one of the passages, which Justinian uses to show the incarnation of Christ, is quoted by Denis Saurat as illustrating the theme of sexual life in God and pantheism in the Renaissance poets[396].

Pedro Galantino (1460-1540) was a Franciscan, Pedro Columna, who took that name. His work *De arcanis* was widely circulated with the Renaissance. Galantino had a bad reputation for plagiarising the *Pugio fidei*.

Cardinal Gil de Viterbo (1465-1532), a mere name in the list of authors who dealt with the Kabbalah, has left a considerable body of work. Gil de Viterbo knew all the Hebraists: besides Justinian and Palatine, Felix del Prado, converted and entered the order of the hermits of St. Augustine. It is known that Felix, who was the Hebrew teacher of Daniel Bomberg, assured in the latter the edition of the Hebrew bible of 1515-1517, later criticised by Elias Levita. In addition, Cardinal Gil de Viterbo had other Jews or converts in his service. We know of Michael ben Sabthai, called Zematus, originally from Africa; Baruch of

---

[396] Ibid., p. 100.

Benevento, of whom Widmandstetter says that he was an excellent kabbalist and the first to have spread the books of the Zohar among Christians through Cardinal Gil de Viterbo; another convert, Nicholas Camerarius archpriest of Benevento, who translated for him a book of the Kabbalah; Joseph Hagri, who copied for him the texts of the Kabbalah in the *Scechinah*.

With Francesco Giorgi (or Zorzi) (1460-1540) we find ourselves in Venice, which played a great role in the spread of Christian Kabbalah. This was the city of the great publishers of Hebrew literature, the city of Bomberg. Giorgi belonged to a patrician family and entered the minors in 1480 after studying in Padua. He had relations with the kabbalistic milieus. He wrote *De harmonia mundi*, which he dedicated in 1525 to Clement VII. The attention attracted by *De armonia* grew with the publication in 1536 of the *Problemata*. The work was censored in Rome and Giorgi had to write an *Apologia*. It has been said of the *De harmonia mundi* that it is one of the most disordered and confused works of Renaissance mysticism, partly pagan and partly Christian, that its author, who was highly educated, although devoid of criticism and all method, brought together Neoplatonic, Neo-Pythagorean, Rabbinic, Kabbalistic doctrines and those of the pretended Dionysius without bothering to bring them into agreement.

The *Problemata* and the *De harmonia* were, with the works of Pico della Mirandola, Reuchlin and Galantin, the main sources of Christian Kabbalah[397].

The development of the Kabbalah in Germany

It has been repeated that the Reformation, favouring literal exegesis, had condemned the Christian Kabbalah. But this does not seem to be true. Kabbalah continued to flourish, as did Hebraic studies. It was the first Reformed religious who studied Hebrew and the Kabbalah. Thus, Conrad Pelican (1478-1556), one of the first Hebraists in Germany, was a shoemaker in the convent. He developed a prodigious activity in translations and commentaries of Kabbalistic texts. Admittedly, Pelican, like Viterbo, Widmandstetter and later Masay, were the best

---

[397] *See F. Secret*, Les Kabbalistes chrétiens de la Renaissance, *p. 138.*

Hebraists and collected most of the texts, but they did not leave behind monuments on a par with their works[398].

Pelican's disciple, Sebastian Munster (1489-1552), on the other hand, produced a good number of grammars, dictionaries, biblical commentaries, geographical works, translations of D. Kimhi and Elias Levita. His testimony of 1523 has been noted: "Fame, which is not always a lie, reported that thanks to the care of the Cardinal of Toledo, who illustrated our Congregation during his lifetime, all the books of the Old Testament were printed in Alcalá de Henares, in Spain, in four languages with a Hebrew dictionary. This we readily believe because Spain has always had learned Jews". Munster, if he was not a great fervent fan of the Kabbalah, made good use of it.

Wolfgang Fabrizio Capito (1478-1541) also had a relative appreciation for the Kabbalah. His pupil Paul Fagio (1504-1550), on the other hand, showed a more decided taste. His commentaries on Scripture, which have been reprinted with those of Munster in the *Critica Sacri*, make it easy to judge, on the same text, the reactions of the two commentators.

While for Capito the Kabbalah was a children's legend, Fagio states twice that the true Kabbalah is the Christian tradition.

John Oecolampadius (1482-1531), who was a pupil of Reuchlin, of W. F. Capito, and a collaborator of Erasmus, did not disdain the Kabbalah either.

> "The Christian Kabbalah in the Reformation milieu must have had as many opponents as sympathisers, but we will adduce the manifestations later when discussing the Kabbalah in the Reformers."

Christian Kabbalah in France

In France, the Kabbalah did not produce a Christian interpreter of the stature of Pico della Mirandola, Galantin, Justinian, Giorgio, Gil de Viterbo, Reuchlin, Pelican, Widmandstetter, until the appearance of William of Postel (1510-1581), one of the most astonishing figures of the Renaissance. His works, in considerable number, are indeed very difficult to find.

---

[398] Ibid., p. 144.

Without going into the meanderings of the myth constructed and lived by Postel, which some of his contemporaries compared to a labyrinth (Kvagala, *Postelliana,* p. 55) and others to "a sewer of all heresies" (T. de Beza, *Hist. Eccl., Hist. Eccl. 2*), 2), and which, as R. Simon said, is "a mixture of the philosophy of Aristotle commented on by Averroes, of Platonism and of the Kabbalah of the Jews" *(Lettre,* Moisiers, 1730, I, p. 211), we will point out its general meaning before giving some idea of the way it uses the Kabbalah.

Having first of all the idea of establishing universal concord by demonstrating the reasons for adopting Christianity, Postel, in a succession of illuminations, came to a millenarianism in which man would find the splendour of reason before the fall. According to him, the world and man, who were created by the mediator between the immobile God and the mobile world, live through four ages: that of the law of nature, that of the written law, that of the law of grace and, finally, that of the law of Concord, in which man is restored to the state of nature. Postel, in order to attract the attention of the spirits, said that he had taken the two great truths of the system of the Cabala: the spirit of the Messiah and the Gilgul or the recirculation of souls. Two aspects of the same truth which the Gospel condenses in a formula applied to Christ: "Omnia in omnibus". For Postel all men, from Adam until then, are members of Christ and have really been made partakers of his substance and not of his divinity... Postel, who has been restored to his pre-fall reason, understands all the secrets hidden from the constitution of the world, and this is what he reveals in his translation of the Zohar[399].

Postel's Zohar is a Postelian Zohar. For Postel there is no doubt that the Zohar is the work of Simon the Just, of whom St Luke praises: "The Holy Spirit had revealed to him that he would not die before he saw the Lord's Christ". The surprising text published by Postel in Venice in Latin and Hebrew is entitled *The Light of the Lamps of the Candlestick to Enlighten the Eyes in the Secrets of the Law, composed with the books Hazoar and Habahir or Summary of the Theories of the Zohar.* In fact, Postel expounds his own doctrine on themes already common to Christian kabbalists[400].

---

[399] Ibid., p. 176.
[400] Ibid., p. 179.

If Postel's great work, which Buxtorf the younger still dreamed of publishing, remained unpublished, it was nevertheless the origin of a whole French school.

The school of William of Postel

Postel, who did not form the Postelian sect, as Catholics and Reformed would reproach him, had disciples and admirers. One of the first was undoubtedly Jean Boulaese (b. 1530), who began to collect Postel's manuscripts while the latter was a prisoner in Rome.

Another disciple of Postel was his admirer Peter Victor Palma Cayet (1525-1610), accused by his former co-religionists of indulging in curious sciences. *Editor of a prodigious and lamentable history of the great doctor Faust*, he is usually called Peter the Magician. And *the Pithoeana* say: "I heard Cayet preach that the Virgin had come to save women"[401]. Cayet multiplies the references to the Zohar on themes that he has no doubt gathered from the Christian kabbalists.

But Postel's favourite disciples were the brothers Guido and Nicolas Le Fèvre de la Boderie, Normans like him. Guido (1541-1598) published a *Syro-Chaldic Dictionary*, which Buxtorf used and which indicates the author's interest in the Kabbalah. Nicolas (1550-1613) wrote a small book published in 1588 in praise of the holy language, and a copious preface to his translation of the *Heptaplo*. The opinion of Nicolas Le Fèvre de la Boderie is that he who dares to explain the Apocalypse without the help of the traditions of the Cabala remains in outer darkness.

Postel also had a great influence on two other less mysterious but very important figures of his time: Gilbert Génebrard (1537-1597) and Blaise de Vigenère (1513-1596).

The former, one of the authors of the ecclesiastical authorisation for the translation of the *Harmonia* and the *Heptaplo*, was not, however, always so favourable to the Cabala. Vigenère became famous for cryptography.

---

[401] Ibid., p. 191.

Christian Kabbalah in England

Erasmus sent Reuchlin's *De arte cabalistica* to John Fischer (1459-1535), who was attracted by the Kabbalah. In the sermon he delivered in 1521 on Luther's condemnation he justifies the traditions of the Kabbalah, traditions not written by the prophets.

It is known that Thomas More translated the biography of Pico della Mirandola through his nephew.

However, it is in the work of a Frenchman that we find mention of the Cabala: Du Guez, who had read Reuchlin, makes this clarification.

Mentions of the Cabala multiply. In 1583 Henry Howard, Earl of Northampton (1539-1614), in a *Defence against the poison of pseudo-prophecies* distinguishes between the Cabala, which is a valid method of expounding scripture, and the methods by which letters are used to indulge in divination.

Reginal Scott (1538-1599), in *The discovery of Witchcraft,* published in 1584, and directed against Bodin's *Demorwmania,* attacks the Cabala as magical and papist.

The Kabbalah is important in Henry Wainsworth (1571-1622), an exegete who lived in Amsterdam and who published, from 1616, *Annotations on the Pentateuch.*

Even Francis Bacon (1560-1626) was interested in the Kabbalah. In *De dignitate et augmentis scientiarum* he criticises the rabbis and kabbalists who seek in Scripture what can only be known through philosophy. Finally, Robert Fludd (1574-1637) is noted for his fondness for the Kabbalah and for distinguishing between a true Kabbalah and a superstitious Kabbalah. The way was open in England for Milton and H. More and many others to associate the Kabbalah with their speculations.

Kabbalah among Protestants

The Renaissance and Counter-Reformation Popes were favourable to the Kabbalah.

Alexander VI established that Pico della Mirandola had not fallen into formal heresy. Leo X received the dedication of the *Historia saeculorum* and that of the *De arte cabalistica,* and if he condemns the *Augen Spiegel* it is as a consequence of the Lutheran movement. His successor, Clement VII, who was preparing to convene a commission of six Jewish and six Christian scholars for a revision of the Bible, hurried the Cardinal of Viterbo to write and publish his works on the Cabala. Cardinal Madruzzi, who in 1543 sponsored the Hebrew printing presses of Rita di Trento, was still in favour of the books to be condemned in 1562. It is true that Paul IV (1555-1559) became famous for his harshness, from the point of view of the Christian Kabbalah, but it should be noted that it was under Pius IV (1559-1565) that a Christian publisher published the Mantua edition of the Zohar.

Among Protestants, sympathy and antipathy for the Kabbalah were more or less equally divided. Luther, who changed his attitude towards the Jews, distinguished a good Kabbalah and a bad Kabbalah[402].

Reuchlin's nephew Melanchton - of whom he wrote a biography, although his uncle had disinherited him - was of a more nuanced opinion: "There are among the doctrines of the Kabbalah many valid things handed down by the ancients to their successors, but the latter have often added the most fanciful theories.

Calvin's (1509-1564) condemnation of the Kabbalah rules out all curiosity. In the commentary on the word *Beresith*, he warns that it is very frivolous to explain that it is Christ, and on the word Elohim, "plural in Moses, of which it has been the habit to say that it denotes the three persons of the Trinity, it seems to me to be an unsound proof, and I do not insist". On the name of Jesus: "It is more than foolish, for the names of Jesus and Jehovah are only alike in two letters and differ in the others, and have no affinity to want to mix them together and make them one name".

Theodore de Beza accuses Postel of having become a Jew because he has fallen into the delusions of the Cabala. Nicolas de Gallars, in his *Commentaries on the Exodus*, dedicated to G. Farel, Calvin and P. Viret, another of Postel's adversaries, allows "the Kabbalists and their ilk to discuss the lucubrations of the Jews about the accents, spirits, winds of voices, from which they claim to draw their wonders. I do not want to be on the lookout for syllables and letters, but to be attentive to the thing itself, indicated by the true meaning of the words. For this

---

[402] *F. Secret*, Les Kabbalistes chrétiens, *p. 275.*

superstition is as dangerous and pernicious in theology as in any other science.

We see that this foolish folly has been invented by the Jews and the audacity or rather folly with which they have depraved the true history. This has also happened to the Christians who have not only accepted such fables, but have developed them and preferred to obscure the redemption of Christ"[403].

The Lutheran theologian Solomon Gesner (1559-1605), in his *Genesis*, published in 1603 in Vitembergg, has nothing but contempt for the claptrap of the rabbis. In the regions won over to Socinianism, the Christian Cabala, which seeks to prove the Trinity, is an object of ridicule. However, it is no less curious to note that these Socinians were sometimes stigmatised with the term Kabbalists.

The fact remains that the great sympathisers and detractors of the Cabal were equally divided in their admiration and detraction.

Christian Kabbalah and Occult Philosophy

This point must begin with the *De Occulta Philosophia* of Agrippa (1486-1535), who worked only under the guidance of the Christian kabbalists: Pico della Mirandola, Reuchlin, Paulo Ricci and Giorgi, to give a kabbalistic colour to his purpose, which was natural magic, celestial magic and ceremonial magic. Agrippa, as M. L. R. Wagner has shown,[404] used for magical purposes themes proposed by Pico della Mirandola, Reuchlin and Giorgi on the correspondences of physics, astrology and magic. But he fell victim both to his overly charlatanic curiosity and to the discredit of sorcery, from which he had tried to separate a more humanistic magic. And Jean Wier wrote against the legend spread by Paul Jove, "that the devil kept company with Agrippa until his last breath". "I have seen and familiarly known the dog in question, who was black... Called Sir... It was a true male dog and had for a female dog a bitch of the same size and colour called Senorita...".

Agrippa, whose influence was so great through his *De Occulta Philosophia*, was no less great through the palinodia of his *De*

---

[403] Ibid., p. 277.
[404] Sorcier et magicien, *p. 165.*

incertitudine scientiarum, where he denounced the Jewish and Christian Kabbalah.

Agrippa's *De Occulta Philosophia,* which is a theosophical conception in which Christian, Neoplatonic and Kabbalistic elements enter with magic, astrology and the art of Lullaby, reflects better than that of Occult Science the crystallisation of the curiosities of the Renaissance.

Historians of philosophy have pointed out that in Giordano Bruno (1550-1600) "the organisation of Lullianism and encyclopaedism recalls not only the four worlds and the ten sefirot, but above all that cabalistic tree which ends in the crown[405]. We have seen in it the importance of death by the kiss. Bruno mentions other themes when in the *Kabbalah of the Pegasus Horse* he develops this theological philosophy, philosophy of kabbalistic theology, theology of philosophical kabbalah...

The correspondences established by Pico, Reuchlin, Giorgi, Agrippa, the Ricci, between Kabbalah and Astrology must have led Jean-Baptiste Morin (1583-1656), a physician and royal professor of mathematics, who was in correspondence with Marsenne and Descartes, and one of Gassendi's adversaries, to publish a *Kabbalah, discovery of the astrological mansions.*

Nor was alchemy forgotten by the Christian Kabbalists. The first to have compared alchemy and Kabbalah was undoubtedly the mysterious John Pantheus, who published an *Art of Metallic Transmutation.*

But all this literature in which the Kabbalah becomes astrology, alchemy, magic, allows us to better understand the occult philosophy of the time, of which Theophrastus Paracelsus (1493-1541) was, with Agrippa, one of the great representatives. He has been made out to be a Kabbalist, but the texts clearly show that he never made a representation like Agrippa's, based on the Christian Kabbalists. The passages in which the word "Cabala" is found show that Paracelsus never bothered to follow the Christian cabalists.

---

[405] C. Bartolomess, *G. Bruno,* l. p. 51; II, p. 20, 107, 168, 309, quoted by F. Secret, *Les kabbalistes chrétiens de la Renaissance,* p. 290.

CHAPTER VIII

THE KABBALAH, ONCE INTRODUCED, WORKS IN THE CHRISTIAN WORLD WITH BOEHME, SPINOZA AND LEIBNIZ

When the Kabbalah made its official entry into the Renaissance, it had the virtue of *cabalising* Christian thought. This action was effected by two ways: that of direct influence, which was noted in a typical and singular way in certain great thinkers, such as Boehme, Spinoza and Leibniz; and by an indirect influence, which had the proper effect of softening and relaxing the great theses of traditional philosophy and giving rise to a more or less irenistic philosophy.

In this chapter we will consider in particular the direct influence on some important thinkers who had a singular importance and influence on all subsequent thought.

The precursors

Nicholas of Cusa (1401-1464) was influenced by the Cabala, at least indirectly, in various currents. It has been said that "Cusa is a broad, curious spirit, open to all the currents and influences of his time. He straddled two worlds"[406], at the point of intersection between the currents of thought coming from the Middle Ages and the new contributions of humanism and the spirit of the new times. His library contains works as significant as those of Proclus, the Hermetic books, John Scotus Eriugena, Raymond Lullius[407]. Suffice it to mention these fundamental influences to see that we are dealing with a mentality of mystical tendency strongly influenced by Neoplatonism, which seeks

---

[406] H. Höffding, *History of Philosophy*, Paris, 1921, p. 89.
[407] G. Fraile, *History of Philosophy*, III, p. 157.

expression in the philosophical field and in mathematical symbolism, whose insufficiency is the cause, on the one hand, of a marked accent of agnosticism regarding the possibility of attaining the truth and, on the other, of a somewhat imprecise language in which the words go beyond the author's thought[408].

First of all, we must say that it was Nicholas of Cusa who was the first to have the merit of putting this idea of the *Absolute* properly in the meaning that he will maintain below, of the transcendent principle and at the same time immanent to the world of experience[409]. Nicholas of Cusa also had the merit of taking from the Heraclitan and Neoplatonic philosophies the idea of *coincidentia oppositorum* and of having placed it at the basis of the concept of the Absolute, in which, thus, maximum and minimum, infinite and finite, necessity and contingency, eternity and time, possibility and actuality, and thus consequently [410] are identified.

We do not know whether the fact of having introduced this novelty can be called a "merit", but a series of disastrous and dangerous consequences will follow, which will alter the most fundamental principles of Catholic doctrine.

For Nicholas of Cusa, in the divine essence all opposites coincide, are confused, harmonised and identified: everything and nothingness, being and non-being, existing and non-existing, created and to be created. Creation *ex nihilo* must also remain insufficiently expressed. It was not without reason that the theologian John Wenck, an Aristotelian from Heidelberg, reproached Cusa for this and other phrases with a pantheistic flavour similar to some found in Eckhardt. Cusa's orthodoxy," says Fraile, "is safe from suspicion. But Giordano Bruno and Spinoza would hardly have to tinker at all with some of his expressions"[411].

Giordano Bruno (1545-1600) was influenced by Renaissance cabalists such as Ficino, Pico della Mirandola, Paracelsus and above all Raymond Lullaby and Nicholas of Cusa, "the divine Worm", whose

---

[408] Ibid., p. 157.
[409] *Italian Philosophical Encyclopaedia*, Rome, 1957, "Assoluto", I, p. 411.
[410] Ibid., p. 411.
[411] Fraile, *History of Philosophy*, III, p. 163.

"genius, if his priestly habit had not infected his genius, would not only have equalled but surpassed that of Pythagoras"[412].

In his intention, Bruno is not a pantheist, as neither are Plotinus and the Neoplatonists, says Friar[413]. But in both of them, the intentions fail because of the lack of a correct concept of creation and because they do not distinguish between *ad intra* and *ad extra* operations. The result of Bruno will be a monism, not static in the manner of Parmenides, but dynamic, evolutionary, in the manner of Heraclitus and the Stoics.

It has been observed that in his system Bruno dominates and centralises everything in cosmology, since the universal cause is the soul, which therefore vivifies the universe from within, and which is endowed with understanding more than any other soul, since it is providence that from within regulates all things[414]. For this reason, Bruno conceives the universe as a single infinite body with a universal intellective soul, also infinite in form.

This universal soul is the active divine power, present in all things, *natura naturata, it* is the *explanation* of the infinite divine *complication*. Spinoza is already anticipated in this metaphysical monism.

The human soul is a particle detached from the soul of the world and its deepest longing is to return to the unity within the Whole, in which its happiness consists. One must love the universe as divine and seek unity over multiplicity[415].

How Bruno reconciles human freedom, which he constantly praises as man's best attribute, with this pantheism subject to the most rigorous necessity, is not clear.

A. Guzzo noted in the article dedicated to him in the *Italian Philosophical Encyclopaedia* that "Bruno agrees with a tradition that came from behind, but which he found close to him in the Neoplatonists, who were so dear to him, of the fourteenth century; the tradition according to which not only the sacred books of the Hebrews

---

[412] Ibid., p. 184.
[413] Ibid., p. 184.
[414] Philosophical Encyclopaedia, *Rome, I, 813.*
[415] Fraile, ibid. p. 195.

and Christians were inspired, but also the writings of the great founders, Eastern and Greek, of the great movements of thought"[416].

Sebastian Franck (1499-1542), *Valentin Weigel* (1533-1588), *Gaspar Schwenckfeld* (1489-1561). These thinkers, also along Gnostic and cabalistic lines, are important in that they prepared the way for Boehme. Franck conceives the immanence of God in all things in such a way that no creature can work except through God. "God is the one who flies and sings in the bird". Man needs redemption, but this is realised within each individual, and Christ is but the symbol of an eternal reality.

Weigel read works by Plato, Plotinus, Proclus, Hermes Trimegistro, Eckhardt, Nicholas of Cusa and above all Paracelsus, from whom he took his philosophy of nature. From all this he formed a mystical-pantheistic system. Everything is in God. In God all things are contained implicitly (*complicite*), but none explicitly (*explicite*). Creation is necessary, and God, in creating the world, creates himself. He becomes personal through creation and acquires self-consciousness through man.

Schwenckfeld altered Christology above all by maintaining that Christ's human nature was not created but begotten by the Father and therefore did not possess holiness by grace, but as something that was His own due[417]. In connection with this doctrine, Luther pronounced the word Eutychianism. He summed it up in these terms: *Dicit creaturam post resurrectionem et glorificationem in Deitatem transformatam et ideo esse adorandam.*

With Jacob Boehme (1575-1624) we enter resolutely into a clear conception of the Kabbalah. F. C. Oetinger, one of Boehme's last supporters, relates in his autobiography that in his youth he asked the Kabbalist Hopel Hecht, who died in 1729, in Frankfort am Main, how he could best understand the Kabbalah, and the latter referred him to a Christian author who, he said, spoke more openly than the Zohar. "I asked him what he meant and he replied:

"Jacob Boehme"; and he went on to tell me of the parallels between his metaphors and those of the Kabbalah"[418].

---

[416] A. Guzzo, Giordano Bruno, *in* Encyclopaedia philosophica, *p. 819.*
[417] Dict. de Theol. Cath., t. 14, col. 1.589.
[418] G. Scholem, Le grandi correnti della mistica ebraica, *p. 254.*

In expounding the thought of Jacob Boehme we will preferably follow Alexander Koyré [419], who is considered to be one of the most authoritative experts on Boehme. We will expose the salient points of his philosophy that show its similarities with the Kabbalah.

The notion of God. "The *Deitas* is but a stage: the first moment which is still in the

"before" this life. For God, Boehme's God, lives, develops, evolves. He is precisely the God who "wird und entwird" eternally in a single *nunc aeternitatis*. He is not outside movement. He understands it and contains it in himself"[420].

"Boehme's God-persona is not "outside" difference and similarity in indistinction outside unity. He contains in himself all difference, all the infinity of opposition and distinction that eternally overcomes and gathers, revivifies and aggregates in himself. It is *in* the movement and the movement is in it.

> "Boehme starts from the constitutive divine being, from the finished God, from the concrete God. And if, at times, it seems to us that we are only witnessing a dialectical ascent from below to above, in which the less engenders the more, let us be disappointed: this dialectic is only possible because the "less" already contains the "more", and because in its chaotic indistinction the germ virtually contains the concrete being that it is called upon to produce"[421].

To the thesis: *Omnis determinatio est negatio,* Boehme implicitly opposes the belief: *omnis determinatio est positio;* the perfection of the finite becomes possible, and therefore the ultimate victory over evil becomes possible.

God, eternal nothingness and chaos

In Boehme, God is the eternal Nothingness[422], which is the eternal One.

> "The first will being therefore an Unfathomable, when we consider it as an Eternal Nothingness, it seems to us like a mirror in which one

---

[419] La philosophie de Jacob Boehme, de Vrin, Paris, 1929.
[420] Ibid., p. 317.
[421] Ibid., p. 318.
[422] Mysterium magnum, I, 2.

sees one's own image, similar to a life, although without being life, but only a figure and a portrait of life"[423].

The only name that can be given to it is that of Absolute, of *Ungrund*, bottomless and groundless abyss, abyss in which not only the foundation or reason of something cannot be found, but where God finds his own foundation[424].

The Ungrund is in the absolute that which is in itself eternally mystery, unrevealed and unexpressed: in its "inner self", that which is before and which is neither manifested nor expressed; "before" that which does not put itself and does not give itself its absolute being. The Absolute is the *Ungrund* realised as absolute. The *Ungrund* is the eternally fecund background of the life of the Absolute, the absolute germ which, being a germ, is still nothing, but which contains within itself everything that will be[425].

"The will belongs essentially to the spirit. God, as spirit, is will, absolute and first will, to which nothing precedes and nothing founds, but the indeterminate Absolute, the *Ungrund* itself. Now, since the Absolute is nothing and founds nothing, it is fairer to say that the will is the very bottom of the Absolute. The Absolute finds its foundation there; nothingness finds something there. The divine will is called, because of the direct emanation that engenders it, the will of the absolute, which does not mean that the will will wills the Absolute, but, on the contrary, that the absolute abyss (the *Ungrund*), which wills "in the will"[426].

A God who begets himself

In fact, as we have seen above, it is on the scheme of the germ that Boehme represents divine life; his God is a living God who begets himself and begets *God*[427].

> "Its evolution is entirely organic; as a spirit, its life is that of a spiritual germ which, starting from the unconscious (the indeterminate Absolute), is engendered as will and thought. It develops, finds itself, becomes aware of itself. It constitutes itself, builds itself into a

---

[423] Sex puncta, I, 7.
[424] *Koyré*, La philosophie de Jacob Boehme, p. 320.
[425] Koyré, p. 323.
[426] Ibid., p. 336.
[427] Ibid., p. 339.

spiritual centre, gives itself a life and a body, becomes personal and expresses itself through will and thought. It rises to love and to action ordered by love"[428].

Creation ex nihilo

For Jacob Boehme, creation *ex nihilo*, as it is commonly taught, makes no sense. Nothing can come out of nothing. "Reason says: God created the world out of nothing. Answer: It was not therefore some essence or matter externally taken in reality; but such a formation was in the eternal power of the will[429]. But, on the other hand, since before God's creative act there was nothing from which God could have made the world, and nothing from which He could have drawn it, it remains only that from Himself, that is, from His nature, He draws it, and from Himself He creates and produces it[430].

This is how, according to Jacob Boehme, the creation of the world can be imagined: God "sees" in his wisdom the possible world, insofar as he expresses it, and divine nature, guided by divine imagination, desires it, engenders it and produces it; God, i.e. divine nature, forms and engenders (magically) temporal nature.

On the other hand, another school of thought asserts that God is the essence of everything and that He manifests Himself in all ways. He is not only light; he is nature, he is anger. Wisdom is also a reflection of the angry eye of God, the overall image of all dark creations[431].

God's creation of evil

Creation is not explicable only by the desire to embody the celestial forms of radiant and luminous wisdom. Nature is not only God's desire; it appears rather as an infinitely fecund Matrix, which seeks to produce everything, to realise everything. Good or evil, darkness and light, anger and love, it produces everything, because everything expresses an aspect of divinity[432].

---

[428] Ibid., p. 339.
[429] Koyré, ibid. p. 417.
[430] Koyré, ibid. p. 417.
[431] Ibid., p. 421.
[432] Ibid., p. 422.

The present world, a mixture of good and evil, can be explained by a cosmic fall.

The world of darkness is not, to tell the truth, the revelation of God, as love, as *God*. It is an expression of God, but not a legitimate one. Struggle is necessary, but it is only necessary to allow opposition, tension, victory. Life implies death, but it is not necessarily agony. Moreover, the state of this world is by no means necessary. It is visibly the effect of a perversion caused and produced by a fall.

What fall, Adam's fall? It is not possible. Because Adam was created on the last day and already before his creation the world was in chaos.

However, if one considers the whole process of creation, it is conceivable that a disruption in one of its phases could influence its final outcome. This is precisely what happened. Creation was by no means complete when Lucifer's rebellion perverted its course and introduced disharmony, evil, death and suffering into the structure of the total universe, as well as into the structure of the sensible and material universe. It is perhaps unfair, or better, it is not always accurate to speak of fall and rebellion. This technique would imply, in fact, that Lucifer at the moment of his fall and rebellion was fully constituted in his being, that he was finished, and that his being and his nature preceded his acts[433].

Anthropology

There is in the still present and fallen world a *quid divini* which enables it to desire God and eternity. Indeed, if there were not such a quid divini in man he could not love God and seek Him as animals and demons do... Man, therefore, has his source in the eternal and is himself eternal; he has come from God, he is the son of God. But he is not only an eternal creature; he also belongs to nature, which, proceeding directly from eternal nature, is itself eternal and thus founds man's independence and perenniality as man. The human species is eternal and necessary, and so is the human individual.

But man also belongs to this temporal world and shares in its properties.

He has a body which is a "possessed" body, he has animal flesh which, far from being an instrument of the spirit, possesses a relatively

---

[433] Ibid., pp. 426, 427 and 431.

independent life. Between the body of man and the body of the world there is a correspondence[434].

Adam did not resemble today's man in the body.

Boehme also maintains that "Adam, created by God in a state of ontological perfection, did not exactly resemble man as he exists on earth. He possessed none of the physiological organs which make man close to the animals. He had neither sexual parts nor digestive apparatus; whether he was nourished by paradisiacal fruits or also indirectly by the divine spirit, it is evident that he possessed neither animal body nor flesh, and that he could not have a body structure comparable to that of animals[435].

Adam, representative of the whole, complete and perfect man, in all the integrity of his essence, was evidently an androgynous being. It is evident that the present state of humanity, i.e. the separation of the sexes, is not essential to man as such[436].

We need not describe in detail the history of the successive falls that have brought Adam to the present state of humanity. Each of these falls corresponds to a hindrance, a progressive materialisation of Adam's body, a deeper disarrangement of his spiritual-bodily organism and an ever greater dependence of the organic body on the spirit, which progressively loses its dominion over nature, sinks deeper into the sensible and into animality[437].

Man saves himself

"We must now, says Koyré, starting from the condition of fallen man, consider the problem of his free return to God, the problem of salvation which, as we well know, was posed for Boehme from the beginning of his thought and which had determined the course of his speculation. Boehme's metaphysics allows us to establish with certainty these cardinal points, fundamental pieces of his religious conception: the Universe is not comprehensible if we do not admit that its source is a living God, a good God and master of the eternal nature that reveals it by his creative action.

---

[434] Ibid., p. 454.
[435] *Mysterium magnum*, ch. 18, 12; 19, 20.
[436] Koyré, ibid. p. 466.
[437] Ibid., p. 467.

In front of God stands a creature as free as God himself, who must collaborate with God in the very work of creation. This creature is man. It is he himself who saves and condemns himself; it is not God as *God* who predestines him to loss or salvation. On the other hand, there is no choice or deliberation in God. His will is one, eternally similar to himself. God wants to manifest Himself in the world and in the soul. God wills the whole of his theophanies. It is up to man to decide his fate; to choose the way of expressing and revealing God; each one is for himself a determining cause; each one carries in himself, says Boehme, paradise and hell, his own God and his own Satan[438].

The soul - man, to be more precise - "imagines" "in God", "imagines" "in Christ", which means in Boehme that he reconstructs himself according to the image of Christ which he forms in himself; plastic and magical power, the *imaginatio* empties man into the "form" imagined by him.

She transforms him into this image which she makes him imitate; she introduces him into Christ, in whom she makes him participate, and this transformation is nothing other than the incarnation of Christ in man, who becomes, in a direct and primitive sense, the image, incarnation and expression of God. One could say: by imagining "in" Christ, the faithful imitate him, and in imitating him, they themselves realise the image of God. *It could also be said that, in doing so, he does nothing but realise and express his own background*[439].

As can be seen, in Boehme's thought, Christ is not the efficient cause of our redemption and salvation. He is only the exemplary cause. Not otherwise taught the Gnostics, who also spoke of the imitation of Christ *alone*. Man saved himself and in so doing imitated Christ.

And here Koyré notices something important: "The renunciation of the self, the death of the "I", abandonment and detachment are themes common to Schwenckfeld, Franck, Jacob Boehme and the *Germanic Theologia*. Annihilation, renunciation of the "I", of *Selbheit, of* the egoism that separates the soul from its divine foundation: the abandonment of the world, from which the soul "separates" in order to return to itself, to immerse itself in its uncreated depths, the eternal *Ungrund*; the theme of the *Entleerung* by which man, destroying

---

[438] Ibid., p. 478.
[439] Underlining is mine, J. M. Ibid., pp. 481-482.

himself (destroying the false individuality which belongs to this world) makes himself nothingness, emptiness, thus finding in this nothingness of himself the eternal Nothingness of God, which, substituting itself for the vanished individuality, takes its place; the necessity of voluntary action, the only means by which this destruction of self-will *(Eigenwille)* and desire can be obtained, which leads us to identification with God and to mystical intuition, which, in a single indistinct vision, enables us to perceive the soul in God and God in the soul"[440].

Man possesses absolute autonomy

In Boehme's conception man's freedom is absolute. There are certainly many factors that hinder the exercise of this freedom: heredity, passions, temperament, false doctrines, the flesh, to put it in a nutshell.

But all these factors, being finite, cannot destroy man's infinite freedom. Indeed, the human personality is infinite; as such, it is "more" than the sensible universe as a whole.

Man, in Boehme's conception, possesses absolute autonomy. Basically, he has no need of anything. Heaven and earth, Paradise and Hell, everything is in him. Grace is in man. Christ is in him. God has been given to him before his birth. Eternity has become incarnate in him - virtually-, but is this virtuality not already a reality of potency?[441].

Judgement on Boehme's thinking

The En-Sof of the Kabalah, which means Nothing, Nothingness which evolves and then realises itself in the Sephiroth, is determining Boehme's whole conception. The God of the Kabalah who is realised and constituted to end in the Universe with man by culmination also appears clearly in Boehme.

In the third chapter of *De Signatura Rerum* entitled "Of the great mystery of all things", Boehme says: "Taken outside of nature, God is a Mystery, understand here, in Nothingness; for outside of nature there is nothingness, that is to say an eye of eternity, an unfathomable eye which does not reside and does not look into anything because it is the Indeterminate; and this eye is a will, understand a desire of

---

[440] Ibid., p. 483.
[441] Koyré, p. 491.

manifestation to find Nothingness"[442]. The indeterminate is nothingness and at the same time will, a bottomless will, a nothingness that "hungers for something"[443] ; a pure freedom, which has no essence[444].

All this, like the Kabbalah, is but a theogonic process, the process of the birth of God in eternity, in the eternal Mystery. Boehme, writes Berdiaeff[445] "is the first in the history of human thought who has made freedom the first foundation of being; it is for him deeper and more primary than all Being, deeper and more primary than God himself".

As the God of the Cabala has a luminous and a shadowy face, so that of Boehme. "For the God of the sacred world and the God of the dark world are not two different gods: there is one God; He is all Being, He is Evil and Good, heaven and hell, light and darkness, eternity and time, the beginning and the end; where His love is hidden in a being, His wrath appears[446].

In the God of the Kabbalah and in the God of Boehme "there are two eternal lives, two different sources, and each resides in its fire. The one burns in love and in the realm of delights; the other in anger, anger and pain, and sorrow, and pain, and its materials are pride, greed, envy and anger, its strength resembling a sulphurous spirit. For the rise of pride is covetousness, envy and anger compose a sulphur in which the fire burns, and in which it is always burning, feeding on this matter[447].

Berdiaeff observes of Boehme's anthropology that "hermaphroditism is a repressive and sickly caricature, whereas the androgynous myth is one of the deepest and oldest of mankind, justified by a more esoteric interpretation of Genesis. The androgynous theory can be found in the *Kabbalah*. The theologies that fear and deny the doctrine of the androgyne are those that deny the Heavenly Man, *Adam Kadmon,* because of its exoteric character and speak only of the natural, empirical terrestrial man, that recognise only the vetero-testamentary anthropology, built retrospectively from the conception of sin. Boehme, however, discovers the celestial and seraphic anthropology, the celestial

---

[442] Vol. IV, 284-285, quoted by N. Berdiaeff in *Jacob Boehme,* Aubier, Paris, 1945, t. I, p. 15.
[443] IV, 286, cit., ibid. p. 15.
[444] IV 429.
[445] *Mysterium magnum,* foreword, p. 18, Aubier, Paris, 1945.
[446] Cited, ibid., p. 20.
[447] Cited, ibid., p. 21.

origin of man. His anthropology is linked to Christology; his cosmology and his Mariology are a function of his doctrine of Sophia and the androgynous.

Finally, the intuition of the Sophia and the androgynous image of man is for him the fundamental intuition of light, just as that of the *Ungrund* is the fundamental intuition of Darkness[448].

In short, that God is abyss, chaos, darkness, and man is light. This is also the teaching of the *Kabbalah*.

Baruch Spinoza

Boehme is a mystic but Spinoza (1632-1677) is a philosopher. If the Kabbalah perverts the world of mysticism, it also alters the world of philosophy. This is where it must infect the whole of life. The relationship between Spinoza and the Kabbalah was already evident in Spinoza's time, writes Claude Tresmontant[449]. The achromatic work he has left us still allows us to discern the fundamental themes of Jewish gnosis. The part of his work that Spinoza burned before his death must have contained more frankly esoteric texts, especially writings on metensomatosis.

The first book devoted to this subject is Joh Georg Wachter's *Der Spinozismus im Judenthumb, oder, die vom dem heutigen Judemthumb, und dessen Geheimem Kabbala Vergötterte Welt*, published in Amsterdam in 1699, and soon followed by a work in which Wachter corrects his earlier theses and affirms the unity of the Spinozan doctrine and the Kabbala, *Elucidarius cabalisticus, sive Reconditae Hebraeorum Philosophiae Brevis et succinta Recensio, Epitomatore* Joh. Sergius Wachterius. Philos. Prof., Romae, Anno 1706.

After Wachter, the following are published: Fr. H. Jacobi, Werke, IV, I, (1819); Elias Benamozegh, *Spinoza et la Kabbale*, 1864; Is. Misses, *Spinoza und die Kabbala* (Zeit für ex. Philos. VIII, 1869, 359-367).

In our days the problem has been restated with considerable erudition by Stanislas von Dunin Borkowski, S. J., *Spinoza*, Zweite auflage Münster, 1933.

---

[448] Berdiaeff, p. 33.
[449] *Estudios de metafísica bíblica*, Gredos, Madrid, 1961, p. 172.

Here are some of the points around which Wachter, in his *Elucidarius Cabalisticus,* groups the analogies and identities between the doctrine of the Cabala and that of Spinoza: 1) The knowledge of truth in the Cabala begins with God, and things are conceived by us in the order in which they have been brought into existence. Cf. *Eth.* pars. 2, schol. prop. 10: *Omnes concedere debent...*

2) The Qabalists call the beginning of their philosophy *En-Sof,* which means *Infinite,* by which they define *God* in Himself considered. The same philosophy founds Spinoza: "Per Deum, inquit..." *(Eth.,* I, def. 6).

3) If we ask in what way these finite things have been produced by the infinite, we have almost the same answers. The Infinite Power does not produce something out of nothing, he opines with the Qabalists. That nothingness becomes something refers him to fictions *(De Emens. int.,* p. 374).

4) From this principle the Kabbalists draw various conclusions, such as that matter is neither created nor, because of the vileness of its essence, can it exist by itself; consequently, either there is no matter in the universe, or spirit and matter are one and the same thing (cf. H. Morus, *Theses Cabbal n Kabbala denudata,* t. I, 1677, part. 2ª, pp. 153 et seq.). In this Spinoza agrees admirably, since he denies that any corporeal and material mass, which is the subject of this world, can be created by God (cf. *Eth.,* I, schol., prop. 15).

5) Hence he frequently warns (Epist. 73) that matter has been wrongly defined by Descartes as being constituted by extension, for extension is wrongly explained by vile nature, which must be in one place, finite and divisible, etc., since matter must be explained by the attribute which expresses the eternal and infinite essence.

Does Spinoza then affirm that God is matter? No. But he denies matter entirely and only retains the word, free from the meaning of the vulgar.

6) According to Spinoza there is no matter in the universe, but what is, is a most excellent thing, that is, as the Qabalists say, spirit... He manifestly teaches *(Eth.* I, Cor. prop. 13 and schol. prop. 15) that no substance, not even corporeal substance, as substance, is divisible. Cf. *Eth.* 3, schol. prop. 2: "that mind and body are one and the same thing, expressed in only two ways..." and *Eth.* II, schol. prop. 7: "that the thinking substance and the substance are one and the same substance which is already known under the attribute of thought and that of extension" (proxime cit.: *Hoc quidam Hebreorum quasi per nebulam...*).

8) That God has produced some things mediately and others immediately is the unanimous judgment of the Qabalists; hence they speak of a first beginning which God had immediately caused to flow from Himself, and by which the other things would be produced in series and order, and this they usually hail by various names, such as Adam Kadmon, Messiah, Christ, Lagos, Word, First-born Son, First Man, Heavenly Man, etc. The same thing was known to Spinoza *(Eth.* I, schol. prop. 28).

9) It is also a doctrine admitted by the Qabalists that God produced a living, animate world, for since there is no matter in the universe, there is no death either, but whatever appears is animate in varying degrees.

13) Human souls exist from eternity before bodies and cannot be killed with bodies.

19) Spinoza affirms that everything is done by an untamed necessity and by a necessary destiny, even more by a necessary requirement of the nature of God Himself, and that this necessity is called Malchut or Kingdom of God.

So much for Wachter.

Dunin Borkowski notes that in 1647 and 1648, when Spinoza was engaged in his Kabbalistic studies, Kabbalists were diligently consulting this work in Amsterdam *(cited above,* p. 171). He also notes that Herrera's *Heaven's Gate*, one of Manasse and Morteira's favourite books, which at that time was very popular in the Jewish quarter of Amsterdam, spoke to him in modern language about the conceptions of the *Zohar (ibid.,* p. 188).

Borkowski points out that it would be a mistake to attribute every relation of resemblance to a relation of dependence. Spinoza starts from the divine being and only then develops the divine attributes. He certainly had no need to learn this preliminary step from the Kabbalists. When further on the Kabbalah taught: "Know therefore that it is not permitted to attribute to the eternal one a will, a desire, an intention and a meaning", we shall find this generally Spinozist phrase, in a more precise and more thoroughly substantiated version, in almost all Jewish religious philosophers; and it is much more probable that the philosopher adopted their decisions, and not those of the Kabbalah. The same is true of the Kabalistic phrase, that every affirmation implies a negation *(ibid.,* p. 171).

Dunin Borkowski shows how Spinoza has sublimated and rationalised the Sephiroth or intermediary beings, thus paying homage to neo-Platonic-Cabalist and neo-Platonic-Arabic speculations *(ibid.,* p. 172). Spinoza's thought does not seem to have been influenced by the seven Sephiroth[450]. On the contrary, the doctrine of the first three Sephiroth seems to have played an important role in the genesis of Spinozism. For Spinoza, the reminiscences of the 1st and 3rd parts of the Zohar were of supreme importance. The Sefirot *Wisdom* together with the *Crown*, and the *En-Sof* compose an absolute unity. They are three heads in one. "All is united and merged into one Whole". "Between the universe and the old man there is no difference". "All is one and the same, without difference or separation". He who presents the Sephiroth separately, destroys the unity of God[451].

Bodily nature is the ultimate expression of wisdom, matter represents a degradation. Space, the inversion of thought. This doctrine is not new. Matter, space, the last stage of emanation, removed from God as far as possible, is the doctrine of Plotinus. We will find it, only slightly transformed, in Bergson. Matter externalises an eternal and infinite essence. For this reason, matter has been ill-defined by *extension* in Descartes, for it must be explained as an attribute expressing the eternal and infinite essence *(Epist.* 83).

Matter proceeds eternally from the Absolute. Marxist materialism refers to Spinoza concerning the eternity of matter; of course, after having put Spinozaism underfoot.

Claude Tresmontant affirms the existence of a close, though not dependent, relationship between the Kabbalah and Spinoza. Leon Dujovne, in his *Spinoza - His Life - His Age - His Work - His Influence*[452] - gives an account of the whole question, focusing on the thesis of Harry Waton[453], in favour of the influence that the Kabbalah would have exerted on Spinoza's system, and against the opinion of Sir

---

[450] P. 186.
[451] *Zohar,* III, 286b and 290a; III, 290.
[452] Four volumes, Instituto de Filosofía, Buenos Aires, 1941-1945, especially vol. II, pp. 135-149.
[453] *The Kabbalah and Spinoza's philosophy,* Spinoza Institute of America, New York, 1931, pp. 20-21.

Frederick Pollock[454], who denies any link between Spinoza and the Kabbalah.

Perhaps Dujovne somewhat downplays Borkowski's opinion, which he judges to be intermediate between those of Waton and Pollock. Dujovne writes: "Spinoza's biographical circumstances therefore justify us in asking whether the Kabbalah had an influence on Spinozaism, whether the latter does not contain thoughts derived from the Kabbalah. Waton answers this question in the affirmative, based on various arguments. In his book he reproduces extracts from Kabbalistic writings in order to point out similarities between the ideas contained in them and some of our philosopher's"[455].

We think that the similarity and diversity between Spinoza and the Kabbalah are due to the method proper to Spinoza's philosophy, who adopted the *mathematical form in the philosophical exposition*. This problem has been very well studied by Dujovne in his aforementioned work, where he expounds the opinion of Ludwig Meyer[456] who brings these significant words of Spinoza regarding the mathematical method employed by Descartes: "To come to his aid I have often wished that a man, equally exercised in the analytical and in the synthetic order, very familiar with Descartes' work and thoroughly acquainted with his philosophy, would wish to set himself the task of arranging in synthetic order what Descartes has presented in analytical order and demonstrating it by conforming to the mode of ordinary geometry. I myself, although fully aware of my weakness and knowing that I am far below such a great task, have more than once had the intention of doing it and have even begun to do it, but other occupations that often distract me have prevented me from carrying it out".

But Spinoza was to expound with Cartesian method, not the philosophy of Descartes, but the philosophy of the Kabbalah. And here we believe that the words of León Dujovne[457] must be understood in a rigorous and radical sense: "Another dissent is that while Descartes - as Spinoza faithfully exposes - admits that "such and such a thing is beyond human comprehension" our philosopher, in turn, believes "that all these things

---

[454] *Spinoza, his life and philosophy*, Duckworth and Co., London, 1899, pp. 92-96.
[455] Dujovne, ibid., II, 145.
[456] *Œuvres de Spinoza*, translated and annotated by Ch. Appunhn, Garnier, Paris, 1904; see Dujovne, ibid, II, p. 274.
[457] Dujovne, ibid., II, p. 275.

and even many other higher and subtler things can not only be clearly and distinctly conceived by us but that it is even possible to explain them with great comfort if the human understanding in the pursuit of truth follows a different path from that which Descartes has opened and cleared, and admits that the foundations of science found by Descartes and the edifice he has erected on them are not sufficient to penetrate and resolve all the most difficult questions found in metaphysics, but that others are required if we wish to raise our understanding to that summit of knowledge". And here Dujovne notes: "In these lines, Spinoza not only rejects certain conceptions of Descartes, but also proposes intellectual *procedures* different from Cartesianism and more appropriate to reach the truth".

León Dujovne will then show how "the idea of God occupies the foreground in Spinoza's mind, and that is why he could say that the common philosophers take creatures as their starting point, while Descartes started from the *self*, and he, Spinoza, from God".

Here Spinoza's Kabbalistic influence is openly reflected in Spinoza. The idea of God occupies the first place in the human mind. This idea cannot be acquired through sensible things, but is first and therefore born of the cognising subject. By making the idea of God the first and total reality, Spinoza has no other recourse than to make man and all other things also a divine reality. There is but one substance. And this is God. Then, everything is God.

Hence the fundamental ideas of Spinoza's system are those of the Kabbalah, expounded, as has been said, in a Cartesian method. "To the thesis of the existence of a unique God, Spinoza adds the thesis of a unique substance. This unique existence is God. There being only one substance, and this being God, God and nature must be the same"[458].

From this first assertion of Spinoza "that there is but one substance and that it is God", the other assertions must rigorously follow. But since this first assertion is fanciful and false, the subsequent propositions must be equally fanciful and false.

"All things produced by God are equally necessary, both those produced in a mediate way and those that derive from Him immediately; God is the cause of all of them, determined to this or that

---

[458] Dujovne, ibid., III, p. 50.

action. Any hint of contingency is thus excluded from reality. Determinism is universalistic. The will is not a free cause; it is a necessary cause, Spinoza maintains in proposition 32" [459]. This universal determinism evidently contradicts experience, but it is ultimately governed by that first proposition which makes of all substance, God.

"Of all the modalities of divine causality, within Spinozism, the one that interests us most here is that of immanence. It and universal determinism constitute far-reaching features of Spinoza's philosophy"[460]. It is clear that with this idea of God's efficient and immanent causality, the whole universe is engendered from the divine substance. Pantheism, universal determinism, and immanent causality are one and the same thing, but said in a different way and in a different perspective.

"Spinoza has already asserted that there is only one substance, God or nature. This nature is the cause of all things; things, in their turn, are not logically independent substances.

One would almost have to distinguish between the one substance as cause and what flows from it as effect: between *natura naturans* and *natura naturata*"[461]. Here is another version, already found in Giordano Bruno, of Spinosa's pantheism, which is also of Kabbalistic origin. For between the *En-sof* and the last of the Qulipoth there is a single reality or substance that flows *homogeneously* throughout the universe.

Such a radical and profound alteration of the concept of God must logically bring about an alteration of the universe and of man. And if this alteration is made in the sense of cabalistic gnosis, as is the case with Spinoza, his whole system must also be gnostic-cabalistic.

Gottfried W. Leibniz

Leibniz (1646-1716) and the Kabbalah has also been discussed by Claude Tresmontant [462], who writes: "Leibniz read and annotated Wachter's book on Spinoza *Elucidarius cabalisticus*.

---

[459] Dujovne, ibid., III, p. 70.
[460] Ibid., p. 85.
[461] Ibid., p. 82.
[462] Studies in Biblical Metaphysics, *p. 177.*

We have the text of these annotations in A. Foucher de Careil's collection entitled *Réfutation inédite de Spinoza par Leibniz*, Paris, 1854. In this important document, Leibniz's observations on Spinoza are often interspersed, as in Wachter's book itself, with reflections on the Kabbalah and other mystical and esoteric doctrines..."[463].

"Leibniz, who was so many things, was also always an occultist whose thought is curious and impregnated with alchemical doctrines. It is often forgotten that, as soon as he left the University of Altdorf in 1667, he joined the Nuremberg Rosicrucians, of whom he became secretary, and that he spent a whole winter absorbed in this activity until his arrival in Boineburg. Although this episode in his career is scarcely known, we would run the risk of deceiving ourselves if we considered it to be devoid of significance[464].

Leibniz is linked to two of the greatest kabbalists of the time, Francis Mercurius van Helmont and Baron Knorr von Rosenroth, author of the *Kabbala denudata, seu doctrina Hebraeorum transcendentalis.*

It is likely that van Helmont and his friend Knorr had a hand in Leibniz's naming his spiritual substances as *monads* after a reading of Giordano Bruno [465]. Knorr used the term *monad* in his *Kabbala denudata* and considered matter as a conglomerate of dormant spiritual monads, *coalitio monadum spiritualium torpentium* (F. van Helmont refers to this passage of Knorr's in his *Princ. Philos.* and also uses the word monad for his terminology).

In 1687, Leibniz spent a month with Knorr von Rosenroth. Leibniz has left us a summary of their conversations, edited by Foucher de Careil[466].

Jorge Rodier, in an article on *One of the origins of Leibniz's philosophy*[467] exposes the doctrine of Plotinus as *"a centon of the Monadology"*, which seems to put beyond doubt the influence of the Neoplatonic system on Leibniz's [468]. Nevertheless," Rodier adds, "Plotinus and Proclus are rarely cited in Leibniz's works published up to now, and Leibniz even conceals their authority in cases where the

---

[463] Friedmann, *Leibniz et Spinoza*, 1946, p. 134.
[464] Ibid., p. 135.
[465] Friedmann, *Opus Laud*, p. 137.
[466] La philosophie juive et la Kabbale, *Paris, 1861.*
[467] Études de philosophie grecque, *1926, pp. 338 ff.*
[468] Ibid.

analogy between his opinions and theirs is flagrant". Rodier supposes that Leibniz had read the Neoplatonists in his youth and that he had forgotten his sources... But perhaps another hypothesis could be put forward: the filiation between Plotinus and Leibniz would pass through the Jewish and Christian kabbalists. The fundamental structure of the Neoplatonist and Kabbalistic metaphysicians is essentially identical. Neoplatonism allied itself with Gnosis, to create the great Gnostic systems of the Kabbalah, and then of German Idealism. Here is a page from the *Kabbala denudata* which can illustrate the affinities between the doctrine of the Kabbala and that of Spinoza and Leibniz.

"The foundations of philosophy... which properly denies all creation, and supposes the divine essence as corporeal-spiritual, and the material world in some way.

1. Nothing is created out of nothing.

2. And therefore neither matter can be created.

3. Nor by the vileness of its nature can it exist of itself; the consequence, or rather the foundation, of which is, that no vile thing can exist.

4. There is therefore no matter of the nature of things.

5. What exists is spirit.

6. That this spirit is uncreated and eternal, intellectual, sensible, vital, self-moving, infinite in breadth and necessarily existing in itself.

7. That therefore this Spirit is really the Divine Essence.

8. That no essence outside the Divine can exist by its own force.

9. Since, apart from the Divine, no essence is made in the university of things, according to exioms 1, 2, 3 and 8, and since it is manifest that any of this one Essence can at present be divided, it is also manifest that the Divine Essence can be divided.

10. When the Divine Essence is made, each of its particles is infinite and can extend and expand in orbits of infinite virtue and amplitude.

11. Now then, as each of the grit and grains of stone and the particles of air, ether, etc., are parts of this Divine Essence, it is equally evident that it can also contract and constrict itself into these very smallest parts.

12. Of these contracted parts consists the world which is called *Material* when it is truly *spiritual,* being certainly composed of divided spirits or

particles of the Divine Essence contracted into monads and physical points.

13. This contraction is *a state of sleep* or slumber and the expansion of these divine particles is *a state of wakefulness*.

14. The degrees *of the waking state* are various, namely, of *vegetative, sensitive, rational* life, and in *Neschamam, Chajah and Jachidah;* moreover, the waking and expansion is made in an infinite orb of power and breadth, so that this particular Divine particle or Spirit can fabricate for itself a world consisting of earth, water, air, sky and elsewhere.

15. This particular Spirit of the dust, for example of the marble, can become Plant, of the gross Plant, of the gross Man, of the gross Man Angel and of the Angel God, Creator of a new Earth and Heaven.

16. The same may be said of each of the necessarily separate or separable parts of the Divine Essence, that is, that all are or may be God, creators of the earth or of the heavens. This is what a child hinted to me in a dream, asking me if I believed in God. And he smilingly replied that he believed in several gods, distinct from each other..."[469].

Conclusion of the chapter

This takeover of modern thought by the Kabbalah in thinkers of the hierarchy of Boehme, Spinoza and Leibniz was to mean an increasingly total domination until it reached German idealism and the contemporary thought derived from it.

---

[469] This page is taken from the *Kabbala denudata,* by Knorr von Rosenroth, in t. I, p. 293, under the title *Fundamentals of Philosophy* or *of the Aito-Paido-Melisean Kabbala,* which denies all creation proper.

CHAPTER IX

THE CABAL ACTS OPENLY THROUGH GERMAN IDEALISM

Boehme was primarily a mystic and not a philosopher. Spinoza was a philosopher, and although he had a great influence on the philosophical currents[470], by the excess of his affirmations and above all by his pantheism, he remained somewhat on the fringe and as a loner in the face of these same currents. It could be said that in a certain sense he was ahead of them. Spinoza was to be fully realised in German idealism, and in this respect it should be noted that Fichte's system was described as an *internalised Spinozism*, which is all the more true of Hegel's system.

Fichte

Georges Rodier has analysed the presence of Neoplatonic and more precisely Plotinian and cabalistic themes in Leibniz's philosophy[471]. With Fichte we meet again the metaphysical principles and themes that we evoked in Plotinus, in the Gnosis and that appeared again in the *De Divisione naturae* of Scotus Eriugena. In Fichte, as in Spinoza, there is no creation of being but division, dispersion, individuality. Going through Plotinus, says Claude Tresmontant[472] we have to go back to the Upanishads to find the first known expression of the fundamental metaphysical theses elaborated by Fichte.

---

[470] León Dujovne, *Spinoza*, t. IV, Instituto de Filosofía, Buenos Aires, 1945.
[471] *Georges Rodier*, Sur une des origines de la philosophie de Leibniz, Paris, 1936, p. 338.
[472] *Claude Tresmontant*, La métaphysique du christianisme et la naissance de la philosophie chrétienne, Au Seuil, Paris, 1961, p. 717.

Here we follow Claude Tresmontant, who in turn analyses one of Fichte's most popular writings, "Die anweisung zum seligen Leben"[473].

1st *The appearance and being of things.* Fichte's starting point is the distinction *between appearance* and *being.* A large proportion of people, throughout their lives, only reach the *exterior* of things, what they perceive with their external senses, believing it to be the reality of things. In contrast to this way of thinking, Fichte opposes an opposite way of thinking, which consists in thinking that behind the *appearance* of external objects lies the true reality of what things *are.* In all things there is to end in a *Being* which is not subject to becoming, and which for this reason does not depend on anyone but exists by itself and of itself and from itself. Within this being there is no change, but it is immutable from eternity. *Being,* in which all things ultimately consist, is *one* and not multiple[474].

Why is it that what in itself is pure unity and remains one in life and in true thought is transformed into the diversity of phenomena, the reality of which we cannot deny?

Fichte responds to this in the fourth lecture, in which, at the beginning, he reminds us that the misery of men consists in their dispersion in the diverse and changeable, and that, on the other hand, the only condition for a happy life is to understand the *One and Eternal* in an intimate love.

There is truly and in the proper sense of the term nothing outside of God, if it is not knowledge; and this knowledge is divine existence itself, pure, simple and immediate, and it is in so far as we are knowledge that we *are ourselves in our deepest root* of *divine existence.*

All that apart from this appears to us as existence - things, bodies, souls, ourselves insofar as we attribute to ourselves an autonomous and independent Being - does not truly and in itself exist. It exists only in consciousness and in itself, as known. Only the one and immutable exists; the changeable and variable does not exist and its manifestation is nothing but appearance[475].

2° *Knowledge, in the act of distinguishing, gives rise to the multiple and diverse.* Consciousness or knowledge, in the act of distinguishing,

---

[473] Medicus, Leipzig, 1923, p. 41, French translation by Rouché.
[474] Claude Tresmontant, ibid. p. 717.
[475] Ibid., p. 719.

transforms into different that which is essentially One and Eternal. Thus the concept transforms into a fixed and present being that which is in itself directly divine life. *The transformation of immediate life into a fixed and dead being*, such is the fundamental character that the Concept causes existence to undergo. The Concept is properly the creator of the world, transforming into a fixed and different being the divine life which is in itself one and eternal.

In the act of *reflection*, by its very nature, what was but one is divided and split into two. Reflection produces the world, and the world, as a consequence of reflection, cannot but be broken and divided. And just as the Concept in general has revealed itself to be the creator of the world, so the free act of reflection here reveals itself to be the creator of diversity and infinite diversity in the world[476].

Just as our sensitive eye is a prism in which the ether of the material world, which in itself is perfectly equal, pure and colourless, is refracted in various colours on the surface of things, so we cannot see the colourless ether, but we can think it colourless, so it is for the intellectual life and for our spiritual eye. *What you see,* Fichte tells us, *you are eternally.* But you are not such as you see yourself, just as you do not see yourself as you are.

You are immutable, pure, colourless and formless. Only the reflection, which is also yourself, and which for this reason you cannot take away from yourself, refracts it into infinite forms and rays[477].

3° *Science or gnosis makes us know our divine reality.* We *are* the immediate life of God, and yet we know nothing of this immediate life. Our being in God, although it may be ours at its root, remains eternally foreign to us. Even if God remains Himself behind all these forms, we do not see Him; or rather we see Him only in the form of stone, grass, animal. The form always hides the essence from us. Rise, Fichte tells us, to the point of view of religion and all veils disappear; the world disappears before your eyes with its dead principle and the divinity itself enters into you, under its first and primitive form, as life, as your own life.

But the point of view of Science - of gnosis - is still superior to that of religion. Science embraces all the points of transformation of the One

---

[476] Ibid., p. 720.
[477] Ibid., p. 721.

into the diverse and of the Absolute into the relative, completely, in their order and in their mutual relations; it can always, and from each isolated point of view, *reduce,* according to law, all that is diverse to unity, or deduce from unity all that is diverse. Science overcomes what religion already perceives, namely, that all that is diverse is already founded in the One and must be reduced to it. Science comes to understand the how of this relation; for it makes genetic what for religion was only an absolute fact[478].

4th *Conclusion of all that has been said.* Claude Tresmontant concludes that in these fundamental themes of Fichte's system we find the theses already expressed in the Upanishads, in Plotinus, in the Christian Gnostics, in Scotus Eriugena and in the Cabala.

The Absolute is the One. But the Absolute is Knowledge, Consciousness, Reflection. The Absolute, the One is known, is reflected upon, and thus the second hypostasis, the *Nous,* is born. "The One is not understanding.

How does the understanding beget? Because it sees by turning to itself; and this sight is the understanding" (Plotinus, *Enn.,* V, 1, 7). This understanding has had the audacity to turn away from the One... *(Enn.,* VI, 6, 9, 5). Within the intelligible world, there is an *apostasy,* a schism, a division. The understanding is dispersed, it is the principle of dispersion. Consciousness is the principle of division. As in the Kabbalah, in which the Sephira *Bina, the* Intelligence is also that which divides and differentiates[479].

This idea of *Trefnnung, Entzweiung,* responsible for the at least apparent diversity of the real, this idea that we find in Schelling and Hegel is a very old idea that we find in Plotinus, in certain Gnostics and in the Cabala. The multiplicity of beings does not come from creation, but is the effect of an action of dividing and separating.

By the teaching of the sage - who is called Spinoza, Plotinus or Fichte - we free ourselves from this multiplicity and recognise the divine substance and the Absolute which, in our innermost being, *we are.* Through gnosis we operate the *conversion* from the illusory point of view to the truth of unity. And in this knowledge that converts us and returns us to the *One* consists the gnostic salvation. It is not a question,

---

[478] Ibid., p. 722.
[479] Ibid., p. 723.

as in Christianity, of health being brought about by the grace that *is added to* man, but of *removing* that which hinders gnosis and of removing the *maya* that hides from us the true divine reality that we are[480].

5th *Fichte believes that his doctrine is the true Christianity.* Fichte believes that his doctrine is confirmed by the Fourth Gospel of St. John and that it is John alone who teaches authentic Christianity, as opposed to St. Paul, who would have allowed the old error of Judaism, the idea of creation, to persist. For John, on the other hand, always according to Fichte, the Concept or the Word is the only creator of the world in general and, by the *divisions* operated in its essence, the creator of the infinite diversity to be found in the world[481].

Schelling

Schelling renews the great themes of pagan philosophy by adopting the theogonic scheme of the Gnostic theosophies. Schelling considers that the God of Christian theology lacks vitality because he is subtracted from becoming and the tragic. But it was Hegel who, in his *Philosophy of Religion* and his *Phenomenology of Spirit*, was to be the greatest exponent of Valentinian gnosis, as Fernando Christian Baur [482] demonstrated in 1835. There, Baur shows how Hegel's philosophy of religion and Valentinian gnosis are related in a common conception by which God, dividing Himself, alienating Himself and turning to Himself, engenders Himself and becomes conscious of Himself.

Hegel

We will extract some pages from Hegel's "Phenomenology of Spirit", where the Gnostic schema clearly appears. We will follow the pages of G. W. F. Hegel's "Phénoménologie de l'Esprit" translated by Jean Hippolite[483].

---

[480] Ibid., p. 724.
[481] Ibid., p. 726.
[482] *Die christliche Gnosis oder die christliche Religions-Philosophie in ihrer geschichtlichen Entwiklung*, Tübingen, 1835.
[483] Aubier, 1939, Paris.

God or the Absolute is not a simple being but moves differentiating itself by the negative. In the famous preface to the *Phenomenology of Spirit*, Hegel criticises Schelling's formalism where the Absolute is the night where all cows are black. And there he proposes the true, not as substance, but precisely also as subject. And Hegel writes: "The life of God and divine knowledge can therefore very well, if you like, be expressed as a play of love with itself; but this idea is reduced to edification and even banality when it lacks the seriousness, the pain, the patience and the work of the negative. *In itself* this is really the serene equality and unity with itself which is not seriously compromised in the other and in alienation, and which is not compromised in the movement to overcome this alienation... The true is the whole. But the whole is the essence fulfilling and completing itself through its development. Of the Absolute it must be said that it is essentially *Result*, that is to say, that it is only at the end when it is in truth; in this properly consists its nature, which is that of being effective reality, subject or development of itself"[484].

Hegel will attempt to break down the representation of God into its original elements and the moments that constitute it, and in doing so he will emphasise the power of the *understanding, an* understanding that must be understood not only as a human faculty but as the understanding inherent in things themselves and in God. And so he writes: "But it is an essential moment that this *separate,* this effective non-reality; it is, in fact, only because the concrete is divided and becomes non-effectively real that it is that which moves. The activity of dividing is the force and the work of the *understanding,* of the most astonishing and greatest power, or rather of the absolute power. The circle which rests in itself closed upon itself, and which, as substance maintains all its moments, is the immediate relation which does not arouse any surprise. But that the accidental as such separated from its outline, that which is bound and effectively real only in its connection with something else, obtains a dasein of its own and a distinct freedom, is through the prodigious power of the negative, of the energy of thought, of the pure I. Death, if that is what we want to call this unreality, is the most fearful thing, and to hold strongly that which is death demands the greatest strength... It is not this life that recoils in horror from death and preserves itself pure from destruction, but the life

---

[484] *La Phénoménologie de l'Esprit,* I, 18, Aubier, 1939, Paris.

that bears death, and maintains itself in death itself, which is the life of the spirit. The spirit conquers its truth only with the consideration of finding itself in absolute brokenness"[485].

With this idea of *separation* and *tearing apart*, Hegel conceives of a God who evolves and who, in this evolution, separates and tears himself apart. God could not be realised without this inner tearing apart. The creation of the world would act as an immolation that would complete God.

Creation would be an alienation and a development of God.

In Catholic theology the universe comes out of God's hands through efficiency, so that without any change in God, the creatures are made as *participations in* the divine being. The created universe increases the spectacle of existing things with new beings, but not with more being. In Hegel's philosophy, as in that of Plotinus and the Kabbalah, creation is not an increase of beings but a *division of* the one being, i.e. an alienation. Thus Hegel writes that "the alienation of substance, its becoming self-consciousness, expresses the passage into the opposite, the unconscious passage of necessity, or expresses that it is *itself* self-consciousness.

Inversely, the alienation of self-consciousness expresses that it is *in itself* the universal essence or - because the Self is the pure being-for-itself that remains itself in its opposite - that it is *for it* that substance is self-consciousness and, by the same token, spirit. One can therefore say that this spirit which has left the form of substance and enters into dasein under the figure of self-consciousness - if one wants to use relations taken from natural generation - that there is an *effective mother*, but a father remaining-in-itself; for the *effectiveness* or self-consciousness and the *in-itself*, like substance are its two moments by mutual alienation of which each becoming the other - the spirit passes into dasein as its unity"[486].

And Hegel describes creation in this way using the concept of alienation or negation or division: "1. The only eternal or abstract spirit makes for itself *an other*, or enters into dasein, and immediately into the *immediate dasein*. *It* thus *creates* a *world*. This "creating" is the mode of representation for the concept itself according to its absolute

---

[485] Ibid., I, 19.
[486] Ibid., II, 263.

movement, or for the process in which the absolutely enunciated Simple, or pure thought, is rather the negative and thus the opposite of itself or the other because the abstract; or to say the same thing in a still different form because what is put as *essence* is simple immediacy or *being;* but as immediacy or being has no *Yes,* and thus lacking interiority it is *passive* or is being *for-another.* This *being-for-another* is at the same time a *world;* the spirit in the determination of being-for-another is the calm subsistence of the moments previously included in pure thought, thus the dissolution of its simple universality and the dislocation of this universality in its own particularity..."[487].

"The world, however, is not only this spirit thrown and dispersed in the integrality of existence and its external order..."[488]. "In order for it to be in effect Yes and spirit it must first become for itself an *other,* just as the eternal essence presents itself as the movement of being equal to itself in its being other"[489]. That is to say that for Hegel creation is a dialectical moment of the genesis of the Absolute, God alienates himself, makes himself other; and in the movement by which he alienates himself and then finds himself overcoming alienation, God develops and realises himself. This is the theme of all the theosophies and gnosticisms that make creation an unfolding of God, a theogony.

Evil within the divine essence

In Hegelian thought, evil enters into the divine essence as a necessary element without which it would not develop. Being given," writes Hegel, "that this self-concentration of consciousness being there is immediately determined as the becoming unequal likewise, evil manifests itself as the first dasein of consciousness concentrated in itself, and, since the thoughts of good and evil are radically opposed to each other, and since this opposition is not yet resolved, then this consciousness is only evil"[490]. "It can be said that the first-born of light, concentrating on itself, is that which fell; but that, in its place, another son was immediately begotten. Such forms, that of the *fall* and that of the *son*, belong to the representation and not to the concept..."[491].

---

[487] Ibid., II, 276.
[488] Ibid., II, 276.
[489] Ibid., II, 276.
[490] Ibid., II, 277.
[491] Ibid., II, 278.

"The extraneity of the divine essence is put in its double mode. The Yes of the spirit and its simple thought are the two moments whose absolute unity is the spirit itself; its extraneation consists in the separation of these moments and in their unequal value in relation to each other. This inequality is therefore the double inequality, and thus two conjunctions take birth whose common moments are those already indicated. In one, *the divine essence* counts as the essential, but natural dasein counts as the inessential, which must be suppressed; in the other, on the contrary, it is *being-for-itself* that counts as the essential and the simple divine as the inessential. Its still empty medium is dasein in general, the simple community of the two moments"[492].

The passion of Christ is an alienation and reconciliation of the divine essence.

The Absolute is generated in creation and in incarnation. The Absolute is engendered by the tragedy of evil and of the uncanny that is unevenly produced in this process of unfolding that takes place throughout human history.

Passion is the culminating moment of the inequality that determines the process of reconciliation and resurrection. Thus Hegel writes: "This is represented as a voluntary operation, but the necessity of its alienation lies in the concept, according to which the being-in-itself, thus determined in opposition, has for this very reason no authentic subsistence. This term, therefore, for which is valid as essence not the being-for-itself, but the simple, is that which alienates itself, goes to death, and thereby reconciles the absolute essence with itself; in this movement, in fact, it presents itself as spirit; the abstract essence becomes foreign to itself; it has a natural dasein and a personal effectiveness; this being-other which is its own or its sensible presence is taken up by the second becoming-other, and is put as suppressed, as *universal*. Hence the divine essence has returned to itself in this sensible presence; the immediate being-there of effectiveness has ceased to be a strange or external being-there, because it has been suppressed, *universal;* this death is therefore its resurrection as spirit"[493]. And in a note Jean Hippolite comments on this passage by saying that "the death of Christ is itself reconciliation". The *presence* is no longer opposed to

---

[492] Ibid., II, 279.
[493] Ibid., II, 280.

the *essence,* through death it has been raised to universality. At the end of this movement, the spirit leaves the kingdom of the Son (the represented world) to enter the kingdom of the Holy Spirit (that of the universal Self-consciousness of the community). This negation by death is in effect the interiorisation of existence, its passage into self-consciousness as spirit[494].

The philosopher must relive this process of alienation and the return to himself of the divine substance in nature and history.

The philosopher, like the Gnostic, must become aware of the theogonic process. He must thus know where he comes from, who he is, where he is going. What is nature and what is history. This is the reason for the great value placed on science and absolute knowledge in Hegelian philosophy. Absolute knowledge is gnosis and "contains in itself this necessity to alienate from itself the form of the pure concept and contains the passage from concept to consciousness"[495].

Because the spirit that knows itself, precisely because it knows its concept, is the immediate equality with itself[496].

But "knowledge, Hegel adds, is not only knowledge of itself but also of the negative of itself, that is, of its limit. And to know its limit means to know how to sacrifice itself"[497]. The spirit knows what it knows and what it does not know in the double knowledge of nature and history. And "nature, the alienated spirit, in its own being-there is nothing other than this eternal alienation of its own *subsistence* and the movement it restores to the subject"[498]. And Hegel adds: "But the other side of the becoming of the spirit, *history,* is the becoming that is actualised in *knowledge,* or the *becoming mediatising itself,* the alienated spirit in time; but this alienation is the alienation of itself; the negative is the negative of itself"[499]. And Hegel explains why history or Science by history must develop slowly and thus writes: "This becoming presents a slow movement and a succession of spirits, a gallery of images of which each is adorned with all the richness of the spirit, and it moves so slowly because the Self must penetrate all this richness of its

---

[494] Ibid., II, 281, in note.
[495] Ibid., II, 311.
[496] Ibid., II, 311.
[497] Ibid., II, 311.
[498] Ibid., II, 311.
[499] Ibid., II, 311.

substance and assimilate it"[500]. This work of assimilation by history must be slow and patient because the philosopher has to assimilate the work of centuries in the evolution of spirits. "The *goal*, writes Hegel, absolute knowledge, or the spirit knowing itself as spirit, has as its way of access the recollection of spirits, as they are in themselves and as they fulfil the organisation of their spiritual realm"[501]. The reason for this slowness and patience is that "not only the substance of the individual, but the spirit of the world itself had the patience to traverse these forms in the whole expanse of time and to undertake the prodigious work of universal history in which it has embodied in each form, as far as it could bear it, the total content of itself..."[502].

We endorse the opinion of Claude Tresmontant who summarises the Hegelian gnosis by saying that "the idea of an alienation of the divine substance is an idea found in several Gnostic systems: in Manichaeism and in Jewish gnosis, the Cabala. Contrary to Manichaeism, Hegel, like Spinoza, does not feel the need to have recourse to two uncreated heterogeneous principles. God is exiled, alienated, but not in an enemy and uncreated matter which would be hostile to him. Nature is God who would have made himself alien to himself. No there is in Hegelianism, a pre-existent matter in which the Absolute would have been exiled, alienated"[503].

---

[500] Ibid., II, 311.
[501] Ibid., II, 312.
[502] Ibid., I, 27.
[503] Claude Tresmontant, *La métaphysique du christianisme*, p. 743.

CHAPTER X

MODERN PHILOSOPHY ON THE WAY TO THE NEGATION OF GOD AND THE DIVINISATION OF MAN

We have previously noted that the heart of all gnosis is ultimately to make all reality, divine and human, good and evil, truth and error, yes and no, nature and grace, the Church and the World, *a single reality, a single dimension of reality*. Here, too, is the heart of the Kabbalah. The *Ein Sof*, which is otherwise confused with nothingness, with the indeterminate, evolves and by more or less insensible degrees becomes *the more of things* - the less becomes the more - and so the universe is made; *nature naturata* comes out of *natura naturans*.

In the Kabbalah and the Gnostic systems there seem to be two processes: first, the one, which takes place in God himself, in the Ein-Sof, in the Pleroma. A process of Ein - nothingness - becoming Ein-Sof - the indeterminate infinite, the darkness, the Abyss, Boehme's Ungrund - and then this Ein-Sof becoming Ein Sof Aur, into light, and into an attributed and personal God who develops into the Sephiroth - the Pleroma. And the process of this God - *natura naturans* - which then unfolds throughout the universe until it reaches matter and the demonic world - the world of the Qulipoth - the *natura naturata*. But in this single or double process there is a *single emanating and emanated reality*, divine and human, spiritual and material.

This is why every creature, and man in particular, is divine in the depths of his being.

It is clear that the duplicity of the process or triplicity of processes seems to dominate. For first there is a path from nothingness to being, from darkness to light, and then from light to darkness, and finally, in the return, from darkness back to light, to the Pleroma. *But there is always only one reality that evolves.*

God and the world are therefore composed of a single reality; God is not *transcendent* to the world, but immanent. By rejecting *creation*, the world, far from coming from absolute nothingness, comes from the substance of God. Therefore, creation, far from being creation, is generation, and God comes out of God and is constituted in God. Now, a God who constitutes the world, and who, before constituting it, comes himself out of nothingness, is perfectly useless. Therefore, in the total immanence of God in the world, God is useless and atheism prevails. On the contrary, atheism implies the total immanence of God in the world and the divinisation of man, which, as we have seen, is also an idea openly expressed in the Kabbalah and in all the Gnostic systems. Hence, to study the atheism of modern philosophy is to study the immanence of God in man and, by the same token, the divinisation of man.

Studying the principle of immanence is therefore the same as studying the atheism of modern philosophy and the divinisation of the creature.

1. *The principle of immanence*

The principle of immanence is a typically modern acquisition. "Whereas until the Renaissance the claims of atheism (and the related claims of monism, pantheism, naturalism...) were the consequence of a "reduction" or lowering of man to the common ontological denominator of matter, and man's being was reduced to one or another form of element or principle of nature, modern thought - and its atheism - is constituted precisely by the claim of man's originality vis-à-vis nature".

That is to say that before the Renaissance those who denied the transcendence of man over matter and nature were atheists, while after the Renaissance, on the contrary, those who affirm this transcendence are atheists. "The claim is expressed by the new principle of immanence, that is, of the elevation of man's being to the *cogito*, that is, of the reduction of the acting of being to the acting of the *cogito*...

Thus, truth is not, as for classical naturalistic atheism, a simple turning from man to nature, but springs from the possibility of man, which presents itself as freedom of being. In other words, in modern atheism there is a divinisation of man, whereas in the old atheism there was a lowering and materialisation of man. Fabro can therefore add that this positivity of the new atheism (be it Marxist or existentialist or neopositivist or pragmatist...) is expressed in the ambitious epithet of "humanism" that the atheists of the modern era claim especially since Feuerbach[504].

2. The principle of immanence implies the negation of the principle of contradiction and atheism

"The thesis of the implication of atheism in the principle of immanence is certainly not new: it is important to retain firmly the profound affinity which circulates in the most opposed systems of modern thought and which is the reason for the combat between them. Rationalism and empiricism, deism, sensism, criticism, idealism, phenomenism, positivism... with the other minor systems that can be indicated, constitute the stages of the authentication of the *cogito*. It is true that in the atheistic resolution of the *cogito*, materialism seems to express an obvious misunderstanding and a patent contradiction, and for this reason, the rationalist and idealist wing always refuted as unworthy the qualification of atheism. But after the work of Nietzsche, Feuerbach and Sartre, such disdain has become rarer and rarer, and one can say that today it has completely disappeared among philosophers: it must be admitted that this constitutes a remarkable contribution of honesty and clarity in the speculative field[505].

To understand the principle of immanence and its implications we must start from the fact that "modern philosophy has undoubtedly constituted the most audacious attempt of the human spirit, which is the self-foundation and formation of thought in itself. Thought, the *cogito*, has set itself up as the first and only principle, from which all reality must emerge. But human thought is empty. It has to be nourished by the being and reality that comes to it from outside. But thought, once it has been fed with reality from outside, can imagine this reality in many different ways and in infinite combinations. It can create these combinations, *entities of reason*, which may or may not respect the principle of contradiction. The idea does not necessarily presuppose being. St. Thomas has lucidly seen this against St. Anselm. The idea of God implies the existence of God, St. Anselm taught. For "knowing what this term *God* means, it is understood in the act that God exists because

---

[504] Cornelio Fabro, *Introduzione all'atheismo moderno*, Editrice Studium, Rome, 1964, p. 33.
[505] Ibid., p. 79.

by this name we express the greatest of all that can be conceived, and greater will be that which exists in the understanding and in reality than that which exists in the understanding". But St Thomas replies: "Even supposing that all understand by the term *God* what is intended, it does not follow that they understand that what is designated by that name exists in reality, but only in the concept of the understanding" *(Summa,* I, 2, 1, ad 2).

That is to say that from the idea, from the pure idea, one cannot pass to being. Just because one has the idea of a thing, it does not follow that this thing exists. It is a principle of common sense which becomes evident to people when they reflect and realise that it is not because they dream of having a fortune that they actually have it. Man's idea, the idea alone, creates nothing and produces nothing.

To arrive at the reality of God we must start from another reality, the reality of the existence of the world. If the world is not capable of giving itself existence, there must be a God who brings that existence out of nothingness.

But modern thought erects thought, the *cogito*, as a creative source. Therefore, God is not necessary. Thought is enough to create the world. If the reality of the world is not independent of and prior to thought, neither is it necessary to seek an explanation of this worldly reality and of thought. Consequently, God does not exist. The principle of immanence implies atheism.

Strictly speaking, it can also be said to imply the assimilation of being and nothingness, that is, the assimilation of contradictories, or of being and non-being. For human intelligence as such can, although not with logical coherence, conceive of both terms as compatible, just as the notion of a square circle can be made.

For intelligence depends on being, as St. Thomas teaches, but properly applied. It can be determined by an *entity of reason* as by a real being, that is to say, it can be deceived or deluded. If the intelligence can take as reality what is not reality and as non-reality what is in truth reality, it can with all the more reason ignore Being par excellence or deny it.

The intellectual affirmation of the existence of God is necessarily connected with the intellectual knowledge of the first principles of intelligence, because it is by virtue of these first principles, and only by virtue of them, that man is intellectually constrained to admit the existence of God. Since man has no intuition of being in common, let alone of Being in itself, his knowledge of God is necessarily mediated and by way of resolution in the first principles.

Hence the whole of modern philosophy, which is governed by the principle of immanence, is a distorted philosophy, *contra naturam*, since it fails in the elementary task of making the creature and the Creator known to us.

3. Descartes introduces the principle of immanence as the first principle of philosophy

"The paradox of modern thought, writes Faber[506], in its ascendant phase and in the period of greatest splendour from Descartes to Hegel, is, on the one hand, the explicit intention of its greatest representatives to make the Absolute, in the demonstrations of the existence of God and his attributes, the principle and centre of philosophising, and, on the other hand, the ever more repeated accusation of atheism on the part of its enemies". And rightly so. For this affirmation of the Absolute was of an abstract reality and not that of a personal God, endowed with intelligence and freedom. Above all, God was not a Creator God, who would have fixed the personal destiny of the intelligent creature. Hence the significance of the denunciation by G.

Hardouin in *Atheists Unmasked*[507] : "The central argument or act of accusation is quickly presented in the brief *Praefatio*: What they present as God is not the God of the believers, but only the Being, the Being of every Being, the essence of all essence, the universal Truth, the universal Goodness, the intelligible Form of all truth... diverse attributes which some of those authors (he alludes especially to Descartes) have thought to gather together in a single term, that of Infinity, *Ens infinite perfectum*. In fact, continues our author, if God were reduced only to such an infinite, atheism would not be possible; everyone, whether in the present or in the past, would have admitted God, they would never have been atheists, and it would be quite useless and out of place to write against atheism".

Hardouin shows that Descartes' God is precisely the *Ens*, the *Ens illimitatum, Ens, Res, Perfectio in genere: Ens propterea ínfinitum,*

---

[506] Ibid., p. 99.
[507] Ibid., footnote, p. 99.

cujus nullum est nomen determinatum; unde et innominabilis a nonnullis appellatur: id fere quod Galli dicunt chose. Thus this philosophy is rightly called, among Catholics, the philosophy of atheists[508].

And attacking Descartes' arguments, Hardouin demonstrates that the Idea of God, like that of infinite being that Descartes celebrates, says nothing more than the idea of *"ens in genere, verum in genere..."*, Entity in general, truth in general... And he concludes: "The metaphysical God is nothing but the infinitised world and the moral God is the infinitised man"[509].

Maurice Blondel has denounced the profound ramifications of the corrosion produced by the *cogito* in all of life: "The personal faith of a Descartes did not prevent Cartesianism from preparing the modern schism of metaphysical speculation and religious meditation. It is not normal for the philosopher to specialise his research (which, unlike the positive sciences, must deal with the whole man and the whole being) to the point of maintaining, even if he is a believer, a partly double compatibility of conscience and to establish watertight partitions where the need for unity, universality and coherence is the higher law of all spiritual life. Conversely, Leibniz's effort to realise and imply nature in grace is both the effect and the cause of a no less serious error. For by showing in the supernatural a simple expansion of deep nature, he prepares to the letter and gives rise to the spirit of the modernist illusion". And Blondel had already warned[510] : "We have already indicated how Descartes has inverted the meaning of philosophy. Not only by inverting the first impulse of the quest and by folding it back on the *cogito,* while the first movement of the mind *primus motus mentis* goes to truth, to being, to God. Another inversion, which undoubtedly results secretly from the preceding one, has prepared, if not the regression, at least the deviation or denaturalisation of the civilising ideal. How is this? Descartes had the firm intention of founding a science and a philosophy intimately associated to ensure their autonomy, their frank and indefinite development, their realm

---

[508] *Hardouin shows that Descartes' God is precisely the* Entity, *the* unlimited Entity, Entity, Thing, Perfection in general: Entity by the same infinite, of which there is no determinate name; whence the unnameable is called by some: almost what the French call thing.
[509] Ibid., p. 177.
[510] Maurice Blondel, *L'Être et les êtres*, 135.

limited, no doubt, to this world and to the human order, but, independently, and basing himself in this domain: *mundus nobis traditur*[511]. Metaphysical, it is above all to establish the certainty of our dominion over nature, to remove, by pacifying them, the restlessness of souls, to offer a definitively assured field for the happy future of an indefinitely increasing culture, almost to the point of prolonging without assignable limits the duration of our earthly existence (...) one can now understand the immense apostasy of a conception which, even when it uses God, uses him, so to speak, against him, takes him literally so that he leaves us to ourselves, dispenses as much as possible with him and is content to organise the world and humanity for our enjoyment, our domination, our self-loathing".

4. Spinoza introduces metaphysical immanence

The second step, writes Fabro[512], and more decisive than the Cartesian one, of modern thought towards atheism is undoubtedly that of Spinoza (1632-1677): but the nature of his contribution and in particular of the inner dynamism of his principles towards the elimination of the theological principle from philosophy is quite evident and at the same time more complex and controversial... It can be said that while the Cartesian *cogito* has introduced gnoseological immanence and, with it, exigential atheism, Spinoza has conceived - from the pantheistic and panentheistic background of Greek, medieval, Hebraic and Renaissance philosophy - metaphysical immanence...

And if Descartes thinks of making the beginning with the act of consciousness... Spinoza goes further and tries to make the beginning with the content "of the principle of belonging" (of the parts in the Whole, of the finite in the infinite, of the world in God).

Spinoza's God, whose freedom is identified with necessity[513], is also identified with nature. He is a blind, mute and paralytic God. "We thus see that men have been accustomed to call natural things perfect or imperfect, more from a prejudice than from a true knowledge of them. We have shown, in the Appendix to the first part, that nature does not work for an end; and that eternal and infinite Being which we call God

---

[511] A world is given to us.
[512] Ibid., p. 127.
[513] *Epistle XLIII*, Ed. Gebbardt, t. IV, p. 211, cit. Faber, ibid. p. 133.

or nature works by the same necessity which brings the same work into existence[514]. The reason or cause by which God, or Nature, works and by which it exists is the same. And just as He does not exist for any cause, so He does not work for the cause of the end, and just as there is no beginning or end to the work of existing, so there is no beginning or end to the work"[515].

Spinoza's God is identified with his famous *natura naturans* and this with *natura naturata*.

God is identified with the world of created things. Just as everything is God, God is nowhere to be found.

It has been said that, by identifying nature with God, Spinoza has introduced into it the expansion of the infinite, characteristic of the baroque age; an infinity of the formless that reduces the finite as such to nothing, according to the principle *omnis determinatio est negatio*, which will later be the key to Hegelian philosophy[516]. Since the creature is divine, man is also divine, who is united to the divinity. Hence the famous *"intellectual love of the mind for God is the very love of God, by which God loves himself, not in so far as it is infinite, but in so far as by the very essence of the human soul, considered under the species of eternity, it can unfold; that is, the intellectual love of the soul for God is part of the infinite love by which God loves himself"*. The immanence of God in man is changed into the immanence of man in God, according to which man's true thought is identified with God's thought and God's thought acts only in man's thought. And thus man is acted as something divine, as the only divine.

5. The Metaphysical and Dynamic Immanence of German Idealism

German idealism must be regarded as the most complete form of modern thought, as the highest theoretical and systematic expression of the principle of immanence and synthesis of the Spinozist metaphysics and the Kantian *ich denke*, i.e. of the monistic and naturalistic principle of being and of the new conception of the productivity of

---

[514] Prop. 16, p. I, Fabro, ibid. p. 137.
[515] Ethicae, P. IV, *Proefatio*, t. 11, p. 206, quoted Faber, ibid. p. 138.
[516] Fabro, ibid. p. 149.

consciousness[517]. A synthesis of elements that today may seem absurd and strange, but which in reality show a fascination that has few comparable points in the history of thought and which belongs from now on to the structure of western consciousness[518].

> "It is that in idealism the most vital aspirations and instances of modern thought - such as the essential belonging of truth to consciousness, the aspiration to gather into a dynamic unity nature and man as well as nature and the absolute, the purpose of penetrating and gathering the One and the whole in the multiple and in the diverse - the nostalgia to gather the eternal in time and to conjugate itself to the first source of life, and finally the creative synthesis of consciousness as a whole extended to absorb in the speculative act the elevation to the first source of life, the nostalgia to gather the eternal in time and to conjugate itself to the first source of life and finally the creative synthesis of the whole consciousness extended to absorb in the speculative act the elevation of the historical religion - had shone the hope to gather at last the enigma of freedom and to put in the hands of man, with the fulfilled sense of history, the solution of the mystery of existence"[519].

Spinoza had reduced his God to nature, to a rigid and immobile block, while idealism had conceived nature as creating as such, pure creation without any object, pure and absolute productivity. But productivity and creation is only of singular objects. And for this philosophy, on the other hand, there can only be a single, eternal and immutable being, that is, the Being of absolute productivity. German idealism had realised a dynamic thorniness: whereas Fichte had made moral consciousness absolute, Schelling had conferred this dignity on "nature", proclaiming it the "... absolute productivity, the sacred creative force of the world which generates and produces by the activity of itself all things, the one true God, the Living"[520].

But in reality in the conception of God-Nature it is not possible without absurdity to identify being and nothingness in the sense of the identity of the Unconditioned with the conditioned, of necessity with reason, of reason with the absurd, of good with evil... that is to say that this

---

[517] Ibid., p. 461.
[518] Fabro, ibid. p. 461.
[519] Ibid., p. 461.
[520] Quoted by Jacobi, *Von den göttlichen Dingen...*, S. W. Bd., III, 342, in Fabro, ibid. p. 524.

philosophy destroys what is at the root of man's dignity, the freedom of reason, and man would have no other superiority over the brute than that of error and lies"[521].

Jacobi showed that "while theism refers the world and all finite beings to the Absolute as first Cause, naturalism resolves the whole reality of the world into the One-all... as infinite foundation and abyss. It is a very symptomatic inversion and substitution to remove the mask from the true face of the new philosophy in its pantheistic variations".

Jacobi repeats for the same reason to Schelling, against transcendental materialism, what he had opposed to Fichte against his transcendental moralism: "Reason without personality is an absurdity, the same absurdity of that *fundamental matter* or of the *original foundation,* which is all and not one, that is, one and none, the perfection of the imperfect, the absolutely indeterminate, and is called God by those who do not want to know the true God, but who still avoid denying it on their lips"[522]. To the naturalists' formula *without the world, there is no God,* Jacobi opposes the formula *without God there is no world.*

Hegel, in his *History of Philosophy*[523], clearly points out that "the substance of the Spinozist philosophy is only a rigid substance, it is not yet the spirit, it is not one in itself. And God is not the Spirit here either, because he is not the triune and one God. The Spinozist substance retains its rigidity, its petrification, without the sources of a Boehme, for the determinations of the understanding are not the source spirits of Boehme, which intertwine and disappear into each other.

Hence Hegel censures Spinozism because it lacks the dynamic of the "negative". Spinozist substance, Hegel writes [524], is conceived as "wholly in the abstract, but not in its vivacity". Lacking the negative - Boehme's "separator" - it lacks movement, becoming, fire, self-consciousness[525].

---

[521] Jacobi, ibid., Fabro, ibid. p. 524.
[522] Ibid., Fabro, ibid. p. 525.
[523] Fondo de Cultura Económica, III, p. 309.
[524] Ibid., p. 310.
[525] Ibid., p. 310.

6. The drama of atheistic humanism

Henri de Lubac published a book with this title[526], in which he gave an account of the currents of atheism in the process of immanence initiated by Descartes and consummated in German idealism. The real author of the atheistic current in the 19th century is Hegel, who for the first time speaks of the *death of God*[527].

Feuerbach drew consequences from Hegel's dialectic of consciousness and demolished this dialectic. He was the great link between Hegel and the revolutionary current of Marx[528].

Hegel died in 1831 and almost immediately the great debate on the problem of God, which divided the Hegelian Left from the Hegelian Right, began. "To explain the mechanism of this theogony, Feuerbach resorts to the Hegelian concept of *alienation*. But whereas Hegel applied it to the Absolute Spirit, Feuerbach, reversing the relation of the "idea" to the "real", applies it to flesh-and-blood man[529].

Alienation, according to him, consists in the fact that man finds himself dispossessed of something that belongs to him by essence for the sake of an illusory reality. Divinity belongs to man, and here it is that man, knowing that he is deprived of it, projects it onto an external being, onto a fantastic subject, and invents the idea of God. By the same act he strips the world of what it contains and transfers it to God. The poor man believes in a rich God... and affirms in God what he denies in himself"[530].

For Feuerbach then "the essence of man is the supreme being... If the divinity of nature is the basis of all religions, including Christianity, the divinity of man is the ultimate goal... The turning point of history will be the moment when man will become aware that only man's God is man himself. *Homo homini Deus*".

Feuerbach had wanted to give the title of *The Essence of Christianity*, the first of his works, the motto of his essential idea: *Gnothi seavton*,

---

[526] *Le drame de l'humanisme athée*, Edt. Spes, Paris, 1945, 3rd ed.
[527] *La phénoménologie de l'Esprit*, Aubier, Paris, 1951, I, p. 287.
[528] *See my book*, The Destructive Power of the Communist Dialectic.
[529] Feuerbach, *L'essence du christianisme*, traduit de l'allemand par Jean-Pierre Osier, François Maspero, Paris, 1968.
[530] Ibid.

know thyself. Man was the true divinity. Gnosis was perfectly fulfilled and consummated in Feuerbach's sensist materialism.

In his time, Feuerbach produced a real revolution. Engels has spoken of the extraordinary impression of liberation that many of the young people of his generation would experience, in November 1841, on reading the *Essence of Christianity*. "The enthusiasm was general... We all immediately became Feuerbachians"[531]. But the great disciple and admirer of Feuerbach was Karl Marx, who has left his admiration stamped on *The Holy Family*, and writes thus:

"The absolute critique, which has never left the cage of the Hegelian conception, rages here within the bars of its prison walls... But who has discovered the mystery of the system? Who has destroyed the dialectic of concepts, the war of the gods, the only thing the philosophers knew? Feuerbach, who has put, not the significance of man - as if man could have any other significance than that of man - but "man" in place of the old trinket, even of "infinite self-consciousness"?

Feuerbach and only *Feuerbach*

But the God of Karl Marx was not to be the individual man of flesh and blood, but the dispossessed social class, the proletarians, who, in a death struggle, were to strip the bourgeois class of the power of money and government and erect the perfect and divine society of mankind. Marx's communism would present itself as the true concrete realisation of humanism and the divinity of man. There the human problem would find a complete solution.

> "This communism, as a fully developed naturalism, is equal to naturalism and is the *genuine* solution of the conflict between man and nature, and between man and man - the true solution of the struggle between existence and essence, between objectification and one's own consistency, between freedom and necessity, between the individual and the species. Communism is the solution of the riddle of history and the knowledge of having achieved this solution"[532].

---

[531] Engels, *Ludwig Feuerbach*, Carthago Ed.
[532] Marx, *Economic and philosophic manuscripts 1844*, Foreign Languages Publishing House, Moscow, p. 162.

"And the religion of the workers, Marx wrote, is godless because it seeks to restore man's divinity"[533].

7. Nietzsche and the Death of God

Nietzsche, in a way, was impressed by Feuerbach. Religion would be the result of a psychological split. God would be nothing but the mirror of man[534]. And religion would be nothing but a case of alteration of the human personality. And in Christianity this process of debasement would reach an extreme degree. The "death of God" had had a correct interpretation in traditional theology, both Catholic and Protestant. But with Hegel it had begun to take on a different accent. In Nietzsche it already translates an option. "Now," says Nietzsche, "our taste decides against Christianity and not the arguments". It is an act and deed as clear-cut and brutal as that of an assassin. The death of God is not only for him a terrible fact, but is willed. If God is dead, "we have killed him. We are the murderers of God"[535]. Few pages have been written as tremendous and as pathetic as those in which Nietzsche describes the announcement of the *death of God*. In the *Gaiety of Science* the madman appears with his unusual announcement of the death of God.

The madman

> "Perhaps you have heard of the madman who, one sunny morning, lit a lantern and ran into the market place shouting, 'I seek God! I seek God! There were many people there who did not believe in God, and it gave them great joy to hear the madman. What is it, is he lost? said one. Is he lost like a child? said another. Is he hiding? Is he afraid of us? Is he perhaps on a sea voyage? Has he emigrated? said the people, shouting and laughing uproariously. The madman stood in their midst and glared at them. Where has God gone? he shouted. Now I'm going to tell! We killed him, you and I! We are all murderers! But how did we do it? How were we able to drink in the sea? Who bit the sponge that allowed us to wipe out the whole horizon? What did we do to separate the earth from its sun? Where is it going now? Where are we going? "Away from all the suns, are we not going on and on? Is there still an above and a below? Are we not wandering, as if we were wandering in the infinite nothingness? Is not empty space still above

---

[533] Letter to Hardmann.
[534] Henri de Lubac, ibid. p. 41.
[535] Ibid., p. 47.

our heads? Is it not getting colder? Is it not true that the night is advancing steadily, getting darker and darker? Perhaps we will have to light lanterns in the middle of the day.

Do we not hear the noise of all the gravediggers who are burying God? does not our nostrils detect the divine putrefaction? for the gods themselves are subject to it. For the gods themselves are subject to it. God is dead! God is still dead! And we have killed him! How shall we, the most abject of murderers, console ourselves? The holiest and highest thing the world has ever had, has shed every drop of blood under our knife. Who shall wipe away the stain of that blood from us? In what water shall we wash?

What ages, what sacred fires will we have to invent for ourselves? Should we not become God just to make ourselves worthy of Him? Nothing of greater proportions has ever happened, and in relation to it all those who are born after us will belong to a higher history than any of the previous ones!

"On arriving here, the madman was silent and looked again at his listeners; they too were silent and looked at him with surprise. At last he threw down his lantern, so that it broke and ceased to shine. "I am too early," he then said, "I have not come at the right time.

This prodigious event is still on its way; it has not yet reached the ears of men. Lightning and thunder, starlight and exploits take time to be seen and heard. This action, for the time being, is further from them than the farthest star - and yet it is they who have done it! It is said that the madman then made his way to several churches that same day and that inside them he intoned the *Requiem aeternam Deo*.

When invited to come out and give an explanation, he always replied: "What else can these churches be now but tombs and mausoleums dedicated to God?

8. *The Principle of Immanence in Modern Politics*

The principle of immanence, which places the Creator in man himself and thus divinises man, while at the same time secularising and humanising God, was to give a secularised and humanised context to a whole Gnostic and cabalistic movement that had been at work in the West, and of which we have already given an account in our discussion of John Scotus Eriugena and Joachim of Fiore. Eric Voegelin, one of today's most perceptive thinkers on politics, in his valuable book *"The New Science of Politics"*, is particularly concerned with this movement.

Eric Voegelin starts from Augustine's *Civitas Dei*, which had dedivinised the pagan world and created the healthy foundations of Christianity, which were maintained for a thousand years in Western society, only to be altered by the intrusion of Gnostic and cabalistic elements that once again redivinised society, albeit in a secularised context.

Eric Voegelin's approach

The clash between the various types of truth in the Roman Empire ended with the victory of Christianity. The desacralisation of the temporal sphere of power was the inevitable result of it. We have already anticipated that the specifically modern problems of representation would have to do with a redivinisation of man and society. These two terms especially need further definition, since the concept of modernity, and with it, the periodisation of history, depends on the meaning given to the redivinisation[536]. Thus, desacralisation is to be understood as the historical process in which the culture of polytheism died of atrophy and man's existence in society was reordered, through the experience of man's destiny and through the world-transcending grace of God, towards eternal life in beatific vision... modern redivinisation has rather its origin in Christianity itself and derives from components that were eliminated as heretical by the universal Church. The nature of this internal tension in Christianity needs to be more precisely defined[537].

In the life of the Church there were, in the early centuries, some cabalistic ferments which speculated *on a new speculation and apocalypse within history*. But this was firmly rejected by the Fathers and Doctors and definitely in St. Augustine's *Civitas Dei*. He clearly abandoned the belief in the millennium as a fable and boldly declared that the reign of the thousand years will be the reign of Christ in His Church in the present age which was to continue until the final judgment and the advent of the eternal kingdom in the hereafter[538].

The Augustinian conception of the Church, without substantial change, remained effective until the end of the Middle Ages. The revolutionary

---

[536] Eric Voegelin, *The New Science of Politics*, The University of Chicago Press, 1952, p. 107, p. 168.
[537] Ibid. p. 107; English ed. p. 168.
[538] *Civitas Dei*, 7, 8 and 9.

expectation of the Second Coming, which was to transfigure the structure of history on earth, was discarded as "ridiculous"... The one Christian society remained articulated in the spiritual and temporal orders. In its temporal articulation it accepted the "conditio humana" without kyletic fantasies, but at the same time it sublimated natural existence with the representation of its spiritual destiny by means of the Church..."[539]. The Church as a historically concrete representation of man's spiritual destiny found its parallel in the Roman Empire as a historically concrete representation of human temporality[540].

> "Christian society in the West was thus articulated in the spiritual and temporal orders, with the Pope and the Emperor as its supreme representatives in both the existential and the transcendental sense. From this society, with its established system of symbols, arose the specifically modern problems of representation with the new emergence of the eschatology of the Kingdom... Joachim of Fiore, whose conception we have already studied[541], breaks with the Augustinian conception of history and introduces a new kingdom of the Spirit within history itself towards which all historical becoming converges".

> "As variations of this symbol are recognisable the humanistic and encyclopaedic periodisation of history into ancient, medieval and modern; the theories of Turgot and Comte on the succession of theological, metaphysical and scientific phases; Hegel's dialectic on the three stages of freedom and self-reflexive fullness; the Marxist dialectic with its three phases of primitive communism, class society and final communism, and finally, the national-socialist symbol of the Third Reich..."[542]

> "The second symbol is that of the leader. It became an immediate reality in the spiritual movement of the Franciscans, who saw in St. Francis the fulfilment of Joachim's prophecy.

> Dante's speculations on the "Doge" of the new spiritual age also reinforced its effectiveness. It is then identifiable in the paraclectic figures, the "homines espirituales" and "homines novi" of the late Middle Ages, the Renaissance and the Reformation; it can be

---

[539] Voegelin, ibid. p. 109; English ed. p. 171.
[540] Ibid. p. 110; English ed. p. 172.
[541] See Chapter V of this work.
[542] Ibid. p. 111; English ed. p. 175.

discerned as one of the components of the Machiavellian "prince"; in the period of secularisation it emerges again in the supermen of Condorcet, Comte and Marx, until it comes to dominate the contemporary scene with the paraclectic leaders of the new kingdoms"[543].

The third symbol is that of the prophet of the new age... Thus the Gnostic prophet or, in the later stages of secularisation, the Gnostic intellectual is an element of modern civilisation[544].

The fourth symbol is the brotherhood that is realised in history with the descent of the Holy Spirit. Joachim conceived of the new age as a brotherhood of monks; the Puritans as churches of saints; and Marxist mysticism as a reign of freedom without the compulsion of the state.

The structure of history is changed. "The movement of history does not take place in a cycle, as Plato and Aristotle had it, but acquires direction and destiny. In the elaboration of his theoretical vision, Augustine distinguished between the deep sphere of history in which empires rose and fell and a sacred history culminating in the appearance of Christ and the establishment of the Church. Furthermore, he situated sacred history in a transcendental history of the *Civitas Dei* that included the events of the gospel sphere and those of the transcendental eternal Sabbath. Only transcendental history, including the pilgrimage of the Church, had a direction towards an eschatological fulfilment. Profane history, on the other hand, had no such direction; it was a waiting for the end; its present mode of being was *saeculorum senescens*, an age growing old.

With Joachimistic speculation, the historical process becomes immanent and brings forth from its very entrails a new age of the Spirit. "The idea of an immanent radical fulfilment grew more rapidly in a long process which may be called "from humanism to Enlightenment"; only in the eighteenth century, with the idea of progress, did it grow in significance in history and become a completely intramundane phenomenon, without transcendental irruptions. This second phase of immanentization can be called "secularization""[545].

---

[543] Ibid. p. 112; English ed. p. 175.
[544] Ibid. p. 112; English ed. p. 176.
[545] Ibid. p. 119; English ed. p. 186.

The immanentization of a Christian objective is secularised because it occurs in the context of the denial of God that we have studied earlier in this chapter. Eric Voegelin warns that in this immanenticised history there is a *historical eidos* that directs the march of history and the result is a *progressive interpretation* of history, which can take the form of a utopia, as in the case of St Thomas More, or of the various forms of idealism that dream of the abolition of war and the unequal distribution of property, fear and necessity, or can ultimately be dressed up in a total revolutionary transfiguration of man as in Marxism[546].

Eric Voegelin shows how this immanentization of a *Christian eschaton* - an ideal state of perfection, realised within history, even if secularised - is opposed to Christian faith, which is an intellectual assent to the word of God and rests instead on a "false experience, on an illumination or gnosis, which must be historically linked with the ancient Gnostic or cabalistic systems". "The Gnostic experience," writes Voegelin, "offers a firm hold and is an expansion of the soul to the point where God is drawn into human existence. This experience can engage the human faculties, and hence, indeed, it is possible to distinguish various kinds of gnostic faculties according to the faculty which predominates in the operation of reaching God. Gnosis can be primarily intellectual and take the form of a speculative penetration of the mystery of creation and existence, as, for example, in the speculative gnosis of Hegel and Schelling. It can be primarily emotional and take the form of an indwelling of the divine substance in the human soul, as for example in the leaders of the paraclete sects. Or it can be primarily volitional and take the form of an activist redemption of man and society, as for example in revolutionary activists like Comte, Marx or Hitler"[547].

And here Voegelin adds a very important caveat: "These Gnostic experiences, in the breadth of their variety, are at the heart of the *redivinisation of society*[548] because the people who fall into these experiences divinise themselves by increasingly replacing faith in the Christian sense with passive modes of participation in divinity[549].

The Gnostic experiences that nourish man today, secularised experiences, are humanism, the enlightenment of the Age of

---

[546] Ibid. p. 121; English ed. p. 189.
[547] Ibid. p. 124; English ed. p. 194.
[548] Underlined by me, J.M.
[549] Ibid. p. 124; English ed. p. 194.

Enlightenment, progressivism, liberalism, positivism and Marxism. And finally, with its prodigious advance since the 17th century, science may become, one is inclined to say inevitably, the symbolic vehicle of Gnostic truth.

In the Gnostic speculation of scientism this particular variant reaches its extreme point when the positivistic perfection of science replaces the age of Christ with the age of Comte. Scientism has remained one of the strongest Gnostic movements in Western society; and the immanentist pride in science is so strong that even the specialised sciences have reached a distinguished sediment in the salvation variants of physics, economics, sociology, biology and psychology[550].

9. The Modern Revolution

With the immanentization of the *Christian eschaton* within the mundane course of history - which is typically Gnostic or Kabbalistic, as we have noted - society becomes changeable and revolutionary. Eric Voegelin studies at length the case of the Puritans, who were undoubtedly the first Gnostic revolutionaries to achieve political domination of a nation. With them, the Revolution triumphs in Western society, rejecting the supernatural destiny of man secured by the Catholic Church and giving rise first to a naturalistic expansion of man, and then to a liberal one which will be followed later by the communist expansion[551].

The British Revolution is the first revolution of a country as a whole to enter the revolutionary society of modernity[552]. This is why Isaac Disraeli, father of Benjamin, Earl Beaconsfield, begins the life of Charles I published in 1851 with these words: "It was predestined that England should be the first of a series of revolutions which is not yet completed".

The English revolution was made by the Puritans, who were "revolutionary Gnostics, engaged in the struggle for existential

---

[550] Ibid. p. 127; English ed. p. 199.
[551] See my book, *El comunismo en la Revolución anticristiana*, Theoria, Buenos Aires, 1964.
[552] A. H. M. Ramsay, *The nameless war*, Britons Publishing Comp., London, 1962, Translated and published by Omnia Veritas Ltd, *The nameless war - Jewish power against the nations*, www.omnia-veritas.com.

representation that resulted in the overthrow of the English social order, the control of the universities by the Puritans and the replacement of common law by scriptural law. Hooker[553] understood perfectly well what is not understood today about Gnostic propaganda being political action and not the search for truth in the theoretical sense. With unerring sensitivity he diagnosed the nihilistic component of Gnosticism in the puritanical belief that its discipline, being the absolute commandment of Almighty God, was to be received as from on high; herein lay the greatest danger". In the political culture of the time it was abundantly clear that the government, not the subjects, represented the order of society.

The Gnostic revolution of the Puritans stemmed in turn from the systematic formulation by Calvin in his *Institutions*, which had created a Gnostic Koran[554].

This first great revolution was to be followed by others, the French, the Russian and the world revolutions, all of them operated with the same structure and configuration, with the same methods and by the same powers. In this respect, the works of Nesta H. Webster, *World Revolution, The plot against civilization and Secret Societies and subversive movements*[555] are definitive in demonstrating that the process is affected by a total dependence on a central focus to be located mainly in the Cabal. The World Revolution would proceed from this focus and would have as its fundamental aim the destruction of the power of the Roman Catholic Church and its civilising work, i.e. Christian civilisation. This cabalistic attempt would have been perpetrated through the Gnostic sects such as the Albigensians, the Templars, occultism, and in the Middle Ages and the Modern Age through the innumerable secret societies which, in their turn, are the driving force behind the communist and anarchist movements. The Judeo-Masonic-Communist danger would be nothing but the practical and political execution of the Kabbalah.

---

[553] Hooker, Richard, *Works*, ed. Keble, (7 Oxford 1888), quoted by Voegelin, ibid. p. 137; English ed. p. 213.
[554] Voegelin, ibid. p. 139; English ed. p. 215.
[555] Britons Publishing Comp., 1964.

For knowledge of these plans and their implementation, it is necessary to refer to expert authors such as Barruel[556], Cretineau-Joly[557], Dom Benoit[558], Drumont[559], Descbamps[560], Mgr Jouin[561], Henri Ford[562], Leon de Poncins[563], Henry Coston[564], Pierre Virion[565], Maurice Carlavilla and many others.

---

[556] *Mémoire sur le Jacobinisme.*
[557] *L'Église romaine en face de la Révolution.*
[558] *La cité antichrétienne*, 2 volumes, 2nd ed., Paris, 1894.
[559] *La France Juive*, 2 volumes, Paris.
[560] *Les sociétés secrètes et la société, Paris, 1880.*
[561] *Le péril iudéo-maconniques; Les protocols des Sages de Sion.*
[562] *The International Jew.*
[563] *Les Forces secrètes de la Révolution*, Beauchesne, Paris, 1932; *Les juifs maitres du monde*, Beauchesne, Paris, 1932.
[564] *Les financiers qui mènent le monde.*
[565] *El gobierno mundial y la Contra-Iglesia; La masonería dentro de la Iglesia*, Cruz y Fierro Editores, Buenos Aires.

CHAPTER XI

VARIOUS WAYS MANIFEST THE INVASION OF THE KABBALAH IN THE CHRISTIAN WORLD

The Kabbalah enters openly with philosophy and politics into the thought and life of the Christian world. From there it is to dominate all other areas of thought and life. Everything is flooded with kabbalistic experiences. Thought, politics, sociology, psychology, economics, literature, everything oozes the kabalistic conception of God, the world and man. The Kabbalah, in the very contradiction and antagonism, has to express the thousand variants of its rich and inexhaustible content. In the present chapter, therefore, we shall draw a general picture of the broad lines along which the Christian world has been inundated by the Jewish Kabbalah. In order to follow a certain order, we shall first of all set out the lines of esotericism, Hinduism and occultism; secondly, the philosophical lines of Hegelianism, Marxism and existentialism; thirdly, the lines of psychologism in Freud and Jung; and fourthly, the lines of sociology, economics, or politics and mass culture.

1. The cabalistic lines of esotericism

René Guénon (1886-1940) represents the highest that esotericism has produced, perhaps in all times[566]. Esotericism is a pure metaphysics,

---

[566] René Guénon's main works are: *Introducción general al estudio de las doctrinas hindúes,* ed. Losada, Buenos Aires, 1945; *L'homme et son devenir selon le Vedanta;* Les Éditions tradidionnelles, Paris, 1952; *Orient et Occident,* Véga, Paris, 1948; *Les etats mu/tiples de l'être,* 1932, 2nd ed, 1947; *Autorité spirituelle et Pouvoir temporel,* Véga, Paris, 1947; *La grande Triade,* Table ronde, Paris, 1947; *Aperr;us sur l'esotérisme chrétien,* Les Éditions traditionnelles, Paris, 1954; *Symboles fondamentaux de la Science sacrée,* Gallimard, Paris, 1962; *Le symbolisme de la Croix,* Véga, Paris, 1934; *Aperçus sur l'initiation,* Les éditions traditionnelles, Paris, 1953; *L'ésotérisme*

which would be, in René Guénon's conception, neither pagan nor Christian, but universal. Religious forms would only be a way of *external* expression of certain truths of this metaphysics. Frithjof Schouon, a disciple of Guénon, has published a book, *"De l'unité transcendante des religions"*[567] where he gives an authoritative account of the main theses of esotericism and, therefore, of René Guénon. In this thought, a first thesis is that of the *gradation of universal reality:* Reality is "affirmed by degrees", but without ceasing to be one. The lower degrees of this affirmation are absorbed by the metaphysical interaction or synthesis in the higher degrees: this is the doctrine of cosmic illusion: the world is not more or less imperfect, "ephemeral", but is in no way with respect to absolute reality, since the reality of the world would limit that of God who only "is"; but being itself, which is none other than the "personal God", is in its turn superseded by the "impersonal" or "suprapersonal divinity", the "Not-being", of which, the personal God or Being, is but the first Determination[568].

These ideas are expressed by René Guénon by saying that the "Self" is the transcendent and permanent principle of which the human being and every other being is but a transitory and contingent modification. Or the supreme, total and universal principle, therefore impersonal, beyond all qualification and beyond all distinction. Or again, the infinite is that which has no limit, which contains everything and outside of which there is nothing. Or again, the universal possibility contains all possibilities, of which Being or also Non-Being are therefore aspects. The unmanifested comprises the possibilities of non-manifestation and the possibilities of manifestation, as such, are not manifested. The state of non-manifestation is always transitory and conditioned.

From this it appears that Guénon's God or reality or infinite possibility coincides completely with that of the *En Soph* of the Kabbalah. God is everything and is also non-being or nothingness. The same must appear in the notion of creation or chaos.

---

de Dante, Les éditions traditionnelles, Paris, 1949. Both published by Omnia Veritas Ltd, www.omnia-veritas.com.
[567] Gallimard, Paris, 1948.
[568] Ibid., p. 51.

The notion of creation *or* chaos.

Creation, as a resolution of *chaos*, is in a sense instantaneous, is properly the Biblical *fiat lux*; but what is really at the origin of the *cosmos* is the primordial Light itself, that is to say, the *pure spirit* in which the essences of things are; and from this the manifested world can in fact only be lowered more and more into *materiality*.

This production of order out of chaos is assimilated by all traditions to an illumination: *fiat lux*. Chaos is symbolically identified with darkness and potentiality. The production of the manifested universe is a production of order out of chaos, chaos being undefined and the cosmos defined[569].

Metaphysical realisation

Man becomes aware of what he has never really ceased to be, namely his essential identity with the principle which is the only real thing[570]. Here appears the pantheism of the Guénonian system, as well as that of the Vedanta and the Kabbalah. Man can access the superhuman by becoming aware that his being is realised in another being that prolongs his self, as the wave realises the sea. Man is not an absolute and complete unity, but is open on high, and metaphysics is the science that fulfils realisation, that is, that makes the knower identify ontologically with the known. In realisation this identification is fulfilled in the "itself", that is, in Brahman, in the metaphysical Zero, in the Non-Being[571].

These ideas on metaphysics would constitute the primordial tradition of all peoples. René Guénon has taken great pains in many valuable works to expound these doctrines and to emphasise the significance and value of the Kabbalah. In *Le Roi du Monde* (1930) he elaborates at length on the interpretations of the *Shekinah* and *Metatron* that bring him dangerously close to the demonic[572].

Although René Guénon met Papus in 1906 and, through him and Saint-Yves d'Alveydre, came into contact with the esoteric circles coming

---

[569] Jacques Marcireau, *René Guénon et son œuvre*, Paris, 1946, p. 61.
[570] Frithjof Schouon, ibid. p. 53.
[571] *Symbolisme de la Croix*, pp. 25, 193 and 203.
[572] *Renovatio*, No. 2, 1967, p. 300.

from Martinez de Pasqually and Louis-Claude Saint-Martin, it is clear that his teachings are higher than those of all of them.

René Guénon has always been a Gnostic, but distancing himself from historical Gnosticism, he will place the Gnostic Church, to which he belonged, in the same category as spiritualism, theosophy and occultism[573]. His line of initiation must be placed in that of the *barabah* of Sheikh Elish who placed it in the line of the 12th century Sufi, lbn'Arahi, one of the most eminent representatives of what specialists like G-C. Anarrabe and Louis Gardet have called, for lack of a better term, an "existential monism"[574].

Lucien Meroz, who has intelligently followed René Guénon's spiritual path, points out that "inspired by a certain view of the Hebrew Kabbalah, he interprets the Genesis account and understands what he calls the "symbol of the universal fall"[575]. Following this kind of mythology, man is represented in the origin as identical with a single principle: the Word or total Truth. He takes the name of *Adam Kadmon*. A new factor comes into play: *Nashah*, the egoism or desire for universal existence. The original Adam Kadmon is segmented and the separate particles from it constitute the *Adam Protoplastes*, i.e., the first formator.

The *Adam Kadmon* could be compared to the Platonic idea of man. It is also the Androgyne. Within the *Adam Kadmon* arises the will of individual existence designated by the name of *Adam Protoplastes*. The two Adams are like two inverted faces, one of light, the other of darkness, and are symbolised in the fig tree of the two elders of the Zohar and in the seal of Solomon[576].

René Guénon could not be said to have been directly influenced by the Kabbalah; rather, these influences are those of the Brahmanic and Sufi traditions, and through them, also of the Kabbalah, for all traditions coincide and converge in the great primordial Tradition of humanity.

---

[573] *Lucien Méroz*, René Guénon et la Sagesse initiatique, Paris, p. 47.
[574] Ibid., p. 48.
[575] Ibid., p. 192.
[576] Ibid., p. 194.

Raymond Abellio, another esoteric author[577]. In his novel *La Fosse de Babel*, Raymond Abellio speaks for the first time of *the absolute structure* as a universal key to being and becoming, to situations and mutations. The absolute structure was based on the universal senary sphere derived from the Bible, interpreted cabalistically. "We consider, says[578], the Bible and the accompanying texts of explanation, the *Sefer Yetzirath, the* book of creation, and the *Sefer-ha-zohar* or book of Splendour, which constitute the Kabbalah, or primordial tradition as the repository and field of the numerical science... The Sephirotic construction and mechanism constitute the very centre of the Kabbalah and the knot of our science..." "The Hebraic documents are par excellence initiatory documents". Abellio's work is in turn based on the work of Fabre d'Olivet[579].

"Numerical science, says Abellio, is the science of the cycles and vibrations that make up the world. Thus, like any science, it is both a mode of representation and a mode of action. I will not give, he says, here, the definition of number which the Pythagorean and Platonic schools have developed at length. The great mystery is not in the number, but in the passage from number to the cycle of numbers, whose relation is the same as that from immobility to movement. The existence of the "itself" considered in isolation establishes in Non-Being no duality, no cleavage and, in the proper sense, no *existence*. It is the absolute unity. And no meditation is possible on the number 1 considered in its static perfection.

The movement begins at number 2, when at the level of the "self" the consciousness of the self appears, an element of imperfection and yet of progression, but of cyclic progression, because immediately the binary brings the ternary and the act of *self-consciousness* objectifies a third term, *Consciousness*. In a single movement are thus indissolubly linked not only the self, but also the act of consciousness itself, that is to say, the conscious, the known and knowledge. It is the first and at the same time the simplest and most general of the cycles. It is the

---

[577] *He has published the following works, all in French, in Gallimard, Paris:* Les yeux d'Ezechiel sont ouverts, *1949;* La Fosse de Babel; Vers un nouveau prophetisme; La Bible, document chiffré *(2 vols.);* La structure absolue; Heureux les pacifiques (Flammarion); Assomption de l'Europe *(Flammarion).*
[578] La Bible, document chiffré, *p. 14.*
[579] *Cosmogonie de Moise; La langue hebraique restitué,* 2 vol. Rorban Ainé, Paris, 1815, Chacornac, 1905.

procession of the Father, the Son and the Holy Spirit that timelessly generates the Son? What is necessary for the incarnation to begin? For the *other*, in the Platonic sense, to be in its turn existent, and thus to pass from the ternary to the quaternary. But this materialisation by the 4 is incomplete. For the procession to continue and be completed, it is necessary that this other in turn acquires its own self-awareness and objectifies its own intelligence, that is to say, that a second ternary be confronted at the primordial end. It is the Incarnation of the Son, through the birth of the number six, the figure of fulfilment in creation, symbolically expressed by the general myth of six stages or six days. The birth of the number six also expresses genesis from its first word: *Bereschit*. The *Sifra di-Tzeniutha* indeed gives the following occult translation: "Six, in the beginning (Bereschith) created six (bara schith)..."[580].

> "One would like to see the Chinese tetragram of Wen Wang which, at the head of the Yi King, gives, according to Matgioi, *La voie métaphysique*, the key to universal phenomenism... one would recognise the mythological expression of the Hebraic *Ein Sof*... And all this to conclude in magic. Magic used to be a direct contact with divine forces..., but today it is the increase of "clear consciousness", psychic vertigo and clear consciousness... Later "the magical efficacy of the word linked to the progressive mastery of cosmic vibrations, will appear more clearly""[581].

This is where René Guénon and Abellio diverge. The former is a harsh critic of the modern world, which is moving further and further away from the primordial tradition and towards the reign of quantity; the latter, on the other hand, tries to combine the Kabbalah with modernity in the phenomenological aspect of Husserl[582] and Heidegger and in the contributions of the mathematical sciences. *"There is not, he writes, a single question posed from this angle by traditional science which does not evoke in a more or less precise way questions of the same nature raised by the highest and most recent mathematical theories, especially those which are in the process of elaboration and which do nothing but*

---

[580] *Abellio*, La Bible, document chiffré, *p. 21*.
[581] Ibid., pp. 24-25.
[582] See in *La structure absolue*, Gallimard, Paris, 1965, how Husserl's phenomenology and Heideggerian ontology are incorporated into esotericism.

presage the possibility of a future and prodigious synthesis between the exoteric sciences and secret knowledge"[583].

And Abellio adds: "And, in another domain, perhaps it is an intersign that mathematics has taken as a symbol of the transfinite names the Hebrew letter *aleph;* you can remove any number from *aleph* and it always remains identical to itself". This sentence taken from a work by Eddington[584] could serve to raise what we call in our genetics the problem of Emanation or creation *ex nihilo*[585].

2. Hindu doctrines and the Christian West

Abellio in *La structure absolue*[586] tells us, repeating the theses of the Kabbalah, that "the problem of the Indeterminate, called Supreme *Brahman* by the Hindus, *Tem* (he who does not exist in form) by the Egyptians, *Ain-Sof* by the Jews, *deity* of God by the master Ekhart and *Ungrund* by Jacob Boehme, is confused with that of the infinity of the possible, and the supreme contingency appears there as the result of an absolute determination... The deity appears to us as the equivalence of an absolute fullness and an absolute emptiness"[587]. From this it appears that gnosis, both ancient and modern, is a mixture of the mysteries of all religions and traditions with a veneer of Christian elements and they all have the same and unique structure, traced on Hinduism, Parseeism, Chaldean and Egyptian religions, Hermeticism and, unfailingly, the fundamental mould of the Kabbalistic gnosis.

Hence, Hindu doctrines play a most important role in this dissemination of the Kabbalistic mentality.

In modern times the spread of Hinduism[588] as a religion or esoteric practice in the West has gained momentum. In the late 17th and early 18th centuries Hinduism seemed moribund as a result of magical or idolatrous practices. The first to reinvigorate it was *Ram Mohan Roy* (1772-1833), the founder of the Brahma Samaj. For him Hinduism is

---

[583] La Bible chiffré, *I, p. 33.*
[584] Espace, Temps, Gravitation, *Hermann, Paris.*
[585] La Bible chiffré, *I, p. 34.*
[586] P. 315.
[587] Ibid., p. 316.
[588] This whole point on neo-Hinduism is taken from the excellent book by Emile Galtier, *La Pensée hindoue, du Seuil,* Paris, 1960.

theistic. God is the author of the universe and must be worshipped only in the spirit, without being allowed to give Him any name or plastic representation. Morality, faith, humility are the ways of salvation. The same path was followed by Debendranath Tagore (1817-1905) and Keshab Chandrasen (1818-1884)[589].

Dayananda Sarasvati (1824-1883), well acquainted with the popular Hinduism and yoga of his time, tried to renew Hinduism. In order to prove in the name of the Vedas the existence of three eternals, God, souls and the world, in order to establish also on the Vedas the foundations of modern science, as far as it had content, he had to request the texts in an unscientific way[590].

Ramakrishna Paramahansa (1834-1886) was the man of extraordinary experiences. His visions are countless and he offers an interesting system of study for the psychologist and the historian of religions. For him, all forms of Hinduism are equally good in themselves, even if devotion to the mother goddess Kali was to him a source of anger. The condition of his experiences was that *all* religious forms were but aspects of the same truth.

He extended this theory also to Islam and Christianity[591].

Vivekananda (1863-1902), his successor, presents himself in a totally opposite aspect. He is above all an extravert, a dynamic. He repeats the lessons of his master on the relativity of all religions. His rhetoric knows how to amplify the ideas received from Ramakrishna, which enables him to take from secular science and all philosophical systems superficial knowledge and to give rise to a syncretism at the summit of which *Advaita* radiates.

His success at the Congress of Religions in 1893 prompted him to found the Ramakrishna Mission.

He did not hesitate to study the constitutions of the Christian monastic orders and to take from them the basis of his own organisation. His disciples are still doing real work in India, publishing books, lecturing, caring for the poor, missionaries, etc. Outside India, they offer to

---

[589] Ibid., p. 11.
[590] Ibid., p. 114.
[591] Ibid., p. 114.

uninformed Americans and Europeans a presentation of Hinduism that differs from that of orthodox Hindus[592].

Theosophy. This society, founded by Mme. Blavatsky and brought to its zenith by Annie Besant, is not Hinduism. It is an unhappy combination of elements drawn from Hinduism, Buddhism and Christianity. At its core, anti-Christianity is one of its fundamental attitudes[593].

Aurobindo Gnose (1872-1950). He is well known in the world. His "ashram", the monastery of Pondichéry, is a beautiful economic realisation, a sort of phalanstery[594].

His yoga wants to show the way to liberation and at the same time to prepare a race of living liberated ones, of supermen. Not like those of Nietzsche, who would surpass humanity in crime, but supermen who, having realised their divine nature, would make happiness radiate. When he explains his metaphysical position, he finds himself again in front of an Advaita, not that of Caneara, in which the world and man would be products of Maya, but a world of multiplicity which must not be sacrificed to unity. A beautiful presentation of the theory of "Chedâbheda", distinction without distinction: distinction and unity are equally true.

The second aspect of his theory states that, if there is evolution, it is because there has been involution, i.e., that everything, even matter, is the aspect of the One, or rather, that the One, appearing in different forms, produces multiplicity as the play of the one.

Many currents run through the position taken by Aurobindo: the Advaitic current, the influences of Plotinus, Bergson, Christianity and others. The complexity of the presentation of the system gives it the appearance of depth, while some borrowed elements give the followers a familiar ground.

Other modern philosophers. One of the best known representatives of modern Hinduism, Shri S. Radhakrishnan, cannot be passed over in silence. His philosophical position is advaitic without Maya. He has an

---

[592] Ibid., p. 115.
[593] Ibid., p. 115.
[594] Ibid., p. 116.

anti-Christian position and it is from India, according to him, that the mystical element of Christianity would have come.

K. Coomaraswammy (1877-1947) was a Hindu esotericist who became acquainted with the books of René Guénon and accepted the idea of a single traditional truth so willingly that his researches kept confirming it. In his main work, *Hindouisme et boudhisme*[595] he tries to re-establish the meaning of the original Buddhism, which had been denatured by the orientalists.

It should be noted that it is not only Hindus who have tried to introduce Hinduism into Western society, but Westerners themselves have endeavoured to re-evaluate the doctrine of the Upanishads. A leading representative of this trend is Aldous Huxley (1894-1963), who in the last years of his life became fond of Hindu philosophy and mysticism and published a number of works reflecting this preoccupation, such as *The perennial philosophy* (1946).

3. The Occult

Occultism, Spiritualism, Theosophy, are interchangeable labels for the same products. The same could be said of esotericism, to which we referred earlier, but which has a more distinguished intellectual presentation. The most relevant modern chorister of occultism is undoubtedly Éliphas Levi, who has said: "Through the veil of all the hieratic and mystic allegories of ancient dogmas, through the darkness and strange proofs of all initiations, under the seal of all sacred scriptures, in the ruins of Nineveh and Thebes, under the corroded stones of ancient temples, and under the blackened face of the sphinxes of Assyria and Egypt, in the monstrous or marvellous paintings which translate for the believers of India the sacred pages of the Vedas, in the strange emblems of our old alchemical books, in the ceremonies of reception practised by all mysterious societies, the traces of the same doctrine are always to be found, everywhere carefully hidden. Occult philosophy seems to be the nurse or godmother of all religions, the secret lever of all intellectual forces, the key to all divine scriptures"[596].

---

[595] Gallimard, Paris, 1949.
[596] Éliphas Levi, *Dogme et rituel de la haute magie*, Paris, Germer-Baillière, 1856, 2 vol.

Occultists invoke the *Genesis of Enoch, which* predates Moses and the prophets and is identical in its substance to the teachings of ancient Egypt. *Hermes Trismegistus*[597] is one of their favourite authors, and above all, the books of the Kabbalah. The occult tradition is linked to the Kabbalah by Nicolas Flamel (died 1413), Pico della Mirandola (1463-1494), the priest Trithemus (1462-1516), Cornelius Agrippa (1486-1536), Paracelsus (1493-1541), William Postel (1510-1581), Jacob Boehme (1575-1625), who inspired the Marquis Claude de Saint-Martin (1743-1803). In the years leading up to the French Revolution, Europe was full of mysterious characters of an equivocal nature: the Count of Saint-Germain (1710-1784), Joseph Balsam (1743-1795), known as the Count of Cagliostro, the magnetiser Mesmer (1733-1815), the Swede Swedenborg (1688-1772). More recently, occultism was inspired by Fabre d'Olivet (1767-1825), who, with the key to the Egyptian sanctuaries, tried to reconstruct the Mosaic cosmogony, and who passed on his powers to Éliphas Lévi, the Catholic priest Alphonse Louis Constant (1810-1875), who expounds the principles and history of occultism in his famous works *La clef des grands mystères*[598], *Histoire de la Magie*[599], *Dogme et rituel de la haute magie*[600], *La science des esprits*[601]. The heirs of Éliphas Levi are Stanislas de Guaita (1860-1899), Josephin Pelladan (t 1920), Saint Yves d'Alveydre (1842-1909) and Dr. Gerard Encause (1865-1916), called Papus, who has published *La Cabbale*[602].

It is not necessary for us to expound the doctrine of the occultists, for it would be necessary to repeat what has been said.

I would just like to highlight the book by Dr. Adolph Weiss, *The Universal Law of Societies*[603], where he studies what he calls the biological lesson given by nine thousand years of human history. This biological lesson would be interpreted through occultism, which would provide the synthesis for understanding what is the ideal government of peoples. This is what the epilogue would lead us to, in which the "historical experiences whose voice is this work, [which] asks of rulers

---

[597] See Festugiere, *La Révélation de Hermes Trismegiste*, Gabalda, Paris.
[598] Librairie Alean, Paris.
[599] Alcan, Paris, 1922.
[600] Alcan, Paris.
[601] Alcan, Paris.
[602] Éditions Dangles, Paris.
[603] Editorial Kier, Buenos Aires, 1945.

more freedom than radicalism, more equality than democracy, more personal aristocracy than nobility of origin, more fraternity than socialism, more authentic hierarchy than the representatives of thrones and altars"[604].

And what would the historical experience of the peoples teach us? That there is a universal biological law of societies: the trinitarian constitution, the three social powers... "This law I have not invented, says Weiss, I have only verified it and brought it to light. The ancient and modern universities that "supplied me with the material of knowledge. India, Iran, Tibet, Ancient Egypt, China, Japan, the Israel of Moses, the Helad of Orpheus, the Rome of Numa, the Judea of the prophets and of Jesus Christ, all of them are witnesses to the truth of this book and of the social law revised by it in the past, this testator of all principles in a state of activity and fulfilment in the present and for the future"[605].

Three bodies must be formed in society: the body of teachers, the body of jurists and the body of economists. Public opinion must be persuaded that only a society governed by the *authority* of wisdom, by the *power* of the state and by the *structuring of* the economy will realise the synarchical peace into which all the cults and universities, all the courts and economic unions of Europe and the world will enter.

That is to say that the universal plan of synarchic occultism of which Saint Yves d'Alveydre outlined the outlines would coincide with the old plan of the secret and masonic societies.

It remains to mention some more vulgar and popular expressions of occultism, such as the spiritualism of Allan Kardec, who believed in reincarnation, the same spiritualism of Arthur Conan Doyle, the famous author of the character Sherlock Holmes, who tried to make contact with the world of the dead; the theosophy of Blavatsky (1831-1891), Annie Besant (1847-1933) and Khrishnamurti (1895-); the anthroposophy of Rudolf Steiner (1861-1925); the esotericists Gurdieff (1877-1949) who counted among his disciples Louis Jouvet, Aldous Huxley, H. O. Lawrence and Lanza del Vasco (1861-1925). O. Lawrence and Lanza del Vasto; the physicist Bennet; Ouspensky, author of the *Tertium Organum*, who at one time in his life maintained

---

[604] Ibid., p. 453.
[605] Ibid., p. 453.

relations with Gurdieff; Louis Pawells, with his famous magazine *Planete*.

4. The Kabbalist line of Hegelian philosophy

We have shown in chapter nine how Hegel is a typically gnostic author. The famous system is nothing but a gnosis in the vocabulary of German philosophy. With Hegel's death in 1831, the system breaks into pieces. On the one hand, the famous Hegelian right and on the other hand the even more famous left. The various gnostic systems indicate only general outlines which each author will then fill in and determine according to his own tastes and preferences.

So it is also with Hegel. Already during Hegel's lifetime, Herbart, in 1822, had warned of the profound contradiction that ran through the entire Hegelian system of law. "Hegel, he said, wants to reconcile the irreconcilable, i.e. Spinozist monism and Kantian freedom"[606].

But the real division was to be established, after the death of the great philosopher, on the occasion of the controversy about religion. "The Hegelian school was then divided, like the French parliament, into a right wing which applied the idea of the unity of divine and human nature, considering the whole of Gospel history as authentic history, to which Goschell, Garbler and Bauer belonged; into a centre which applied it only in part, in the sense of the right wing, to which Rosenkranz belonged; and a left wing represented by Strauss, which applied it in the sense of not considering the biblical account as history in its entirety"[607].

The left merely emphasised Hegel's Gnostic position, which regarded the divine life as manifesting itself in the great historical personalities, but by no means fully and absolutely, and as the highest degree that could be attained by the human person in that of self-consciousness in a self-unity in God. Jesus Christ would have possessed this consciousness to a degree that no other mortal had[608]. Behind Strauss, Feuerbach and Marx were to arrive at more radical positions, but always within the Gnostic line or accentuating its characters.

---

[606] *Encyclopaedia Philosophica*, Firenze, 1957, t. II, col. 1.018.
[607] Ibid., col. 1.023.
[608] Ibid., col. 1.023.

The moments of the Hegelian-communist dialectic as a profane transposition of Christian mysteries. To understand Marx one must understand Hegel, and to understand Hegel one must understand the deepest mysteries of Christianity. For both Hegel and Marx have done nothing but transpose the Christian mysteries: the former on a philosophical plane, the latter on a social economic plane.

The Christian looks up to a transcendent, infinitely transcendent God. While recognising that by his presence God makes himself immanent in creatures, he knows that his very special way of being - subsistent Being - is outside and above all that is created. God - fullness of being - has not created man not out of an intrinsic need to complement himself but by a completely gratuitous act of the superabundance of his goodness.

The transcendent God, fullness of Being, without mixture of finitude or imperfection, encloses in his Deity two communications of his very essence: one, by way of intelligence; the other, by way of love - two processions - that of the Word and that of the spirit. But they are fulfilled in the immanence of the Divine Essence. The inborn Father from eternity begets the Son, communicating to him his very essence, and the Father and the Son give rise to the Holy Spirit by way of love. The mystery of the Trinity is the most august and impenetrable of all mysteries. But there is another mystery, also august and impenetrable, and that is the Incarnation of the Word: "And the Word - the Logos - became flesh". It is true that God is sufficient unto Himself and has no need of the creature. Nevertheless, he communicates himself freely to them. The greatest communication takes place in Christ. The Son, the Second Person, without ceasing to be God, takes on human nature in unity of person. The Son becomes man. In the mystery of the Incarnation, two natures, the divine and the human, are united in the same person. St. Paul describes this mystery as the *denial of God* and tells us so in the *Letter to the Philippians*, 2, 5:

> "Have the same mind that was in Christ Jesus, who, being in the form of God, did not count it robbery to be equal with God, but emptied himself, taking the form of a servant, and being made in the likeness of men; *But emptied himself,* taking the form of a servant, and being made in the likeness of men, and being found in fashion as a man, he humbled himself, obedient unto death, even death on a cross; wherefore God hath highly exalted him, and given him a name above every name: that at the name of Jesus the knee should bow, whatsoever is in heaven, and in earth, and in the depths; and that every

tongue should confess that Jesus Christ is Lord, to the glory of God the Father".

In this teaching of St. Paul, special attention must be paid to this *"he was annihilated"*, which in Latin the Vulgate translates as *"exinanivit"*, he became nothing, and the original Greek as ἑαυτὸν ἐκένωσεν, he emptied himself. For this is the origin of the whole false theological interpretation which Lutheranism was to introduce, and which was to influence Hegel in the philosophical creation of dialectics, which, as we have pointed out, rests in a particular way on the principle of the "second moment", that of "antithesis" or "negation", or "contradiction", or "alienation".

St. Paul, when he speaks of this "annihilation", or "emptying" of Christ, does not do so ontologically as if Christ ceased to be God and became something else, but simply wants to draw the attention of Christians to the example of humility that Jesus gave us, who, being God, showed himself to be a simple man hiding the glory and power of divinity.

Christian doctrine adulterated by Lutheranism

These Christian dogmas were to be adulterated by the Protestant movement born out of Luther's reformation.

Catholicism maintained a speculative and sapiential attitude to the Christian mysteries. It considered them in themselves, in their "speculative" reality. With Luther, however, a theological movement of *action and practical knowledge* began. Dogmas are not of interest as truths *in themselves*, truths that are the object of pure contemplation, but as truths for us, and in so far as they concern our justification. Luther pays attention to what he calls *theologia crucis*, as opposed to *theologia gloriae*. The metaphysical aspect of Christology does not interest him either, but its dramatic aspect does. It matters little to him that Christ has two natures: instead he is interested in the fact that he came to take our sins and to give us his righteousness. And so he also conceived in a *practical* way what theologians call the *communicatio idiomatum*, i.e. the fact that to a *single concrete subject*, Christ, the Incarnate Word, the properties of the human nature and of the divine nature can be applied indistinctly. *"God died for us"*, it is said, and rightly so. And this by virtue of this *"communicatio idiomatum"* without this meaning that He suffered and died, as God, in His Deity. He suffered and died in His humanity, which is created and passible, but since this humanity belongs to the Divine Person of the Word, it is legitimate to affirm that God - the Divine Person of the Word - suffered and died on the Cross.

Luther, on the other hand, *begins* to understand this *"God became man and sin"* in Jesus Christ as a *"change"* of the virtues and the situation of the two natures taken as concrete realities. God, taking in Jesus our weaknesses and even taking our sin, but attributing to us his Righteousness, and then, later on, his Glory[609].

This lack of speculative rigour and sapiential consideration will determine that the text of the Apostle to the Philippians in which he speaks of God's self-emptying is interpreted as if God, on becoming incarnate, stripped himself of his attributes of divine essence, of his immutability, and acquired creaturely conditions. A theological movement then began which would culminate in what is known as the *theology of Kenosis,* in which the Protestant theologians of the 18th and 19th centuries would maintain that the Logos has the power to limit himself in his being and activity and that in Christ's career on earth the divinity has been limited, and thus the *"communicatio idiomatum"* is interpreted as *"Logos non extra carnem nec caro extra Logos";* namely, as if the Word had no being outside humanity and humanity outside the Word[610].

Beneath these purely theological errors there is in Lutheranism a fundamental philosophical error arising from nominalism. Nominalism has no exact notion of being, which is predicated not univocally but analogically of the various beings who realise it differently. God is Being by essence, and the creature is being by participation. There is an analogical predication. The diversity of being permits its unity. In nominalism, on the other hand, being is *univocal,* so that there is, we would say, a single mass of being which is distributed, part to some beings, part to others; part to God and part to the creatures. There are not two essentially different ways of possessing being - in the case of God, Being by essence, and in the case of the creature, being partaken of and derived from God - but only one way, from which it follows that what God has, the creature does not have, and what the creature has, God does not have.

The philosophy of the univocity of Being tends to *set* the creature *in opposition* to the Creator; it tends to exalt the divine transcendence over

---

[609] Yves Congar, *Le Christ, Marie et l'Église,* Paris, 1952, pp. 32-38; Georges M.-M. Cottier, *L'athéisme du jeune Marx,* J. Vrin, Paris, 1959, p. 140. Cottier, *L'athéisme du jeune Marx,* J. Vrin, Paris, 1959, p. 140.
[610] Dict. de Théologie, *de* Vacant-Kénose.

the creature, as if in order to exalt God it were necessary to humiliate and despise the creature.

The Hegelian gnosis. On this adulterated theology Hegel elaborated his philosophical system. Today it is sufficiently proven that Hegel was strongly impregnated with Lutheran theology. Paul Asveld, in his excellent study *La pensée religieuse du jeune Hegel,* states that "Hegel never adhered to Lutheran orthodoxy, although he was literally besieged by it".

The whole background of Hegel's system is profoundly theological. After the studies of Nohl[611], Dilthey[612], Enrico de Negri[613], Jean Wahl[614], Hippolite[615], Asveld[616], Grégoire[617], nobody doubts this. The Dominican Georges M. M. Cottier[618] has made a demonstration of this thesis in the first hundred pages of *L'Athéisme du Jeune Marx,* which makes a striking impression.

And indeed, Hegel's entire system is built on the notion of *Entäusserung* which the authors translate by the term *alienation.* Enrico de Negri in his excellent article *L'elaborazione hegeliana di temi agostiniani,* says of *entäusserung:* "The self-movement of the idea or of the absolute spirit or of the system insofar as the system develops or should develop on a ground cleansed of all impurity".

This term *entäusserung* is the noun form of the word *hat sich selbs geeussert,* with which Luther translates from the Vulgate that *"he was struck down"* of St. Paul to the Philippians of which we spoke above.

Just as in the Incarnation, interpreted in the doctrine of kenosis, the Logos *empties himself* of divinity and clothes himself with humanity in order to be exalted in the community of the Church by the Spirit, so in the Hegelian system, the Logos, the Spirit, empties himself in different

---

[611] Hegel Theologische Jungendschriften, *Tübingen, 1907.*
[612] *Hegel y el idealismo,* Fondo de Cultura Económica, Mexico, Buenos Aires, 1956.
[613] *L'elaborazione hegeliana di temí agostiniani,* in Revue Internationale de Philosophie, t. VI, 1952, No. 19, pp. 62-68.
[614] *Le malheur de la conscience dans la philosophie de Hegel,* Presses Universitaires de France, *1951.*
[615] *Genèse et structure de la phénoménologie de l'esprit de Hegel,* Aubier, Paris, *1945.*
[616] *La pensée religieuse du jeune Hegel,* Desclée, Paris, *1952.*
[617] *Aux sources de la pensée de Marx,* Vrin, Paris, 1952. Études hégéliennes, Louvain, 1958.
[618] J. Vrin, Paris, 1959.

figures until he reaches his complete realisation in the Absolute Spirit, which comprises the infinite and the finite, the identity of identity and non-identity.

In this process that the Logos accomplishes we can consider a double movement, a movement of negation, of alienation, in which the Logos is stripped of all transcendence, and a second movement, negation of the negation or appropriation -aufhebenen, in which the Logos appropriates in its immanence the divinity represented in the previous transcendence.

First movement, the negation. Here we have to consider that God becomes Christ, Menschwerdung, becomes incarnate, understood as an incessant action or becoming, or better, "God identifies himself with history, which is a continuous process of revelations, manifestations, incarnations. Here we have the meaning of the phenomenology of the Spirit, which develops in successive figures"[619].

In these successive figures God dies, i.e. the death of Christ is negation, which in Hegel constitutes the life-giving soul of the movement. The death of Christ - alienation - is also mediation, because one figure leads us to a higher figure, and thus through the series of figures we arrive at absolute knowledge. The figures that are the negation of the Logos, the other of the Logos, are also its negation.

But Hegel wants first of all to deny a transcendent God; therefore, in this process of *entäusserung*, kenosis, which takes place in the whole of the Hegelian system, a series of alienations takes place. Hegel rejects the transcendent God of the Judeo-Christian tradition, he rages against the God of Abraham. And in the famous figure of the master and the slave, the master is the transcendent God and the slave is consciousness; but the slave will eventually become master of his master, when he succeeds in reabsorbing divinity into the magnetisation of consciousness.

The second movement of entäusserung. The first movement, the negation of *entäusserung*, constitutes only the first stage of a circular movement. Loss is followed by re-appropriation; splitting is followed by reconciliation; negation is followed by negation of negation. The annihilation of which the Apostle speaks to us is followed by the

---

[619] Cottier, ibid.

exaltation of which also speaks to us. Denial suppresses and preserves. Divinity is denied as transcendent, but is preserved in immanence.

In short, that Hegel takes from the Christian mystery of the Trinity the idea of *process* or *procession,* which, although in good theology does not imply movement or change, Hegel takes it as if it were a self-movement. Where does Hegel get this idea of self-movement which develops in three moments? He takes it from the mystery of the Incarnation, misunderstood through the theology of Kenosis, as if the Logos were transformed into the humanity of Christ and then transformed, in his passion and death, into the exaltation of the Church. This confusion and simplification of the highest Christian mysteries is transferred from the level of theology to that of philosophy, to that of the "concept". In the concept all transcendence has been reabsorbed and the concept is a self-moving and self-creating subject. The concept is *causa sui,* not only in relation to its own determinations, but it is the effectiveness. The inner dialectical movement was already a play of the same and the other. But the Logos must also have its other, natura. *Natura* and *Logos* are thus the two moments of a dialectical unity, but this victory cannot last because it would signal the victory of duality and splitting. In turn, Logos and nature are "suppressed" in the spirit. Logos evolves through natura into spirit, which is identity of identity and non-identity. The spirit is realised historically in *art, religion and philosophy,* God is confused with history. And since history is humanity on the move, God is confused with the life of humanity, with human becoming, which is to say that it is realised through philosophical praxis.

5. *The gnosis of the revolutionary communist dialectics* [620]

The three moments of Hegel's dialectic are a transformation *on the plane of human reason* of the Christian mysteries, and especially of the falsely understood mystery of the Incarnation. It is thus a perverse theology, and a perverse philosophy. The other mysteries of the Trinity, of the Incarnation, of the Passion and Death of the Lord and of the vivification of humanity in the Mystical Body by the Holy Spirit, are

---

[620] Both the communist gnosis and the Hegelian gnosis, which are published here, are reproductions of what is written in my work *The Destructive Power of the Communist Dialectic.*

used to construct an atheistic and evolutionary system which will turn modern philosophy into a divinity, into an atheistic and dangerous gnosis. It is called gnosis, in a pejorative sense, any system that rationalises the Christian mysteries. It is the great heresy that tries to destroy Christianity from the first moment of its existence and that perseveres under various names in all Christian ages. Nevertheless, the Hegelian gnosis will not be the most dangerous of all possible gnosticisms. Hegel maintains the superiority of spirit over matter. The legitimacy with which Hegel admits this superiority of the spirit is debatable. For strictly speaking, since the dialectic is constituted by contradiction and negativity as its essential and constitutive element, it is moved not precisely by being but by nothingness. It does not therefore tend upwards, towards the Spirit, but downwards, towards matter. However, although the coherence of Hegel's system may be questioned, the fact remains that in it Spirit has primacy. Marx, on the other hand, with his famous inversion of the idea in the socio-economic sphere, will create a more perverse and revolutionary gnosis by bringing this gnostic Christianity as a factor of social dissolution to the level of the life of peoples and human societies. Christianity, in fact, substantially disfigured and sustaining this terrible monstrosity which is the atheistic communism of Karl Marx and Lenin. We have seen how Marx maintains as an essential piece of his system that of *process, change* and *movement*. Nothing is stable, everything is pure process. He takes this idea from Hegel, who, in his sacrilegious transposition, takes it from the *processions* that are fulfilled in the immanence of the Trinity.

This process unfolds in the three great moments of affirmation, negation and negation of negation. Hegel's dialectic is a dialectic that unfolds in a triadic rhythm. This system is also taken, as we have explained, from the Christian mystery of Christ's humiliation. In the Incarnation, when the Word becomes Man, there is an affirmation, the Word, there is a negation - man - and a negation of the negation or overcoming - which is Christ exalted above all creation. Marx is going to bring these three moments of the dialectic to the level of the present history of humanity.

The central point of Marx's system is constituted by what is called *the great law of history,* or *Marx's prophecy,* which consists, in short, in the *dialectical transition* from capitalism to communism. This law has three culminating moments. *The first moment,* the humanity of primitive communism, when, because of the lack of division of labour, and because of the primitive character of technology, there is no *private possession of the means of production*. In the Marxist conception this is a purely "negative", "poor", "empty" communism, something like the "idea" of Hegel's logic. To become rich, to pass from the empty to the full and rich, this humanity has to alienate itself, to lose itself; just as the "idea" of logic, before it reaches the richness of the Absolute Spirit, has to pass through all the phases of nature and history. And the enriching factor is negation or contradiction. Man cannot be enriched by technical progress unless he denies and alienates himself. In reality, Marx assigns no reason for the necessity of this alienation. Why does not man from primitive communism pass directly and in a continuous process to the man of communism with high technical progress without the necessity of passing through the stage of alienated labour of the epoch of slavery, feudalism, and capitalism? Marx assigns no reason for this necessity.

It is imposed by the dialectical game. And why does the dialectical play with its triadic movement impose it? Marx, like Hegel, does not assign any reason either. The Christian heritage, from which the modern world has not been able to detach itself, even in the deepest epoch of its aberrations, is nourishing and sustaining a thought which would otherwise be exhausted in pure nihilism.

We pass to the *second moment* of the communist dialectic, when humanity, whose essence is constituted by social labour, is alienated or lost through the private ownership of the means of production. This second moment has a long and chequered historical trajectory that runs through the regime of slavery, the feudal regime and finally the regime of capitalism. Technical progress determines the division of labour, which, in turn, results in certain men who own the means of production subjecting to labour those who are deprived of these means. Society becomes two irreconcilable classes, that of the exploiters and that of the exploited, which at the present stage of dialectical development are the bourgeoisie and the proletariat. Each of these classes dialectically constitutes the other and, in turn, opposes the other and fights and struggles against the other.

The tragedy of the Christian drama in which the Word-God gives Himself up to the great humiliation of taking our passible humanity and making it go through the various steps of a rugged and opprobrious passion, finds its corresponding parallel in the labouring mass of humanity - slaves, serfs and proletarians - who with their sufferings and struggles engage in the great struggle to liberate humanity.

This economic alienation determined by the ownership of the means of production must in turn engender another alienation on the social, political, philosophical and religious level. The economic infrastructure also determines and engenders the superstructure. The man who feels himself a slave before the boss, his master, in the bourgeois regime, feels himself also, through a purely imaginative alienation, a slave before his master, a transcendent God, above all that of the Judeo-Christian tradition. And man, the proletarian, will not wage his fight to the death against the economic master, his master, if he does not first wage it against his religious master - the God of religion - because to overcome the alienation that has lost him, he needs to have confidence in his creative power, which would not be possible as long as he is cowed and cowed by putting his trust in a Creator outside himself. For the proletarian to become conscious of his creative power, of his own life and of history, he must convince himself that he alone is his divinity for himself, that man is the *supreme essence of man*[621] and therefore like another Prometheus he must exclaim "I hate all gods" and make his own the words of Prometheus himself to Hermes, the messenger of the gods: "I will never exchange my chains for the servility of a slave. It is better to be chained to a rock than bound to the service of Zeus"[622]. From this we see that atheism - the war on religion - is an essential and inseparable element of Marx's communism.

And thus we can understand the *third moment of the communist dialectic*, that of the negation of the negation, when the proletariat, equipped with the revolutionary theory of scientific socialism, engages in its merciless struggle against the world which it calls bourgeois, and which is to a large extent so, since by the effect of the anti-Christian revolution, the ancient Catholic city which flourished in the Middle Ages has been transformed into the bourgeois Christian society of the Western world. Communism holds that in this third moment the proletariat will win a crushing victory over the bourgeoisie and that, after a laborious process, the communist world city will finally be established. Just as the Word humbles itself and wins the victory over sin, so the humiliated, redeeming proletariat saves humanity.

Of this communism, Marx says in his famous *Manifesto* of 1844: "It is the genuine solution of the conflict between man and nature, and between man and man, the true solution of the struggle between existence and essence, between objectification and self-assertion, between freedom and necessity, between the individual and the species.

---

[621] Marx, *Critique of Hegel's Philosophy of Right*.
[622] *Philosophy of Democritus and Epicurus*.

Communism is the solution of the enigma of history, and the very consciousness of being this solution".

Thus, the affirmation of humanity, its loss in capitalism and its recovery and salvation in communism, responds to the profane and economic-social version of the Christian mystery of the Incarnation, of St. Paul's "he was emptied" to the Philippians. The proletariat acquires the attributes of messianity which in Christianity correspond to Christ, the Saviour, and the communist labour city is the Marxist version of the Mystical Body of Christ, which is the Church. Marx's historical materialism is indeed an operative gnosis of the Anti-Christian Revolution.

6. The Schopenhauerian Kabbalist line

Opposing the intellectualist line of Hegel and the materialist line of Marx, Schopenhauer (1788-1860) affirms *the will* as a creative force, an irrational and evil will, working towards death and nirvana. It has been said of Schopenhauer that he was a synthesis of Kantianism and Buddhism. The fact is that Kabbalistic theses, through Hinduism, appear in Schopenhauer through every pore of his works. "The only philosophical system whose knowledge is indispensable for the understanding of my work is therefore the philosophy of Kant. Better still is a knowledge of Platonic philosophy. And if, in addition to this, the reader were initiated into the wisdom of the *Vedas*, whose secrets the Upanishads have revealed to us, he would be perfectly able to understand what I say"[623]. And Schopenhauer could say that what the Upanishads reveal is also revealed to him by Spinoza, Bruno, the Gnostics and the Kabbalah: "None of us knows immediately more than one thing: our own will is our own inner consciousness. Everything else we know by mediation and judge by analogy with it. This depends on the fact that in reality there is only one being; the illusion of plurality *(Maya)*, which is derived from the forms of the extensive objective understanding that has not been able to penetrate the inner consciousness, so that the latter knows only one being"[624]. And this single being is the self: "But can the one who feels this way believe himself to be in contradiction with nature, imperishable, completely

---

[623] Schopenhauer, *The World as Will and Representation*, Aguilar, Buenos Aires, I, 25.
[624] Ibid., 11, 157.

mortal? On the contrary, he will understand the profound meaning of the sentence of Upanishad in the Vedas. *All these creatures in totality am I, and outside of me there is no other entity*[625].

And the themes of the Kabbalah and Spinoza appear in the hypostasised and creative nature: "At the same time we will be convinced that the primitive force, the *natura naturans,* is immediately present, whole and undivided, in each of its innumerable works, in the most perfect as well as in the most insignificant, from which it follows that the creative nature knows neither time nor space by itself"[626].

In turn, this "I" is the same as the will. "The world is, on the one hand, representation and nothing but representation; on the other, will and nothing but will"[627]. The world is then creation or representation made by my will and the only reality is "I" or my "will", which is, in turn, Kant's *thing-in-itself,* that is, negation or nothingness. "My doctrine, according to these principles, takes on a negative character when it reaches its culminating point and ends in a negation which, having reached this point, can only speak of what is renounced, what is repudiated; as for what is gained or found on the other hand, it is obliged to call it nothingness; only by way of consolation does it add that it is not an absolute nothingness, but a relative nothingness. Indeed, when a thing is nothing of what we know, it is in reality nothing for us. But this does not mean that it is nothing, speaking in absolute terms, that is to say, that it is nothing in all respects and in all senses..."[628].

It is clear that this nihilism cannot but end in absolute pessimism. And so says Schopenhauer, putting him in the mouth of St. Clement of Alexandria: "At the same time, full of it he does not want to leave to the Marcionites even the merit of originality, and armed with his well-known erudition, he shows them with numerous quotations that the ancient philosophers Heraclitus and Empedocles, Pythagoras and Plato; Orpheus and Pindar, Herodotus and Euripides, and in addition the Sibyl, lamented the wretched condition of the world and consequently taught pessimism"[629].

---

[625] Ibid., 195.
[626] Ibid., 157.
[627] Ibid., I, 38.
[628] Ibid., III, 230.
[629] Ibid., 253.

There Schopenhauer himself gives a Gnostic view of the Old Testament and Christianity, assimilating it with Brahmanism and Buddhism and the Gnostic and Persian sects[630], and finally teaching the doctrine of pantheism. "The doctrine of the έν και μαν, that is, of the absolute unity and identity, of the essence of things, after having been taught by the Eleatians, by Scotus Eriugena, Giordano Bruno and Spinoza, and having been refreshed by Schelling, was already admitted and understood in my time; but the problem lay in knowing what this one principle is and how it comes to be made manifold, and I believe I was the first to give the solution"[631]. It is clear that this monistic doctrine, in absolute terms, and pessimistic, can only tend towards *nothingness*, towards *nirvana*. And so Schopenhauer writes: "The calmness and peace which are visible on the face of most of the dead seem to have this origin. They voluntarily renounce this existence as we know it. The one that will be given instead to our eyes is *nothingness*. Buddhism calls it *nirvana*, which means extinction"[632].

7. *Nietzsche's nihilism*

With Nietzsche we are back to total pessimism. "Alas, man returns eternally, the little man returns eternally! One day I saw the biggest and the smallest man naked: too much like each other; too human, even the biggest.

Too small the biggest! This is what disgusted me in man, and also the eternal return of the smallest! This was what made me disgusted with everything in existence. Alas, disgust! disgust! disgust! disgust! disgust! disgust! disgust! disgust! Thus Zarathustra spoke, sighing and shuddering, because he remembered his illness"[633].

If Nietzsche, with Schopenhauer, makes the will the essence of being, the will to life, the will to will, the will to power, the will is the original source of being. There is no question of an end outside this original will; there is no point in asking: why, whence and for what? The eternal becoming and pleasure of the will has nothing that can transcend it.

---

[630] Ibid., 111, 237.
[631] Ibid., III, 152.
[632] Ibid., 111, 239.
[633] *Así hablaba Zaratustra*, Ediciones ibéricas, Madrid, p. 264.

Think of this instant," I continued; "from this portico of the moment a long eternal street leads *backwards*; behind us lies an eternity.

"Everything that *can* run, must it not have run down this street? And if everything has already happened, what do you think, dwarf, of this moment? This very porch, must it not have been here again?"[634].

I therefore return to the cosmic monism of the ἐν και μαν according to which there is a complete interpenetration of being and will. No longer just untenable theism, but transcendental and meaningless pantheism. Schopenhauer and Nietzsche accept in substance Feuerbach's critique of theological idealism with a slight modification: theology is not anthropology, but anthropologism[635].

There is no doubt that Nietzsche's negation had no radical meaning; God is dead, not only the God of Christianity, although this was especially so, but also Buddha and all the gods of all times and religions are dead. It is therefore an affirmation and a verification in the history of the spirit: that in the modern age it has rid itself of God and religion, that modern man has radically exorcised himself of the divine... Nietzsche takes stock of modern man and proclaims, like Feuerbach and the Hegelian left, like Schopenhauer, that there is no longer any place for God in modern man. But unlike Schopenhauer's quietist thought, Nietzsche wants to fill this vacuum left by God, God's place cannot be left vacant; and this is the aim of the doctrine of the "superman" which forms the theme of *Thus Spake Zarathustra*.

It is clear that this will to power that animates Nietzsche's superman actually has its foundation and meaning in the acting out of the *will to Nothingness*, since it does not close in any given thing, but is a becoming of an endless chain of things eternally moved by necessity. The life of human beings and of all beings is meaningless. It is absolute *nirvana*. A nirvanic hell. Total nihilism. Man is a structure of death. Nietzsche is aware of the drama he poses to his generation and thus says: "It was not worth sacrificing God himself for cruelty to himself and worshipping stones, stupidity, gravity, fate, nothingness. Sacrificing God to nothingness, this paradoxical mystery of supreme

---

[634] Ibid., p. 162.
[635] *Fabro*, Introduzione all'atheismo moderno, *p. 829.*

cruelty, was reserved for the present generation; of that we all know something"[636].

8. Freud and Jung, or the psychoanalytical current of the Kabbalah

The Nirvanic instinct that runs through the works of Schopenhauer and Nietzsche also pervades the psychoanalysis of Freud and Jung. Freud, in 1920, studied in some detail the death instinct in relation to the libido or pleasure instinct in *Beyond the Pleasure Principle*[637].

It is well known that Freud moves within Darwinian evolution and thus imagines an evolutionary state in which life would have arisen from non-life. And this is why he says: "If as experience, without exception, we have to accept that all living things die on *internal* grounds, returning to the inorganic, we can say: *The goal of all life is death*. And with equal foundation: *the inanimate was before the animate*"[638]. And further on he insists: *"The instinct of self-preservation, which we recognise in every living being, is in curious contradiction with the hypothesis that the total instinctive life serves to lead the living being towards death"*[639].

Thus, in Freud's opinion, a struggle or opposition was established between the instincts of self-preservation, derived from the pleasure instinct, and the death instinct, which would come from the original state of inanimate beings. "The instincts of the self come from the vivification of inanimate matter and want to re-establish the inanimate state"[640]. And do not think that this death instinct can be secondary, but, on the contrary, Freud considers its dominant and fundamental character in the whole psychic life of man. "To have recognised as the dominant tendency of psychic life, and perhaps also of nervous life, the aspiration to lessen, to keep constant or to make the tension of internal excitations cease, the principle of nirvana, according to Barbara Low's expression), as this aspiration manifests itself in the pleasure principle,

---

[636] Nietzsche, *Beyond Good and Evil*, Aubier, bilingual edition, Paris, 111, 55.
[637] *Obras completas*, Biblioteca Nueva, Madrid, 1948, I, p. 1111.
[638] Ibid., p. 1,126.
[639] Ibid., p. 1.127.
[640] Ibid., p. 1.129.

is one of the most important reasons for believing in the existence of death instincts"[641].

In this study, Freud argues that in the beginning human nature was very different.

> "Primitively, he says, there were three sexes; three and not two, as nowadays; next to the male and female there lived a third sex which participated in equal measure in the other two...". Also these human beings were double; they had four feet, four hands, two faces, double genitals, etc. But one day Jupiter decided to divide each of them into two parts, as pears are usually divided for baking". "When the whole of nature was thus divided in two, there appeared in each man the desire to be reunited with his own other half, and the two halves embraced each other, intertwined their bodies and wanted to form one being again".

Freud notes here that he owes these ideas on the Platonic myth to Professor Heinrich Gomperz of Vienna, and that they are to be found in the *Brihad-Aranyaka-Upanishad*[642]. But it is clear that these ideas are also from the Kabbalah, though not in the details of the Platonic myth, but simply of the first celestial Adam, who later became androgynous. The distinction between male and female would coexist even in God, according to the Kabbalist Abulafia[643]. Henri Serouya adds that "Adam, a faithful reflection of the superior or primordial Adam, must as his model have united in him the double principle of male and female. He was created primitively androgynous, man and woman were linked back to back; God separated the woman and brought her to Adam, so that they could see each other face to face"[644].

If Freud must be linked by the nirvanic instinct of his doctrine with the cabalistic current, Jung must be linked with it with much more reason. Strictly speaking, this famous psychiatrist proposes a system of ideas which goes beyond the purely psychological field and reaches metaphysics and theology. In the *Answer to Job* we find the complete systematisation of his thought[645].

---

[641] Ibid., p. 1.135.
[642] Ibid., p. 1,136.
[643] Henri Serouya, *La Kabbale*, Grasset, Paris, 1967, p. 264.
[644] The Kabbalistic origin of Freud is the subject of Prof. David Barkan's work, "Freud and the jewish mystical tradition".
[645] *Reply to Job*, Fondo de Cultura, 1964.

Jung starts from a God who is "in contradiction with himself, and this, moreover, in such a total way, that Job is sure to find a protective God and an advocate against God himself; a Jahweh... who is an *antinomy*, a total internal contradiction"[646], an antinomy that "is the necessary presupposition of his tremendous dynamism, of his omnipotence and omnicience"[647]; an amoral Yahweh with devastating fits of rage; an unconscious God, with three quarters of animality and only one quarter of humanity, of an unbearable behaviour "[648]. Needless to say, the familiar ideas of the Kabbalah, Boehme and the Gnostics appear here.

This contradictory, unjust and evil God will approach "with the Hebrew *jojma*"[649], with the idea of *Sophia*, or *Sapientia Dei, a pneuma of feminine nature*[650]; a cosmogonic pneuma that crosses heaven and earth and all creatures[651]; with the character of "shaper of the world, of *maya*"[652]; which will determine a *status* of transformation of Jahweh[653], a transformation that would take place in the face of the failure of the attempt to pervert Job that Jahweh himself would have undergone[654].

Just as there would be an analogy between Adam and Yahweh, there would be an analogy between Satan, the son of God, and Cain and the serpent[655]. Adam would have had a lurid relationship with Lilith, who is the satanic correspondence of wisdom[656]. Satan is a trickster and a spoilsport, who takes pleasure in organising unpleasant incidents[657]. It is not clear to what extent Eve represents wisdom, nor to what extent she represents Lilith. But Adam possesses the priority in any respect. Eve came secondarily from the side, and therefore comes second[658].

In the idea of creation "out of nothing" we also find reminiscences of Kabbalism and Scutus Eriugena. "When Yahweh, says Jung[659], created

---

[646] Ibid., p. 16.
[647] Ibid., p. 17.
[648] Ibid., p. 32.
[649] Ibid., p. 36.
[650] Ibid., p. 36.
[651] Ibid., p. 36.
[652] Ibid., p. 36.
[653] Ibid., p. 40.
[654] Ibid., p. 42.
[655] Ibid., p. 42.
[656] Ibid., p. 43.
[657] Ibid., p. 43.
[658] Ibid., p. 47.
[659] Ibid., p. 53.

the world out of "nothing", he could do nothing other than secretly introduce himself into creation, every part of which is himself". And he further stresses this same idea. "These indications and prefigurations of the Incarnation may seem to some to be totally unintelligible or superfluous, since the whole of creation, which came forth *ex nihilo* from God, consists of nothing else but God, and therefore man, like every creature, is God objectified"[660].

Out of creation comes a world in which, as in God its author, injustice, deceit, immorality and contradiction dominate. But now, when Yahweh decides to become incarnate, it is not the world that must be transformed, but God who wants to transform his own essence. And now humanity is not to be annihilated but *saved*. Now no new men are to be created, but only one. The masculine *Adam secundus* is not to spring immediately from the hands of the creator, like the first Adam, but is to be born of a human woman. This is the *second Eve*, who has priority, and not only in a temporal sense, but also in a substantial sense[661]. "It is nothing less than a revolutionary transformation of God; it represents something akin to what creation once meant, that is, the objectification of God"[662].

This transformation of God signifies Job's victory over Yahweh's outbursts and immorality: "Job had a higher moral stature than Yahweh. The creature had surpassed the Creator in in this respect"[663]. In Christ divinity reaches its human essence, that is, the moment when God has the experience of mortal man, and experiences the very thing that he made his faithful servant Job suffer"[664].

With the transformation of Yahweh into Christ comes the historical separation, definitive for the time being, of Yahweh from his dark son. Satan has been banished from heaven and no longer has the opportunity to convince his Father to embark on troublesome enterprises. "This event may explain why Satan, whenever he appears in the story of the incarnation, has such a secondary role that bears no resemblance to his previous relationship of trust with Yahweh"[665]. "As a result of this

---

[660] Ibid., p. 54.
[661] Ibid., p. 49.
[662] Ibid., p. 57.
[663] Ibid., p. 61.
[664] Ibid., p. 63.
[665] Ibid., p. 64.

relative restraint of Satan, Yahweh has identified himself with his luminous aspect and has become a good God and a loving father"[666].

"The immediate and continuous working of the Holy Spirit in those called to divine sonship means *de facto* a progressive incarnation. Christ, as God's begotten son, is the first-born, followed by a whole series of human beings born after him... Man has an intimate relationship of trust with God as Father and with Christ as "brother". These radical transformations in human *status* are directly caused by the work of Christ's *redemption*[667].

After this brief exposition of Jung's thesis it is not necessary to clarify that there is in this author a theogony, a cosmogony, an anthropogony in no way different from those of the ancient Gnostics and mysteries. The only novelty that Jung asserts is the power of the *unconscious* and of the archetype into which these symbolic magnitudes of Yahweh, Satan, Christ, Eve and Mary are translated. Jung grants "to the archetype a certain degree of autonomy, and to the consciousness a certain creative freedom, corresponding to its degree of consciousness. From this arises a mutual interaction between two relatively autonomous factors, and this obliges us, in the description and application of phenomena, to present one factor and the other as the acting subject; this is the case when God becomes man. The solution which has been given up to now has circumvented this difficulty by recognising only one man-God, Christ. But the indwelling of the third divine person, that is, of the Holy Spirit, in man, gives rise to a christification of a number of men; and then the problem arises as to whether these God-men are fully so"[668].

There is in Jung, as can be seen, a naturalisation and even a psychic materialisation of the Christian mystery. Here we can establish a relationship between Jung and the occultists of all ages. "Nothing is created and nothing is destroyed: it is the victorious formula over death". Jacobi, an authoritative interpreter of Jungian thought, states: "Death is no less important than birth and is, like birth, inseparable from life. Nature herself, if we understand her, takes us into her protective arms. The older we get, the more the outer world is hidden from us and loses its colour and fascination, and the more intensely the inner world

---

[666] Ibid., pp. 68-69.
[667] Ibid., pp. 68-69.
[668] Ibid., p. 131.

claims us and occupies us. The ageing man tends to return to that collective psychic state from which he emerged with great fatigue as a child. Thus the cycle of human life closes and the beginning and the end coincide, as the symbol of the Ouroburo, the snake that bites its own tail, has expressed since time immemorial. The spirit is in fact never linked to the consciousness, like the understanding, but contains, shapes and dominates the whole depth of the unconscious, of the primordial nature"[669].

Thus, what in Freud was a desperate monism of death is transformed in Jung into a monism of eternal life, into a true and proper pantheism[670]. And the unconscious fills the function of chaos in the ancient theogonies and of the Abyss and Silence in the early Gnostic systems.

9. Heidegger's cabalist line

Heidegger has had the great wisdom to focus philosophy on the problem of the truth of being and of the "being that transcends entities". The problem of idealism and realism, of subjectivism and objectivism would no longer be fundamental, but the problem of "being", which is prior to and more fundamental than all the divisions that are formulated within "essence", when in reality it is necessary to look for some agreement that makes possible the essences themselves.

The entity with respect to being is something founded and derived. Being, on the other hand, is the opening and illuminating of entities. "In Greek philosophy the two meanings of *on*, the authentic and the spurious, coexist side by side. As was seen with regard to Plato's *idea*, the same is said of Aristotle's *energy*, of Heraclitus' *Logos*, of Parmenides' *moira*, of Anaximander's *Jreon*. The deviation - from which the confusion of the "systems" of philosophy was born - began when the *einai* of the *on* (the esse of the ens) was extended and translated as *actualitas* in the sense of actualisation of a "subject" (which is the essence) with respect to which the entity would be indebted for its foundation. And so it is that from *actualitas* one passes

---

[669] Quoted in *Renovatio*, II, p. 293.
[670] Ibid.

to "reality" and from this to "objectivity" and takes the latter as the main one, when it is the last one, forgetting the "presence"[671].

In all this, Heidegger's approach is correct. The real problem begins when it comes to determining what this being *that transcends entities* is. The matter is all the more serious when we know that Heidegger finds the Christian idea of creation inadmissible insofar as it entails production from nothingness, and thus denies the truth of the principle *ex nihilo nihil fit*. Nothingness thus becomes for Heidegger in the Christian conception, the opposite concept to what it properly is, to *Summum Ens*, to God as *ens increatum;* but it is for Heidegger a passing beyond the fundamental point, since the problems of being and nothingness are overlooked and especially the very problem that "if God produces out of nothing, he must precisely be able to enter into relation with nothingness. But if God is God, he cannot know nothingness, since as an Absolute he "excludes from himself all nothingness" (What is metaphysics?). The only valid concept of nothingness is not that which is opposed to being, but that which makes it belong to the being of the entity and therefore identifies it, in the theoretical seat, with being itself according to the Hegelian principle that pure being and pure nothingness are the same thing"[672].

Heidegger was accused of nihilism and atheism. The pretext for the accusation of nihilism had been found in the thesis of *Was ist Metaphysik?*, which placed nothingness together, or rather, as the foundation of being, but also the whole orientation of *Dasein* in *Sein und Zeit* as "being for the end", which resolves itself into being for death. To this Heidegger replied with *Brief über Humanismus* (1947) with the following formula: "Since the truth of being consists in the openness to the presence of the being of the being of the being of the being, only from the presentience of the being of the being can the problem of whether God exists or not, and how He exists, be settled."

But Heidegger, by altering the concept of creation, closes the only rational way to God. He then has to invent a "gnostic way", the discovery of "the sacred", which, starting from the truth of being, leads us to the divine. Heidegger has shown that Hölderlin put special emphasis on the latter writings and that the terms "nature", "chaos",

---

[671] Fabro, *Historia de la Filosofía*, Rialp, Madrid, 1965. II, p. 630.
[672] Hegel, *Science of Logic,* translated by Augusta and Rodolfo Mondolfo, Hacrette, Buenos Aires, 1956, p. 107.

"sacred", "open" are equivalent in him[673]. The Heideggerian being then has the sacred[674], the indeterminate, the impersonal on its back. In other words, a gnostic god that does not go beyond the sphere of indeterminacy of the absolute.

We believe that Karl Löwith's statement that "in writing *On Humanism*, Heidegger comes so close to Hegel's metaphysical historicism that there is hardly any difference in his *History of Being* and Hegel's History of the Absolute Spirit" is correct. And Hegel is merely renewing Valentino's Gnostic system in modern language, as we have noted above[675].

10. Kabbalah and mass culture

All this expansion of the Kabbalah in the higher manifestations of religion and intelligence is to cascade down through the intermediate groups of advertising, press, radio, television and cinema, until it reaches the masses. "The world could be called both the incarnation of music and the incarnation of will"[676]. This formula, which summarises Schopenhauer's ontology, is also the foundation of mass culture, understood as an instrument for the education of man in the mysticism of the collective, that is, in the transcendence of that superpersonal and superrational being that Teilhard de Chardin defines as the "planetary totalisation of human consciousness"[677].

But it is "the discovery of the unconscious and the reduction of its latent thought into logic, a double of human logic, which constitutes the principle of the great Freudian system... Freud seeks to reveal the secret of absolute man by means of pure scientific observation. He transforms man's situation and reality into an *anthropogram* and reduces man to the immanence of the thing, of matter. Hence it is not by chance that a visible fruit of Freudianism is mass culture. Rationalist humanism has already been surpassed. Today we are in a consumer civilisation in which the drama of the renunciation of all intellectual pretensions is

---

[673] Fabro, *Introduzione all'atheismo moderno*, Studium, Rome, 1964, page 867.
[674] Brief über Humanismus, *p. 102*.
[675] *Heidegger, pensador de un tiempo indigente*, Rialp, Madrid, 1956, p. 126.
[676] Schopenhauer, passim.
[677] Renovatio, 1967, III, p. 467, article by Piero Vasallo on *Fundamento neopagano della cultura de massa*.

represented, the "intellectual eclipse", to use Zolla's expression: an eclipse that means the real transcendence of things with respect to the will, and to human understanding"[678]. The rationalist gnosis founded by Kant and Hegel converges in the scientistic gnosis founded by the Viennese doctor[679].

"And so Sartre draws the "categorical" formula of the very new philosophy, the famous "to live is to make the absurd live", from the study of the Freudian work, whose strictly Gnostic nature he first intuited. Humanistic philosophy recognises that the negation of transcendence necessarily implies the negation of the transcendence of the understanding of things. The desperate Sartrian cry, the "everything exists" is but the philosophical formula of Freud's scientific formula: "Life is nothing but the dialectic of the path from life to death""[680]. In the phenomenology of Husserl and his followers, we can also find the perfect synthesis of Freudianism and humanist philosophy[681].

Immanentism in matter directly links Freudian gnosis with Marxism. In *Beyond the Pleasure Principle*, Freud himself seeks to link the death instinct, which as an instinct belongs to psychology, to ageing, to consumption, to the irreversibility of time, to entropy. Final satisfaction for Freud tends to peace, according to that principle that Barbara Low calls the "principle of nirvana"[682]. Life is a process that includes death. Life is a constant journey towards death.

On the other hand, to live for death, to externalise myself, to fulfil myself as a man, I must satisfy my needs with goods. Life is doubly consumption: to live for death I must consume. The final satisfaction is the fulfilment of the nirvanic instinct[683].

That is why the great science today is *psychosociology*, the science of crowd management, the science of managing the masses for death. And the great enemy, which has to be defeated with this science of psychosociology, is the Christian idea of *Transcendence*. For today nothing must remain standing but the absolute immanentism of all

---

[678] *Gnose e psicoanalisi*, Piero V assallo, in Renovatio, I, 1967, pp. 142-143.
[679] Ibid.
[680] Renovatio ibid. p. 143.
[681] Ibid., p. 143.
[682] Ibid.
[683] Ibid.

gnosis which seeks the glorification of man in his purely material needs of the masses.

CHAPTER XII

THE CABAL WITHIN THE CHURCH OR CHRISTIAN PROGRESSIVISM

It would be a mistake to understand Christian progressivism as the effect of a *direct* influence of the Kabbalah. We do not think so; at least not in relation to the mainstream of theologians in whom the movement is taking place to move the Church from the traditional Church, the Church of old, to the new Church, which is in gestation. We think that the influence is indirect, though real and effective, through the modern culture which has been entirely won over by Gnostic and cabalistic influences.

These influences, in turn, do not take place in a general and total way, but are partial influences on each of the doctrinal elements and on the facts - liturgical, societal, spiritual and pastoral life and government - taken separately. The change thus brought about will, if things do not change their course, take on a sweeping global rhythm, of a universal character, which will substantially modify the whole doctrine and life of the Catholic Church.

We are going to study each of these changes in order to reach the conclusion that *a new religion* is in movement and gestation within the Roman Catholic Church, *substantially different from the one left by Christ, and that it takes on the characteristics of a perfectly configured pagan and cabalistic gnosis.*

1. Relativism in Revelation and theology

The Church's teaching on the immutability of revealed dogmas is well known. The First Vatican Council in the "Constitution on the Catholic Faith" clearly states this teaching. There it says: "For the doctrine which God revealed is not proposed to human ingenuity to be perfected as a philosophical invention, but has been given to the Bride of Christ as a divine deposit to be faithfully guarded and infallibly declared. Hence this is the sense to be retained of the sacred dogmas which Holy Mother Church once declared, and it is never to be departed from by a kind and name of higher intelligence. "Let the intelligence, the knowledge, the wisdom of each and of all, whether of one man or of the whole Church, but in their own kind, in the same dogma, with the same sense and in the same sentence, grow and increase to a high degree"[684].

Another doctrine is taught by Karl Rahner in a conference of the Association "Paulus" at the Faculty of Theology in S. Cugat del Vallés in May 1966[685], where he defends the historicity of Revelation and theology. Rahner first of all upholds "the historicity of the Revelation" and apparently criticises the traditional exposition which would reduce "revelation to a series of separate affirmations (?)[686], which God notifies one after the other in a simply additive manner, thus gradually increasing the "depositum fidei" until it reaches its definitive measure with the Christian revelation, and so that it only remains for the Church afterwards to administer and distribute this deposit".

In criticising the traditional understanding of the growth and formation of revelation, it is not clear whether Rahner holds that revelation can grow even after the death of the last apostle. It seems that he does, for he immediately adds: "The cultural, religious and secular situation is also a growth stimulus for the history of revelation, an assumption without which this history cannot be thought of at all". And since it is evident that the cultural situation of the world has been changing since the time of the Church of the apostles and martyrs, and then of the doctors and scholasticism, one would have to suppose that Revelation is also changing, which is completely gratuitous and whimsical.

It is clear that, when moving on to the second point, *historicity of theology*, Rahner promptly resolves the question because "only if there is a history of Revelation can there be a proper history of theology that makes real historicity an element of its essence"[687].

In order to prove that Revelation and Theology must change and change substantially, contrary to the clear teaching of the First Vatican Council,

---

[684] Denz., ed. 31, Herder, Fribourg, no. 1800.
[685] *Selecciones de teología*, Barcelona, No. 22, p. 148.
[686] The question mark is put by me to question the odious and false way in which traditional teaching is proposed, as if it did not have the organic cohesion of a living tradition.
[687] Ibid., p. 149.

Rahner adduces a threefold characteristic of the present situation, from which and about which theology must express itself. 1) the rational-scientific image of the world, which would be a dynamic, evolving system; 2) the dialogue between theology and the world would be co-determined by sin; 3) there would be the possibility and reality of erring in theology.

But to this it must be replied that the evolutionary system is not a scientific acquisition, proved by facts, but a merely hypothetical opinion of palaeontologists, distorted and denied by biologists[688]. That there is contamination of sin in theologians and the possibility of error shows that there may be variety in theological *opinions* on matters of opinion, but not several truths firmly affirmed in Revelation and theology on the same point. Ultimately, it is a question of whether the teaching of Vincent of Lerins, mentioned in the above transcription of Vatican I, is to stand. If Rahner authorises with an ambiguous and justification-prone article the change in Revelation and theology, why should one be surprised that theologians then call into question the most evident truths sanctioned by the extraordinary magisterium of the universal Councils themselves?

For this reason, Paul VI's speech of 3 April 1968, while documenting the seriousness of the situation in theological circles, in allowing themselves to be invaded by this "transforming historicism", testifies that "the word of Christ is the truth which does not change and which always remains identical and the same as itself". The Pope says: "This phenomenon also invades the religious field, which many would like to subject to a radical revision, trying to strip it of those dogmas, that is to say, of those teachings which seem to be outdated and surpassed by scientific progress and which are incomprehensible to modern thought. In the attempt to give the Catholic religion an expression more suited to the common language and mentality, that is to say, to "aggiornare" the religious teaching, its inner reality is often unfortunately upset and a way is sought to make it "comprehensible", first of all by changing the formulas with which the teaching Church has clothed it and, as it were, sealed it so that it would jealously preserve its identity through the centuries, and then by altering the very content of the traditional doctrine, subjecting it to the dominant law of transforming historicism.

---

[688] See this question more extensively studied in my work *Teilhard de Chardin or the religion of evolution*.

In this way, the word of Christ is no longer the truth, which does not change and which remains always identical and the same as itself, always living, always fruitful, always luminous, even if often superior to our rational understanding. The word of Christ is reduced to a partial truth, like all others, which the mind measures and shapes within its own limits, ready to give it in successive generations a different expression, according to a free examination which strips it of all objective and transcendent authority".

Humani Generis (1950) already denounced this error of theological relativism, which later developed and which seeks to diminish and relativise the power and value of reason. With regard to theology," we read there, "what some seek to do is to diminish as much as possible the meaning of dogmas and to free them from the traditional way of speaking already in the Church, and from the philosophical concepts used by Catholic doctors, in order to dissolve, in the exposition of Catholic doctrine, the expressions used by the Holy Scriptures and the Holy Fathers. They hope that thus the dogma, stripped of elements which they call extrinsic to divine revelation, may be fruitfully compared with the dogmatic opinions of those outside the Church, and that by this means they may gradually arrive at the assimilation of Catholic dogma with dissenting opinions".

"By reducing Catholic doctrine to such conditions, they believe that the way is also opened to obtain, as modern needs demand, that the dogma be formulated with the categories of modern philosophy, whether it be immanentism, idealism or any other system".

And further on he adds:

"And while they despise this philosophy (that of St. Thomas), they exalt others, ancient or modern, Eastern or Western, in such a way that they seem to insinuate that any philosophy or doctrine of opinion, with the addition of some corrections or complements, if necessary, can be reconciled with Catholic dogma; Which no Catholic can doubt to be altogether false, especially when it concerns the false systems called *immanentism, idealism* or *materialism,* whether *historical* or *dialectical,* or even *existentialism,* whether it defends atheism or at least contests the value of metaphysical reasoning".

Because the problem that lies at the heart of this is to know whether a philosophy that is modelled by the *essences* and the *being* of things, or on the other hand another that is modelled by the *immanence* or the *idea* or the existence of the subject who would be, in the end, the author and creator of reality, is sustained and advocated. There is only one philosophy that fully and completely fulfils these conditions of being fully and completely modelled by the reality of things. There is only one philosophy which, shaped by the extramental being, can rationally arrive at God. Hence, adherence to false philosophies which alter or distort the value of human reason must also lead to the elaboration of false theologies, because a distorted reason, when applied to revelation, can only produce a distorted theology. Hence the falsehood of the existentialist, dialecticist, immanentist, historicist theologies with which the new theology and the new theologians want to replace traditional theology. They can only do this, as we shall see later, by seriously altering the dogmas and by creating a new religion which will not be the one left to us by Jesus Christ, but another one, of Gnostic and cabalistic origin.

On the other hand, by applying to Revelation an *immanentist, dialecticist, idealistic* and *existentialist* philosophical treatment that uses an eminently *subjectivist* and *anthropological* method that necessarily downgrades the revealed content from an eminently transcendent sphere, in which the divine plan of salvation of a transcendent God has been conceived, to a specifically human and worldly sphere, one falls into the typical error of Gnosticism, which consists in assigning a single dimension to God and the creature, to good and evil, to nature and grace, to the Church and the world. This is the way to worldly or secularise or immanentise the whole mystery of faith in man, whether individual or communal, from which the words of the Apostle Paul are to be fulfilled: "Christ sent me not to baptise but to evangelise, and not with cunning words, *lest the cross of Christ be misrepresented*". The artifices and words of the new theological systems devised by man *must completely empty the cross of Christ,* contrary to the Apostle's command, *non evacuetur Crux Christi*[689].

2. The historical character of Scripture is questioned

Antonino Romeo, in an article *L'Enciclica Divino afflante Spiritu*, published in the prestigious review "Divinitas" [690], denounced in

---

[689] 1 *Cor.*, 1, 17.
[690] December 1960.

particular the excesses of an article by Fr. Luis Alonso Schökel, entitled *Where is Catholic exegesis going?*

Karl Rahner called Romeo's article "hateful" "against the professors of the Pontifical Biblical Institute"[691], but, on the other hand, echoed the same criticism when he exhorted today's exegetes not to forget that *"Catholic exegesis is a science of faith, and not only philosophy and religious science, and that it has a positive relationship to the faith of the Church and its magisterium"*[692].

It is well known that the tendencies which dominate today in the interpretation of the Holy Books are all, more or less closely, in the orbit of the Protestant exegetes, and in particular of Bultmann, who, as is well known, is in the midst of the task of demythologising the sacred books of the Old and New Testament. In fact, Bultmann renews in a variant, with a more scientific colouring, the errors of the impious Strauss, who maintained that the facts of the New Testament lacked *historical value* and were reduced to myths or fables. It is evident that with the displacement of the historical and supra-historical event which is summed up in the name of the crucified and risen Christ, the Christian faith as a whole is also displaced. We do not believe in the resurrection of Christ because that was the faith of the first Christian community, but we believe in it because that fact has been verified in reality and historically.

Rudolf Bultmann has become today the symbol of a dangerous theological radicalism...

His disciples continued his critical exegetical work with cool determination. Some critics urge him to rid himself of the concept of *kerygma*, as of a last mythological residue, and to assimilate his Christianity frankly with a philosophy[693].

In reality, Bultmann renews a gnosis. One only has to read the article that F. Mussner devotes to *"Demythologisation of the New Testament"* in "Encyclopedia of the Bible". Let us read what Mussner says: "Since what had been announced about this historical Jesus in the post-Easter *kerygma* had the significance of underlining with the help of

---

[691] Various authors, *Exégèse et dogmatique*, Desclée de Brouwer, Paris, 1966, p. 30.
[692] Ibid., p. 32.
[693] Giovanni Miegge, *L'Évangile et le mythe dans la pensée de Rudolf Bultmann*, Delachaux et Niestlé, S. A., Paris, 1958, p. 117.

mythological ideas, especially from the apocalyptic myth of late Judaism and the Gnostic myth of redemption, the "transcendence" of Jesus and his cross for the attainment of a true, Christian understanding of himself (selbstverständnis)". The prophetic announcement by Jesus of the imminence of the end of historical events would have had the significance of a "decisive call" to men, which was intended to free them from their fall into worldliness and the "flesh" and lead them to the "authenticity" and "unworldliness" of existence... Always, according to Bultmann, "resurrection to life" means, by demythologising it, to achieve the authenticity of existence... In reality, salvation has not happened (then and there) but always happens, when through the word of preaching I succeed in my existence... Therefore, demythologisation is not, according to Bultmann, an eliminative or subtractive procedure, but a hermeneutic or interpretative process, in which, by means of the interpretation of the myth, I arrive at the true understanding of myself before God.

In reality, Bultmann's attempt at demythologisation is characterised as an attempt to empty the New Testament of Christian truth, which is based on the historical fact of the Resurrection of the Lord, and to clothe it in a *Gnostic myth*. The New Testament, deprived of historical truth, would contain a Gnostic significance, which would be the very understanding of authentic existence. The *kerygma* would not be the preaching of a historical truth but the call from worldly existence to authentic existence. The famous demythologisation would be a Gnostic mythologisation. The schema of Kabbalistic Gnosticism is fulfilled in the Bultmannian demythologisation. Through the hermeneutic process man discovers his worldliness and finds himself in his authenticity. Man saves himself and Christ is but a paradigm of this process of salvation.

With his demythologisation of the New Testament, Bultmann renews the transformation of the Old Testament, and especially of Genesis, into Kabbalah, which the ancient Kabbalists did.

3. The theologians of the new theology made the Primum movens of the Church

The Church is governed by the Spirit of God. And the Holy Spirit has constituted the bishops to shepherd the Church of God[694], and, in a particular way, the Bishop of Rome, on whom the universal Church has been founded. But *in the change,* which Progressivism is bringing about in the Church, not only is the value of reason and revelation weakened, but theologians - and theologians of the new theology - are made the cornerstone of the Church. This tendency, obscurely expressed, is perfectly expressed in a very suggestive article by the well-known theologian M. Chenu, O.P., who at the same time reveals the action accomplished by the theologians at Vatican II[695]. The theological task would no longer consist in the application of metaphysical intelligence to the revealed data in order to deduce theological conclusions from it in a perfectly homogeneous way, but would consist in something more ambiguous, which had already been tried to be put into practice at Vatican II. First, "an internal orientation of the debates" which would determine "the exact axis" of the problematic in each of the questions and, through this methodological procedure, would also determine the solution of the problems in a given sense. Secondly, the elaboration of a world view in which the light of faith is refracted and introduced. Thirdly, elaboration of the concepts and words used to enunciate the word of God, so that in transmitting it it can be understood correctly and fruitfully, so that it incarnates the Gospel message today in its actual human truth.

Fourthly, the introduction into the language of the Church of a whole family of terms such as *socializatio, communio, communitas, history, evolutio, progressio, dynamism.* Finally, in these forms and at these levels we must place the argument from expediency, whose name betrays a little its density for the epistemology of faith, and which is undoubtedly the most appropriate both for the object of faith and for the discretion of the believer"[696].

This extension of theology and of the task of the theologian beyond the strictly theological terrain does not fail to have very serious

---

[694] I. Peter, 5, 2.
[695] Concilium, No. 21, *Theology as an Ecclesial Science,* p. 96ff.
[696] Ibid., p. 106.

consequences which can authorise the theologian, or the supposed theologian, to venture, in the name of theology, into fields which are either alien to such knowledge, or, if not alien, to contribute debatable and purely human opinions, which have nothing to do with this divine science. The problem is all the more delicate when today, as we find ourselves in a *politicised* world, politicised by the sinister forces of the Revolution, theology can believe itself entitled to pronounce itself in favour of the Revolution and become a weapon of subversion. The issue is not merely hypothetical when we see so many clerics who, with the vision of Hegel or Marx, have taken a "theological" stand in today's world.

Cardinal John Heenan denounces current contempt for the magisterium

This is what[697] says: "In today's theology there is no subject as delicate as this one. What is the magisterium? Leaf through your old dogmatic theology books (say those of 1960) and you will read there that the ordinary magisterium is the one that guarantees that the faithful will learn the revealed truth through the teachings of the Pope and the bishops *("qui fidelibus oralem veritatem revelatam seu Traditionem dispensant"*, says an old popular manual that has been widely used for the last ten years). Today, defining the magisterium is a little more difficult. It certainly has authority, but who can exercise authority that is not duly recognised?

The ordinary magisterium of the Pope is manifested in his encyclicals, allocutions and letters. It is no secret that contemporary theologians have less respect for an encyclical than - for example - for an article in "Concilium".

"The lone voice of the Pope. The magisterium has thus become a very risky subject to discuss, not only because it is widely ignored by those whose duty it is to pass on its directives, but also because it is exercised with less confidence by those who possess its authority. It is very difficult for the bishop or the local hierarchy to condemn a theory, however unusual or fragile. According to recent reports from Rome, Paul VI wept in a public audience as he spoke of the disloyalty and disobedience of many who speak and teach in the name of the Catholic Church. These reports may not be accurate, but it is certain that the Pope

---

[697] L'Osservatore romano, arg. ed. of 25-6-6-68.

regularly insists on the dangers of theological innovations. No other authority follows his example. During the Synod of Bishops, one cardinal pointed out that the voice of the Pope is becoming a lonely voice.

Perhaps the global notion of the ordinary magisterium of the Church is changing. After the conclusion of the Council, it is rare for the world Episcopate to echo the anguished calls of the Bishop of Rome.

"The words "magisterium" and "hierarchy" have become unpleasant terms. This is perhaps why few bishops are willing to risk their popularity by exercising the magisterium. It is true that in the past the magisterium has often been exercised more to condemn than to guide. Outside of Rome, the magisterium today has become so self-confident that it is rare for it to even attempt to lead. Dangerous contemporary writings on ecumenism and the Eucharist know no episcopal censure. Distinguished ecumenists seem to see no significant difference between Catholicism and other confessions. In seeking solutions to the distressing problems of mixed marriages, for example, they claim that a Catholic has neither the right nor the duty to safeguard the faith of his children. This doctrine is preached without any protest from the magisterium".

Through the progressive propaganda, promoted by the great organs of world publicity, a very dangerous substitution of the magisterium is taking place, shifting from the Pope and the bishops to the theologians of the new theology. An article in "Concilium" by any contemporary theologian has more audience, as Cardinal Heenan says, than a directive from the Roman magisterium.

The matter is all the more serious because it merited a warning from the Holy Father at the Second General Assembly of the Latin American Episcopate, meeting in Bogota on 23 August 1968, on the occasion of the International Eucharistic Congress. The Pope said there that "faith is the basis, the root, the source, the primary raison d'être of the Church, as we well know. And we also know how faith is undermined by the most subversive currents of modern thought. The distrust which has spread even in Catholic circles concerning the validity of the fundamental principles of reason, that is, of our "philosophia perennis", has disarmed us in the face of the not infrequently radical and captious assaults of fashionable thinkers. The "vacuum" produced in our philosophical schools by the abandonment of confidence in the great masters of Christian thought is often invaded by a superficial and almost slavish acceptance of fashionable philosophies...

"Unfortunately, even among us some theologians are not always on the right path. We have great esteem and great need of the function of good and courageous theologians; they can be providential scholars and courageous expounders of the faith, if they remain intelligent disciples of the ecclesiastical magisterium, constituted by Christ as custodian and interpreter, through the work of the Holy Spirit, of his message of eternal truth. But today some resort to ambiguous doctrinal expressions, arrogate to themselves the liberty of enunciating their own opinions, attributing to them that authority which they themselves, more or less openly, dispute to the one who by divine right possesses charisms so formidable and so vigilantly guarded, they even allow everyone in the Church to think and believe what he wishes, thus falling back on the free examination which has broken the unity of the Church itself and confusing the legitimate freedom of moral conscience with a misunderstood freedom of thought which often errs through insufficient knowledge of genuine religious truths".

4. Progressivism tends to weaken the firm truth of God's existence

If there is a first and fundamental truth in the Catholic Church, it is undoubtedly the existence of God. St Thomas places it at the head of his Summa Theologica. Indeed, if God does not exist or if I do not have absolute certainty of His existence, the whole edifice of theology and revelation falls. Progressivism appreciably weakens such an august and fundamental truth in two ways: by revaluing atheism, and by denying demonstrative efficacy to the proofs of God's existence.

Reassessing atheism in progressivism

The Catholic doctrine on atheism immediately translates what the Scriptures reveal. There it is clearly taught that "the fool said in his heart, 'There is no God'"[698]. And St. Paul openly teaches that "from the creation of the world, God's invisible, eternal power and divinity are known through the creatures. So that they are inexcusable"[699]. And among the conditions for salvation, *the Letter to the Hebrews* places two as necessary with the necessity of a means, that is to say that without them salvation is totally and absolutely impossible: "He who

---

[698] *Psalms,* 14, 1.
[699] *Rom.* 1, 20.

comes to God must believe that he exists and that he is the rewarder of those who seek him"[700]. From this it is evident that the word of God teaches that atheism is a sin which makes salvation impossible. This is the objective teaching of Revelation. What happens *subjectively* in the heart of the atheist and what chances he has of salvation, God alone knows, according to Ecclesiastes: "When I pondered all this in my heart, I saw that the righteous and the wise and their works are in the hands of God, and man does not even know whether he is the object of love or hatred; everything is hidden from him"[701].

This is the clear doctrine of the Holy Roman Church. But now the progressive theologians, with Rahner at their head, teach another doctrine, the fundamentals of which they do not and cannot assign.

In an article, *On the Doctrine of Vatican II on Atheism*[702], Karl Rahner sets out his doctrine, which is now shared by countless theologians and which can be summarised in three propositions. First, the Council modifies the traditional doctrine, which taught that an adult atheist who professes atheism cannot exist without moral guilt. Second, consequently, the new position must be admitted and it must be accepted that there can be an atheist without moral guilt. Thirdly, this atheist can have saving faith.

First question: *the Council modifies traditional doctrine*, according to Rahner[703]. Well, read numbers 19-21 of the Constitution "Gaudium et Spes", which refers especially to atheism and which Rahner invokes, and you will find nothing to justify the position of this theologian. On the contrary, the opposite of Rahner's proposition is affirmed. For we read:

> "Those who willfully seek to put God out of their hearts and to avoid religious matters are disregarding the dictates of their conscience and are therefore not without guilt". There it is stated that the *voluntary and deliberate act* of denying God is guilty. From this no one has the right to conclude, as Rahner does, that the *involuntary or indeliberate act* of denying God is not culpable. For the Council teaches nothing on this point. It is not logical to ascribe to the Council an affirmation because the Council is silent. The responsibility for an involuntary act

---

[700] *Hebr.*, 11, 6.
[701] *Eccles*, 9, 1.
[702] Concilium, No. 23.
[703] Ibid., p. 380.

can only be known to God. It is a question of a responsibility *in causa*, in which a thousand *subjective* motivations enter, which cannot be discerned in this way in general and which have to be determined in each concrete case; and which in the end can only be known by God, the "searcher of the heart"[704].

It is true that in "Lumen Gentium"[705] we read: "Divine Providence does not deny the help necessary for salvation to those who, through no fault of their own, have not yet attained a clear knowledge of God and yet strive, aided by divine grace, to attain a righteous life". In this case, however, it refers to "those who through no fault of their own have not yet attained a clear knowledge of God". Whoever does not have a clear knowledge of God is not necessarily an atheist. This is why Rahnes' interpretation of this paragraph, which certainly includes atheists, does not seem to us to be correct[706]. Moreover, for this obscuring of the idea of God, those who suffer from it will undoubtedly have to be excused from *personal* guilt, but this guilt, which always exists, will have to be unloaded on those responsible for modern societies who, with their culture, work to obscure and not to clarify the existence of God.

In this case, the guilt in this case is diluted in society and in those responsible for this social state that determines the existence of people who do not succeed in putting into operation their own discourse that easily leads to God. The text of Vatican II does not clarify whether it is a question of precarious semi-Atheists who would become explicit theists before their death, because in this case, which is the most probable one, there would be no special difficulty. For in the case of *permanent* semi-Atheists, there would be a new difficulty, which would be that of the practice of a righteous life. If this is already difficult for a believer, so much the more for an unbeliever who would not have the possibility of asking repentance from a God whose existence he does not admit.

Second question: that there can be an atheist without moral guilt. *Objectively* there cannot be atheists without moral guilt, because St. Paul teaches[707] that they are *inexcusable* and the Psalm says that they are *fools*, and man is obliged to behave like a *man* and not like a fool.

---

[704] *Psalm,* 7, 10.
[705] No. 16.
[706] Ibid., p. 383.
[707] *Romans,* 1, 20.

For there to be guiltless atheists it would be necessary that the knowledge of God should be a difficult thing to acquire and that it should not be a thing indispensable and obligatory on man. And both hypotheses are not true. Man can easily know God by a simple reasoning based on the first principles of speculative reason. When he sees the splendid spectacle of creation, he is moved to affirm the existence of the Creator. There is a simple and sure reasoning. No doubt the *scientific* demonstration which the five ways of St. Thomas can provide are not within the reach of everyone, but the demonstrative and conclusive illumination imposes itself on anyone whose intelligence is not perverted.

Today, it is true, there may exist in many this perversion of intelligence that renders the simplest metaphysical reasoning unfit for the simplest metaphysical reasoning. But *objectively* there is guilt in the perversion of intelligence. However, in each concrete case the *subjective* responsibility for this guilt is not in the power of man to measure it.

Third question: that an atheist can be saved. The "Letter to the Hebrews" strictly excludes that an atheist can be saved and the reason is very simple. I cannot have theological faith if I do not accept God. Karl Rahner, on the contrary, affirms that, "on the basis of the doctrine of the Epistle to the Hebrews we can begin by affirming: yes [he can be saved], *provided that* in this content of conscience there is *at least* an *implicit* knowledge of God and furthermore that this "content" is affirmed in a free act, elevated by grace according to the mode of faith"[708]. But the Letter to the Hebrews speaks of an *explicit* knowledge of God.

Moreover, what is this implicit knowledge, what content of consciousness can *contain* God and demand that it be *made explicit?* If it is not *made explicit, it* is a sign of a *perversion* of intelligence, which cannot but be *objectively* culpable.

Karl Rahner in this whole question speaks of a "transcendental experience", i.e. of an experience of the unlimited openness of the spirit towards absolute being, since all knowledge - on the subjective level - is a real knowledge of God, albeit implicit, i.e. not necessarily objectified and concrete"[709].

---

[708] Concilium, Rahner, p. 388.
[709] Ibid., p. 389.

But what is this transcendental experience of God in the first place? If it is experience, it is immediate knowledge. But of God, as St. Thomas has definitively shown, we cannot have *a priori* or immediate knowledge. There is only one means of knowing God, and that is by reasoning through sensible things. If it is by reasoning, it is necessarily *mediate*. Therefore there can be no *experience* since it presupposes *immediate* knowledge.

That all knowledge implies an opening of the spirit to the absolute, we have no difficulty in admitting; but this does not authorise us to affirm that this opening is directly known in every cognitive act, and that therefore God is known in all knowledge. There is no other way of knowing God than through the metaphysical analysis of all worldly reality, even of all human knowledge, and this, therefore, by means of a reasoning that investigates the ultimate instance of all finite reality. Karl Rahner's thesis smacks of ontologism because implicit in it is the assertion that in all knowledge there is an immediate knowledge of God.

Another claim that Rahner makes, which is entirely fanciful, is that there is the possibility of a transcendental openness to God; but that on the objective plane, it is interpreted falsely, or in a way that is not entirely correct, and within a categorical atheism[710]. This is to repeat in another way what has gone before, namely, that of a transcendental experience of God which would ignore itself and which could not be translated into categorical terms. There is, as we have said, no such transcendental experience of God, for then there would be an immediate knowledge of God which would be an evidence. The human spirit in all knowledge may be *ontologically* open to God; but this relation of ontological openness to God cannot be known except by reasoning, i.e. by mediate knowledge. Therefore there is no such transcendental experience of God, as Rahner gratuitously affirms. And in the event, not being known in categorical terms, it is not known at all, since all human knowledge must be expressed categorically, even if it is expressed in virtue of the evidence of reasoning, founded on the first principles of being and reason, and with value for the supracategorical or transcendental world. Rahner, who affirms the openness of the spirit to God, the transcendental experience of God, which would not be translated into categorical terms, cannot psychologically ground the

---

[710] Ibid., p. 392.

possibility of this openness. His assertion is whimsical and arbitrary, based on idealistic presuppositions.

The proofs of God's existence

The entry that has been given among Catholics to existentialist, historicist, dialecticist, evolutionist and other systems, leads to the questioning of a philosophy founded on the first principles of metaphysics. We saw above[711] that the only way to God is that of reason, and that of metaphysical reason, and that this can only be reached through the *evidence and certainty* of the first principles of being. Inquiring into the cause of being, we arrive at a Self-subsistent Being, the cause of all being. Herein lies the *scientific* exposition of the rational demonstration of the existence of God claimed by Vatican Council I. "Holy Mother Church herself holds and teaches that God, the beginning and end of all things, can certainly be known by the natural light of human reason"[712]. And here the Council appeals to the words of the Apostle: "for since the creation of the world, the invisible God... has been known through creatures"[713].

The rational demonstration of the existence of God raises the question of the value of the five ways of St Thomas, in his famous text I, 2, 3 of the *Summa Theologica*. In a way, the whole Thomistic school is involved in this task, from Cajetan, who posed the question of what the ways really prove, to Garrigou-Lagrange, who develops and completes it.

But nowadays, in addition to exercising the instruments of historical and doctrinal criticism on the arguments of St Thomas (especially a study of the various sources that converge in the elaboration of the Angelicus), the arguments are sifted according to the demands of the positive sciences and of the philosophy marked by the Kantian crisis.

It is very important to determine what the famous v *iae* can say to 20th century man. In reality, this problem is framed within a larger one: what access can contemporary thought, dispossessed of a healthy metaphysics and drowned in immanence, have to the variegated world of concepts and realities of the Thomistic synthesis?

---

[711] Chapter VI of this book.
[712] Denz., ed. 31, no. 1.785.
[713] *Rom.* 1, 20.

Within the Catholic camp there are two very different attitudes or lines of interpretation of St Thomas' "proof of God". One confers on it a rigorous value, emphasising the level of metaphysical depth at which the ways are developed, a level at which they are strictly scientific and evidential. Another line dilutes this value and considers them no longer "proofs" but simply "ways", that is, "approaches"; they would not be sure arguments that lead in a complete and satisfactory way to affirm the existence of God. This second attitude is often seen as a reaction against a short-sighted and manualistic presentation and repetition of the "ways", which would not take into account the richness of the Thomistic text and the difficulties of interpretation that it contains.

The works of Fabro[714] and Guérard des Lauriers[715], for example, can be placed in the first attitude; in the second, F. van Steenberghen[716]. According to this Lovanian, the fourth way is useless, the first and second incomplete, the third and fifth in need of correction and complementation. In other words, none of the five ways constitutes in its literal tenor a complete and satisfactory proof of the existence of God. On the other hand, he tries to extract from the following questions of the Summa (deduction of the divine attributes) the elements of what he calls a genuine metaphysical proof. From this he would have to extract the principles of a complete and rigorous demonstration, inspired by Thomism, to be presented to the man of today.

Bernhard Welte represents a less clear position perhaps, but much more nuanced, in the publication of the course he gave in Buenos Aires[717]. In it, there is a whole attempt to arrive, by the phenomenological method, at demonstrating the existence of God. Needless to say, the impossibility that this attempt represents. The demonstration of the existence of God can only be based on the metaphysical analysis of first principles. If something exists, and this is self-evident, it has its raison d'être in itself or in another. Thus it cannot have it in itself, since the existing reality is affected by a determination which rejects necessary existence, and so we must turn to another being, which does not depend on anyone and is perfectly absolute. The demonstration is based in the near future on the principle of causality, but in the last analysis and in

---

[714] *L'uomo e il rischio di Dio.*
[715] *La preuve de Dieu et les cinq voies,* Cathedra Sanchi Thomae, 1 vol. of 232 p., Rome, University of Letron, 1966.
[716] *Dios oculto,* Desclée de Browuer, Veritas et Justitia collection, 1965.
[717] *Atheism and Religion, Theology,* vol. VI, no. 12, 1968, pp. 75-122.

the last instance, on the principle of non-contradiction. In other words, the principle of non-contradiction would fall if the existence of God is not accepted. This is what the famous five ways of St. Thomas boil down to. And to question the validity of the five ways is, by the same token, to question the value of reason in arriving at God. And if reason does not lead us to God, there is no other *legitimate* way to reach Him. And therefore faith, which can only rest on reason as a preamble to faith, is destroyed.

All modern criticisms of the five ways are equally valid for any rational demonstration of the existence of God. These criticisms are ultimately based on Kantian agnosticism, which in turn rests on the impossibility of metaphysics. For every modern man, whatever philosophical current he comes from, metaphysics is impossible, and thus it is impossible to reach the *noumenon,* reality, being, and thus the Subsistent Being. Reason can only reach the phenomenon and the world of appearance. There is a radical impossibility for the human mind to reach God. This impossibility is based on the fact that the human mind is *distorted* and therefore *radically* incapable of reaching the natural object of reason, which is being.

Theologians, who in one way or another accept the modern approach, also fall into the agnosticism which characterises all modern thought, and are compelled, if they were consistent, to call into question the first principles and even the principle of non-contradiction. By denying the existence of God and, consequently, the validity of the first principles, one has to affirm that the world is ultimately divine and that the flowing reality is nothing but appearance and *maya*. This is where one falls into the kabalistic gnosis, which is but a variant of the Brahmanic gnosis that teaches that all is *brahman, the* divine, and that the world is but *maya* or appearance.

5. Some new theologians question the mystery of the Holy Trinity and the mystery of the Incarnation

We read on page 249 of the third issue of the 1966 issue of the journal "Tijdschift voor theologie":

"The Healthy Presence of God in the Man Jesus Christ. Dialogue on the mystery of Christ. The following article brings together three contributions; the starting point and the object of this dialogue are to be found in the study of Fr. A. Hulsbosch, on which the other two authors leave free rein to their reflections. True to the fundamental intention of the ecclesial confession of faith, Hulsbosch does not wish to refrain from criticising - in the constructive sense of the word - the simple formulation, "Two natures in one person". He considers that the exceptional uniqueness of the man Jesus can be sufficiently understood when it is understood as a grace, conceived and assimilated to a creation. Thus "hypostatic unity" seems to him to be a conceptual superstructure on the datum of faith, a superstructure which may have been necessary at one time, but which is empty of meaning for us. E. Schillebeckx considers the "hypostatic unity" to be an ineluctable implication of the new and absolutely unique way in which Jesus is man, but criticises the unqualified representation of "two births" in Christ.

Schoonenberg criticises above all the idea of what is called the pre-existence of the divine persons and asks whether, when this idea is abandoned, there is still room for admitting a divine hypostasis in Christ, in order to be faithful to his unique importance for our salvation.

"To doubt the orthodox intention of such a reflective faith would be not only uncharitable but also narrow-minded. These studies loyally seek to renew the preaching of the mystery of Christ, to which they want to give an existential meaning.

Moreover, the publication of such a dialogue in a scientific journal seems perfectly justified. This is mainly because the people of the Dutch Church (Catholic and Reformed), whether they like it or not, have the problem of Jesus. This problem has reached the public, or rather, it has arisen in the public. Moreover, to want to keep the public from reflecting on this problem is to want to play ostrich politics. To reject the problem by opposing it with the heavy artillery of uninterpreted dogmatic formulas is simply to confess one's kerygmatic impotence and, in the end, to be unfaithful to the living Christ. Moreover, the best censure is the public opinion (in the scientific occurrence) which, in a dialogue constantly preoccupied with the word of God, progressively realises where exactly the moment of connection is to be found. The deepest meaning of our Christianity is finally nothing other than the will to link ourselves to the Word of God; and this ultimate meaning is realised precisely by the power of the grace that God gives us in Christ". "The authors".

So far, "Tijdschift voor Theologie".

What are we to think, objectively, of the formulation of Trinitarian and Christological dogma in the contributions of these authors? A.

Hulsbosch questions nothing less than the divinity of Christ. He claims that the exceptional uniqueness of the man Jesus can be understood as "created grace". And to top it all off, he speaks of the "hypostatic unity" as nothing more than a conceptual superstructure that makes no sense to us. Consequently, with Hulsbosch's words reflecting the intelligence of Christological dogma, the man Jesus would not have the uncreated grace of union, that is, he would not be the divine person of the Son in whom the humanity of Jesus would subsist. He would therefore not be God.

In E. Schillebeckx's formulation there would not be two births in Christ, one eternal, by the generation of the Father, the other temporal, in the womb of Mary. Consequently, there would not be two natures united in the hypostatic union of a single person.

In Schoonenberg's formulation, the lack of a pre-existence of the divine persons to the Christological mystery would call into question the mystery of the Trinity and the mystery of the incarnation itself.

And let it not be said that the content of the mysteries would not be touched here, but only their formulation.

For the dogmatic formulae are but the expression of this content, and they cannot be substantially altered without altering the understanding of these divine mysteries. For it is clear that with formulae which contradict the mysteries, and such is the case which we here denounce in these theologians, these same mysteries cannot be affirmed.

One more word about the position taken by E. Schillebeeckx in the article in question. On p. 275 he writes: "I adhere one hundred per cent to the 'new' approach to the mystery of Christ advocated by Hulsbosch". But since Hulsbosch, as we have seen, denies the hypostatic union, Schillebeeckx must therefore also deny it.

And on page 276 Schillebeeckx himself writes: "Since 1953 I have always opposed the formulation "Christ is God and man", and also the puzzling expression "the man Jesus is God"". In a note, he warns: "In doing this, I was in good company. Thomas himself says: "Therefore the proposition, *Christ, as man, has the grace of union,* is true, but the proposition *Christ, as man, is God,* is not true"".

One cannot see how the hypostatic union can be affirmed if one does not accept the formula "Christ is God and man". For the unity of hypostasis is verified precisely because the Word, the very Word, the hypostasis of the Second Person, with the divine nature, assumed the human nature. Hence we must also accept the formula: "The man Jesus is God, because the human nature is attributed to the person of the Word, who is God". On the other hand, it is not appropriate to say "Christ, as man, is God", because this is precisely the expression of Christ's humanity, which, being created, cannot be God.

6. There is no shortage of theologians who doubt the existence of Satan

Ambiguity in the exposition of doctrine is today a tactic used by new theologians who should be firm in the exposition and defence of the faith. But more dangerous than ambiguity is doubt, and doubt is also used to speak of angels and the Prince of evil angels, Satan. Thus, in the French Dominican magazine, *Lumiere et Vie*, Christian Duquoc, O.P., published an article[718] with the suggestive title of *Satan, symbol or reality?*, which contains paragraphs such as the following: "It is not the scientific mentality that requires the disappearance of Satan; it is the seriousness of faith. It was once believed that the Christian combat was between the super-terrestrial Powers; today we know that this combat is futile. Evil is our product, and it is a question of pushing it back in our world and by ourselves". And further on: "In the present situation, we will say, theology could not answer with full certainty that Revelation affirms, with all the authority conferred on it by the word of God, the existence of Satan. It must be said with no less vigour that the theologian would not be able to hold Satan's personal non-existence as certain"? And he adds: "Disillusioning as it may be, it is the only honest answer in the present situation".

However, there is no truth so firmly stated in the Holy Books, in the Letters of the Apostle Paul and in the Gospels themselves. If such firm truth is called into question by invoking mythologisation, it must also be invoked to cast doubt on the very existence of the Lord Jesus Christ.

7. Original sin is denied as originating

The question of original sin in modern culture is one of the most difficult to maintain.

---

[718] May-August 1966.

Above all, but not only, because of the evolutionary thesis, and of the total evolutionism which has been irrationally imposed, but which, in any case, has gained ground among scholars. And indeed, if man is the product of evolution, and comes from the most formless matter, which is perfected and arrives first at the chemical species and from these to the living species, plants and animals, and from here to man, it is clear that the first state of man has been one of imperfection that has progressed towards a more developed and perfect one[719]. On the other hand, the account of original sin as it appears in Genesis is that of a perfect man, who in the fullness of his reason and will deliberately chose evil and *fell* into guilt and its consequences, in a state of notorious imperfection and misery. Hence, it is not possible to sustain evolutionism by maintaining the classical theses of St. Augustine and St. Thomas on the state of perfection in which man would have been constituted, not only in the gifts of original justice, but also in the preternatural gifts of immortality, knowledge and freedom from concupiscence. Moreover, if evolutionism is admitted, it is not possible then not to accept polygenism, since it is to be supposed that evolution would have been effected by various ancestries of animal species which would have given rise to various human species or lines. And then, how would the Apostle Paul's words "as by one man sin entered into the world, and death by sin, and so death passed upon all men, for that all have sinned" be fulfilled[720].

Up to now, theologians had held firm to the doctrine of original sin in all its chapters and pointed out that the thesis of evolutionism was a scientific hypothesis which was far from being supported by the facts and that the facts, especially the biological facts, were opposed to this hypothesis. Things have changed in recent years, and already in 1950 *Humani Generis* had seriously drawn attention to the danger of taking polygenism and even evolutionism for granted. A number of works in the main theological faculties have appeared in recent years which question the traditional doctrine and simply deny it. In this connection we refer in particular to *Il peccato originale in prospettiva evoluzionistica* by Zoltan Alszeghy, S. J., and Maurice Flick, S. J.,

---

[719] Labourdette, O.P., argues that the first man, coming by evolution from the lower species, would have been endowed with supernatural and natural gifts when he became man, and then would have lost them when he sinned, falling into the state he would have been in before receiving those gifts.
[720] *Rom.*, 5, 12.

which appeared in Gregorianum, 47 (1966), 201-225, to the book by Henri Rondet, S. J., *Le Peché Originel dans la Tradition Patristique et théologique*[721], and to *The Power of Sin* by Piet Schoonenberg, S. J.[722].

The solution sought in these studies to the problem of "reconciling the dogma of original sin with polygenism" consists in identifying "the original sin of origin with the sin of the world", that is, with all the personal sins of mankind[723]. This solution is sought "in order to harmonise faith in the dogma of original sin with the new vision of the world which is the common heritage of contemporary culture"[724].

It is evident that such a purpose must result in the softening of the interpretation of the theological sources of original sin, namely *Genesis* 2-3, *Romans* 5, 12-21 and the Decree of Trent on original sin. The agreement among exegetes is realised on the basis of defending that *Genesis* 2-3 explains the entrance of evil (especially moral evil) into the world, revealing the reality of a sinful resistance to the divine will, which is the cause of the perJmc10 suffered by humanity. Everything else (state of original righteousness, uniqueness of the sinful couple, etc.) does not formally belong to the message of *Genesis*[725]. Paul's text in *Rom.* 5, 12-21 is visibly tempered by saying that the salvation of the one Christ who embraces all men is to be emphasised there and that the existence and influence of Adam is not affirmed with the same intensity as the existence and influence of Christ and that Paul tells us nothing about the way in which Adam transmits sin and death to other men. That, consequently, it cannot be concluded that *Rom.* 5, 12-21 demands that all sinners through Adam's transgression are descended from him by physical generation[726].

Finally, with regard to the decree of Trent, it is said that "while it is true that the Council wants to affirm categorically that everything has original sin before it can imitate Adam's sin, it is not true that the same value is given to the affirmation that physical descent from Adam is necessary to contract original sin"[727].

---

[721] Le Signe Fayard, Paris, 1967.
[722] Ediciones Carlos Lohlé, Buenos Aires, 1968.
[723] Selections in Theology, No. 23, 1967, p. 127.
[724] Ibid., p. 218.
[725] Ibid., p. 219.
[726] Ibid., p. 219.
[727] Ibid., p. 220.

The proposed hypothesis differs from the traditional description of man's origins, mainly in the conception of the *state of original justice*, since this hypothesis does not admit that man lived in a state of grace, immortality and integrity[728].

It is clear that the new theologians actually destroy the original sin of origin. The Apostle's definite teaching would no longer be true: "Just as through one man sin entered the world, and death through sin, and so death spread to all men, because they had sinned". Sin would not have entered by one man. Nor would sin and death have passed upon all men. At most, it would have passed *in imitation* as the Pelagians taught. Adam would have had influence on his descendants only by bad example. Hence, the Decree of Trent states categorically: *Si quis hoc Adae peccatum, quod origine unum est et propagatione.* If anyone affirms that this sin of Adam, that it is one by origin and propagation. And canon 2: If anyone affirms that Adam's prevarication harmed him alone and not his offspring...

On the other hand, with regard to *Gen.* 2-3, it must be said that although Genesis is such a special genre of history that there must always remain doubts about certain details, nevertheless this must not prevent the revealed core from being drawn with certainty. From this the following conclusions can be drawn:

1. The Genesis account is not a jubilant hymn to progress. It is the explanation of the origin of evil by the fall of our first parents.

2. The first couple had been created to live in innocence, divine familiarity, happiness and immortality of body.

3. At the instigation of a mysterious evil being, in whom later revelation will clearly show us the devil, he wanted by a fault of the spirit to attain to the divine likeness.

4. This fault will cause him and his descendants to incur the divine punishment, which consists in the loss of divine familiarity, concupiscence, suffering and death.

5. God does not abandon man completely. His Providence continues to protect him after the first fault; it gives him courage for new struggles and gives him a glimpse of triumph over the serpent and his posterity.

---

[728] Ibid., p. 222.

6. Thus, this story is not about the transmission of Adam's guilt to all his descendants. He does not appear as the source of sin but as the source of an unhappy state, of a ruin into which he drags his whole family... Only in the light of the following pages, in the light of Calvary, will St Paul reveal to Christians the solidarity with Adam, the source of sin for the whole race[729].

The teaching of Tridentine, authoritatively interpreting Scripture, clearly teaches that original sin is transmitted with *generation*, and thus biological solidarity is necessary for original sin, which can proceed only from a single original sin of origin. And the Fathers of the Tridentine Council defined the decree of original sin not as men of their time, who knew only monogenism, but as Bishops in hierarchical communication with the Pope, under the assistance of the Holy Spirit, who assured them of inerrancy in the faith.

Pope Paul VI has closed with memorable words all attempts to accommodate, and therefore to distort, the traditional doctrine of original sin, affirmed in definitive form at the Council of Trent. Paul VI said on 16 July 1966 to the participants in the Symposium on the Mystery of Original Sin: "It is clear, therefore, that the explanation of original sin given by certain modern authors must seem to you to be irreconcilable with genuine Catholic doctrine. These authors, starting from the unproven presupposition of polygenism, deny more or less clearly that the sin from which so many evils have befallen humanity is above all the disobedience of Adam, the 'first man', the figure of that future man, committed at the beginning of history. Consequently, such explanations are not consistent with the teachings of Sacred Scripture, Sacred Tradition and the Magisterium of the Church, according to which the sin of the first man was transmitted to all his descendants, not by imitation but by propagation".

8. An all too human image of the Person of Christ is constructed

In theology as in philosophy everything is perfectly united, so that one part cannot be weakened without the other parts and the whole suffering detriment. Sin cannot be touched without redemption and incarnation

---

[729] H. Gaudel, in Dictionn. Théol. Cath., t. 12, col. 286.

suffering. The weakening of the notion of original sin was to be followed by that of the personality of Christ.

The mysteries of the infancy of Jesus. Catholic exegesis, which in many of its most publicised representatives has embarked on a very dangerous path, as we pointed out above, shows itself particularly in the historicity of the mysteries of the Saviour's infancy to be extremely mean-spirited and even purely negative. Ugo Emilio Lattanzi has shown[730] that the genre of *midrash* with which the *midrashic school* catalogues the mysteries of the Saviour's infancy, narrated by Matthew and Luke in the first two chapters of their respective Gospels, is nothing but the resurrection of the concept of myth with which, in the last century, Strauss qualified the historical character of the life of Jesus.

According to this school they would undoubtedly have a midrashic content:

1. The announcement of the birth of Jesus, which, according to León-Dufour, would be traced according to the five moments of this type of announcement: appearance, disturbance of the protagonist, message, doubt, sign and name[731].

2. St. Joseph's dreams are inspired by the midrashim of Moses' birth[732].

3. The account of Herod's persecutions resembles the midrashim relating to the childhood of Moses, found in the Jerusalem Targum, the Chronicle of Moses and the Hiddrash Rabbath[733].

4. The appearance of the star imitates some midrashim which is not the case to describe[734].

5. The flight to Egypt is modelled on a midrash[735] in which Jacob is said to have taken refuge in Egypt to escape the persecutions of Laban[736].

---

[730] Il vangelo dell'infanzia è verità o mito?, *Renovatio, I, 1968, p. 9.*
[731] Annonce à Joseph, in Études d'Évangile, *Paris, 1965, p. 77.*
[732] L. Dubiere, *La révélation par songe dans l'Évangile de Saint Matthieu,* in *Mélanges,* Levy, Bruxelles, 1955, p. 665.
[733] R. Bloch, *Quelques aspects de la figure de Moïse dans la tradition rabbinique,* Cahiers Sion, Paris, p. 95.
[734] X. Muñoz Iglesias, *El género literario del Evangelio de la infancia en San Mateo,* Estudios Bíblicos, 1958, pp. 264-268.
[735] *Deut.,* 26, 5-8.
[736] D. Daube, *The earliest structure of the Gospels,* New Test. Studies, 5, 1959, pp. 174-187.

6. The hecatomb of the innocents is related to the midrashim of Laban's persecutions against Jacob[737].

In Luke, they would be midrashic in content:

1. The two announcements of the birth of John and the Lord[738].

2. The visitation is modelled on the journey of the Ark of Yahweh from the house of Obededom to Jerusalem[739] and also on the three months of its stay[740].

3. Elizabeth's canticle repeats the Paleo-Testament blessings, especially those of Judith (13, 18)[741].

4. The canticles of the *Benedictus* and the *Magnificat* were not pronounced respectively by Zechariah and the Virgin[742].

5. The birth of Jesus is a midrash to the prophetic text of Micah (4, 7-5, 5) with which Luke describes an event on the basis of a prophetic text according to its purpose[743].

6. The announcement to the shepherds falls within the genre of the announcements described in its moments[744].

7. The encounter with the prophetess Hannah is a midrash which is like a Kabbalah (given the caveat to the number of Hannah's years)[745].

And this authorises Hugo Lattanzi to conclude that in the minds of these authors "the whole Gospel of childhood is nothing but haggadic midrash".

The infancy of Jesus would have no historical value. And since there is no essential difference between the infancy and the public life of the Lord, if the former has no historical value, neither does the latter. And the life of Jesus is a novel, a fable and a myth, as Strauss and Renan

---

[737] D. Daube, art. cit.
[738] X. Muñoz Iglesias, *El Evangelio de la infancia en San Lucas*, Est. Bíblicos, 16, 1957, pp. 329-382.
[739] 2 *Sam*, 6, 11.
[740] René Laurentin, *Structure et Théologie de Luc*, 1-2, Paris, 1957, p. 79.
[741] René Laurentin, *op. cit.*, pp. 81-82.
[742] J. R. Forrestel, *Old Testament background of the Magnificat*, Marianical Studies 12 (1961), pp. 205-244.
[743] René Laurentin, *op. cit.*, pp. 86-88.
[744] F. Neirynck, *L'évangile de Noel*, Paris, 1960, pp. 42-45.
[745] E. Burrows, *The Gospel of the infancy*, London, 1940, p. 42.

taught years ago. This is what J.J. Schierse, S.J., who has the rare merit of speaking clearly, says. He says in effect: "He who would read the testimonies with the aim of satisfying his thirst for historical knowledge, whether it be with the lousy intention of following exactly Mary's earthly life, of describing to us her thoughts, impressions and feelings, would have gone astray. The relationship we have with Mary is not different from the relationship we have with the historical Jesus and with the Christ of faith; Mary also enters into the pneumatic process of formation which together with the tradition of Jesus has interested us and which leaves us little room for the historicity of the facts". And Fr. Schierse continues: "The historical Jesus has been transformed into the Christ of Faith, that is, to use the terms of the Apostolic Symbol: "Jesus" Christ, born of the Virgin Mary, etc... has risen from the dead on the third day, has ascended into heaven where he sits at the right hand of God the Father omnipotent. The Gospels proclaim this living Lord Jesus, who continues to operate in the Church, as Saviour and Teacher, even in the history of infancy. His theatre is therefore not primarily Nazareth, Bethlehem or Jerusalem, but the Church. It is in the Church that the angel's annunciation takes place; it is there that Christ is born, there that He is presented to the Father, there that He is to be sought and found. The historical quality of the lives of Jesus and Mary becomes a symbol of heaven and earth, of the boundless space of the Church, in which the events of the past are made present and perpetuated as mysteries of salvation"[746].

The Gospel of the infancy, therefore, is not a complex of historical narratives, but of *mysteries of faith.*

However, no matter how many assertions are made by these scriptural scholars who know the hidden secrets of how the Sacred Books have been put together and how they have come down to us, it is wise to listen to the Evangelist Luke himself, who, in the prologue of his Gospel, tells us simply and truthfully how he has documented himself in order to relate these historical facts to us: "Since many have tried to write the history of what happened among us, as it has been handed down to us by those who, from the beginning, were eyewitnesses and ministers of the word, it has seemed to me also, after informing myself exactly of everything from the beginning, to write to you in orderly

---

[746] *Weihnachtliche Christusverkündigung,* Bibel und Le ben 1 (1960), pp. 221-222.

fashion, optimal Theophilus, so that you may know the firmness of the doctrine you have received"[747].

The image of Christ in contemporary theology

If exegesis does not authorise us for anything other than a *Christ of faith and not of history,* all theology is built on a fragile foundation, which cannot provide us with the unshakeable certainty of reason and the word of God. But theologians, and not the lesser ones, will take it upon themselves to weaken the divine word by calling traditional theology into question. Bishop Antonio Piolanti has written a remarkable article in *Divinitas* [748] in which he gives an account of the attempts of contemporary theologians to create a "new image of Christ", in which Christ appears more human and less divine than in traditional theology.

These theologians begin by attacking the "ontological method" which would have, they say, the pretension, starting from the revealed datum, to leap to the knowledge of what God and Christ are in themselves, beyond the salvific event. And so the theological-metaphysical disquisition of the mystery of God in himself, considered prior to any revelatory economy, leaves the latter to appear as a purely contingent and relative fact, unworthy of consideration as such[749].

On the other hand, they ponder the "historical-functional" method which shows us the God of Revelation not manifested in himself, but in his free activity *ad extra,* in his salvific function which he exercises through Christ: the centre of salvation history... We do not think of a pre-existence of Christ in God as a divine person, independent of his revelatory function, but we always speak exclusively of a pre-existence as a "totally dynamic and functional hypostasis, for whom the Logos is essentially his revelatory action"[750].

In this way the whole theology of Nicea, Ephesus and Chalcedon is called into question and presented as unfounded. Catholic theologians may not yet reach these excesses of Protestant exegesis, but they nevertheless affirm that the biblical data are not favourable to a "theology of nature" or to the idea of a Son of God who can be

---

[747] *Luke,* 1, 1.
[748] January 1968.
[749] Ibid., p. 152.
[750] V. Cullmann, *Christologie du Nouveau Testament,* Paris, 1960, p. 230.

expressed independently of his revelatory function[751]. The reality of Christ the Saviour is not to be studied in an ontological way, but must begin with soteriology, and an "economic and functional image of the Redeemer" must be given precedence over his theological image[752].

Thus, the "Christology from above", the traditional theology of union, which highlights the divine in Christ and illustrates the hypostatic union by resorting to the ontological unity of the divine being of the Word and to a rigid hegemony in the psychological order, is opposed in preference to a "Christology from below", which starts from the human experience of the Saviour, from the affirmation of his messiahship, from his function of mediation, from the human reality of the affirmations in which the non-consciousness of Christ appears.

Hence there is a whole tendency to maintain the autonomy of the human life of the Saviour in relation to the Word[753], showing how, by the fact of the hypostatic union, no change in the human nature of Christ would have taken place[754]. Above all, Karl Rahner, in *Current Problems of Christology*[755] would be the great defender and, in a certain sense, initiator of this current, which maintains that Christ the man does not know his belonging to the Logos and that the only human knowledge of his divine being would be along the lines of self-consciousness. Christ's knowledge of his own belonging to God would come from the pole of consciousness and not from science, that is, on the line of subjective and not objective knowledge. Christ the man would not have, at least at the beginning of the Incarnation, an objective representation of God, to whom his intentionality of human consciousness could refer. It is undoubtedly an intrinsic and immediate moment of the hypostatic union, but it is not an objective vision. Such an immediate self-consciousness would be in an area of obscurity that would become clearer on reflection, and thus one could speak of an evolution, even a religious one, in the original self-consciousness of Jesus[756].

Observations on the image of Christ in contemporary theology

---

[751] J. Dupont, Essais sur la Christologie de Saint Jean, Bruges, 1951, p. 7.
[752] See L. Cerfaux, *Le Christ dans la théologie de Saint Paul*, Paris, 1951, p. 392.
[753] Grillmeier, Zum Christusbild der heutigen katholischen Theologie, *p. 117*.
[754] Ibid., p. 117.
[755] *Escritos de Teología*, Taurus, Madrid, 1961, I, p. 169.
[756] Ibid., p. 178.

This all-too-human image of Christ in contemporary theology is not without concern, especially if it is placed, as it should be, in an exegesis overly influenced by Bultmann. There is a danger that the historical figure of Christ's divinity will evaporate and leave us with a Christ who is a great prophet and founder of religions, as Confucius and Buddha might be.

And to refer to the historical-functional method of the new theology, it must be noted that there is nothing really original in it which is not already true, not in revealed theology, but in purely natural theology. In fact, even in the latter, it starts from the creatures and the operations of the creatures in order to know the existence of God and his divine nature.

On the other hand, it is not true that the Holy Scriptures ignore the essential attributes and substantial determinations of God and Christ. For the whole prologue of St. John's Gospel is but a hymn of adoration to the Word who in the beginning was in God and was God; and St. Paul invites us to rise to the adoration of the depth of God's riches, wisdom and knowledge[757] and to submit our intelligence to the divine plan of salvation, a plan which is before the Saviour's own saving operations. Moreover, the Trinitarian mystery presented in an exclusively functional light, according to an idea that is no longer transcendent but "economic", runs the risk of compromising the personal distinction of the Father, the Son and the Holy Spirit, and of giving us a modalistic and Sabellian concept of the Trinity[758].

And coming to Christology, can it be affirmed that the titles *Logos, Son of God, Only-begotten* are to be considered in the functional salvific light and that they tell us nothing about the Person of Christ Himself?[759]

It may be conceded that the concept of "instrument" as applied to Christ's humanity may be misinterpreted as if Christ's human nature were totally passive to the detriment of the originality and activity of his human will, but this is not the thought of the Angelic Doctor, who valued the *free human action of Christ's Redemption*[760].

---

[757] *Ephesians*, 1. 3-14.
[758] Piolanti, ibid. p. 163.
[759] Ibid., p. 163.
[760] Ibid., p. 163.

But it must also be noted that the messianic mediatorial function of Christ, a central and indispensable dogma of the Catholic faith, cannot absorb the full reality of Christ's action, which moves in the theandric unity of Christ's work as the Son of God[761].

Observations on the psychological understanding of Christ's human nature in relation to the divine Self

Karl Rahner, while admitting an immediate contact of the human consciousness of Christ with the divine Self, with God therefore, maintains that this contact and knowledge would be confused and that it would not become objectively clear, but only gradually; that, consequently, there would also be a religious evolution in Jesus Christ.

Against this attempt at historicism in the human consciousness of Christ it must be insisted that Jesus Christ, even in his human soul, enjoyed the immediate vision of God, and a vision which did not exclude, but on the contrary demanded, the beatific vision[762]. Only in this way can we give full satisfaction to the words of the Apostle John who in his famous prologue to his Gospel tells us that "we have seen his glory, glory as of the only begotten Son of the Father, full of grace and truth"[763]. St. John speaks to us of the fullness of the truth that was in Christ, that is, an absolute fullness that also includes the beatific vision, and this at every moment of his earthly life.

That fullness of truth flowed from the Only Begotten, that is, from the divinity of the Word who became flesh, that is, from the theandric compound[764]. *For from his fullness we all receive grace upon grace*[765]. The absolute fullness of Jesus Christ and our participation in this fullness is emphasised. *No one has ever seen God; the only-begotten God, who is in the bosom of the Father, he has made him known to us* [766]. The lack of vision of God, which creatures do not have, is contrasted with the only-begotten of the Father, made flesh, who has come to reveal the Father to us. If he came to reveal him to us, it is a sign that

---

[761] Ibid., p. 167.
[762] Ibid., pp. 168-169.
[763] 1, 14.
[764] 1, 14.
[765] 1, 16.
[766] 1, 18.

he had a clear and full vision of the Father himself, of whom he made him known to us.

Karl Rahner's restriction of the immediate vision of God, which Christ's humanity would have had, is fanciful, and tends to limit the words of St. John, which evidently demand the beatific vision in Christ's soul during the whole earthly pilgrimage.

The same argument could be made with the joyful words of Christ that Matthew brings us[767] : "All things have been delivered to me by my Father, and no one knows the Son except the Father, and no one knows the Father except the Son and anyone to whom the Son chooses to reveal them".

Archbishop Piolanti, quite rightly, calls this attempt of the new theologians to nullify the divine reflections which the assumption of his humanity by his divinity would require *a total eclipse of the divine in the humanity of Christ*. Moreover, all this would not only imply a serious diminution of the privileges with which the holy humanity of the Lord was endowed, but would serve to diminish, and ultimately to suppress, the cult of adoration which this same humanity, sanctified by the presence of the divinity of the Only-Begotten Word, deserves among the Christian people.

9. *Marian privileges and, in particular, her virginity are curtailed.*

Before touching the divine figure of the Son, the new theologians have had the audacity to touch the Mother. We have already seen how the mysteries of Jesus' infancy recounted by Matthew and Luke are called into question. These mysteries are directly related to the mysteries of Mary and, in particular, to her virginity, so clearly affirmed in both evangelists. We have also seen how the Jesuit Schierse has the rare merit of openly questioning the historical truth of the Mariological mysteries. But today it is very common in the Catholic camp to question, or openly deny, the virginity of the Mother of God.

The magazine "Time"[768] states that "many Dutch theologians hint that the perpetual virginity of the Mother of God may be a myth". J. van

---

[767] 11, 27
[768] March. 1967.

Kilsdonk, S.J., professor at the Dutch Catechetical Institute, was known to deny the virginal conception, in the obvious sense of the term, of Jesus Christ by the Virgin Mary, and was invited by Rome to explain himself. But according to "De Tijd" of October 12, 1966, nothing has changed because in a broadcast of the Dutch Catholic Radio Broadcasting on October 11, 1966, he declared that he was convinced that Jesus Christ was not conceived virgins by his Mother, although the apposition of the word "Virgin" to the name of Mary remained valid for anyone who understands the religious poetic art of the New Testament and the Ancient Church".

10. Downgrading of the character and authority of the Church

Progressivism, even or especially in the most qualified theologians, tends to weaken the great dogmas of the Catholic Church. No wonder, then, that the criticisms had to be directed particularly against the Church itself, its fundamental structures, and especially against the authority of the sovereign Pontiff, the living rock on which the Holy Church was founded.

This was already seen at Vatican II, where, under the pretext of collegiality, the primatial authority of the Roman Pontiff was seriously questioned. The Pontiff himself had to intervene directly with the famous *nota praevia,* thus closing the way to any possible misunderstanding that might tend to weaken the authority of the Roman Chair.

Hans Küng, a prominent theologian from Tübingen, was to take the lead with his writings in this task of weakening the Church in its dogmas, in its unity and holiness, and especially in its authority. Already in the middle of the Council, in 1963, he published his *Structures de l'Église*[769], and now in 1968 he was to bring out his two volumes on *L'Église*[770].

In *Structures de l'Église,* Hans Küng points out, not without some satisfaction, the ironic fate that "he who is the great foundation of the Church is denounced as the main factor in the persistence of schism

---

[769] Desclée de Brouwer, Paris, 1963.
[770] Desclée de Brouwer, Paris, 1968.

among Christians"[771]. "Even he who is in favour of the primacy of *Peter* remains, in spite of everything, resolutely opposed to the primacy of the *Pope*". And he continues: "The problem of the ministry of Peter cannot be developed here in all its breadth. The difficulties range from the interpretation given to the history of the Church, the history of the constitutions and the history of dogmas, to the concrete way in which the ministry of Peter is represented and exercised in our own day. Historical trials and sufferings, anti-Protestant and anti-Roman passions, and a host of non-ideological factors weigh in all this controversy. Thus, until this is purified, at least in some way, exegetical and dogmatic discussion will hardly advance"[772].

Further on, Hans Küng picks up on the secular accusations that Protestantism still echoes today. Evangelical Christians cannot, he says, fail to see in these titles of *Successor Petri, Vicarius Christi*, more than proud pretensions, if there is no demonstration of the Spirit and Power that are authentically theirs. The "Roman apparatus" and the "Roman system", the unevangelical pomp and external power, the Byzantine etiquette, the baroque forms of expression and absolutist methods of government make it difficult for separated Christians to recognise in the Pope the Fisherman of Galilee to whom he claims to be the successor"[773].

But Hans Küng, both in *Structures de l'Église* and in *L'Église*, accumulates a series of difficulties for the recognition of the primacy of Peter, and it is not clear whether he considers it justified. He tells us there that the East "had never understood nor accepted the doctrine of the Primacy, which had developed little by little in the West and which had been masterfully formulated in particular by Leo the Great[774]; and that "it relied on the New Testament conception of the Church when it refused a Church of the absolutist and centralist monarchical type, such as was gradually developing in the West"[775]; that the construction of the Church, completed by dint of centralism and absolutism, was obtained at the price of the division of a Christendom which could

---

[771] Ibid., p. 265.
[772] Ibid., p. 265.
[773] Ibid., p. 267.
[774] *L'Église*, II, p. 612.
[775] Ibid., p. 613.

accommodate itself less and less to this absolutist system and its abuses[776].

Hans Küng goes on to contrast Vatican II, "with its clear awareness of community, *communio*, collegiality, solidarity, service", and "the basic mentality of the majority of Vatican I, which was clearly marked by the political, cultural and religious world of the Restoration period, of romantic traditionalism and political absolutism"[777]. And to present Vatican I's definition of the primacy of the Pope in a more odious way, Hans Küng points to "the exaggerations of many popular and scholastic Catholic expositions of the primacy and also, finally, the style of government of Popes such as Pius X (with regard to the modernists) and Pius XII with regard to theologians, bishops and in particular with regard to working priests"[778].

Hans Küng makes no argument against the primacy of the Pope, but lets it be understood that it is the end of a long process in which the Roman Church, against the Churches dependent on it, would have closed itself in an absolutist centralism, contrary to the New Testament teachings which would have been preserved in the East. And to round off this odious and malevolent insinuation, he denounces the precipitousness of Vatican I, which would conclude "from the primacy of Peter to an unfailing permanence of this primacy. The primacy, he says, having been instituted for eternal salvation and for the lasting good of the Church, must also necessarily endure according to Christ's order. No scriptural text is cited in support, but it is decreed in every way". Therefore, "he who says that it is not by virtue of the institution of Christ Our Lord Himself, that is, by virtue of divine right, that St. Peter and his perpetual successors have the primacy over the whole Church... let him be anathema"[779].

But in the intention, at least the objective one, of this theologian, representative of the new currents, an attempt is made to weaken such a fundamental truth as the dogmatic definition of the Primacy of Peter and his successor, the Roman Pontiff. With this weakening the firm

---

[776] Ibid., p. 614.
[777] Ibid., p. 617.
[778] Ibid., p. 617.
[779] Ibid., p. 627.

structure of the Church is shaken. But the weakening also affects other firm truths of the Church itself, as we shall immediately see.

Vatican II's *Lumen Gentium* confirms the current doctrine that identifies the Church with the Kingdom of God. It says that "Our Lord Jesus founded his Church by preaching the good news, that is, the Kingdom of God promised many centuries before in the Scriptures..." and then adds that "the Church, enriched with the gifts of her founder, faithfully observing his precepts of charity, humanity and self-denial, receives the mission of announcing the Kingdom of Christ and of God, of establishing it among the nations and constitutes on earth the seed and the beginning of that kingdom"[780]. It is clear that the earthly Church is not the consummated kingdom of God, but *the beginning* of that kingdom, as is also the Church militant. This is where Hans Küng's whimsical argumentation falls down, which on pages 129 to 151 wants to emphasise the *differences* between the Church and the kingdom of God. How Hans Küng can write: "In the New Testament already - and this could excuse many things in the history of the Church and theology - the original message of Jesus concerning the kingdom of God has not been stripped away in the Church and by the Church?"[781]. "The *identification of* the Church and the *Basileia* is tempting, writes[782]. And shortly afterwards he explains how "the Christian Empire, the realisation of the messianic age of salvation... an episcopal theocracy of the West as advocated by Athanasius, Ambrose, Hilary and the bishops of Rome, implied a broad identification of the kingdom of God with the earthly reality, in this case with the hierarchical Church"[783]. And Hans Küng concludes: "Instead of identity, it is necessary to affirm the fundamental *difference* between the Church and the kingdom of God"[784]. It is true that shortly afterwards Hans Küng softens the harshness and says that "the message of Jesus, as we can see it today, no longer allows us to dissociate the Church and the kingdom of God or to identify them"[785]. And he adds mischievously, placing the future in brackets: "The Church is not, in truth, the (future) kingdom of God,

---

[780] *Lumen Gentium No. 5.*
[781] *L'Église*, p. 129.
[782] Ibid., p. 132.
[783] Ibid., p. 132.
[784] Ibid., p. 136.
[785] Ibid., p. 139.

but it is henceforth subject to the kingdom of God which is breaking into the world"[786].

Later he adds: "Jesus announced the kingdom of God as a kingdom essentially *future, eschatological and definitive*. And then: "At this end of time, the Church does not have the right, in spite of all her extreme efforts in the service of the kingdom of God, to want to create the kingdom of God herself"[787]. The Church has not consummated this kingdom, it will not consummate it, it can only bear witness to it"[788]. It would be interesting if Hans Küng would clarify that if the coming kingdom of God, which is *within us,* and which is like a *seed sown by a man in his field*[789], is not the Church on earth but an *essentially future kingdom*[790], on which planet is this kingdom? And if he would also clarify that the *kingdom is religious thinking* and that the *Church cannot behave like a politico-religious theocracy,* that it must not establish an imperium of power that is both spiritual and non-spiritual, but a ministerium in the form of service?

For all this can take the passive form and show that the Church behaves like a politico-religious theocracy and a temporal empire. Hans Küng would echo and willingly take up the odious accusations of the Protestants against the juridicity and against the social bonds that the Church must necessarily have while on pilgrimage here on earth, where it cannot have a purely pneumatic character.

This hatred against the Church, against the Roman Church, which Hans Küng exudes, is increased in the long pages he devotes to L'Église et les juifs and in which he imputes to the Church the responsibility for the sufferings of the Jews throughout history. But Hans Küng, so addicted to biblical theology, should not forget the words of St. Paul in the Second Letter to the Thessalonians, when he says: "The Jews, those who put to death the Lord Jesus, and the prophets, and persecute us, and who do not please God and are against all men; who prevent the Gentiles from being spoken to and their salvation from being procured". In this way, he would have realised the biblical foundation of the denunciations of the Fathers, Doctors, Pontiffs and saints, throughout

---

[786] Ibid., pp. 142-143.
[787] Ibid., p. 143.
[788] Ibid., p. 143.
[789] Mt. 3, 2; 4, 17; Le. 17, 21; Mt. 13, 14.
[790] Hans Küng, L'Église, II, 142.

the history of the Church, of the insidiousness and persecution that the Jews have plotted at all times[791].

11. The new theology also questions transubstantiation

Today's theologians are engaged in a task of revision which does not always remain within the limits that the integrity of faith demands. The theological work of two millennia has achieved through the speculation of the Fathers and Doctors a precision and adjustment in some notions incorporated into the intellection of the faith which, although not explicitly found in the sources of Revelation, it would be dangerous to abandon or call into question, since they are irreplaceable. One of these is precisely transubstantiation, which has been incorporated into Catholic dogma by the Tridentine Council and which is unique in explaining "conveniently and properly" the real presence of Jesus Christ in the Eucharist.

The Eucharist is in fact the sacrament in which, under the species of bread and wine, there is truly, really and substantially the Body and Blood of Jesus Christ, which is offered in sacrifice and distributed as spiritual food for souls. Leo XIII considered this sacrament as the prolongation of the Incarnation: Just as the Word of God made himself present in human form to procure salvation for us, rendering to God the homage due and full satisfaction for sin, so Christ makes himself present under the veils of the Eucharist to carry out for us the work of redemption, in its ascending phase, renewing the Sacrifice of the Cross, and in its descending movement, distributing grace through the sacramental rite of communion. The Eucharistic mystery thus embraces the Real Presence, the Sacrifice of the Mass and the Sacrament of Communion.

The Real Presence is the dogma according to which, under the species of bread and wine, the Body, Blood, Soul and Divinity of Jesus Christ Our Lord is present. The way by which the Body of Christ is made present under the Eucharistic species is transubstantiation. The real content of this term is specified by the Council of Trent with these words: :

---

[791] See my book *The Jew in the Mystery of History*, 4th ed. Theoria, 1964.

> "Admirable and singular conversion of the whole substance of the bread into the Body and of the whole substance of the wine into the Blood of Christ, the external appearances remaining unchanged"[792].

Conversion is the passage from one thing to another; Transubstantiation is a singular conversion, that is to say, unique in every order of nature; for all the conversions which usually take place in the created world are either limited to the quantitative or qualitative mutation of things, or, at the most, vary the substantial form, as occurs in the passage from wine to vinegar; but in nature no conversion is found which changes matter, the common substratum on which the infinite variety of sensible things is embroidered. This, which cannot occur naturally, takes place in the Eucharist by the omnipotence of God.

There the matter and form of the bread and wine are completely changed into the Body and blood of Christ, with only the accidents remaining intact. For these reasons, Transubstantiation is a unique conversion, totally outside the realm of experience and the natural scope of human reason. For this reason it is admirable, that is to say, mysterious, since, removed from experience - from which the human understanding naturally ascends to the idea - we cannot form an adequate concept of it, but only an imperfect one, elaborated by analogy.

This doctrine is logically deduced from an in-depth analysis of the words of the Institution:

> "This is my Body", in the light of the teaching of tradition, which created new terms to express, less inadequately, this truth: "Transmutatio, transelementatio, transformatio", which preluded the felicitous term "'transubstantiatio", which the Council of Trent defined to be the optimal expression of Catholic dogma[793].

Against this doctrine the authors of the "new theology" are nowadays raising their voices and proposing instead the theory of transignification and transfinalisation. For these authors, this new theory does not mean that, because of the real, true and substantial presence of Christ, verified by Transubstantiation, the species of bread and wine acquire a new meaning for the intelligence enlightened by faith, and a new end for the will, moved by charity, according to Paul VI in his recent encyclical

---

[792] Denz. 884.
[793] Denz. 884.

"Mysterium Fidei", On the contrary, they seek to change the content of the Faith itself, maintaining that Christ gives himself to man through the bread and wine, which, by virtue of this gift, acquire a transfinalisation and ontological transignification, as a result of which the bread and wine are no longer such, but become the real presence offered of Christ.

In this way the new theology reverses the order of causes in the present matter.

While Paul VI in "Mysterium Fidei" considers transfinalisation and transignification as effects, and not as causes, of the real presence brought about by transubstantiation, the "new theology" considers them as causes that bring about the real presence. Of course, for this approach the "new theology" is based on two postulates, i.e. on two unproven and gratuitous principles.

The first is the completely arbitrary - and unproven - assertion that transfinalisation and trans-signification would be ontological insofar as they are capable of transubstantiating this bread and wine from their own being; to the point that the reality, that is, the substance - in its components of matter and form - would no longer be bread and wine, but Christ in his real presence offered to man under the sign of a food and drink.

But this postulate, besides being gratuitous, is absurd. For the end, to which transfinalisation obviously corresponds, is one of the four causes of all being. Now this cause can only exercise its causality in the order in which it has being. And since the end has being only in the ideal order, it can exercise causality only in the ideal or intentional order, unlike the efficient cause, which, as a real cause, has a physical causality and produces effects in the very order of real things. The end, in fact, can do nothing other than influence as Bonum aprehensum ac desideratum the efficient cause, which, thus influenced, then chooses the means and moves to action in order to bring the end into existence. Sicut autem influere causae efficientis est agere, ita influere causae finalis est appeti et desiderari, just as the influencing of the efficient cause is to act, so the influencing of the final cause is to be desired and desired[794] ; and also the famous axiom finis primus est in intentione et ultimum in assecutione, the end is first in intention and last in execution.

---

[794] St. Thomas, De veritate, XXII, art. 2.

Even if Michelangelo has the idea of making the Pietà out of marble, it becomes so only to the extent that he sets about the execution of the work. The end always remains in the order of ideas and only becomes reality through the action of the efficient cause. Consequently, to attribute the quality of "ontological" to transfinalisation implies the absurdity of a metaphysical somersault from the final cause, that is, from the ideal order in which it only has being and in which it can only exercise its intentional causality, to the real order. In other words, this would imply the passage from the idea of a thing to the thing itself.

For transfinalisation to be able to influence directly in ordine essendi, in the order of being, it would be necessary for the essence of material things to consist in the destination that man assigns to them; in such a way that if the destination of a thing were changed, the essence itself would automatically be changed. This hypothesis constitutes the second postulate - also absurd - on which the theory of the new theology is more or less explicitly based. And it is absurd because there is confusion between the destination of a thing and its nature, even if by hypothesis we are dealing with the finis operis and not with the finis operantis. For even if it is true that the finis operis enters in a certain sense into the nature of the thing, but it enters as a tendency or impulse and not as constitutive of its very nature. This is why we say that once the finis operis is obtained, the thing is enriched, though not precisely in its very nature. In other words, the end of a material thing does not constitute its essence, but necessarily presupposes it; nevertheless, once obtained, it is an enrichment of the thing itself in ordine rerum, in the order of things. Sic ergo secundum primum esse, quod est substantiale, dicitur aliquid ens simpliciter et bonum secundum quid, i.e. inquantum est ens.

Secundum vero ultimum actum dicitur aliquid esse ens secundum quid est bonum simpliciter, according to this, when we consider the first being of things, which is the substantial, we say that they are absolutely beings, and in some way good. On the other hand, when we consider them in possession of their ultimate actuality, we say that they are good at all and in some way beings[795].

On the other hand, if the equation were true: the nature of the material thing is equal to the destination assigned to it by man, it would be necessary to conclude, against the principle of contradiction, that the

---

[795] I, 5, ad. 1.

same meat would have a different nature if it were destined for a man or for an animal.

And following logically it would also be necessary to conclude that the infinite number of material things which are not immediately intended for man - or which are intended for his own vision - are no more than mere shadows or pure phenomena.

And furthermore, if we examine this postulate in the light of Revelation, it would also be necessary to conclude that the things that God created, before He created man, had no nature of their own until man gave them a purpose. All this would be contrary to what Revelation tells us when it describes the particular nature of all things and also of those things destined to be man's food[796].

Finally, according to Revelation, every created thing corresponds to an idea of God the Creator; it is an imitation ad extra of the Divine Essence. And this is true not only of man but of every creature. Now God, not being a mere name, but the ipsum ese subsistens[797], is the creator not of shadows but of real things, which participate in his being as substances consistent in themselves and as original nuclei of action.

We can therefore conclude that these theologians of transignification to transfinalisation are forced to admit either that the ideal cause - the end - becomes the real cause, or that the ideal cause does not change the profound reality of the bread and wine at all. In the first case, the "new theology" falls into the metaphysical absurdity of passing from the intentional order to the real order. In the second, it incurs in the simple and plain denial of the presence of Christ in the Eucharist.

On the other hand, these authors, drawing consequences from their principles, fall into another very serious error, which is to distinguish in the real presence that which is simply offered - that of Christ in the Tabernacle - from the other, which is also offered and accepted. The former would be secondary to the "offered and accepted" which would be the complete one. In other words, Christ's presence in the tabernacle becomes perfect on condition that it is accepted by the faithful. This is a very serious error, because in ordine essendi, in the order of reality, the real, true and substantial presence of Christ in the Holy Eucharist is

---

[796] Gen., 1, 29.
[797] Exodus, 3, 14.

verified in instanti, instantaneously, excluding any kind of successive process of realisation.

It is easy to see how all these errors of the "new theology" are similar to and perhaps inspired by the heresy of the sacramental Protestants (Zwingli, Carlostadius, Scholampadius), who reduced the Eucharist to an empty symbol of the Body of Christ, as well as that of Calvin and the Anglicans, who saw in the sacrament of the altar only a bread imbued with a mysterious power, emanating from the body of Christ, present only in heaven. Against these errors, the Council of Trent, in its S. 13, defined that in the Eucharist the Eucharist is the sacrament of the altar. 13 defined that in the Eucharist "the Body, Blood, Soul and Divinity of Our Lord Jesus Christ are truly, really and substantially contained", and condemned those who affirmed that it was only "as present in sign or figure or only virtually"[798], and recently the encyclical "Mysterium Fidei"affirms against the same errors that the bread and wine in so far as they acquire a new meaning and a new purpose, in so far as they contain a new reality, which is rightly called ontological". Pius XII, in Humani Generis[799], had already warned that "there are not lacking today those who maintain that the doctrine of transubstantiation, based as it is on an outdated philosophical concept of substance, must be corrected, so that the real presence of Christ in the Most Holy Eucharist is reduced to a symbolism in which the consecrated species are only external signs of the spiritual presence of Christ and of his intimate action with the faithful who are his members in the Mystical Body".

We could examine this attempt of the "new theology" in the revision of the Eucharistic doctrine in the context of the totality of questions that are currently being asked in the entire field of theological science, and we would come to the very serious conclusion that Catholic doctrine is being emptied of its real content, taught by Christ and handed down by the apostles, and that it is being inoculated with a "new content", similar to that practised in all times by the Gnostic errors[800].

---

[798] Denz., 883.
[799] 12 August 1950.
[800] Catholic doctrine is a realistic doctrine and Gnosticism, on the other hand, is unrealistic.

12. The historical value of the Gospel accounts, including that of the Lord's resurrection, is questioned.

In "Tijdschift voor Theologie" [801], Fr. Luc Grollenberg denied practically all historical value to the Gospel accounts, including that of the Resurrection of the Lord.

13. Karl Rahner's Anonymous Christianity

Karl Rahner has invented a new doctrine of "anonymous", "implicit" or "incognito" Christianity, which has gained wide acceptance in progressive circles and which, in a certain sense, could be connected with Teilhard de Chardin's famous cosmic Christ. The exposition of this anonymous Christianity can be found in an article, "Incorporation into the Church according to Pius XII's encyclical "Mystici Corporis Christi", published in volume II of "Writings on Theology"[802].

There Rahner argues that "when man, as a spiritual person, acts according to his nature in the total decision about himself, such a personal decision is always in concrete terms inevitably a taking of a stand for or against the supernatural vocation of man in the participation in the life of the triune God"[803].

If this were true, it would follow that human nature would have been christified and, consequently, man's personal decision would be capable of attaining a supernatural dimension. Otherwise, if this christification had not taken place, a human act on the purely natural plane could not attain a supernatural dimension.

This is what Karl Rahner affirms; he says: "By the Word of God becoming man, humanity has been converted real-ontologically into the people of the children of God, even prior to the effective sanctification of each one by grace"[804]. But this is a purely gratuitous affirmation which is not based on any directly or indirectly revealed data. But this is a purely gratuitous affirmation that is not based on any directly or indirectly revealed data. By what means does Rahner know that

---

[801] NO. 1, 1964.
[802] Taurus Ediciones, Madrid, 1961, p. 9.
[803] Ibid., p. 10.
[804] Ibid., p. 11.

humanity has been consecrated and christified? By means of reason? Impossible, because it is a supernatural fact which depends on divine free will. By revelation? Why does he not state the source from which he derives such a truth?

On the other hand, we know from Revelation that no one is saved, no one comes to God, if he does not at least believe that God exists and that he is the rewarder of those who seek him. Man comes into this world in sin, and he has no alternative but faith, by which the righteous live, or the wrath of God[805]. He who believes in the Son has eternal life; he who refuses to believe in the Son will not see life, but the wrath of God is upon him[806]. He may not believe in the Son if he does not know Him, but he must at least believe that God is rewarding. A supernatural act of faith, the principle of justification, is necessary, absolutely necessary, in order to be justified. Otherwise justification would be automatic, without man's doing anything supernatural on his part, a thing hitherto unheard of in the Christian world. "For by grace you have been saved through faith, and this is not of yourselves, it is the gift of God; it is not of works, lest any man should boast[807].

Rahner does not justify his affirmation, which serves as the basis and foundation for all the rest of the subsequent affirmations, which will therefore have the solidity that the basis can give them. Hence he goes on to maintain that humanity is the people of God before it is and before it is called the Church. But the Apostle teaches us that humanity and mankind are by nature given over to the wrath of God[808]. How far all this is from the notion of the people of God with which "Lumen Gentium" qualifies the Church! How forced all this theology of anonymous Christianity, of a humanity that would have been sanctified by Christ only by the fact of the Incarnation! What is the scriptural or magisterial tradition basis for the assertion that the Church embraces a double reality: the Church as a juridical-sacral organisation and the Church as humanity consecrated by the Incarnation?

The question raised by Rahner has been considered by St Thomas in article 3 of Part Three of his "Summa Theologica". The saintly doctor asks there: "Whether Christ is the head of all men", and answers: "The

---

[805] Rom. 1, 17 and 18,
[806] St. John, 3, 35.
[807] Ephesians, 2, 8.
[808] Ephesians, 2, 3, in "La Sainte Bible", Jerusalem.

members of the natural body all coexist at the same time, but not those of the Mystical Body, and this is the difference between the natural body and the mystical body of the Church. The non-coexistence at the same time can be considered either in relation to their natural being - the Church, in fact, is constituted by men who existed from the beginning to the end of the world - or in relation to the being of grace; and thus among the members of the Church, even among those who live at the same time, there are those who do not possess grace, but who will possess it, and there are those who are deprived of grace, having previously possessed it. Thus, not only those who are members of the Mystical Body in act, but also those who are members in potential, are to be considered as members of the Mystical Body. Among the latter there are those who will never belong in act to the Mystical Body; but there are those who will belong at a given moment, according to a threefold degree: by faith, by charity in this life, by beatitude in heaven.

"Considering in general all the ages of the world, Christ is the head of all men, but in different degrees. First and chiefly, He is the head of those who are presently united to Him in glory; secondly, He is the head of those who are united to Him only in potency, and who, according to the designs of divine predestination, are to belong to Him in act at a certain time. Lastly, he is the head of all those who are united to him in potency and will never be united to him in act, and such are the men who live in this world and who are not predestined. As for the latter, from the moment they leave this world, they will no longer be members of the Body of Christ, for they will no longer be in potency to be united to him".

To be potentially united means that they can be united, but not that they are actually united; in Rahner, on the other hand, the union of humanity in Christ would be radical, that is to say, at root, and therefore actual, although not complete. This actuality of union is what is new in Rahner and also what is whimsical and false. It is this idea that E. Schillebeckx for his lucubration in which he identifies Church and humanity[809].

Serious, in Rahner's teaching, is that man's salvation, which is verified in union with Christ, does not derive from a free act of man, but is produced automatically and by the fact of being man. Every human being is radically Christian. Christianity is a stamp that hides any reality

---

[809] Concilium, no. 1, January 1965, p. 65.

of man. From here it is only one step to affirming a secularised Christianity, i.e. a non-Christian Christianity.

14. *Justification in Karl Barth and Luther*

Hans Küng set out to re-evaluate the Protestant doctrine of justification by faith. On 10 November 1967 he gave a lecture, "The Catholic Interpretation of Justification according to Luther" at the Centre for Ecumenical Studies in Strasbourg, and before that he had already published a work, "Justification", La doctrine de Karl Barth - Réflexion catholique"[810]. It must be acknowledged that this is a serious work, which first examines Karl Barth's doctrine of justification, then, in a second part, outlines "an essay of a Catholic response", to reach the conclusion of a substantial identity of doctrine in one and the other exposition.

Karl Barth starts from justification as an act of God. "By intervening in justification, God works in a matter that is his own. Certainly, justification is God's grace coming to man. But it is more than this: in justification, God executes his own eternal will for man, he works in virtue of his eternal faithfulness, his eternal right.

God justifies himself in the justification of man as man's creator and his covenant Lord. As Creator, He does not consent to the chaotic eruption and the shameful stain of sin in His creation. As Lord of the covenant, man is God's confederate, and God does not allow himself to be torn away from this confederate.

Justification is done in Jesus Christ. It is the divine right of the Son to be humbly obedient to the Father, so that he executes the divine decision which is also his own.

Recognising and executing the Father's right, he executes his own right as a Son.

Man's justification is fulfilled in the acceptance of the Son of God, that is, in his awakening from the dead. By paternal right and not by tyrannical arbitration, God demands the obedience of the Son, and in the revelation of this same right, He awakens Him, and us with Him,

---

[810] Desclée de Brouwer Paris, 1965; published in Spanish, Editorial Estela, Barcelona, 1967.

from the dead. Thus it can be said: the fulfilment of our justification was also God's self-justification.

In the justification of man, there is the self-justification of God by which a magnificent and gracious sovereignty of God has been brought into full light".

Hans Küng shows how "faith alone justifies", "glory is due to God alone", and the declaratory justification of the reformers can be interpreted in a benevolent way, so that it coincides with the Catholic doctrine advocated by the Council of Trent. And Hans Küng can conclude: "In the ecumenical dialogue on these problems, the essential thing is never to lose sight of the unity of theology and life. That behind a good Catholic theology there is not always a good Catholic life explains why Barth does not remain consistent with his own thinking on these questions.

Subject to these clarifications, we would like to maintain our conclusion that in the doctrine of justification taken as a whole, there is a basic unity between the doctrine of Barth and that of the Catholic Church; in these matters, there is no valid reason for Barth to separate himself from the ancient Church".

However, despite this basic agreement between Barth's doctrine and that of the Catholic Church, Hans Küng does not fail to recognise that in Barth's basic position there are certain tendencies which, in a coherent synthesis, are not erroneous but which, if misunderstood, could easily lead to dangerous errors. Barth's fundamental desire to exalt God's gracious sovereignty over all things tends, in the doctrine of predestination, to apocatastasis; in the doctrine of creation, to the depreciation of the autonomy of the creature; in the doctrine of sin, to dialectical indifference with regard to sin and its justification; in soteriology, to neglect the ontic and created aspect. In the doctrine of justification in the strict sense, it is worth mentioning the tendency to emphasise the peccator, alien justice, in spe, to the detriment of justus, of justitia mea, of in re; the tendency to suppress the existential difference between righteous and sinners, between tares and wheat, between good fish and bad fish, between faithful and unfaithful; the tendency to dissolve justification into a flow without a real cut, without the clear censure that the word of God operates in the hic et nunc of the justification of a given man. A tendency, finally, to refuse genuine progress and growth in grace and the possibility of defection from grace.

These tendencies exist, but, in Barth's fundamental position, they have not become errors or unforgivable exaggerations. They constitute the natural slope of Barth's theology, a natural tendency which would otherwise be found also in Catholic theologians and even in St. Thomas Aquinas.

Hans Küng's book is relatively successful. But isn't there a tendency in it to conflate Catholic doctrine too closely with Protestant doctrine on such an essential point as justification? The doubt persists, even after a careful reading of the book, and this constitutes the danger of a false ecumenism that is dominant today.

15. They question heaven and hell

The magazine "Time"[811] states that the Dominican theologian Willern van der Marck considers that "it should not concern us in any way whether there is a heaven or a hell".

16. Replacement of traditional morality, based on theology and natural law, by a morality based on Christology and the situation.

Morality is also renewed in various ways, all of which call into question the immutability of the moral law. Let us first turn to a purely domestic question among theologians, which is somewhat debatable, but from which situationist theologians and philosophers must draw a further reason to speak of the need to abandon traditional morality and to go down new paths in search of moral principles.

A Christocentric morality instead of a theocentric morality: Until now, moral theology had been centred on God. Man, created by God in the image of God, with the grace of Christ, and following Christ as an example, became more and more God-like and thus more perfect. The ultimate end, the beatifying possession of God, provided the ultimate criterion and reason by which the morality of human actions was measured. God was thus the central and supreme idea of moral theology as a science. This, at least, is how the whole moral theology of St Thomas moved. Today, however, authors speak of a new Christocentric

---

[811] March 31, 1967.

morality, which has Christ in his human nature as the central and supreme idea of theology, whom we should imitate and follow. This would be a "new", "autonomous", "dynamic", "vital", "true" and "effective" morality [812], in contrast to the traditional legalistic, scholastic, heteronomous morality, with universal and abstract norms, which do not fit in with the progress of modern life.

But this Christocentric morality, which is opposed to theocentric morality, does not correspond. For it is possible to consider Christ as exemplary in the whole of human moral life, but in this case the resulting morality is not opposed to but subordinate to the theocentric morality, since Christ's "food was to do the will of him who sent him to finish his work"[813]. Moreover, Christ invited us to "be perfect as the heavenly Father is perfect"[814].

Christ's morality in the Gospels is also authoritative and heteronomous. "Think not that I am come to abolish the Law or the Prophets: I am not come to abolish them, but to fulfil them..." "If any man therefore shall neglect one of these least precepts, and shall teach men so, he shall be least in the kingdom of heaven"[815].

Moral theology is a science which establishes the universal laws of moral and virtuous acts down to the species; it is not to be confused with asceticism and mysticism, nor with pastoral theology.

There is no science except of the universal. That theology is not sufficient to regulate the human act in all its dimensions is quite possible. For the human act has psychological, sociological and other conditions which must be considered, but not in order to determine its moral character as such. In this campaign against legalistic and authoritative morality, one is actually against all morality. For morality is necessarily authoritative and prescriptive. If man is, on the one hand, free and, on the other hand, capable of evil, this means that there must be an objective criterion which distinguishes evil from good.

A morality of situation instead of traditional morality: Strictly speaking, those who criticise traditional morality want to construct a morality of

---

[812] J. Kunicic, O.P., Systema moralis Christocentrica, in Divinitas, January 1968, p. 211.
[813] John 4, 34.
[814] Mt., 5, 43.
[815] Mt., 5, 19.

situation. This is clear from Marc Oraison[816], who devotes the first chapters of his book A Morality for Our Time to criticising traditional morality under the pretext of criticising odious formulations of this morality as coming from fundamentalists and post-Constantinian confusion. We read there: "For my part, I would tend to think that the post-Constantinian confusion between the temporal city and the Kingdom of heaven is not strange. The terrible delay which the theocratic confusion of the government of men in time has introduced is far from having been studied. And the tendency to return to this theocratic conception of political society is not about to disappear, even if it is a strongly archaic regression to a primitive tribal mentality from nomadism to sedentism"[817].

But it is forgotten that the authority of God as the source of all human authority, whether familial, social or political, is openly taught by the apostle: "You must all be subject to the higher authorities, for there is no authority except from God, and those that exist are ordained by God, so that whoever resists the authority resists the ordinance of God"[818].

The same author adds: "The example is still given by the attitude which has been called "fundamentalist". These are the same personalities who react violently against any evolution or any adaptation to new situations as soon as their emotional security is threatened at a very deep level and almost inaccessible to reflection; such is the confusion of a certain mystique of the "fatherland" or the "nation". These are the same people who react violently against the acquisitions of modern psychology in the name of "morality". In the limit - it is not so rare - the same personalities go, without clearly realising what this can mean, to the point of irritating injustice, if necessary to the point of crime, in order to defend what they believe to be "Christian" morality or civilisation.

Marc Oraison is perfectly X-rayed in this and the previous paragraph, which we have transcribed. His allergy to "fundamentalism", which is apparently a characteristic "taboo" for him; His allergy to the rights and traditions of nations and homelands, his revaluation of certain "acquisitions of modern psychology", i.e. Freudian, and the sting he feels for the morals of Christian civilisation in the face of the attitudes adopted in the face of irritating injustices, show that he has taken a clear

---

[816] *Une morale pour notre temps*, Arthème Fayard, Paris, 1964.
[817] Ibid., p. 56.
[818] Rom., 13, 1.

stand for modern "psycho-sociology" which systematically dissolves traditional and moral values in the life of individuals and peoples.

For this reason, the headings at the beginning of the various paragraphs of the second part inform us of the direction he is taking in the problem of morality: "The moral life is always "in a situation""[819]. "There are only situations"[820]. "We are never but in a situation"[821]. We are told there that "the other and the relation to the other constitutes the objectivity of morality"[822] without it ever being made clear how the moral norm is determined and what kind of compliance is due to it. For if man is not pure freedom, pure indeterminacy, but has an essence, a universal nature that can determine him in advance of his free decision, then there is a rightness or wrongness of his actions, which must be determined by the moral law. Situational morality is not compatible with a sound psychology and metaphysics, which give a full account of the human composite.

E. Schillebeeckx, O.P., classifies three trends in situation ethics. The first is that of the existentialists, especially atheists such as J. P. Sartre, S. de Beauvoir and Fr. Janson, who maintain that the freedom with which man fulfils himself is the only criterion of morality; Protestant situation ethics, which maintains that no law, no authority, no Church, can reveal what is hic et nunc the will of God; and finally, that of certain theorists, who maintain that the will of God is the only criterion of morality; and finally, that of certain Catholic theologians such as Steinbückel, Schiller and Rahner himself with his "individual" ethics, who say that no situation can arise in which man can act against the negative precepts of the natural law, but that neither, in the positive prescription, can there be a universally valid norm for all individuals[823].

A morality according to the sense of history instead of traditional morality. l. Lobo argues in Concilium[824], in an article Towards a morality according to the sense of history - The condition and the renewal of morality, that man progressively acquires the sense of history, that he dominates and integrates more and more strongly the

---

[819] Ibid., p. 129.
[820] Ibid., p. 133.
[821] Ibid., p. 137.
[822] Ibid., p. 129.
[823] *Dieu et l'homme*, Éditions du cerf, Paris, p. 252.
[824] May 1967, no. 25.

matter and is socialised at all levels. From this he concludes, not the establishment "of an unhealthy relativism in moral matters, but an application of the principle of the historical catholicity of our religion, the axis of which is the same natural law of the evolutionary process as that laid down by God"[825].

The new morality that Lobo favours is based on the reality of progress that would be fulfilled in all fields of human affairs. And "a practical consequence of what we have been saying will be that whoever considers this morality of progress will not fall into the error of evaluating the Christian according to the fact that in the present moment he sins not much, fulfils or not what is commanded (moral of sin and moral or not legalistic) but the fundamental attitude before the call of God"[826].

But it is precisely here that the misunderstanding is expressed that vitiates Lobo's entire problematic.

How does one measure man's progress, and is there truly human progress in the history of man? Lobo himself acknowledges that there are those who maintain that "history is moving towards a collective suicide of mankind"[827]. And this is supported by scientists such as Jean Rostand and essayists such as Bernanos and Gabriel Marcel; and Lobo adds that Charles Chaplin has made a critique of the modern world in his films and draws attention to the contradictions of history.

It is a fact that there can be progress in one aspect and return in another, that man can make magnificent conquests on the level of knowledge with real aberrations on the level of conduct. It is therefore objectionable that Lobo does not clarify in what sense the progress is verified and speaks in general of man's progress as if it were something self-evident and admitted by all. It is not for nothing that René Guénon, in "La crise du monde moderne" and in "Le règne de la quantité", has argued the involutionary process that modern civilisation undergoes, precisely in modernity.

The fundamental attitude to measure man's progress or return lies precisely in the attitude with which he places himself before God and this, in turn, with the attitude he takes towards sin. And it is evident that

---

[825] Ibid., p. 218.
[826] Ibid., p. 220.
[827] Ibid., p. 307.

the process of atheisation of culture and of modern man is far from speaking to us of human progress. This is where all the theories, which Lobo uses to reason his new morality according to the sense of history, fall down. l. Lobo considers it progress that "the Church loses its privileged and dominant place in culture, in art, even in politics, etc."[828]

But it is curious the mentality of this author who does not realise that if the Church loses its privileged place, it has to be occupied by another, which can only be that of a world driven by the lust for money or pleasure. And a materialistic society will hardly be able to fulfil the primordial condition of caring for one's neighbour and, therefore, of building "a new and better world".

Antoine, whom Lobo quotes[829], may present magnificent graphs relating the constant time to progress and evolution, whereby "the remarkable acceleration of history is made clear"[830], but what neither Antoine nor Lobo explain is what process is involved, because the fact is that man has never been so conditioned as he is today by the machine society[831].

Ignace Lepp's "new morality". Today a new morality is sought, one that leaves behind the legalistic and authoritative morality of the past and accommodates itself to the evolutionary change dictated by modern life. This is repeated in a thousand ways, more or less unprecedented, in Catholic and non-Catholic literature. The favourite theme, especially in sexual morality, is that relationships of this kind should be determined by love, and only by love, and that what is determined by love is already good and sacred. On the other hand, it is insisted above all that science justifies Freudian theories and that, consequently, great care must be taken not to repress the sexual instinct, which would be basic in the human species, because this would determine inhibitions, complexes, and neuroses that are especially studied by psychoanalysis. Ignatius Lepp is a representative author of this tendency which authorises

---

[828] Ibid., p. 223.
[829] Ibid., p. *273*.
[830] Ibid. p. 224.
[831] Ibid., see Julio Meinvielle, *Iglesia y mundo moderno*, Ed. Theoria, Buenos Aires, 1966.

onanism [832], masturbation [833], which values to a lesser degree the virginity so celebrated by the Church[834], and which tends to justify love and everything done for love. "Even sexual union requires love to be morally justifiable", writes this author[835]. There is nothing strange, then, in that he also justifies divorce, especially of non-believers [836], forgetting that marriage is indissoluble by natural law.

To the same kind of literature, which is widely circulated in Catholic circles, belongs "Man and Woman - The Relationship of the Sexes in a Changed World"[837]. Its author, C. Trimbos, insists on all its pages that "modern problems, such as artificial insemination, birth control, population control, homosexuality, mixed marriages, divorce, marriage between divorced persons, etc., can hardly be solved within tradition", and that therefore all dykes must be broken and practically everyone must be left free to solve these problems without moral, legal or any other kind of inhibitions or coercion.

The theology of homosexuality. It is clear that if love is the only law of life, marriage must be justified when it is for love. And since couples can decide to marry because they feel love today, which they will not feel tomorrow, then divorce and the abandonment of children in order to build a new family based on a new love will be justified. And since the most unique aberrations are to be found in human love, and there are men who do not react with love towards women, just as there are women who do not experience love towards men, it follows that homosexuality must be justified in the name of Catholic theology. It is therefore not surprising that a theologian, Fr Callewaert, O.P., made public a document, approved by the Commission on sexuality of the University of Louvain, in a debate in which doctors, psychologists and homosexuals of both sexes took part. Father Callewaert, O.P.[838] said there : "Today, even if the new attitude is not accepted by the whole Church, I believe that many theologians and many of the faithful would like to take a step forward. Certainly, this doctrine has not been officially approved. Its proponents would at least like to help

---

[832] La nueva moral, Carlos Lohlé, Buenos Aires, 1964, p. 190.
[833] Ibid., p. 194.
[834] Ibid., p. 197.
[835] Ibid., p. 202.
[836] Ibid., pp. 204-205.
[837] Ediciones Carlos Lohlé, Buenos Aires, 1968.
[838] See Il Borghese magazine, 20 April 1967.

homosexuals, like all other human beings, in their attempt to live well, even with one another. And I would like to propose to adult homosexuals, as a kind of ideal, to try to realise in their lives a stable relationship of friendship; to take care of each other; to assume responsibility for each other on the economic level, in social life. And also to realise a union of feelings. And also, since we are dealing with men and not purely spiritual creatures, to translate these feelings on the erotic and sexual level in a way that is congenial to them".

17. The secularisation of Christianity, even among Catholic theologians

We have indicated which truths of the faith are touched by theologians, either to adulterate them or to soften them. In reality, no fundamental truth of Catholic dogma is left standing. And the most singular thing is that, as one truth is touched by one theologian and another by another, all are finally affected and called into question; and as in the houses of learning all questions are dealt with, they appear in their entirety questioned, so that nothing of Catholic truth is safe from destruction.

This internal weakening of the truths of the faith has to be seen in the context of another process, which continues its course and which is the weakening of the whole of Christianity itself in the context of universal culture. For centuries we have been engaged in a process of secularisation. The order of medieval Christianity has been broken, first of all by a naturalistic universal city[839] which filled the 16th, 17th and 18th centuries; then by a liberal and animalistic city which filled the whole of the 19th century; and finally by the materialistic and communist city which has pervaded the whole of the 20th century. This process of secularisation of life is putting pressure on the Catholic and Protestant sectors in what remains of the Christian world and is leading them to enter into secularisation.

The curious thing is that the theologians who were supposed to proclaim highly the rights of God, also enter willingly into this universal tide of secularisation, and it is they who demand a desacralised and secularised Christianity, and even this in the name of Christianity itself.

---

[839] See Julio Meinvielle, *El comunismo en la revolución anticristiana*, Edic. Theoria, Buenos Aires, 1965.

It would take a long time to explain and expose the process that leads them to such unusual and absurd positions. But it is because they have allowed clear truths of Catholic theology to weaken.

a) The fundamental distinction between nature and grace. It is a fundamental truth of Catholic theology that in the order of the universal values of man's creation and regeneration there are two kinds of perfectly characterised values. The values of creation, which are natural values, and those of salvation, which are supernatural values. Although God has created the world and man in a supernatural state, this state is not due to the creature, but has been bestowed by a gracious gift of the Creator Himself. Man lost his supernatural creaturehood in which he was created. Adam decayed from the primitive state of grace and brought about the ruin of the human race. Jesus Christ came to restore the lost order and to restore to the human race the supernatural state of grace and glory in which it had been created. This state and this condition are entirely gratuitous. "Eye hath not seen, nor ear heard, neither hath it entered into the mind of man, what God hath prepared for them that love him"[840]. The vision of God in glory is wholly undue to every creature. It is a supernatural gift, which is above the powers and demands of every angelic or human nature. Hence there are two orders, the natural and the supernatural. And to these two orders correspond two lives: one, the present, in which man must provide for his earthly welfare; the other, the future, that of heaven, which man must now procure for himself, but which he can only acquire in the life hereafter.

To these two lives correspond already now two perfect and complete societies, each in its own order. The political society or society of civilisation, the State, which is to provide directly for the goods of earthly life; and the society of the Church or society of the supernatural and religious life, which is to provide directly, and already here on earth, for the goods of faith, hope and charity which serve for eternal life. These two kinds of goods are distinct, but they are united, and united by the subordination of the lower, natural goods to the higher, supernatural goods. Although the State and the Church are autonomous and perfect, each in its own order, there must be an indirect subordination of the State and of civilisation to the Church. This teaching was a common truth in the magisterium of the Church and in

---

[840] I Cor., 2, 19.

Christian pedagogy until a few years ago, and was enunciated in a masterly manner by the great Pope St. Pius X[841] : "Besides these goods, there are many others which belong to the natural order, to which the mission of the Church is not directly ordered in itself, but which also derive from it as a natural consequence of it. The Church, by preaching Christ crucified, scandal and folly in the eyes of the world[842], has become the first inspirer and author of civilisation... The civilisation of the world is Christian civilisation... the more it declines, to the immense harm of social welfare, the more it is removed from the Christian idea... In this fact lay the relations between the Church and the States... the concord of the two powers, of the State and of the Church, in procuring in such a way the temporal good of the people that the eternal good should not suffer harm".

The relations between the two lives, the life of grace and the life of nature, determine the relations of Church and Civilisation and also determine the relations of Church and World. In the present providence, the world can only be saved by the Church. "And the world has been put to evil"[843]. "Love not the world, neither the things that are in the world. If any man love the world, the love of the Father is not in him. For all that is in the world, the lust of the flesh, and the lust of the eyes, and the pride of life, is not of the Father, but is of the world"[844]. But the world that is evil can be saved by Christ, if it submits to the law of Christ. "God did not send his Son into the world to judge the world, but to save the world through him"[845]. From this teaching it follows that the world, being evil, leads mankind to catastrophe, from which only Jesus Christ can save it. This is why God created the world good, but the world fell into the catastrophe of sin; God raised it up, but the world was plunged into the flood; He raised it up again, but the world was filled with pride, plunged into the confusion of the languages of the tower of Babel; God separated the people of Israel, and they were unfaithful to the Lord. And in the Christian world the same law of unfaithfulness of the world and of salvation through Jesus Christ is fulfilled.

---

[841] Il fermo proposito.
[842] I Cor., 1, 23.
[843] 1, John, 5, 19.
[844] 1, John, 2, 15.
[845] John, 3, 17.

b) The law of history in nature and grace. The relations of nature and grace, Church and State, God and world, had hitherto been explained by Augustine's great law of the two cities. The pedagogy of the Church saved the world, and the world, which without the Church was evil, could not solve the same problems as the world. The world, as a result of sin, had been wounded in the natural. The Church, which came to give supernatural health to the world, by the way and as a consequence also ensured the natural order of civilisation. Without the Church, the world would drift into barbarism, into the barbarism of the jungle, or into the barbarism of the slave society[846].

This order of the relations of nature and grace, which translated into the political order in the relations between Church and State, in the harmony between priesthood and Empire, was in full force throughout Christian Europe until the Reformation. When the Reformation began a movement of separation and rupture - separation of Church and State, of philosophy and theology, which was then to embrace ever deeper areas of the human being - the intelligence was to be separated from the will, the speculative order from the practical order, and then the order of intelligence from the order of sensibility, the economy from politics, technology from the economy itself. Today, each sector of science and technology stands on its own side and the human being is torn and shattered into a thousand fragments. On the other hand, a process of false unification is taking place through the psycho-sociological disciplines, and man is thus becoming a robot and an automaton, controlled by powerful world groups which ultimately aspire to world government through the psycho-technical control of man.

We are thus moving towards a unification in a single dimension of all that is human; a unification that encompasses all religions, all cultures, all politics, all economies, and the whole human species would be unified in a matter-cultural-religious syncretism. The entire human species would be unified in a matter-cultural-religious syncretism. And the Church? The Catholic Church? The Church would practically merge with the other cults, and would thus be fused, as an emanation of the spiritual (?), of this unified mass of humanity, totally secularised and materialised.

---

[846] Today's society, as it moves away from the Church, falls into the technocratic society, the communist variant or the variant of the Western world.

In other words, if until now the relationship between the Church and the world was marked by the distinction between the two realities, with the definitive predominance of the Church as the most exalted and transcendent reality; now, on the other hand, it must be marked by the absorption of the Church into the world, which would remain the only and totalitarian reality.

Hence the significance of this invitation of today's world to the Church to build the world in the sense of the world itself. This calls for a new approach to the problems of nature and grace, Church and civilisation, God and world, which we will immediately set out in a series of staggered points.

c) The new Christianity of Lamennais and Maritain. Christianity was the correct translation of Church and State, of nature and grace, in the order of life and history. The totality of life in its temporal and supernatural aspect, each of these aspects maintaining its autonomy, slipped under the gentle dominion of the Church, which acted on man from within man himself. The world rejected the sovereignty of the Church and stood up for its own rights, invoking freedom of conscience, freedom of speech and freedom of thought.

Lamennais, in 1830, was the first to legitimise this uprising of the world against the Christian order, and from within the Church itself, he advocated a New Christianity founded on the acceptance and recognition of false liberties, which were in turn the negation of the correct idea of Christianity. Lamennais was censured by the Church and failed, at least officially, to gain support for his new formulations. But a century later, a Thomist philosopher of high prominence in the Church was to erect the idea of the New Christianity as a norm to be cherished and applied. A Christianity that must accept the course of history and, consequently, the modern world, which, if it had been liberal, was now moving towards the communist city. This was a secular and secularised Christianity. In fact, a Christianity that denied itself. A Christianity against Christianity.

Such an absurd attempt met with no resistance in the Catholic camp, but on the contrary, encouragement and support[847].

---

[847] See Julio Meinvielle, *De Lamennais a Maritain*, Ed. Theoría, Buenos Aires, 1968.

Maritain was above all a speculative man. A man of greater drive in action, he was to spread Maritain's New Christianity under the label of Christian personalism. Maritainian ideas, which spread rapidly throughout the world through the work of Emmanuel Mounier, would shape a whole generation of clergy and laity[848]. With the loss of the correct idea of Christianity, the right approach and formulation of the relationships of nature and grace, of Church and civilisation, of God and the world was lost.

d) Theologians formulate a new approach to the relationship between Church and world. French theologians renewed in a particular way the problematic of Church and World. Chenu, O.P., and Yves Congar, O.P., touched by the ideas of Maritain and Mounier, and therefore lacking a correct formulation of the relationship between nature and grace, took up the idea that the Church, since the time of Constantine, had forged a Manichean conception of the world, as if it had to be conceived on the basis of the life of the monks, as a pure means to eternal life, and that it had therefore been rejected by the laity and had failed; Consequently, the Church, from today, must be in solidarity with the world, which tends to liberate man and must accompany him in this task of building a world because "the future of the Church consists in its presence in the future of the world"[849].

We will not dwell on the ideas of Chenu, O.P., and Congar, O.P., which I have done in my book The Church and the Modern World. Instead, I will present the approach formulated by E. Schillebeeckx in a lecture published in the second issue of "Documentation hollandaise du Concile", and by Johannes B. Metz in "A Christian Understanding of the Modern World". Metz in "Christian understanding of today's world".

e) The Church and the world in E. Schillebeeckx, O. P. Congar argues, in short, that the Church, after Constantine, suffocated the world, and he advocates, consequently, that it should now become the servant of the world in the construction that the world builds for itself. E.

---

[848] The works of Emmanuel Mounier.
[849] Congar expounds these ideas in his works in general and in particular in an article entitled *L'Église et le monde*, which appeared in "Esprit", March 1965, and which we have analysed in The Church and the Modern World.

Schillebeeckx, O.P., will accelerate this process of identification of the world and the Church.

He starts from the idea that the world is an implicit Christianity. "Should we accept, he asks, human history and our whole earthly life as a hidden reality enveloped in the love of God? And he answers: "Working for the world and working for ourselves, we are always in the presence and under the wings of the Mystery that gives itself freely"...

"The world is the profane, earthly and temporal reality with its own structures, its own immediate end, but which in Christ is assumed in the absolute and gratuitous presence of God".... "This is equivalent to saying that in the economy of salvation the concrete world is by definition an implicit Christianity, an objective, not sacral, but holy and justified expression of the communion of men with the living God, while the Church, as the institution of salvation, with its explicit confession of faith, its worship and its sacraments, is the direct and sacral expression of that same reality, the 'separata a mundo'".... "To speak of the relationship between the Church and the world is not, therefore, to enter into a dialogue between the properly Christian dimension and the non-Christian dimension of our human life; it is not a dialogue between the religious and the profane, between the supernatural and the natural or the unworldly, but a dialogue between the two authentically Christian complementary expressions of one and the same theological life, hidden in the mystery of Christ".

Everything is Christian, the world and the Church. The one, implicit; the other, explicit. And E. Schillebeeckx continues: "Within this still anonymous theological life, the building of the world and the promotion of peoples, the two great hopes of earthly humanity, become an activity which has, not only by intention, but intrinsically, a relationship with the Kingdom of God".

And Schillebeeckx, like Congar and Chenu, never clarifies whether this construction of the world, which would be identified with the kingdom of God, is the construction of a world in conformity with the dictates of the Church. On the contrary, it seems to exclude the opposite hypothesis. There will no longer be on earth the city of Cain. Everything will be the kingdom of God. "A dualistic anthropological conception has led Christians in the past to conceive of grace and redemption as a matter between God and the soul of man... There was a risk of depreciating the properly Christian value of world-building and the promotion of peoples, leaving the task to those who called themselves non-believers". And the necessary dualism of good and evil, of the city of the devil and the city of God?

It is clear that, if the world is implicit Christianity, it is no longer true what the Apostle John said that the world "has been put to evil"; on the contrary, it has a congenital goodness and therefore the Church has to be receptive and critical at the same time, attentive to the truth that is elaborated in this world of men because that voice of the world would not be "a foreign voice coming from outside, but that of the living Christ who is the head of the Church and the Lord of the world".

E. Schillebeeckx forgets that the "prince of this world"[850] is the other, and that, by confusing things so notoriously determined by the Lord, he is confusing the whole of Christianity.

f) Johannes B. Metz also "Christianises" today's world. Metz begins by opposing the theology of earthly realities that would seek "to give Christianity an openness to the world that would make it capable of being rooted anew in the mystery of Christ. Such, he says, sometimes lack historical perspective, and easily presuppose that the worldliness of the world is something that contradicts the Christian worldview in its origin and is therefore something that must be overcome". It is clear that with this exordium it is hardly surprising that for Metz the current process of secularisation is "at its core Christian..." and that "the spirit of Christianity remains embedded in the flesh of irreversible worldly history". This means that the process of secularisation which the world has been contemplating for five centuries and which today leads to communism and the machine society is "at its core Christian". And he goes on to say: "The worldliness of the world, as a result of the recent process of secularisation, and as it appears to us today in an intensified form, is elaborated in its foundations (though not in all its historical coinages) only through Christianity: it is originally a Christian event, and bears witness to the intra-historical power of the hour of Christ in our present situation".

On the contrary, says Metz, a worldly and secular world, which reaffirms its autonomy and independence from God, thus takes on "the deepest form of its belonging to God" and "is called by God to his intra-Trinitarian life".

---

[850] John, 12, 31.

Thus there is the laughable spectacle of theologians, who by their profession ought to go out on God's rights, teaching that the more one renounces these rights, the closer one is to God.

This is truly the most typical and incredible example of a theology of contradiction.

"To Christianise the world," he adds, "means to worldise it, to keep it in the unsuspected height and depth of its worldly being, which grace made possible and buried sin". It is a pity that St. Paul had not known these effective methods of "Christianisation" used so wisely by Voltaire, Karl Marx and Nietzsche.

This is a move towards a secularised Christianity. Today this is a popular theme. A few years ago, it would have been considered madness just to mention it. Theologians, even Catholics, now take Nietzsche's "God is dead" seriously. Society cannot but be secularised. A theistic society is absurd. John H. T. Robinson, the author of Honest to God, goes so far as to ask: "Can a truly contemporary person not be an atheist?"[851].

g) Robinson's secularised Christianity. Robinson was the first, with his book Honest to God, to popularise the idea of a secularised Christianity. It is clear that before speaking of a "secular Christianity", Maritain had spoken of a "secular Christianity", and theologians such as Chenu, Congar, Schillebeeckx, Metz, had revalued the world and worldliness as a Christian phenomenon, at least of implicit Christianity. Robinson argues that after Bultmann's studies it is not possible to advocate a supernatural Christianity; that after Bonhoeffer's studies it is not possible to speak of a religious Christianity; and that after Paul Tillich's studies there is no need to refer to a transcendent Christianity. God would be the deepest part of the being of every creature and Jesus the expression of the most authentic self-giving in favour of the neighbour. Therefore, all supernatural, religious and transcendent references should give way to a "naturalistic", "secular" and "immanent" Christianity.

h) Radical theology and the death of God in William Hamilton and Thomas J. Altizer: The process of the "death of God" and that of "secularisation" go hand in hand. In both processes, Protestant

---

[851] *La nouvelle réforme*, Delachaux et Niestlé, Neuchatel, 1966, p. 107.

theologians are taking the lead, although Catholics, who are lagging behind, are following rather quickly. Ouwerkek warns[852] that "voices from the Reformation will often appear, but this is due to the fact that in Protestant literature the phenomenon of secularity appears more explicitly and more frequently. In Catholic thought there is undoubtedly a certain secular mentality, but it manifests itself less clearly in writings than in conversation and oral discussions".

Thomas J. Altizer and William Hamilton are Protestants, as are John Robinson and Harvey Cox of "'The secular city".

Both Altizer and Hamilton have touched on this point with a frankness that is surprising. "If theology is truly to die, it must desire the death of God, it must desire the death of Christianity, it must freely choose its fate and therefore cease to be itself". And he goes on to long for the radical destruction of theology: "All that theology has been up to now must be denied, and not simply because it is dead, but rather because theology cannot be reborn unless it passes through the trance of its own freely decreed death and dissolution"[853].

This death of the God of Christianity means the resurrection of the God of Kabbalah. Thomas J. Altizer makes this confession, which is of great significance: "Without any doubt, theology must abandon Christianity, and as we have already seen, this word can imply all the significant resonances which the term "Christian" suggests to us. A country which since Emerson's time has welcomed Vedanta, which even recently has been deeply moved by Zen Buddhism, which has been sensitive even to the vague speculations of Jung and Toynbee, and which has been initiated into the history of religions by Mircea Eliade, such a country is certain to reject a Christocentrism which is far from universal. Perhaps the most prophetic thinker in North America today is Norman O. Brown, who is trying to combine radical Freudianism with left wing mysticism (Kabbalah, Boehme, Blake, Taoism and Tantrism)"[854]. As we can see, a universal cabalistic syncretism is attempted, which may have a certain colouring, but which is identified with the deep longing of the gnosis of all times, which in a special way has acclimatised in the East. Here, in the East," he continues, "we can find a form of the sacred

---

[852] Concilium, no. 25, p. 275.
[853] Thomas J. Altizer, William Hamilton, *Teología radical y la muerte de Dios*, Grijalbo, S. A., Barcelona, Mexico, 1967, p. 32.
[854] Ibid., p. 35.

which Christianity has never known, and which is becoming more and more significant for our historical situation. By opening ourselves to the radically profane form of contemporary Existenz, we can prepare ourselves for a new reality of the Incarnation, an Incarnation that will be a definitive coincidentia oppositorum"[855].

Altizer realises that this attempt leads to Gnosticism and thus confesses: "From the religious point of view, the danger lies in Gnosticism, which is so elusive that it is not possible to define or circumscribe it"[856]. And Altizer, by adhering to history and the historical moment, is effectively defending himself from falling into the timeless instance of gnosticism. "He who says no to our historical present, who rejects existence in it, who stands in the face of our common destiny, and furthermore seeks rest in a timeless or pre-temporal instance, in a moment or "eternity" with no relation - or only a negative relation - to the present moment, is thereby succumbing to the gnostic danger"[857]. But this Eastern religious syncretism, even if it takes the form of a perfect secularity and responds to the more temporal historical demands of the present moment, is nothing but the Gnostic fable of all times, which aims to satisfy the religious cravings of the moment.

i) Secular Christianity is spreading frighteningly: C. A. J. Ouwerkerk is a Dutch theologian, specialised in moral theology, who has made a very interesting study in "Concilium" [858] on "Secularity and Christian ethics". In it he examines the various expressions of the theology of secularity in the Protestant and Catholic fields. He rightly takes the issue from situation ethics and passes it through the ethics of theonomy versus heteronomy and the ethics of a world that has come of age. Strictly speaking, these are variants that express the fundamental theme of secularity, which consists in turning theology into anthropology and transcendence into immanence, and, in the final analysis, in uprooting all religiosity from the depths of man. The Gnostic and cabalistic programme is faithfully expressed here. The author parades John Robinson, Bonhoeffer, Tillich, Bultmann, Ebeling, Fuchs, Dorothea Solle, van Buren, Altizer, Hamilton, Cox, and then studies "the function of the Church in relation to a secular Christian ethic"[859], to arrive at the

---

[855] Ibid., p. 35.
[856] Ibid., p. 36.
[857] Ibid., p. 36.
[858] No. 21, p. 274.
[859] Ibid., p. 300.

conclusion that "generalising a little, we could say that the fundamental thesis which appears in the whole theology of secularity in various forms is that the Church must place itself at the service of the world and its noble ideals". And he gives the reason for this thesis. "Salvation has been promised to the world; it is in the world that salvation must be realised, and the Church can in no way claim to monopolise salvation"[860]. The problem is to determine what constitutes the salvation of the world. It is quite different to admit a transcendent and personal God above the world than to have the divinity that saves it wrested from the world itself; it is quite different to make salvation consist in the supernatural grace of Christ than to make it consist in the earthly construction of a world that saves itself. The service which the Church must render to the world is first of all a supernatural service and then, in addition, a temporal service. The Lord fixed this in definite terms: "Seek ye first the kingdom of God and his righteousness, and the rest will be given you besides"[861].

j) The secular city of Harvey Cox[862] : "Secularisation designates the coming of age, urbanisation designates the context of this event"[863]. It returns to the hackneyed themes in the theology of secularisation that man has come of age to practise a supernatural, transcendent, religious Christianity. Man has come a long way since The Ancient City described by Fustel de Coulanges as a religious event.

The secular city appears today, and this by virtue of the process of desacralisation brought about by the Bible itself, so that one can rightfully speak of "the biblical sources of secularisation"[864].

Harvey Cox recognises that historical relativism is the terminal product of secularisation[865] and that there is a danger that the relativisation of values can lead to moral anarchism and religious nihilism, though not necessarily[866]. The death of God must, however, make man understand that he must truly become man[867].

---

[860] Ibid., p. 301.
[861] Mt., 6, 33.
[862] French translation. *La cité seculière*, Casterman, Paris, 1968.
[863] Ibid., p. 34.
[864] Ibid., p. 47.
[865] Ibid., p. 62.
[866] Ibid., p. 63.
[867] Ibid., p. 63.

Harvey Cox is candid enough to say that "the growing interest of modern theologians in a theology of history is closely linked to the need for a theology of revolution"[868], which is "the theology of revolutionary social change"[869]. Man, therefore, must embrace revolutionary social change as the Kingdom of God.

However, Cox corrects these points of identification of the Kingdom of God and the secular city: 1° While the Kingdom of God is the work of God alone, the secular city is the realisation of man.

2° While the Kingdom of God demands renunciation and penance, the secular City demands nothing but skill and knowledge.

3° While the Kingdom of God is placed above and outside history (or in the hearts of believers), the secular City is fully of this world"[870].

But despite these differences, "the kingdom of God, inscribed in the life of Jesus of Nazareth, is the most perfect revelation of the God-man partnership in history. When we strive for the formation of the secular City, we respond faithfully to this reality"[871].

For Harvey Cox, the secular City, which is the version of the Kingdom of God in our historical situation, is inextricably linked with urbanisation, which, although it also happens in the life of man, represents here the effort made by man to adapt to the new historical reality with a more just way of living with other human beings in a regime of increasingly generous reciprocity"[872].

In this enterprise of the secular City, the Church, which is not primarily an institution but the people of God[873], must be God's vanguard with a kerygmatic function that announces the revolution in progress[874], with a diaconal function that heals the wounds of the city[875], combating the tension between inner city and suburb, between the powerful and the economically weak, between black and white, and between political

---

[868] Ibid., p. 133.
[869] Ibid., p. 133.
[870] Ibid., p. 136.
[871] Ibid., p. 138.
[872] Ibid., p. 148.
[873] Ibid., p. 150.
[874] Ibid., p. 152.
[875] Ibid., p. 157.

parties[876], as well as a function of koinonia, making visible a kind of living picture of the character and composition of the true city of man"[877].

We must consider the physiognomy of Harvey Cox's secular city as a large urban complex of the American concentration-type, in which people are exclusively dedicated to solving their problems of work, housing, food, culture and sports.

> "We have already let it be understood, says Harvey Cox, that God comes to us today in the incidence of social change, in what theologians call history, and what we call politics.
>
> But incidences of social change are not necessarily convulsions and revolutions. The events of life are also the effects of social change..."[878].

k) The divinisation of the masses by the Dominican John Cardonnel: If one looks closely, there is a continuous process of secularisation, starting with Maritain's attempt to secularise Christianity, followed by the position of theologians who speak of a Christianity and a Church at the service of the construction of the world along the lines of worldliness, i.e. the revolutionary process that leads the world to communism and the machine society. By not assigning to the Church a position above the world, which helps the world, but from above, judging the construction of the world itself and making its help conditional on the sense of this construction, the Church is made a partner in the wrong course the world is taking. It is true that these theologians split the mission of the Church into a supernatural mission to save souls and another, in solidarity with the world, which serves the world in the task of secularisation. This Manichaeism cannot be maintained dialectically and must give way to another position, that of the theologians of the death of God and secularisation, whose radical expression we find in Robinson, Altizer, Hamilton, van Buren and Cox. The latter speaks of a revolutionary social mission of the Church, but this seems to be fulfilled within the moulds of the bourgeois world. Hence the importance of the attitude of the Dominican John Cardonnel, who resolutely pushes the Church, Christ and God into a total

---

[876] Ibid., p. 158.
[877] Ibid., p. 168.
[878] Ibid., p. 279.

functionalism of identification with the masses and with the Marxist masses.

Jean Cardonnel, a Dominican from the convent of Montpellier, disciple of Fr Chenu and friend of Fr Congar, presented on 6 October 1967 a work programme, "The theological option presented to the Church today", which was to serve as an orientation and a work plan for the weekly magazine "Temoignage Chrétien". Notre Combat published this work in its 25th issue of November 1967.

For Father Cardonnel, the Second Vatican Council did not consider the renewal of the Church except on the institutional level, making its organisation stronger, but leaving aside the necessary revolution of mentality and attitude of Christians towards the world. It is necessary to renew our conception of the Church and to take up resolutely our defence of the weak and the little ones, which involves socialism in France, the support of the struggle for independence and freedom of the countries of the Third World, the organisation of an international solidarity which bridges the gap between the satisfied and the oppressed, and the recognition as Christians that Christ is in our struggle. Cardonnel believes that salvation lies in a communist and atheist Christianity.

Cardonnel's system, first, is founded on the Hegelian-Marxist principle of the dialectic of master and slave; second, it develops into a total self-criticism of the Catholic religion, denounced as a capitalist superstructure and an alienation of the peoples; third, it exhibits itself as a deification of the revolutionary masses, and fourth, as an incarnation of the word.

1º The Hegelian-Marxist principle of the master and the slave. For Cardonnel, humanity is divided into two classes of men, the exploiters and the exploited. We are in the time of the massacre of the innocent, of the oppression of the poor by the rich, but the hour of revenge has come with the exasperation of the poor and the oppressed. The white man has not learnt to love and, worse still, the black man has learnt to hate.

The human birth of a mass is the awakening of consciousness by which a quality emerges from a quantity that gives being and existence to all participants. This awakening of the masses is the revolution. The masses can only realise themselves in the violent, implacable insurrection against those who oppress them materially and deprive them of their freedom in order to prevent them from becoming conscious of their own life, of their strength of solidarity, of their capacity to transform mankind. The future of the world lies in liberation. Salvation is there, that is to say that God expresses everything in the salvation of mankind, of the whole world, that there is nothing of God that is not given for salvation, there is only one urgent problem: how to save, how to liberate when all is lost? In the heart of lucid despair, what does it mean to hope? It is the Christian problem par excellence...".

2nd Total criticism of the Catholic Church, denounced as a capitalist superstructure. The Church society is content with speeches, but does nothing to remedy the unbalanced situation of the present society between the exploited and the exploiters. The Church is afraid of the masses... In its most beautiful outbursts of generosity, of fraternal sympathy, the Church, with "Populorum Progressio", turns to its clientele of wise, sympathetic, benevolent elites, in favour of the compassionate fate of the disinherited masses. In this way, these successes only engendered a ritual of pious approval in those satisfied with good will and never reached the masses. Herein lies the crux of the Church society; its essential failure, that which causes it to lose the audience of the masses. The traditional Church, functionally chattering, not engaging, while the Word is at work...

"The liberal, capitalist civilisation, in which the Church is involved, from the point of view that it is society, has consecrated the double divorce of act and thought, of word and intelligence. The prostitution of the Word is the supreme sign of debasement. And this debased Church, lost in the grimoires of "theological systems", in the development of theses, the composition of homilies, sermons, encyclicals, has betrayed the Word and has lost itself in vain words with which it participates in the enslavement of the masses. The masses are violated, flattered, courted... But the creative Word reveals Himself only by the elimination of worldly formulas. It is necessary to choose between elite phrases and the Word that speaks to the masses... "Speeches and adherence to words constitute a world that is self-sufficient: speaking for the sake of speaking". And this world of dreams and alienation is the Church!

Fr. Cardonnel steps forward and expresses his fundamental disagreement with Fr.

He wants to remain in Vatican II, in a Church distinct from the world but at the service of the world. Cardonnel wants a Church identified with the popular masses and fused with them.

It is unthinkable, he says, that the Church should "come" to the world. If it goes in the direction of the world, it is because in the first instance, let us say in a first form of existence, the Church dwells elsewhere, higher up or to the side, it matters little; it is elsewhere... Going to the masses presupposes that one comes from elsewhere, and that one exists only in a world foreign to the masses, that of the elites, of the place apart, of power. No path brings the masses into communication with the privileged. If I come to the masses, my habitual residence is in the rich neighbourhoods. To go to the masses is not to be with them. In such conditions, it is very serious, says Father Cardonnel, that Father Congar reproaches me that by insisting on the solidarity of the Church with men I would neglect the first time, the moment when she is before the world, an abstraction made from the world (although sent into the world to make God triumph in it), the vertical instant, before the divine offers of grace. On several occasions, Father Congar writes that before going into the world, the Church takes care to ensure her in-itself, and that it is necessary for her to be strong in what she knows of her own destiny in order to face the world without danger... But this is precisely the very essence of the worldly march which Christ came to combat: the Church needs a first period of narcissistic contemplation which would make her strong in relation to others!

3° The divinisation of the revolutionary masses. Cardonnel, after having criticised the Church for its claim to preserve its institutional reality and its refusal to be totally confused with the masses, explains why theologians as open-minded as Fr Congar are concerned with securing the in-itself of the Church and finds the reason in the fear that God will evaporate and disappear in his transcendence. They want to defend the in-itself of God. But Jean Paul Sartre effectively ruins the idea of God as an impossible synthesis of the "in-itself" and the "for-itself". One cannot be centred on the self, preoccupied with one's own glory and at the same time be given, surrendered. Sartre is right. The idea of God is incompatible with revelation.

For Cardonnel, God has no transcendence of his own, distinct and free. Men and the Church, he continues, from the angle of their belonging to the hierarchical and societal order, think of greatness, transcendence, in the form of absolute Autonomy, of the "Ens a se", the "Being for itself", the in-itself which has no need of others. However, the Judeo-Christian Revelation does not manifest any such thing... Transcendence is situated in conscious Relativity... Sartre has well seen that Self-Sufficiency could not be given - how could God maintain his transcendence in the shelter of the risks of the Incarnation?

Consequently, Cardonnel continues, if there is no in-itself of God and of the Church, there are no things of faith, there are no things of God either. God is all in his Word, which is his act.

God is all in His Act of the Exodus to Jesus Christ. There is nothing of God that is outside his Act, the salvation, the liberation of the masses. God is nothing other than the "divinisation of the dark forces at work in humanity". And he adds: "Jesus Christ means that there is no God in the pure state, that God is always mixed with man, in the purpose, conscious or not, of the divinisation of men"[879].

4° The revolutionary masses, incarnation of the Word. From all that has been said it follows that the Incarnation is nothing but the appearance of Christ in the womb of the masses, signalling the annihilation of the transcendent God, the death of God in the birth of humanity.

"Catholic theology, says Cardonnel, has neglected in its task the implications of the central fact: the annihilation of God, as sung in Paul's Christological hymn in Chapter II of the Epistle to the Philippians. He has been annihilated, emptied of himself. He has taken no interest in his private, individual self. He has taken no capital, no revenue, no property, in anything. Or he does not yet stand in the rank of God, but takes the rank of a slave... God is the man who espouses the human mass, who lives in it in permanent solidarity.

The Cardonnel-Congar polemic on horizontalism. Jean Pierre Jossua, O.P., reported in "Parole et Mission"[880] under the title Horizontal or vertical Christianity? the controversy that arose from an article by Fr Thomas Jean Cardonnel entitled "Scheme XIII: a disappointment. Conversation with Fr Cardonnel"[881], and that of Fr Yves Congar in "Informations Catholiques Internationales"[882] on Une analyse critique des tendances actuelles.

Criticising certain aspects of the XIII scheme, Father Cardonnel was particularly critical: first, of the Church-world dualism: "We are decidedly allergic to the very idea of a relationship that would be established between the Church and the world...; the whole scheme

---

[879] *Témoignage chrétien*, 16 February 1967.
[880] No. 41, April 1968.
[881] Frères du monde, no. 37, 1965, pp. 105-111.
[882] No. 286 of 15 April 1967.

would be flawed by this people of God which would be something other than the communion of men". The whole scheme would be vitiated by this people of God which would be something other than the communion of men"; secondly, he also took on the natural-supernatural dualism, as if the divine contribution which Christ would bring were not in reality "a provocation to the emergence of the total human", and as if "Jesus Christ does not consist entirely in the passion of being human to the end"; thirdly, he finally took on the idea of a transcendent God, as if he were beyond his communion with humans, thus provoking a dualism between God and universal brotherhood.

Father Congar denounced as horizontalism this attempt by Father Cardonnel, who refused to consider the first moment of the Church as anything other than the world. If Gaudium et Spes has been able to point out a frank entry into the service of mankind, it is because the Council had first secured the in-itself of the Church (faith, liturgy, ecclesiology). There is no "pure in-itself", certainly, but neither is there "pure for men" which is not the normal consequence of this in-itself. No pure verticalism or pure horizontalism.

Cardonnel responded to this with an article[883], "The great myth of being only human", in which, after acknowledging the decisive contributions of Fr Congar in the field of the ecclesiology of service, he concentrates his attack on the in-itself of the Church and the verticality of the relationship with God. For Cardonnel, it is not possible to have a time of recollection in the in-itself of the Church before going out into the world. If one is not with the poor from the beginning, one cannot go to them. "The Church is Christ's, the Church is God's people to the strict extent that it does not recognise itself with an in-itself". Nor is there a vertical time in God. "Congar now places on the level of God and man the relations of power... whose harmfulness for the Church he had shown".

And the relationship of verticality is "divine autocracy".

Cardonnel refuses to accept a "theology of transcendence, whose purpose is to secure the power of the Church-Institution, especially when it is engaged in the effort to live the Gospel on the Way of the Revolution". "Any confession of "transcendence" that leads away from

---

[883] Frères du monde, no. 46-47, 1967.

an effective commitment to the service of justice and peace is a poison for humanity".

Congar was rejected on all the fronts where he had made his attacks, he was forced to confess that "we differed much less on the substance than on the feeling of priority urgencies". But Fr Congar was not convinced. "Is there an opposition? I'm not sure, but I'm not sure there isn't either, he says. Cardonnel justifies the transcendence of the supernatural in Bonhoeffer's position, who adopts that of a 'Christ for others', but I don't know whether this recognises the 'supernatural character of Christ and of the life he gives us'".

The doubt remains, in the controversy of Congar and Cardonnel, whether the latter maintains the supernatural sense of Christianity, or whether he converts it into a purely naturalistic humanitarianism. But we say, there is no such doubt. Cardonnel's Christianity is anti-Christianity.

18. Worship and prayer in a secularised world

If a totally secularised Christianity is promoted, the question immediately arises as to the place of worship and prayer in this Christianity. The Jesuit Pierre Antoine has not failed to refer to this question in the review "Études" of Paris[884], and Alfonso Álvarez Bolado, also a Jesuit, touches on it in an article, Worship and Prayer in a Secularised World, which is reproduced in Selections of Theology[885]. Antoine invites us to "free ourselves from ready-made ideas, from habits canonised into dogmas, and return to a healthy empiricism and rational analysis of situations, as something necessary and urgent today to free the imagination and the creative spirit indispensable to the Church to face the present task"[886]. "Under present conditions, he says, it would seem normal to conceive of this meeting place (of the ecclesial assembly) as the image of the community's activities, as a multifunctional place, usable for purposes other than liturgical ceremonies alone"[887]. And he continues: "Thus, a domus ecclesiae (the house of the Christian assembly), which could be on one or two floors

---

[884] March 1967.
[885] No. 26, April-June 1968.
[886] Ibid., p. 441.
[887] Ibid., p. 442.

of a large building, would comprise, in addition to some small rooms (one of which could be adapted as an oratory for private prayer and the visit to the Blessed Sacrament) and the permanent offices, a large hall arranged for various uses (conferences, meetings, feasts, receptions, liturgy, etc.) by means of truly "mobile" furniture"[888].

Antoine insists on "the inadequacy of the parish institution in modern urban society"[889] and on the "enormous financial cost and the considerable burden of material concerns" involved in the construction of churches... and that we must honestly admit that, in the present conditions, because of carelessness or laziness to devise other possible solutions, we build too many churches"[890].

Antoine also insists that already today, "that there is no sacred place, there is no sacred time either"[891], and that the serious thing would be that, in our efforts to build places of worship, "in the choice between the clear force of the Gospel and our ecclesiastical traditions, it is the latter that seems to us to be more secure and ends up imposing itself"[892].

Álvarez Bolado's article is not as concrete and clear as that of Antoine. For one thing, Álvarez Bolado puts himself in Robinson's context in Honest to God, trying to explain what prayer life and worship would be there. It has to be said that Robinson has already been overtaken, and by far, in his attempts at secularisation in the face of the experience proposed by Hamilton and Harvey Cox. However, Álvarez Bolado censures Robinson for "really exposing himself to "a certain" reduction that "empties Christianity of its marrow"[893].

Accepting Robinson, with some critical remarks, Álvarez Bolado endorses his criticism of classical methods of prayer, which assume "that prayer is defined as an attitude developed in the hours of disengagement", in a "neo-Platonic scheme", by "beings concerned with "having to pray"", who spend energy searching for "times of prayer" and in making viable "methods" that never prove valid[894]. Robinson is right, he says, therefore to ask "whether Christian prayer,

---

[888] Ibid., p. 442.
[889] Ibid., p. 443.
[890] Ibid., p. 444.
[891] Ibid., p. 445.
[892] Ibid., p. 447.
[893] Selecciones de Teología, no. 26, p. 197.
[894] Ibid., p. 201.

that which arises in us, in the light of the Incarnation, is not to be defined in terms which imply a penetration of the world so that through it we turn to God, and not a withdrawal from the world in order thus to set us right with God"[895].

Álvarez Bolado shows timidity, so that he is not representative as an author of the theme of prayer and worship in a secularised world. He proposes "to make the mystery of Christ present to a secularised world, but not to secularise Christianity to the point of turning it into a conventional neo-humanism"[896]. He warns of the danger of his attempt, but he does not fail to expose with pleasure the general tendency today, even if impossible, to maintain sacred things in a totally secularised world.

19. *Some facts that anticipate the new secularised Church*

As interesting as the alteration of the doctrine proposed by the new theologians are the many facts which are taking place in all countries, old and young, and which tend towards the total liquidation to which the Church is today committed. It is already common in the new mentality that the two thousand years of the Church's history must be liquidated, plainly and simply, as an anti-evangelical history, a history of pure power, and of external and monastic power against the laity. When the word Constantinian is used to characterise this Church, it also anathematises all that the Fathers and Doctors have written and preached, all that the saints have taught by their example, and all that the great pontiffs of all times have commanded.

On the other hand, the new generations are being pushed to take the path of a new priesthood, without celibacy, engaged in the world and the pleasures of the world, engaged in the sensualism of cinema, television, psychoanalysis. Hence the psychoanalytical experiences of the Benedictine convent of Cuernavaca were only a first step - happily frustrated by the energetic intervention of Rome - which should not be separated from the wave of sexuality which dominates all religious environments and which threatens to burst into convents and religious houses. With this new atmosphere, which is radically opposed to that

---

[895] Ibid., p. 201.
[896] Ibid., p. 204.

of ascetic austerity which was previously inculcated, we must relate the desertions of priests and nuns which are being noted all over the world.

Entire religious orders have gone down the road of sexual licence and social violence. Sin is no longer sin. It simply does not exist and therefore is not confessed. The masturbation is the order of the day. Premarital sex is simply encouraged. Love, and sexual love, is the great principle that regulates the relations of man and woman. Everything is permitted in the attendance of film shows and everything is authorised under the pretext of art.

The Church has become a factor of social revolution, and the guerrilla priests, the Camilo Torres, are proposed as examples for imitation. The great exponents of the new social order are Fidel Castro, Che Guevara and Mao Tse Tung.

The purpose of the Church is not the salvation of souls but the prophetic commitment to the world and to the building of a future society from which hunger, misery and war must be banished.

The Church is no longer a beacon of truth and holiness in the world but a real factor of subversion and agitation. The Church, the Church of publicity, the Church that appears in the press and on television, has become the vanguard of the Revolution.

CHAPTER XIII

TOWARDS A KABBALISTIC CHRISTIANITY

The new theologians deny or question the main and most fundamental dogmas of the Church. We must ask ourselves: where are they going, what image of the Church do they want? It is evident that in all these attempts there is the purpose to soften the Church and to accommodate it to the world, and to the modern world. But this is precisely the modernist attempt, and this attempt is nothing but the construction of the Gnostic system.

This has been lucidly noted by Bishop Rudolf Graber in the magnificent document where he shrewdly studies "the attitude of Paul VI and the internal crisis of the Church"[897]. There Graber shows how Paul VI has noticed the persistence of the modernist heresy in the present errors of the Church. Paul VI himself states this clearly in Ecclesiam Suam in the key paragraph in which he characterises modernism. The Pope says: "All this, like the waves of the tempest of the sea, envelops and shakes the Church herself; the spirits of the men entrusted to her are strongly influenced by the climate of the temporal world. This influence is so strong that a danger as of vertigo, of dizziness, of aberration (veluti vertiginis stuporis ac trepidationis periculum), can shake her very solidity and induce many to go after the strangest thoughts, imagining as if the Church must deny herself and embrace new and unthinkable forms of life". And then the Pope cites Modernism, continuing: "The errors of Modernism - which we see revived today (reviviscere cernimus) in various attempts at heterogeneous expressions foreign to the authentic reality of the Catholic religion - were not they precisely such an episode of the predominance of psychological and cultural

---

[897] Revista Roma, Buenos Aires, November 1967.

tendencies, proper to the profane world, over the faithful and genuine expression of the doctrine and norm of the Church of Christ?

The Pope sees in the predominance of the psychological and cultural tendencies of the profane world over the conception proposed by the Church the very essence of modernism. And this is precisely the typical phenomenon of progressivism that we have described in the previous chapter. Modern culture dominates and rules Catholic doctrine. The modern world rules Catholic doctrine. The modern world devours, in a certain sense, the Church.

And this culture is reflected in all fields: philosophical, historical, sociological, psychological, and is then manifested in exegesis, theology and the history of the Church.

Note how the errors we have denounced in the current progressivism are the errors denounced by St. Pius X in the decree Lamentabili[898], as characteristic of modernism. Suffice it to cite a few:

2 "The Church's interpretation of the Sacred Books is not to be despised, but it must be submitted to the most careful judgement and correction of exegetes"[899].

18 "John presents himself as a witness of Christ; but in reality he is only an exemplary witness of the Christian life, or the life of Christ in the Church at the end of the first century"[900].

20 "Revelation could be nothing other than man's acquired awareness of his relationship with God"[901].

31 "The doctrine of Christ taught by Paul, John and the councils of Nicea, Ephesus and Caledonia, is not what Christ taught, but what the Christian conscience conceived of Jesus"[902].

36 "The Resurrection of the Saviour is not properly a fact of historical being, but a fact of the merely supernatural order, neither demonstrated

---

[898] Denz., 2001 to 2006.
[899] Denz, 2002.
[900] Denz., 2.018.
[901] Denz., 2.020.
[902] Denz., 2.031.

nor demonstrable, which Christian consciousness gradually derived from other facts"[903].

53 "The organic constitution of the Church is not immutable, but Christian society, like human society, is subject to perpetual evolution"[904].

58 "Truth is no more immutable than man himself, for in him, with him and through him it unfolds"[905].

60 "Christian doctrine was at first Jewish, but it was made by successive evolutions, first Pauline, then Johannine, then Hellenic and universal"[906].

64 "The progress of science calls for a reform of the concepts of Christian doctrine on God, creation, revelation, the person of the incarnate Word, redemption"[907].

65 "Catholicism today cannot be reconciled with true science unless it is transformed into a certain non-dogmatic Christianity, i.e. open and liberal Protestantism"[908].

The impact of modern culture, founded on a subjectivist philosophy, on religious dogmas produces modernism and the current progressivism, which is nothing more than the concrete and historical realisation of modernist aspirations. Progressivism, like modernism, is nothing but the evacuation of the secular dogmatic content of Catholicism and its replacement by a Protestant ideology elaborated around a vague Christ, man-God, more man than God.

Bishop Rudolf Graber has seen that this is nothing but the elaboration of a gnosis and asks: But isn't this the problem that has accompanied the Church and Christianity from its origins, from the temptations of Christ, from the gnosis of the 2nd and 3rd centuries, from the beginning of capitalism at the time of the "Poverello" and the introduction of

---

[903] Denz., 2.036.
[904] Denz., 2.053.
[905] Denz., 2.058.
[906] Denz., 2.060.
[907] Denz., 2.064.
[908] Denz., 2.065.

Aristotelian philosophy, humanism and the Renaissance, up to modernism and the atomic age?[909].

The impulse of all modernism and progressivism leads the Church to merge with the world in order to make the Church an epiphenomenon or a product emanating from the world itself.

It is therefore not purely accidental that all the errors that emerge in today's progressivism end in the secularisation or worldliness of Christianity.

In this secularisation lies the inner energy of progressivism itself. This had already been denounced by Pius IX in the Syllabus when he made the conciliation of the Church and the modern world the key error which closed and summed up the whole of this document[910]. But herein lies essentially the Gnostic and cabalistic character of progressivism.

However, this gnostic and cabalistic character of present-day progressivism has to be seen in two stages; the first stage is that of a system in the making, which is still in the process of elaboration and has not yet reached a finished crystallisation. It is a gnostic system in the making.

Such are the partial and unconnected errors in which progressivism expresses itself today, and which we have described in the preceding chapter. Progressivism can also manifest itself in a complete and complete Gnostic system, as for example in Theilhardism, which, however, is only one of the many variants into which a Gnostic system can be translated. Just as in the second and third centuries the gnosis of Simon Magus, Marcion, Saturninus and Valentinus multiplied, so now there must also appear diverse Gnostic constructions which bring together in a syncretistic amalgam the scientific, philosophical and religious knowledge of the time.

The essence of Gnostic and Kabbalistic error

It is very difficult to determine the essence of Gnostic and Kabalistic error as the present book reveals in all its development. It is possible to indicate a number of characters which individualise a Gnostic system.

---

[909] Ibid., p. 24.
[910] Prop. 80 in Denz., 1780.

But the hard part is to indicate the essential nucleus or the distinctive note that constitutes it. We are going to try to establish hierarchically a series of notes which, in our opinion, determine the Gnostic or Kabbalistic error. We say gnostic or kabbalistic on the understanding that the word "gnosis" has a wider scope than the word "Kabbalah", since the latter restricts the term "gnosis" to the Jewish world. There has been and there is a pagan gnosis, typically Hindu, Iranian or Egyptian. We think, however, that the gnosis operating in the Christian world is influenced by typically Jewish causes and elements, whether direct as in the case of Boehme and Spinoza, or indirect as in Hegel or in the modern movements of Teilhard de Chardin or Jung.

To elucidate this problem we shall consider the Gnosticism of the Qabalah. And as we have argued for the Egyptian origin of the Qabalah in the first Egyptian captivity, back in the 13th century B.C., we also affirm here the Egyptian origin of the Jewish Qabalah. The texts telling us about creation that have come down to us from ancient Egypt belong to all periods of Pharaonic history, from the Ancient Empire to the time when Egypt was part of the Roman Empire: they are material and direct witnesses to more than three thousand years of theological elaboration.

There is reason to suppose that the oldest of them, engraved on the pyramids of the 5th and 6th dynasties (2600-2300 BC) had been composed orally, at least in part, by the prehistoric Egyptians, during the 4th millennium BC, from beliefs born in the mists of time[911].

Extracts from the Pyramid Texts

1. Before creation: "This [king] has been placed in the world in the Noum[912] when heaven did not exist, when the earth did not exist, when nothing yet existed that was established, when disorder did not yet exist, when the terror that was to be born from the eye of Horus had not yet been produced".

2. Appearance of the demiurge: "Hail to thee, Tuna! Hail to thee, Khrepri, who hast come by thyself into existence! Thou culminate in this thy name of "hill", thou comest into existence in this thy name of Khrepri".

---

[911] *La naissance du monde*, Aux éditions du Seuil, Paris, 1959, p. 46.
[912] Noum means "abyss".

3. The divine throat: "Atun-Khepri, thou hast culminated in a hill, thou hast risen in the form of a phoenix, which is the master of the betilo[913] in the Castle of the Phoenix in Heliopolis. Thou hast cast forth a throat, which is Shu, thou hast cast forth a spit (tfen), which is Tefnut".

4. The solitary Creator: "Tuna has manifested himself in the form of a masturbator in Heliopolis.

He grasped his member with his fist: the twins were put into the world, Shu with Tefnut".

5. The God Shu: "O Shu, son of Tuna, you are the Great (=the Ancient), son of Tuna, his first offspring. Tuna has spat thee out of his mouth. He has said: "Raise me up, then, to his sons".

In this very ancient Egyptian writing, God comes out of the abyss, out of nothingness, out of the indeterminate. And this god manufactures the other gods and the world sexually. From this the Israelites could derive their cabalistic conception.

The conception of the Kabbalah thus contains five fundamental ideas. 1st, God, in the last analysis, is nothing coming out of nothing; 2nd, this nothingness, by evolution, becomes the world and man; 3rd, God manufactures the world by sexual action; 4th, evil is in God and the evil of the world has a divine origin; 5th, God perfectly fulfilled and realised culminates in Man, in Humanity.

1. God is Nothing coming out of Nothing

In the Kabbalah this notion that God is Nothing is clearly expressed: "The Ancient One bears the name of Nothing"[914]. And in Kabbalistic language, and even in Biblical language, to bear the name is the same as to be. And elsewhere: "The Father proceeds from the sacred Elder as it is written: 'Wisdom proceeds from Nothing'"[915]. Gershom Scholem acknowledges with his undisputed authority that, for example, "the early Spanish Kabbalists make use of speculative paraphrases such as "root of all roots", "great truth", "undifferentiated unity", and, principally, "En-Sof". This last qualification especially proves, as clearly as all the others, and perhaps even more than they, the character of impersonality which is proper to the God hidden from men. It does

---

[913] A stone from sacred places that represented divinity.
[914] Zohar III, 288 b.
[915] Zohar III, 290 a.

not mean, as it has often been translated, "He who is infinite", but, on the contrary, "That which is infinite", just as Isaac the Blind, the first Qabalist of whom definite news has come down to us, calls this hidden God, "that which is not graspable", and not, with an allusion of a personal character, "The ungraspable"[916].

2. *This Nothingness by evolution becomes the world and man*

Gershom Scholem goes on to say after the paragraph transcribed above: "Kabbalistic thought in formulating this theosophical assertion of an impersonal cause in God - who therefore appears as a person only in his creation and revelation - abandons the personalistic foundation of the biblical concept of God; therefore, one could say that the author of that mystical aphorism was right when he said that not a word is said about En-sof in the Bible or in the Talmud"[917].

After acknowledging that this indeterminate God, impersonal and properly equal to Nothing, evolves and is realised in the sephiroth, which in their totality constitute the world and humanity, Scholem says: "The hidden God - as it were the innermost subjectivity of divinity - has neither quality nor attributes. It, its innermost essence, is willingly called by the Zohar and by most kabbalists by the name of En-Sof, that is, 'the Infinite'. Inasmuch, however, as this hidden essence manifests itself in the cosmic process, positive attributes which represent the profound reality of the divine life suit it, such attributes being degrees of the divine being and divine manifestations in which its secret life flows"[918].

And Scholem continues: "In the emanation of the sephiroth something flows into God himself and bursts through the enclosed crust of his hidden being: this thing is the creative power of God, which does not live only in the earthly creation although it naturally lives in it and is immanent to it and recognisable by it"[919].

There is thus a true "creative evolution", in the manner of Bergson or Teilhard de Chardin, in the Kabalistic conception, according to which

---

[916] Gershom Scholem, *Le grandi correnti della mistica ebraica*, p. 29.
[917] Ibid., p. 29.
[918] Ibid., p. 286.
[919] Ibid., p. 287.

the various worlds of the Kabalah are formed until the perfect Humanity is reached.

It is easy to see how the Kabalistic conception is opposed to the Catholic doctrine. In the former, God is a most perfect personal being who out of His goodness and freely creates the universe out of nothing, in accordance with the plan which He has formed from eternity. In the latter, on the other hand, God, coming out of the indeterminate and the Nothing, is made by evolution until culminating in Humanity, which is God realised. Starting from Nothingness, God is made in the Universe and in Man.

3. The sexual is fulfilled in God

In the text of the Pyramids transcribed above, we saw how Tuna, masturbating, engenders the other gods and with them the world and Man. Something similar must be conveyed to us by the Kabbalah. The emanation and evolution of God - theogony - is done through a sexual path. Gershom Scholem, who studies at length this sexual aspect of the Zohar, notes that the ninth sefira Yesod, united in the image of the King, flow into the Sekhina - the Matron - and engender the secret life of the world[920]. The phallic symbolism, connected with the speculations of the sefira Yesod [921], anticipates in a very suggestive way Freud's lucubrations.

We shall bring only one text from the Zohar, which is of great significance. It reads: "Rabbi Simeon adds: All that I have just said of the sacred Elder and the Little Face designates one and the same thing: all is one and there is no separation... notice that the first point, called Father, is contained in the letter Yod... therefore this letter encloses all letters. The yod is the beginning and the end of all things. It is the river that flows outwards and is called the "future world". It is the future world of the future that will not cease to exist. The future world has been created by the yod, so it is written: And a river flows out of it to water the garden..."[922].

---

[920] Ibid., p. 308.
[921] Ibid., p. 308, Zohar I, 162 a; II, 128 a/b; III, 5 a/b and 26 a.
[922] Zohar III, 290 b.

4. Evil is in God

In God are the two complementary sexes, yes and no, thesis and antithesis[923], good and evil. Gersom Scholem argues that, according to the Zohar, the ultimate causes of evil are even deeper and are to be found in God himself. The divine forces form a harmonious whole and neither is good or holy unless united with the other in a living relationship[924]. This is especially true for justice or severity - in God and from God, which is the deepest cause of evil. God's anger is like his left hand in intimate relationship with the quality of grace and love, his right hand[925]. The one cannot manifest itself without the other. This sefirah of severity is thus the great "focus of wrath" that burns in God, but is continually sweetened and restrained by grace. If, in an enormous, hypertrophic development, it bursts outwards and breaks its union with grace, then it flees from the world of divinity and becomes radical evil, the world of Satan opposed to that divine one[926]. We will bring a single text from the Zohar: "...Discord came from the left side, for as long as there was only the right side, discord was impossible. But inasmuch as by the elevation of the middle, the two sides formed, one right and one left, it is the left side that gives rise to discord and from which hell, Gehinom, emanates[927].

5. God perfectly fulfilled and realised culminates in the man of Humanity

Let us remember what Gersom Scholem tells us that "God is an impersonal reality, who only becomes a person in the process of Creation and Revelation"[928]. And the process of Creation culminates in the emanation of man... therefore only in Man does God attain the totality of his being, the finished personality of God[929].

Hence, and here again we follow Scholem, that the most ancient Hebraic mysticism is the mysticism of the throne, of the Merkaba. "Here it is not a question of immersing oneself in meditation on the true nature of God, but in the vision of His appearance on the throne, of

---

[923] Gersom Scholem, op. cit., p. 297.
[924] Ibid., p. 318.
[925] Ibid., p. 318.
[926] Ibid., p. 318.
[927] Zohar, I, 17 a.
[928] *Le grandi correnti della mística ebraica*, p. 29.
[929] Ibid., p. 30.

which Ezekiel speaks, and of the knowledge of the mysteries of this heavenly world of the throne. The world of the throne means, for the Hebrew mystic, what for the Hellenistic and proto-Christian mystics of that time, known in the history of religion by the name of Gnostics and Hermeticists; this world is the pleroma, the luminous world of the divinity, with its power, its aeons and dominations... the pre-existent throne of God - which contains within itself in exemplary form all the forms of creation - is the goal and object of mystical rapture and mystical vision"[930]. And in a note Scholem explains the preponderant part that the new cosmos or man plays in this mysticism of the throne[931]. Hence the great significance of the Adam Kadmon, the archetypal man, who represents the fullness of the sephiroth or the realised Creation[932].

These five notes of Kabalistic Gnosticism can be expressed by an equivalent fundamental, which virtually contains them, a fundamental note which only strongly emphasises one aspect in preference to the others, which are not excluded but only obscured. Whether this fundamental note is one in preference to another will depend on each system and on the preferences of its author. But by excluding a most perfect and personal God, who by a free action brings the Universe out of nothing, one already falls, by an ineluctable logic, into the cabalistic conception, which will be called evolutionism, materialism, idealism, humanism, according to the one-dimensional character of the substance which makes up the totality of God, the world and man.

Each of these fundamental notes has a special force because, placed as the central idea of the system, it ends by conditioning and modelling the system itself in each and every one of its parts. Thus evolutionism in any system, no matter how many precautions are taken, affirmed as the first and metaphysical truth, must end by conditioning the idea of God, of the world and of man, giving us a simple variant of cabalistic gnosticism.

---

[930] Scholem, ibid. p. 68.
[931] Ibid., p. 110, note 8.
[932] Ibid., p. 294.

The essence of Gnostic error expressed equivalently by some predominant note

1. The totality of a single substance. Both the Kabbalah and the various Gnostic systems are distinguished primarily by the note of "totality". They are systems which embrace the totality of God, of the world and of man. They leave nothing out of the totality and explain everything. The same fundamental current of being runs through all beings in the universe, ascending or descending, but without breaking the fundamental continuity between them all. For this reason, they are emanatist and univocist systems. The liberating creative act of a personal God does not establish a rupture between the sphere of God and the sphere of the creature. One can move without interruption from one sphere to the other. Likewise there is no rupture or discontinuity between the spheres of good and evil. Evil is nothing but imperfect and unfinished good, as in René Guénon, or residues of the evolutionary process, as Teilhard de Chardin would have it, or crusts, as the Kabbalah imagines.

From the En-sof, through the Sephiroth to the quliphah, there is in the Kabalah an unbroken continuity. And likewise, in the classical Gnostic systems, there is an unbroken continuity from the Pleroma through the Intermediary to our universe[933].

Likewise in Hegel's system, in which indeterminate being ends in the Absolute Spirit, or in Teilhard de Chardin's, in which "the multiple" culminates in the Pleroma.

2. An evolutionary emanation of being. We have seen that both the Kabbalah and the Gnostic systems conceive of God, the world and man as a homogeneous totality of being.

For if one does not want to accept the free creative act, which both the Kabbalah and the Gnostic systems reject, there is no other way of explaining the appearance of the new being than by an emanation of this being from the previously existing being. The same substance, the same numerically, unfolds and develops. That is to say, it evolves. Strictly speaking, there is no increase of substance or of being. There is an appearance of new being, but it is an apparent appearance, that is to say, phenomenal, not ontological, metaphysical and not real. At most a

---

[933] Sagnard, *La Gnose Valentinienne*, De Vrin, Paris, 1947, p. 569.

passage from virtual to formal being can be granted. At the most, I say, because this increase of formal being over virtual being could not be sufficiently explained either.

3° Evolutionary emanation can be understood as an ascending or descending path. Evolutionary emanation, both in the Qabalah and in the ancient Gnostic systems, was an involutionary or degrading emanation, or a path of descent. In the Kabalah, at least at one stage of the Kabalah, there was a descending path, from the world of the Aziluth to the world of Briah, from Briah to the world of Iesirah, and finally to the world of Asiah and the Quliphah. In the Gnostic systems and in Plotinus, the pleroma or the "One" by a path of degradation reached the ultimate limit of the material creature. In contrast, in the modern Gnostic systems, that of Hegel or Teilhard de Chardin, the process is evolutionary and more and more perfected beings appear.

4° Either way, evolutionary emanation must start from a First Subsistent Being. Whichever way evolutionary emanation is conceived, whether ascending or descending, it must start from a first being. Nothingness cannot evolve upwards or downwards. If there was nothingness before being, there could never have been being. However one thinks of things, being cannot spring from nothingness. Being springs from being and only from being. Now, this First Being that existed before the process of evolutionary emanation began, was either a First Being, a Pure Act with the fullness of all being, or it was a First Being that has been coming into being, and has therefore been subject to an evolutionary or ascending process.

In the first case, it is the God of the Christian tradition, who contains infinitely the perfections of a personal, intelligent and free Being, and who, out of an excess of goodness and freedom, creates the finite world, not out of its substance, but simply out of nothing, ex nihilo. If we do not accept this first case, we fall into a first being or god of the Kabbalah, a god who makes himself and from whom the world emanates as a necessity of this making of God. Hence the Kabbalah, like the Gnostic systems and Hegel and Teilhard himself, implies an evolution of God from the indeterminate to the more determined, a theogonic process that is confused with the cosmogonic and anthropogonic process of the history of the world and of God.

This first being, not being the Subsistent Being which characterises God in the theology of St Thomas, must necessarily be characterised as an indeterminate being which, in the limit, approaches Nothingness. Hence Teilhard de Chardin calls it Positive Nothing, or Creatable

Nothing, or Manifold, all names which imply contradiction. For if it is Nothing, it cannot be positive.

The pure indeterminate is Nothing, and Nothing has no quality that determines and perfects it. If there is no Subsistent Being or Pure Act, as the most perfect and personal Being, there can be absolutely nothing. St. Thomas has given the definitive reason for this when he affirms that "it is necessary that the first entity be in act and in no way in potency"[934]. For if the first entity were in indeterminacy or potency, it could not come out of its indeterminacy or potency, for there would be no being in act to make it come out.

5° The evolutionary God contains the essential contradiction of the Kabbalah and the Gnostic systems that "the more" comes out of "the less". Absolutely not, the more cannot come out of the less, nor the act out of the potency. St. Thomas has seen this perfectly and has left it in a definitive form. Licet enim in uno et eodem quod exit de potentia in actum, prius sit potentia quam actus tempore, simpliciter tamen actus prior est potencia[935]. Although in the being that passes from potency to act, potency is chronologically prior to act, in no way is act prior to potency, since what is in potency cannot pass into act except by virtue of something that is in act. Herein lies the essential contradiction of "a God who is becoming", both in the Kabbalah and in the Gnostic systems. A god that is becoming is a god that is acquiring perfections that it did not have, and which therefore come out of nothingness. In this case, Being comes out of nothingness. Nothingness equals Being. The ontological and logical principle of non-contradiction is simply denied.

6° In the Gnostic systems and in the Kabbalah, the world and man are made a "totalised God" superior to God Himself. The manifested God is superior to the unmanifested God. The unfolded God is superior to the unmanifested God. The universe, which is an emanation of God, adds perfections to the God from whom it emanates. Humanity, therefore, which is the culmination of the world of stone and life, represents a value immeasurably superior to God alone, and to God unfolded in stone and life. Humanity is God developed in the fullness of His virtualities.

---

[934] 1, 3, 1.
[935] 1, 3, 1.

This is a direct consequence of rejecting creation. Indeed, by accepting creation, the creature, the effect of the free and gratuitous act of the Creator, does not have a being that adds something to the Creator. For the creature's being is a pure and participatory reflection of the Creator. The being of the creature and the being of the Creator may be more beings, but not more being. On the other hand, if one rejects creation and with it that of the creature, a purely participatory and dependent being, one makes of the world and of man a reality emanating from the divine substance which complements and perfects God Himself.

7° This idea of a total emanationism that evolves into a God that culminates in humanity can be expressed by the absolute immanence of God in the world. Today we speak of immanence versus transcendence. We do not want to admit the idea of a God, Lord of the world, who creates it by a free way of his will and who has to submit it to judgement. God is in the world and is one with the world itself. Either the world comes out of God by emanation or it is constructed in the entrails of the world that is constructed. In either case God's immanence with the world is narrow and total. Transcendence is likewise excluded. God is neither outside nor above the world. Immanence is absolute and total. This immanence is but a consequence of that total emanationism which encloses God, the world and man in a way of expressing this emanationism. If God is the totality of the world, God identifies himself with the world or is perfectly and absolutely immanent to it, being identical with it.

8° Another way of expressing this total emanatism is to reject all extrinsicism and to affirm that God is intrinsic to humanity. For if God is absolutely intrinsic, or is within humanity, he forms with it a completely united whole. This idea of the rejection of extrinsicism is important in the treatise on grace and man's destination to the supernatural. One would like to exclude grace and the supernatural vocation of man to glory and grace as purely gratuitous gifts, as gifts that come from outside. One would like to insinuate that, in some way, there is a demand on man. Henri de Lubac, with his "Surnaturel"[936], is the most representative author of this current, which is evidently Gnostic or cabalistic.

---

[936] Aubier, Paris. De Lubac has notably corrected this deficiency in *Le mystère du Surnaturel* by teaching that God's supernatural desire for human nature is ineffective.

9° This idea of total emanatism can also be expressed by that of absolute monism. If man and the world are beings emanating from the substance of God, it is evident that man, the world and God form a single substance and a single being. Absolute monism adequately expresses the idea of total immanentism.

10° In this total emanatism the oppositions of matter and spirit, nature and grace, good and evil, yes and no, disappear. This is a typical characteristic of both the Kabbalah and the Gnostic systems. As all beings and realities proceed by emanation from one and the same substance, no essential diversity can be established between them. And since the divine substance, the Ain Sof of the Kabbalah, evolves in order to perfect and determine itself, and this can only be done at the expense of an essential contradiction enclosed within it, as we have seen in point 5; the yes and the no are found in its very substance, and negation is the motor of the very evolutionary movement of beings, as Hegel teaches in his Logic[937]. This is why Hegel is led to admit the absurdity of self-movement, i.e. a movement which is verified by identifying the motor and the mover; the motor which, as such, gives, and the mover which, as such, receives.

If contradiction forms the very core of beings, everything is one and the same thing, yes and no, good and evil, truth and falsehood, nature and grace, the Church and the world, God and the creature.

11° Hence the Kabbalah and the Gnostic systems end in a total unification of all religions, races, peoples and cultures. This idea of religious syncretism and the disappearance of all differentiations, even or especially religious ones, is a typical feature of every Kabalistic and Gnostic movement. It is found in the Kabbalah and in the various ancient and modern Gnostic systems, and is therefore the distinctive feature of all esoteric and Masonic movements.

12. The Kabbalah and the Gnostic systems also demand a single dimension of nature and grace, reason and revelation, philosophy and theology, church and world. This is an inescapable consequence of the Kabalistic and Gnostic conception, derived from its total emanatism, which tends to confuse and unify everything. Hence the essentially cabalistic and gnostic nature of Maritain's attempt, in his Integral

---

[937] *Ciencia de la Lógica*, translated by Augusto and Rodolfo Nondolfo, Hachette, Buenos Aires, 1956, II, p. 72.

Humanism[938], to promote his "lay Christianity", i.e. a Christian world with a single dimension. This is why, by rejecting the subordination of the world to the Church, a movement first of all towards equality between the world and the Church, and then towards the fusion of the Church with the world, and thus towards secularisation, must be favoured. The secular and secular Christianity advocated by progressive theologians is but a consequence of secular Christianity.

There is total continuity between Maritain with his secular Christianity, Congar with his autonomy of the world from the Church, Schillebeeckx and Rahner with the implicit Christianity of the world, and Robinson, Altizer, Hamilton, Harvey Cox with their complete secularisation of Christianity. One thing brings the other. The logic follows a rigorous and irreversible path. Indeed, Maritain begins his campaign against the Christian public order. Cangar continues against the triumphalist and Constantinian Church, that is to say, against a world and a culture subjected to the Church. Instead, he calls for a Church which is the servant of the world and which, by the same token, has to stimulate the unhealthy aspirations of the world. Finally, the ultimate programme of the Kabbalah and the Gnostic systems is to be proclaimed, which is a totally unified world in the religious aspect, from which the Church totally loses its transcendence vis-à-vis the world.

13° By making God, the world and man a single dimension, everything is either divine or purely human, everything is either spirit or purely matter, everything is either sacred or purely secular. This is also the conclusion of the previous premises. By making God, the world and man a single ontological substance, the totality of the substance of all things is unified under a single dimension. This dimension is given a dominant one which, if it is the divine, turns everything into pantheism; if it is the terrestrial, or the purely human, into pure positivism, a la Comte; if it is the spirit, it gives rise to Hegelianism; and finally, if it is matter, it will become any variant of materialism, whether empiricist or dialectical. When it is admitted that everything is sacred, Gnostic systems arise in the Valentinian manner, and when it is held that everything is secular, we have gnosis such as modern secularism or atheism.

---

[938] See my book *De Lamennais a Maritain*, Ed. Theoría, Buenos Aires, 1967.

14° As there is only one ontological dimension of realities, everything that exists either returns to God, if its existence is assumed, or returns to nothingness, if this is the first presupposition.

We consider this point to be of the greatest importance, because it shows the existence of Gnostic systems which are not only non-religious but which, for the same reason, do not imply a return to God or to the Pleroma, as was the case in the Gnosis of the first centuries of Christianity. At that time it was not possible to imagine non-religious gnostic systems because the gnostic systems wanted precisely to satisfy the religious aspirations of the people; but today, when the profane, earthly and secular has manifested itself with vigour, the different gnoses that are exogitated come to satisfy human aspirations of purely earthly well-being. There is no belief in the "hereafter" and the ultimate aspiration is placed in the "here", and since man must inevitably die, he ends up by accepting nothingness as the absolute and definitive end of life.

Hence, Gnostic Nirvanic systems such as those of Freud, Marx, Schopenhauer, Nietzsche and all the materialists, including Sartre, Camus and Merleau Ponty, must be admitted.

15° If a single ontological dimension of God, the world and man is established, there is no salvation for man except in man himself. This is also a consequence of all the notes that we have been pointing out as constitutive of the Kabbalah and of the various Gnostic systems. Man's salvation does not come from outside man, from a redeemer extrinsic to man, as Christianity clearly professes. Man, by his sin, had become at enmity with God, his Creator, and God, in His goodness, would have sent His only begotten Son Jesus Christ to become man, to suffer and die on the Cross in order to redeem man.

All Gnostic systems reject this notion of redemption from outside man himself, and if they admit the great initiates, as Schuré does, they are but paradigms and exemplars of what is to be realised in each individual man.

Man's salvation is achieved by man's own efforts, by appealing to inner forces as in the esoteric systems of René Guénon and the various theosophies and Rosicrucianism, or to outer forces as in Marx's dialectical materialism.

16° Both the Kabbalah and almost all the various Gnostic systems reject a personal God distinct from the world and from man, and make the world an eternal continuity of eternally succeeding phenomena. This point is also an explanation of all that has been said above. Hence the importance of Brahmanical and Buddhist thought to illustrate the gnosis appearing in the West, whether of a religious or secular character. Hence also the fate of all esotericisms that make the world a mere manifestation of the unmanifested. Hence the importance of Kantian thought, which, by denying human intelligence access to the noumenon, i.e. to the metaphysical reality of things, has made of them a world of pure appearances or phenomena. Philosophy and metaphysics have since then become phenomenology, which may know various variants in Hegel, Husserl and Teilhard de Chardin and, in general, in historicism. The world, since then, is a world of mayhem, nirvanic, phenomenological, in which all realities, in the last analysis and in the last instance, will be reabsorbed into the nothingness from which they came.

17° Modern science is also orbited by a Gnostic and cabalistic philosophy. Modern science has detached itself from all metaphysics, since, after Kant's pretended demonstration, it would be impossible and absurd. Consequently, we cannot arrive by rational means at the intelligibility of things, not even of the most sensible and accessible to the sense. We cannot speculatively distinguish a stone from a horse or from a man, since we cannot penetrate with our intelligence into the noun. Only what appears, the phenomenon, the surface of reality, is accessible to us. Philosophy of nature and metaphysics are impossible.

All that remains is a quantitative science of phenomena, i.e. the possibility of subjecting the sensible data to measurements, and thus measured, to coordinate it by means of approximate and changeable theories. In other words, only a science of utilisation of the things that appear as they appear is possible. Utilisation is made for practical purposes of human welfare. Hence all sciences ultimately end up in a technology and finally in a technocracy or science of the domination of man by man through technology.

The regulation of things does not come from the sciences themselves, since they tell us nothing about the reality and laws of things in themselves, but from the regulation that man wants to assign to them.

He invents philosophical and religious systems - gnostic systems - with which he interprets the science of things. All these systems reject the way to arrive rationally at God and, consequently, to give the necessary negative basis for all religion. For if we do not know God by reason we cannot worship Him in a religion founded on reason. Hence, by denying the rational way to God, atheism is imposed, and science and philosophy must be atheistic. If God does not exist, there is no other way to explain the existence of the world and of man than man himself. The universe would have been made by small increments which, starting from the indeterminate, or from Brahman, or from Ain-Sof or from Nothingness, in millions and millions of years would have arrived at more and more perfected beings until giving us homo sapiens, first the Neolithic one and then the Collective Superman that is being manufactured.

The Universe is a God who makes himself. Such is the teaching of the Kabbalah, which is the same as that of Spinoza, Hegel and all modern thinkers, and which is also the modern mass culture that has come to dominate.

The universe is a God who is made in man, with man and for man. Therefore, man is the only great reality of the universe. The construction of man for himself, on the basis of science and technology, is at its peak, and today, with the sciences of conditioning, psychology and sociology, the Great Man-Machine, into which modern society will be transformed, is about to be created. A man who will be scientifically dosed in the consumption of food, housing, clothing, transport, pleasures, use of sexuality, multiplication of the species in order to determine the quality and quantity of men on the planet on the basis of semen banks.

The sciences, therefore, are not to be directed towards the knowledge of the Creator, but, with the great machine-society produced by technology, towards the exaltation and glorification of man.

18° The new theologians are not to suppress theology as having no object of its own, since God does not exist, but they will make it serve secularisation. Someone might think that in the new structure of science theology should be suppressed, since theology, as a specific science of the supernatural, will have nothing to do in a secularised world in which the supernatural is suppressed. A profound error! The theologians of secularisation reject such an error, and speak of theology determining how the secular city is to be realised according to biblical prescriptions. That is why the works of Robinson and Harvey Cox are full of biblical quotations, and the famous Pleroma of Teilhard de Chardin is the pleroma of the mystical and cosmic Body of Christ that St. Paul and St. John would propose to us.

19° The Kabbalah and the modern Gnostic systems propose to us today the Happy City. The Christian city was built in Christian Europe on the institutions of natural law - family, property and civil authority - crowned by the divine grace of the Catholic Church. The Kabbalah and modern gnosis dealt fierce blows to that society and succeeded in breaking it. First came the naturalistic society of natural reason in the 16th, 17th and 18th centuries. Then came the animal city of capitalism, the bourgeois city of the 19th century, in which man sought the satisfaction of his material and sensible needs. Then came the communist city, conceived by Marx and implemented by Lenin, which required the use of the means of terror to break down the opposing bourgeois resistance. This is the city that is being built in the first half of the 20th century. But today, the Happy City of the 21st century, announced by Aldous Huxley, is already being projected[939]. A city for man, organised by modern science and technology, a machine society in which man will live in pleasant slavery, where everything will be scientifically dosed and planned.

20° The happy city will be the city of perfect nihilism, where all transcendence over man will have been suppressed. If man comes from nothingness and ends up in nothingness, the city that will make him happy and save him will also be the city of nothingness, of nihilism. The Kabbalah and the Gnostic systems build the Great City of perfect nihilism.

21° The Kabbalah and the Gnostic systems build the City of the Superman of modern thinkers. The Qabalah and the Gnostic systems aim at the erection of Man as the unification of God and the world. They are all to end in the Superman. The progressive Superman of Condorcet who is realised through the acquisitions and progress of human history. The positivist Superman of Comte who, passing through the theological and metaphysical states, reaches the summit of positivism, in which, through the positive sciences, he builds himself, in plenitude. Marx's materialistic superman, who, passing through the stages of slavery, servility and the proletariat, reaches the fullness of communism. Nietzsche's Dionysian superman, who, overcoming all the Christian virtues of ressentiment, discovers the fullness of his own species. Heidegger's authentic man, who discovers and nurtures the being that transcends all entities. Hegel's man of the absolute spirit, who with the dialectic of the spirit goes through all the stages of consciousness in order to identify himself with the divine trinity. Teilhard's man of the

---

[939] *A Brave New World*, 1932.

pleroma of Christ, who, by universal evolution and starting from the creatable nothingness, arrives at the fully christified planetary man. Freud's nirvanic man, who, made for sex and death, ends in death. Jung's archetypal man, who identifies himself with the divinity of his own self in the collective archetypes. Sartre's absurd and perverse man, Saint-Génet, who gives satisfaction to his basest instincts in order to achieve his full recovery.

The progressivism of theologians, a first stage of Christian Gnosticism

We said above that the progressivism of theologians represents a first stage of Gnosticism. In other words, theologians weaken the firm truths of the faith and thus destroy the coherence of Christian dogmas, which, not being articulated in a synthesis and architecture that is also Catholic, remain in a condition to be articulated and unified in another synthesis that would empty them of the content that Catholic theology has hitherto assigned to them. If, for example, the notion of original sin, which was sanctioned by the Council of Trent, is destroyed, or at least weakened, all the dogmas of Christology, justification and the sacraments are equally weakened or destroyed. This was clearly seen by the great Pope St. Pius X, who, in Ad diem illud, February 2, 1904, taught: "Where do the enemies of religion start from in order to sow so many and such grave errors, with which the faith of so great a number is shaken? They begin by denying the primitive fall of man and his descendants.... The edifice of faith is utterly destroyed...".

The point could not be clearer. If Adam did not sin with a sin that is passed on to mankind by way of generation, the present evils of mankind do not come from a first sin. Man today is not corrupt and malformed. There is no fall. Both Adam and mankind, his descendants, come thus, as they come today, from the hand of God.

Therefore they do not need to be redeemed and saved. Christ is a matter of luxury for a humanity that does not need Him to fulfil its end and vocation.

Christ may bring man a supererogatory good, but not a necessary and inescapable one.

Moreover, it would be false to say of St. Paul that "as by one man sin entered into the world, and death by sin... For if by one man's trespass many die, much more by the grace of one man, Jesus Christ... shall they reign in life"[940]. As the necessity of Jesus Christ falls, the person of Christ, God and man, ceases to have reason. Justification and Baptism and the Eucharist cease to have reason.

With Christ falls also the divine motherhood of the Virgin Mary with all the other sublime privileges with which she is endowed.

Since there is no fall in original sin, neither is there any loss of the supernatural gifts of grace, nor of the preternatural gifts of integrity and immortality. The ancient heresy of Pelagius, against which St. Augustine so intrepidly fought, is once again prevailing in the Christian world and is destroying the whole splendid edifice of the Christian faith.

Theology, losing with such a transcendental truth the cohesion and coherence of all its other truths, is automatically disorganised and calls for another principle of cohesion.

Add to this the lack of an infallible magisterium to assure the value of Revelation and the ongoing process of secularisation by which the secular and profane world tends to absorb the sacred, the supernatural and the transcendent into the immanence of the world, and it will be easy to understand how the single dimension of the mundane will end up imposing the full virtualities of a broad and total Gnosticism. For if Christ is questioned, how is the supernatural order of grace, and with it the Church, secured? And if the Church loses its raison d'être, how is it prevented that the powers of the world do not totally dominate man and impose their law on him? And if man is absorbed by the immanence of the world, how can he be saved by an extramundane principle?

But it is possible to show in more detail how within the Church itself key truths of Catholic doctrine are being weakened, leading logically towards total Gnosticism.

First and foremost, the concept of God, which is basic to Catholic doctrine. This concept is fading away due to the convergent action of various factors. First and foremost, because of the weakening of the rational ways to reach Him. By questioning the way of access to God, one questions His existence and, a fortiori, His nature. This leads to a vague and indeterminate notion of "the divine", which provides the basis for the indeterminate god of the Kabbalah and the Gnostic systems. The weakening of reason and the critical rationalism of the

---

[940] 940 Rom. 5, 12-21.

Bible which has entered the Catholic camp greatly help to create this confusion in the very notion of God.

Secondly, there is a real appreciation of atheism among Catholic theologians. This assessment is determined by the overestimation of modern culture and modern thought. It is evident that atheism grows with modern culture, as we have repeatedly argued in this book. This should have led theologians to a blanket censure of modern culture as intrinsically perverse and to a more thorough examination of this culture as a cause of atheism. But far from this, theologians, in an idolatrous admiration of modern culture, are led, by an intrinsic logic, to value the atheism that is connected with this culture[941]. Hence the tendency of the theologians noted above to justify the secularisation and atheisation of the old Christian society and to seek the survival of Christianity in the secularised society.

Thirdly, the tendency of modern theologians to reject the transcendence of God and to immanentise him in man's consciousness leads to a Gnostic notion of God. The author most characteristically of this tendency is, as is well known, Paul Tillich, but it has gained wide currency through the writings of John Robinson in *Honest do God* and through all the abundant literature on the death of God.

Fourthly, the transformation of theology into anthropology also leads to an imposition of Gnosticism. It is true that this tendency is far from reaching the excess with which it was expressed in Ludwig Feuerbach's The Essence of Christianity[942]. But the fact of speaking of "overcoming the God or man dilemma and the opposition between "vertical" and "horizontal", between "from without" and "from within", is significant enough[943]. As if emphasising the part of God were to the detriment of that of man and the affirmation of verticality were at the expense of horizontal dialogue, and the word that comes "from outside" subtracts something from the welcome that must come "from within"". We have already seen something of this in the polemic between Cardonnel and Congar on the subject of "horizontalism". In the Lord's Prayer, Jesus Christ had no qualms about clearly affirming verticality, Our Father, who art in heaven, and that the kingdom does not come from within

---

[941] This attitude is typified by Jules Girardi in *L'Athéisme dans la vie et la culture contemporaines*, Desclée, Paris, 1967, pp. 20 and 24.
[942] François Maspero, Paris, 1968.
[943] L. Bakker, *The Place of Man in Divine Revelation*, Concilium, no. 21.

man but from without, thy kingdom come; and that the essential and first thing is that the will of the Father be done, thy will be done on earth as it is in heaven[944].

By downgrading in one way or another the ineffable transcendence of the Father, there is also a tendency to forget the divine character of the person of the Son made man and to emphasise almost exclusively his human character. We have seen this at length in the previous chapter. The same method used in Christology, which is purely functional, tends to make us forget the divine pre-existence of the second hypostasis, even though it is clearly affirmed in the prologue of the Gospel of John. This tendency is all the more dangerous because it is accompanied by a manifest undermining of the adoration of the person of the Word made flesh in the Holy Eucharist, since this mystery is obscured in a thousand different ways: either by denying transubstantiation, that is to say the radical character which alone gives full account of the real presence of the person of Christ under the species of bread and wine; or by affirming transfiguration or transignification, as if it were a purely functional or dynamic presence as opposed to an ontological one; or by failing to pay to the Eucharist, the real presence, the central and permanent homage of the whole liturgical worship which moves from there towards the community of the faithful.

By lowering the theandric mystery of the person of Christ and his Eucharistic actualisation in the Church, the privileges of the Virgin Mother are also undermined, and her role in the Work of Redemption is reduced to a vulgar and inconsequential level.

Despite the fact that Vatican II strongly affirmed the institutionality of the Church, which revolved around the jurisdictional primacy of the Sovereign Pontiff, this authority is questioned in progressive circles, especially with regard to the ordinary magisterium and the necessity of universal consent for its validity, as if authority did not come from above, from Jesus Christ, but from below, from the society of mankind. This point is especially studied in the statements of the Swiss theologian Hans Küng, who is representative in the present matter.

These errors of theologians do not remain at the high level of theology. They reach down to the Christian people, who are becoming impregnated with a new religious mentality. In France, a compulsory

---

[944] Mt., 6, 9.

catechism for children from nine to eleven years old has been imposed by the will of the Episcopate, in which it is not said that Jesus is true God and true man. It does not say that the Blessed Virgin is the Mother of God. There is no mention of original sin. Nor is there any mention of the Sacraments of Confirmation, Extreme Unction, Holy Orders and Marriage. Numerous texts concerning sacrifice and priesthood are omitted. There is no mention of the commandments of God.

The Gnosticism of the Dutch Catechism

But much more serious is the case of the Dutch Catechism[945]. This catechism claims to be a theology for the laity. Starting from the Mystery of human existence, it explains the religious history of mankind as a journey of peoples towards Christ, especially in the journey of Israel. Humanity comes to Christ, the Son of Man. And the way of Christ in the Church founded by Him remains open in doctrine, liturgy and sacraments. It is the Way to the end that leads us finally to God.

But this catechism is already typically Gnostic. In fact, the whole Christian fact unfolds against a cabalistic background. It is well known that Catholic theology, although it is a supernatural fact which we know from Revelation, has as its background what St. Thomas calls preambula fidei, that is, truths of pure reason which are presupposed and are the negative foundations on which faith rests. Indeed, the word of God revealing his plans for man has no value if we do not know that God exists and that God has spoken to man. This is why, prior to supernatural theology, it is indispensable to found natural theology. And in order to found natural theology, by which reason reaches God, it is necessary to have metaphysics, which teaches us this rational way to God. Not a word about this in the Dutch Catechism. On the other hand, it presupposes as accepted truths those of evolutionism, and of an evolutionism not only anthropological evolutionism giving as a proven fact the ancestry of homo sapiens, through Neanderthal man and Australopithecus, but of an evolutionism extended to the whole world[946]. We read there:

---

[945] *A new Catechism, Catholic Faith for Adults*, Born and Oates (Herder and Herder), New York, 1967.
[946] Ibid., p. 10.

"Science tells us that the history of man has been preceded by a much longer ancestry, the coming of life. Its origin takes us back to ages of incalculable antiquity, when, in a cooled globe of stone, air and water, there appeared the carbon which forms the cells of living matter. And however old this matter may be, it is young compared with inanimate matter, whose origins are lost in the expanding galaxies...". And the catechism asks: "Where does matter come from, doesn't it come from anywhere?

"What does it mean that all this exists and grows? In the growth of life chance and selection play a great part. But who explains this? Is it an accident that things strive to progress through new and admirable phases - existence, life, feeling, thought? What is this progress, and can we see any significance in it?

"Are we to believe that human history, past, present and future, the whole evolution of the universe, with its sorrows and anxieties, with its love, its joys, and its final end, is it a meaningless joke? Is it an aimless trajectory, coming from who knows where, going to who knows where, like a universe that contracts and expands indefinitely? There is no one in the world who can answer us"[947].

"The mystery of existence is definitively resolved in "The Word of God". The word that has come into the world since in Jesus of Nazareth the Infinite has revealed Himself...".

"Jesus is the most wonderful answer that man could ever dream of. The Son of God has plunged into our misery.... Through the cross God has opened his heart to reveal the deepest mystery - God made one with the victim"[948].

But in the exposition of the Dutch Catechism, the great questions of man are neither explained nor solved: where does the universe and man come from? Why does God exist? God appears at the end, as if crowning the process of the evolution of the universe. How do we know that Jesus Christ is God? But evolution seems to solve the enigma of the origin, the plan and the destiny of the universe. So, by obscuring the idea of God, who appears as a Deux ex machina to satisfy man's infinite aspirations, and by giving evolution as the explanatory cause of the origin and order of the universe, we fall into the Cabala, which explains the world starting from an indeterminate God who explains and reveals

---

[947] Ibid., p. 12.
[948] Ibid., p. 20.

himself in the very unfolding of creation. The universe does not appear as coming out of the mind and will of God, as an effect coming out of the intelligent cause which first devised it and then willed it into existence, but the universe comes into being by evolution in a continuous progress.

The resemblance of the worldview of the Dutch Catechism to that of the Kabbalah and the Gnostic systems becomes even greater if we ask ourselves about the origin of evil. At no point does sin appear as a deliberate act of the rational creature. The "sin of the world"[949] appears as an anonymous sin that is diluted in the totality of the sins and imperfections of the universe. A sin that, in a certain sense, was inevitable, committed with a certain freedom[950]. We read there: "Every sin committed is not inevitable, but the evil that takes place is perhaps inevitable in practice"[951]. Moreover, sin is not a fully responsible act but "is an imperfection that is not inculpable". For "in a world of upward evolution it is nothing other than the refusal to grow in the direction that conscience reveals"[952].

The transgression of the law, and of the law engraved in the human heart by the author of the universe, does not appear. How can this transgression appear if the Lord and Creator of the Universe Himself does not appear?

But in reality, the Dutch Catechism alters the very idea of God by bringing pain and tragedy into it. Giovanni Baget Bozzo has warned of this in a critical note in Renovatio[953]. There he observes that "the structure of human existence is seen as problematic and that its solution is God as crucified. Through the cross, God has opened his heart to reveal his deepest mystery. God appears as one with the victim". "The ancestry, says Baget Bozzo, of these propositions is to be sought in contemporary Protestant theology. But to attribute to God what in itself belongs to the humanity of Christ and to understand as an ordinary logic that of the communicatio idiomatum leads to disturbing prospective of a Gnostic type", as if the crucifixion were the deepest mystery of God as such.

---

[949] Ibid., p. 259.
[950] Ibid., p. 264.
[951] Ibid., p. 264.
[952] Ibid., p. 264.
[953] Renovatio, February-March 1968, p. 123.

But there is more. Gnosis emerges in the Dutch Catechism as soon as evil appears as an autonomous power in the face of God. It says, in effect:

> "When we affirm of each thing in itself or of each event taken in isolation that in each case it comes entirely from God, we affirm more than what we know as the matter of faith..."[954].

It goes on to say:

> "From God's revelation we know as a matter of faith that anything comes from Him. But this does not mean that we are justified in ascribing every particular event entirely to Him. Men and things also possess a certain real efficacy of their own, they go their own way in a certain sense. And this can be unfavourable, a path in itself contrary to the whole... Hence we can no longer affirm that a bad situation, a catastrophe or a crime comes from God. Pain and evil as such are contrary to the whole, contrary to God's plan. They are in contact with that which is not God"[955].

By not clarifying that the cause of evil is a purely deficient cause, since evil as such does not imply any reality [956], the Dutch Catechism oscillates between the autonomy of evil, which would lead to a metaphysical dualism, or to the assertion that not everything is governed by divine Providence[957].

In the whole delicate problem of evil and sin, the Dutch Catechism is seriously deficient in confusing the evil of guilt and the evil of sorrow and in not explicitly recognising that evil comes from a deliberate and full act of the rational creature. This recognition, in turn, must have been lacking when evolutionism served as the background for the whole development of the universe. Indeed, if the rational creature, in this case man, is the product of the blind forces of the universe following an upward process, at what point have they sinned? Can they sin at any point, or do they rather allow themselves to be swept along by their uncontainable impulses? In the case of the conception of St. Augustine and St. Thomas, the rational creature comes with the fullness of his faculties out of the hand of God and sins with lucidity and because he

---

[954] A New Catechism, p. 493.
[955] Ibid., p. 499.
[956] St. Thomas, Summa, I, 48 and 49.
[957] Summa, I, 103.

wills. Sin is not mixed up in the world as an imperfect act of development, as the Dutch Catechism would have it, which assigns "two roots of misery... the evolution of the world and sin".[958] Sin enters as a disordered act of the creature that knowingly and willingly violates the divine order of creation. This violation, lucid and responsible, cannot appear in a conception of the world in which evolution governs the whole process of the universe.

For this reason, the Dutch Catechism defends a timid evolutionism which fails to develop the virtualities which fully express it. The Dutch Catechism demands a fully evolutionary conception of the universe, in the manner of Teilhard de Chardin. An evolutionary conception which has a right of citizenship in Catholic theology[959] and which, however, needs to be elucidated in more detail. For there can be an evolutionary conception of the universe that is compatible with Catholic truth as long as it obeys a divine plan totally regulated by the divine will. But an almost automatic evolutionism in which the progression of beings is verified by the very force of evolution, as if evolution were a creative evolution, is in no way compatible either with the wisdom and creative freedom of God or with the free act of the rational creature.

Karl Rahner's Gnosticism

In order to refer to Karl Rahner's Gnosticism, we will refer to a remarkable work written by the Dominican Guérard des Lauriers and published in "La Pensée Catholique"[960].

The article we are commenting on is of exemplary sobriety. Its "object" is Rahner's "Theological Writings", originally published in German and translated into French and Spanish[961]. Each statement of G. d. L. responds to a quotation from R. His intention is to discover the principles of the theological inspiration of P. R. and to show how his whole doctrine, that is to say, his interpretation of Christian doctrine,

---

[958] A new catechism, p. 492.
[959] Rahner, Christology within an evolutionary worldview, in *Theological Writings*, V, p. 181.
[960] Paris No. 117, 1968.
[961] Karl Rahner, *Schriten zur Theologie*; Einsiedeln; Benziger, Verlag, t. I-VI, 1954-1965. Translated into Spanish by Taurus Ediciones; the quotations, where volume and page are indicated, are from the German edition, those in the first term, and those in the second term, from the Spanish edition.

proceeds systematically from these principles. He seems to have found the key, the internal vertebration of Rahner's thought, of what the German Jesuit calls his "transcendental hermeneutics" (his theological method, one might say).

For G. d. L. this principle of inspiration is a thesis of the order of the theory of knowledge, a thesis which determines R.'s anthropology and through it, with rigorous logic, the theology laid down in his writings. He finds such a principle in the conclusion of "The Spirit in the World"[962] :

"For St. Thomas, abstractio and conversio are the same thing: Man". R. identifies (and incorrectly attributes this identification to the Angelic Doctor) the process of formation or utterance of the mental verb (the term of the act of intellection), which puts the spirit in possession of reality, of the essence, of the "logos" or intimate ordering of being, with the "return to the phantasm" or sensible image, that is, with the process by which one acquires consciousness of the configuration of the intellectual act insofar as such an act proceeds from a sensible and singular term. In other words, he identifies objectivity, the structure of being that can be conceived and expressed in a definition, with subjectivity, the contemplation of the internal organisation of the cognitive act, of its origin and of the bond that roots it in the sensible and singular.

"Reality is only grasped as immanent to Man: that is the whole of rahnerism", says G. d. L. Man thus becomes the measure of all things, of every relationship between creation and God. L. Man thus becomes the measure of all things, of every relationship between creation and God. The rahnerian man is open to the infinite, but by virtue of a "self-transcendence" of an entitative order, of an ontological nature, which is immanent and connatural to him[963].

According to G. d. L., R.'s theology is an interpretation of the whole of Christian doctrine in terms of such a conception of man and his immanent power of self-transcendence. This is the norm, the "transcendental hermeneutic", even if R. invokes Scripture, the ecclesiastical Magisterium and traditional doctrine.

---

[962] Geist in Welt, Kösel Verlag Munchen, 1957 (Zweite Auflage), p. 407. In English, Spirit in the World, Herder, 1963, p. 388.
[963] V, 192; V, 190.

A first proof of the systematic application of this principle of rahnerian humanism and of its value as a rule of interpretation can be found in G. d. L.'s work on the doctrine of the beatific vision which Christ had during his earthly life. L. on the doctrine of the beatific vision which Christ had during his earthly life. On the one hand, R. admits that it is not permissible for the exegete to question this teaching imposed by the Magisterium, but this does not mean, in his opinion, that the exegete "working according to the method of fundamental theology must or can take this theological doctrine into account"[964]. He then proposes his version:

> "A theologically accurate interpretation of this immediate vision of God is to conceive of it as a background, a-thematic and radical, a-determined and primitive behaviour of the created spiritual nature of Jesus"[965].

According to R., the immediate vision of God is identified, in Christ, with "the awareness he has of his immediate contact with God"[966]; an "awareness that concerns the subjective pole of Jesus' consciousness"[967].

This Christological thesis - explains G. d. L. - comes from the position taken on the theory of knowledge and at the same time allows us to understand another rahnerian assertion: man, in the blessed eternity, "can only contemplate the Father through the Humanity of Jesus" and this is an immediate contemplation, because "the immediacy of the divinity is in no way opposed to the mediation of Christ as man"[968]. Fr. R. criticises man's apprehension of God as an object, and dislikes the terms of the Constitution of Benedict XII (Denz. 530), where "it deals only with the divine essence, to which is attributed what is most intimately personal: the manifestation of itself"[969].

Then G. d. L. examines the formulations that R. proposes of the dogmas of the Incarnation, the Redemption, the Trinity and the Eucharist. We will follow his reasoning and his presentation of the texts.

---

[964] V, 244; V, 243.
[965] V, 245; V, 243.
[966] V, 245; V, 243.
[967] V, 237; v, 235.
[968] III, 57, III, 57.
[969] IV, 107, note 9; IX, 109.

The Incarnation

First of all, G. d. L. that R. conceives the relations of the Person of the Word in the divine Nature and with the human nature as relations of the same order. Both relations would play the same role with respect to the divine Person. Faith," says R., "professes a substantial, durable, indissoluble, hypostatic unity, and the disembodiment of two natures in virtue of the same Person"[970].

The Word, as He is Himself according to the divine nature (and remaining in Himself immutable), becomes truly Himself by virtue of the human nature, inasmuch as He is constituted (by the Incarnation) distinct from Himself and united to Himself (t. I, p. 202).

Human nature," concludes G. d. L. - conditions the Word in his Being, just as the divine Nature is identical with his Being. And he brings together a series of rahnerian texts to support this conclusion. Let us see.

> "What does it (the communication of languages) mean if the true human reality attributed to the Word, insofar as He is a Person, does not change Him; as if that humanity does not make Him that which without it He would not be?"[971].

There is a change in the Word. God, even though He is immutable, can be subject to becoming ("God can become something, He who is immutable in Himself can be changed into another"[972]). The Word is changed in human nature. "It is necessary to say (since God is in Himself immutable) that the God who is immutable in Himself can change, become another (properly speaking: He can become man); and "changing Himself into another" is not in contradiction with the divine immutability nor is it, on the other hand, reducible to a "change of the other"[973].

In other words, the human nature of Christ, like the divine nature, is the very reality of the Word. The humanity of Christ", R. argues, "in its concrete (by no means abstract) reality can only have theological significance if it is, as such and not only in so far as it is formally united

---

[970] I, 195; I, 195.
[971] I, 200; I 200.
[972] IV, 147; IV, 149.
[973] IV, 147, note 3; IV, 149.

to the Word a posteriori, the manifestation of God in the world. Because it is the reality of the Word, it forms a unity with the Word"[974].

Thus, by presenting the human nature in parity with the divine nature in its reference to the Word, R. conceives of Christ's humanity in a contradictory way. On the one hand, this human nature is the very reality of the Word. On the other hand, this humanity of God, considered in itself, "cannot and does not receive the grace to approach and encounter God in a way essentially other or essentially superior to that which, by grace, is effectively reserved for each man"[975]. Moreover, sketching a kind of inverted kenosis, R. explains: "God has assumed a human nature because it is in itself open and assumable; because only it (unlike non-transcendent beings, the object of definition) can exist in a total detachment from itself, which allows it to realise the completion of its essential tendency, which is incomprehensible"[976].

Finally, what is the meaning of the Incarnation in the rahnerian interpretation? "That God should arouse man's self-transcendence and induce him to penetrate into his own bosom, that God on the other hand should work in this way by virtue of his absolute self-communication, that the two things should concur to realise the promise made to all men and completed in one: this is the hypostatic union"[977].

G. d. L. understands that according to R., Christ is simply the Man who in an individual reaches the perfection of which he carries within himself a connatural requirement: "Christ is the unique and supreme case of the fulfilment of human reality in its essence; this fulfilment consists in the fact that man exists by renouncing himself"[978]. It is a question - always following the reading of G. d. L. - of an ascent of man (and not a descent of God) inserted in a generalised evolutionism[979].

The Redemption

According to his interpretation of the mystery of the Incarnation, the Redemption (the gift of grace) is considered by Fr. R. as a result, for

---

[974] I, 212; I, 212.
[975] IV, 145; IV, 147.
[976] IV, 143; IV, 146.
[977] V, 210; V, 207.
[978] IV, 142; IV, 145.
[979] V, 191-193; V, 188-191.

each man, of a power of humanity to God's self-communication. It is worked by God, but results from a power immanent in man, as G. d. L. understands. L. Here is the rahnerian text:

> "If it is admitted that this original communication of grace has been made to mankind before sin, not only as a requirement but as a potentiality already firmly established, since at its very source it was ordered to the Incarnation and therefore to the irrevocable self-communication of God to all mankind (and not on the grounds that it had already begun to act in Adam)... then one has the exact idea of Christian redemption..."[980].

G. d. L. points out two observations of R. on the historical manifestation of such a divine self-communication which confirm this interpretation of the Redemption. First: "The concept of Saviour does not imply that this self-communication (made) to the world by God according to His spiritual Subjectivity began at the same time as the Saviour Himself. There is no need for it to do so. And it can instead be conceived of as having already begun before the Saviour, as co-existing with the whole spiritual history of mankind and the world... "(vol. V, p. 202). Second: History finds its completion in Christ: "... this Redemption in Christ (one could also say: brought to Christ) was always operative from the origin of humanity"[981].

Recalling the "original confusion of the rahnerian epistemology", G. d. L. thus seals his survey of the subject: "The Saviour is not gratuitously the Envoy from on high; he is necessarily immanent in the development of Man; the object is identified with the Subject, just as according to R. the verb is absorbed in the phantasm and identified with it".

The Trinity

According to R., the thesis that sheds light on the mystery of the Trinity "as a mystery of salvation (in its reality and not only as a doctrine), could be formulated as follows: the Trinity of the economy of salvation is the immanent Trinity, and inversely"[982].

---

[980] V, 216; V, 213.
[981] V, 202; V, 199.
[982] IV, 115; IV, 117.

G. d. L. observes that this identification of the Trinity in itself with the Trinity as manifested in the history of salvation is an error stemming from R.'s subjectivism.

Point out three landmarks:

- Bearing in mind that something (the Incarnation) has taken place in the world "which belongs to the Word alone, which is the history of one of the divine Persons and not of the others"[983], R. concludes that all that concerns the "economy" (God's salvific design realised in history) "can be said of the Triune God as a whole and of each person in particular"[984].

G. d. L. notices a contradiction in the rahnerian deduction, for if the Word is a distinct Person (which is manifested in the "economy"), then the Father and the Holy Spirit are also distinct Persons. And since the Word only became incarnate, it is evident that the manifestation of the Trinity in salvation history is not always simply the immanent Trinity.

- R. argues that "one cannot adequately distinguish between the doctrine of the Trinity and the doctrine of economy"[985]. But in reality," objects G. d. L. -, there are affirmations which concern the Trinity in itself, distinctly, even if in fact these affirmations are linked more or less directly to the history of salvation. This is what tradition has understood from the word of the Lord in John 8, 38: "I say what I have seen with my Father".

- R. calls into question a fundamental metaphysical truth: God cannot have a real relation or reference to a reality other than Himself[986]. G. d. L. deduces that from the rahnerian thesis necessarily follows the negation of this truth itself. Indeed, if one identifies the immanent Trinity with the Trinity of the "economy", and therefore the incarnate Word according to His humanity with the intimate Logos of the Trinity, then the relations which the incarnate Word has according to His humanity with something other than Himself, relations which belong to the order of the created, become relations of God to the created.

---

[983] IV, 116; IV, 118.
[984] Ibid.
[985] Ibid.
[986] IV, 116, note 15; IV, 118.

If his thesis is not accepted," R. finally argues, "the mystery of God can only be grasped "in a verbal and notional way, by pure verbal revelation, as opposed to a revelation by God's salvific action in us". G. d. L. replies: Again R. has supplanted the verb by the phantasm imposed as self-sufficient; for the truth is that on this earth "the immanent Trinity which the believer embraces in his verb is absolutely above any manifestation however intimate it may be of the Trinity perceived by the believer in his own interiority".

The Eucharist

On the Presence of Christ in the Sacrament of the Lord's Supper[987] R. distinguishes two kinds of interpretation. One, which he calls logical and which consists in analysing the words "This is my Body" in themselves, is the explanation expressed in the dogmatic formulae. The other, the ontic explanation, which corresponds to his "transcendental hermeneutics", excludes such an analysis and consists in relating the fact constituted by the utterance of these words to other facts.

His interpretation, which he himself claims to express in a polemical tone, can be found in the following text by G. d. L. in the following text[988] : "One wants to confine God's action to the purely divine sphere; then this action is no longer present and transforming in the things of the world (peace, morals, the grave, etc.). In this way, such action remains not only beyond the experience of the unbeliever (which is always true), but also beyond the very realities of the earth; God remains in heaven; where the bread is, nothing happens. In these conditions, it seems to me more coherent to say: Christ (of the Eucharist) is only in faith, only by virtue of faith is he present". On the other hand, continues R., Catholic theologians could learn something from Evangelical Christians and their theory of the presence "in usu", that is, during the celebration of the Sacrament[989].

As for the Real Presence after communion, R. holds that "the Real Presence of Christ subsists only as long as the sensible unity of the bread constitutes a human datum"[990].

---

[987] IV, 357-385; IV, 367.
[988] IV, 379; IV, 390.
[989] IV, 383; IV, 394.
[990] IV, 390; IV, 400.

In other words, it ceases immediately after swallowing, since the bread cannot then be perceived as such by the external senses[991]. G. d. L. objects as a subjectivist deformation the support that R. seeks in the teaching of St. Thomas (the Presence ceases if a particle is too small) and replies that the criterion of real Presence is objective, like the Presence itself (which only ceases if the particle corresponds to a disintegration of the molecule).

So much for this astonishing review. The conclusion has been expressed by G. d. L. throughout his article, and it is already stated in the detection of the "inspiration" of the R. theologian. According to the wise Dominican, this inspiration is the ancient and ever-renewed inspiration of gnosis: Man, who is evolving towards the divine force that naturally inhabits him, is the measure of all things, even the measure of the mystery of God. For this reason, in all Rahner's work, it is necessary to highlight the text in which he affirms the generalised evolutionism, that is, that by a process of internal self-dynamics matter becomes life, life becomes consciousness, consciousness becomes spirit and spirit, open to the infinite, becomes God. This text reads as follows:

> "Now, this discontinuity, this essential diversity between matter, life, consciousness, spirit, in no way excludes evolution, if it is true that there is becoming, if becoming is or can be in its own sense an active self-transcendence, if self-transcendence is or can be equally and at least an entitative self-transcendence"[992].

Theilhardism, a stage full of Gnosticism

The Gnosticism of Teilhard de Chardin has already been denounced by authoritative voices. The learned theologian and historian Mgr André Combes formulated his denunciation in a magnificent article, A propos de theodicée teilhardienne, which appeared in December 1965 in "Les Etudes Philosophiques" and was reproduced in "La Pensée Catholique"[993]. There, after demonstrating Mgr.

Combes, how the cosmic Christ, which is the centrepiece of the whole Teilhardian system, must be understood in the full force of his word as a true panchristism, as an organic and total conjugation of the

---

[991] IV, 390; IV, 400.
[992] V, 193; V, 190.
[993] NO. 108.

evolutionary universe in a single being and substance with Christ, so that Christ would have assumed a third nature, neither human nor divine, but cosmic, goes on to point out influences that would have produced in Teilhard this Gnosticism.

Mgr Combes finds the influence of Edouard Schuré, with his famous book The Great Initiates, which Teilhard had read in November 1918 and which would have "immersed him in enthusiasm"[994]. S churé, says Teilhard, gave him food for thought. Undoubtedly, he found it "fanciful", "artificial", "insufficient", but, because of its defects, this master encouraged him to defend, to free "the most beautiful initiations" from this "childish air", from this "note of illuminism", in order to cultivate "true esotericism, true gnosis"[995].

Moreover, it should be remembered that the expression Cosmic Christ, associated with speculations on "planetary evolution and the origin of man", is read under the pen of Edouard Schuré himself, and this since 1912. "The question is to know, writes Mgr André Combes, whether Teilhard was not satisfied with "The Great Initiates", but has also read "Divine Evolution".

No text read by me proves this. The analogy, on the other hand, may be superficial and very limited. Nevertheless, one cannot help wondering whether Schuré might not have merely stimulated Teilhard to develop a gnosis less childish or fanciful than his own, but which would have offered to his original speculation the very theme and expression of the Cosmic Christ.

André Combes concludes by noting that Teilhard de Chardin's aim was to elaborate, by virtue of the "cosmic sense" rather than of long observations or rational requirements, less a theology than a christified cosmogony which would provide him with a global "vision" of the universe. Basically, Teilhard is much more akin to the "wise men" who proceed by "superior clairvoyance" and for whom "contemporary science is on the edge of the Invisible and often swims in the occult without knowing it" than to his colleagues who are wisely devoted to scientific research and who consider that the technical disciplines are not meant to be arbitrarily transcended but scrupulously respected.

---

[994] Letter from Teilhard de Chardin to his niece, 8 November 1918, in Genese dúne pensée, p. 323.
[995] Ibid., p. 334.

Louis Salleron published in "Itinéraires"[996] an article with the title The Gnosticism of Teilhard de Chardin. There he notes that, according to the little book by H. Cornely and A. Léonard, The Eternal Gnosis, one finds in all the Gnostics what is typical of Teilhard, the will for an integral vision of the world. Teilhard wants to build a rigorous system in which all the sciences, grouped in the notion of Evolution, are totally combined with all the faith, grouped in his notion of Christ, from which the Cosmic Christ would emerge. And Salleron points out how Serge Hutin in his book Les Gnostiques states that "it is still curious to see how a thinker like Father Teilhard de Chardin, starting from biology and anthropology, has ended up by reaching grandiose Gnostic perspectives (in the broad and Catholic sense of the term)". Salleron then quotes long paragraphs from Edouard Schuré where he shows that "Schuré's cosmogony, foreign to the exact sciences, is different from Teilhard's; but the concern is the same and the profound orientation is the same".

A study on "Teilhard's Gnosticism" has been published in the review "Aujourd'hui Quebec" by J. M. Jourdain. It notes that in the Teilhardian system, "from the outset, there is no Creator, but chaos, the great whole, indeterminate matter, the infinite receptacle of the possible.

Interdiction to reason, to seek the reasons of Being, the cause of beings. And the great formless whole determines itself progressively, by itself, by internal drive, intrinsic virtue; formal beings proceed spontaneously, more and more perfected". "The more emanates from the "less", thanks to mutation. And the gradation of mutations constitutes evolution - evolution that is made to work as it can".

Jourdain adds:

> "This is the essential creed of the counter-religion. This is the common background of the Kabbalah, of esotericism, of René Guénon's "metaphysics", of gnosis, of Freemasonry, of theosophy, of pantheism. It is said: the world has unity, otherwise it would be unintelligible; this unity excludes all dichotomies - e.g. matter and spirit, matter and life, nature and grace - and does not admit any intrinsic intervention. Nothing but the new immanence, and progress by degrees. Thus the world rises irreversibly, becomes divinised - evolution becomes God".

---

[996] No. 109, January 1967.

"And morality follows cosmogenesis. He who loves himself with all his proud and joyous self, loves the world, and he who loves the world with his most ardent concupiscence enters into the evolutionary movement, and pushes there with his whole energy, strives, with as much fervour as the world is about to reach its fullness by effecting its definitive mutation".

Some very serious studies on the Gnosticism of Teilhard de Chardin were published in the Brazilian magazine "Catolicismo". One, by Alberto Luiz du Plessis with the title Influencias gnósticas no pensamiento do Padre Teilhard de Chardin[997], and the other, Da paleontologia à metafisica, historia de una extrapolaçao, by Giocondo Mario Vita[998].

Teilhard de Chardin's Gnosticism is evident for many reasons which we will be pointing out, and which are consistent with the twenty-one points on which we have characterised the Kabbalah and the Gnostic systems. We will dispense with many notes and references which the reader can consult in my book "Teilhard de Chardin or the Religion of Evolution"[999].

1. A scientific-religious vision of totality. First of all, Teilhard de Chardin, without recourse to a personal God who would have freely chosen and created the present world from among the many possible worlds, excogitates a total, scientific-religious vision of the totality of being. Science and religion, phenomenology and Christianity, evolution and Christ, come together in a closed system which, in a certain sense, forms itself automatically, passing from cosmogenesis to biogenesis, from biogenesis to noogenesis and finally to Christogenesis and to Theogenesis itself.

Everything is integrated in the Pleroma, in the cosmic Christ, all the currents of life, the profane and the religious, good and evil, everything marches towards the total convergence where it is unified.

2nd There is no God who creates the Universe out of nothing. Teilhard de Chardin is categorical. As early as 1917, in L'Union Creatrice, he rejects creation ex nihilo and the idea of a Creator by efficient cause[1000].

---

[997] In issue 156, December 1963.
[998] No. 183 and 184, May and April 1966.
[999] Ediciones Theoría, 1965.
[1000] *Écrits du temps de guerre* (1916-1919), Grasset, Paris, 1965, p. 184.

Thus, the creation of the Universe does not have an extrinsic cause, but is the result of an immanent, intrinsic process of internal evolution. God, or the Omega Point, acts from the beginning, but not as a cause that gives being, but as a principle of orientation and convergence. Just as Teilhar uses much force to reject creation ex nihilo by efficient cause, he uses much more to place a "unifying Centre of the monads (...) real and transcendent". "Extracosmic energy in its origin (though immanent in term) animating ad extra the material elements, and welding them together by the influx of a power foreign to them"[1001].

This is why Philippe de la Trinité, O.C.D., in setting out the postulates of the Teilhardian system, places the postulate of evolution first, but then, as a second postulate, the primacy of the Spirit, i.e. God. Teilhard is not an atheist or pantheist, or, explicitly, he does not present us, like Hegel or the Kabbalah, with a "God who makes himself", in becoming; although the "Teilhardian God" is enriched by creation and is in need of it.

3° In the Theilhardian system, evolution creates the universe. If the universe does not come from God, from nothing, by an efficient cause, it must be produced by evolution itself. This was pointed out by one of Teilhard's admirers, Madeleine Barthelemy-Madaule[1002] : "Evolution was first discovered by Teilhard in its full extent, and in the form of a creative emotion, where religion, metaphysics and science were in a state of ardent fusion.

But, once it has sprouted, intuition develops its fecundity on all planes. It seeks its maximum expansion and only ends when it has structured a synthetic vision". "... Evolution is, in the full sense of its content, the whole of the Theilhardian vision"[1003]. And further on:

> "A single underlying movement animates matter, life, thought. This movement takes the form of a convergence. From this theory of evolution seen as the action of the one in the heart of the multiple, and the transfiguration of matter into spirit, the whole Theilhardian cosmic and religious perspective becomes clear. Being at the heart of the synthesis"*[1004]*.

[1001] Ibid., p. 181.
[1002] Bergson et Teilhard de Chardin, Éditions du Seuil, Paris, 1963, p. 77.
[1003] Ibid., p. 155.
[1004] Ibid., p. 600.

4° In the Kabbalah and the known Gnostic systems, the starting point is an indeterminate divine absolute, which, at a certain point in time, would divide itself and begin the evolutionary process of the universe. In Teilhard's case, this is not really the case. "At the origin, he says, there were at the two poles of being, God and the Multitude. And God, however, was alone, since the sovereignly dissociated multitude did not exist. Of all eternity, God saw beneath his feet, the scattered shadow of his unity, and this shadow, being an absolute aptitude to give something, was not another God, because it itself was not, nor had ever been, nor could ever have been, since its essence was to be infinitely divided in itself, that is, to lean upon Nothingness. Infinitely vast and infinitely rarefied, the Manifold, made nothing in its essence, slept at the antipodes of being One and concentrated..."[1005].

With Teilhard, therefore, it does not happen as in Brahmanism, where Brahman, the neutral absolute, has a desire[1006] and the division of being takes place; or as in the Kabalah, where Ein-Sof, or its first determination, Kether, divides into Binah, the intelligence; but from the first moment God and his antipode and shadow, the pure manifold, the Multitude, the physical nothingness, which, under divine attraction, without efficient cause, begins to condense, concentrate, organise and unify itself, meet"[1007]. Herein lies the fundamental starting point of the whole Theilhardian system.

5th Claude Tresmontant denounces Teilhard's Gnosticism. Claude Tresmontant comments on these Teilhardian pages as follows: "The idea of a "struggle" between the One and the Multiple recalls these Babylonian cosmogonies in which we see the demiurge in struggle with Chaos...

"We are in the midst of metaphysical mythology; Teilhard is in good company, moreover, since he places himself alongside Anaxagoras and Aristotle.

"To avoid the Charybdis of a Universe created in a contingent and arbitrary way, Teilhard falls into the Scilla of a well-known mythology: God complements himself by creating the world, God undertakes a struggle with the Multiple (the ancient Chaos) to find himself at the end

---

[1005] *Écrits du temps de guerre* (1916-1919), Grasset, Paris, 1965, p. 114.
[1006] *La naissance du monde*, Aux Éditions du Seuil, Paris, 1959, p. 337.
[1007] *Écrits du temps de guerre*, p. 114.

of this work, richer and pacified: an old Gnostic idea found in Boehme, in Hegel, in Schelling..."[1008].

6° The concept of creative union, by which Teilhard's evolution produces the universe, eliminates creation ex nihilo and unites it with God. For Teilhard, the affirmation of a creatable nothingness is not a vain subtlety, an excess of refined dilettantism. At issue here is the very theory of creative Union which is by definition opposed to efficiency ex nihilo, since to "create" is to unite and not, formally, to produce[1009]. Teilhard wrote a letter on 10 February 1955[1010] in which he clarifies his thinking, making it clear that creation is not only to unite but to unite with the Creator, so that the universe is part of the divine being. He says there: "I truly think that, under the word "creation", two conceptions very different from each other are confused; one (the classical "creation of the cosmos") which sees the world as the work of a Worker, by analogy with "efficient causality"; and the other (not yet clearly formulated, "creation of cosmogenesis") looking at the Creator as constituting the universe by and in the very act of uniting it (by analogy with a "formal causality") because the Union creates - even in the eyes of physics, for which motion begets mass".

7° The universe, with its immense mineral, vegetable, animal, human and even christic riches, would emerge, by the law of recurrence, from a first initial matter. Teilhard insists in several passages of his works on the existence of a "stock of the universe", Weltstoff, which would contain all the higher forms, which would then appear as the various mineral, vegetable, animal, human and even christic species. The christic, noospheric, biospheric and cosmospheric worlds would be contained, by the law of recurrence,[1011], in the stock of the universe, and from there they would emerge, following the law of complexity-consciousness. And so Teilhard writes: "... the human being is born, not from an accident, but from the prolonged interplay of the forces of cosmogenesis, its roots must theoretically be able (and indeed can to an alert eye) to recognise and follow with loss of sight into the past, backwards: not only in the neuropsychic mutation from which, towards the end of the Tertiary, the first thinking animal on earth emerged, but

---

[1008] *Introduction à la pensée de Teilhard*..., pp 112-116.
[1009] Philippe de la Trinité, O. C. D., *Teilhard de Chardin, vision cosmique et christique*, La Table Ronde, Paris, 1968, p. 59.
[1010] Lettres.
[1011] See in my book, Importance in Theilhardian work of the law of recurrence, p. 124.

further still, down into the lowest primate stock; and lower still, into the very mechanisms by which, for billions of years, the fabric of the universe has been incessantly woven"[1012].

The Theilhardian Weltstoff would then contain in an initial primitive nucleus the whole universe, from which it would emerge by an evolutionary unfolding until it reached the highest degrees of socialisation and of the Cosmic Christ. The ascent from the initial Stofa to the Universe of the Universal Christ would take place according to a dialectic, very similar to the Hegelian one, in the three times of union of differences, qualitative leap and convergence.

8° From the stock of the universe would also come the spirit, and the human spirit. Teilhard is categorical in this respect. Spirit would not be, as Christian philosophy has so far taught, a reality totally independent of matter, but would be a special state of matter, in a degree of condensation also special, attained by a given degree of the law of complexity-consciousness. "Matter and Spirit, he writes, not two things but two states, two faces of the same cosmic stock, depending on whether one looks at them, or prolongs them in the sense that (as Bergson would have said) they become or, on the contrary, in the sense that they fall apart."[1013]. "Finally, it can be said that if the most refined psychism coincides in our universe with the most complicated material support, it is by construction. By virtue of the mechanism of Evolution, in the cycle of our creation, the one is born of the multiple, the simple is formed by uniting the complex, the spirit is made by means of matter"[1014]. And Teilhard assigns this explanation: "Between the perishable souls of the beasts and the immortal spirit of man there is possibly no hiatus, but passage from one degree to another through a critical point: the diffuse becomes punctiform, the section of the cone becomes the summit. Do we not experience this continuity under a sensible form when we think we recognise in ourselves that thought is transformed sensation?"[1015].

This consequence derives from the Gnostic character of Theilhardian thought which constructs the universe with a single homogeneous substance in which matter, life, consciousness and spirit; nature and

---

[1012] Teilhard de Chardin, *L'Apparition de l'homme*, p. 298.
[1013] Quoted by Philippe de la Trinité, op cit. p. 117.
[1014] *Écrits du temps de guerre*, p. 179.
[1015] Ibid., p. 179.

grace; good and evil all converge to a point of total unification, which is the Omega Point, or the Cosmic Christ.

9° The Theilhardian Gnostic system suppresses sin itself. It is characteristic of all gnosis, in one way or another, to derive sin and moral evil from the divinity itself or from the cosmic world. Teilhard will place the origin of guilt in the evolutionary process, as an inevitable by-product of the path of unification[1016]. Sin would not be caused by the free action of the intelligence that knowingly breaks the order established by its Creator.

10° Another note, typically Gnostic, is the fatalistic and necessary character in which the whole evolutionary process unfolds. "By no means through impotence, says Teilhard, but by virtue of the structure of nothingness, on which he leans, God, in order to create, can proceed in only one way: to order, to unify little by little, under his attractive influence, by groping the game of the great numbers, an immense multitude of elements, first infinitely numerous, extremely simple and scarcely conscious; then gradually rarer, more complex, and finally, endowed with reflection"[1017]. And following this paragraph he explains evil in the world as a by-product or a residue, necessarily inevitable, given the nature of creation. The path of convergence, starting from the manifold and passing through cosmogenesis, biogenesis, noogenesis and Christogenesis, follows an obligatory and necessary route until it reaches theogenesis. Creation is not the work of intelligence but of fatality.

11° The great Christian mysteries of the Incarnation, Redemption and Resurrection are also interpreted within this evolutionary Gnostic system. In my book Teilhard de Chardin or the Religion of Evolution I have abundantly demonstrated with quotations from the main Teilhardian works how the Christian mysteries would not be the loving response of the Creator to the insolence of the free creature, who had broken the order of creation, but would be determined, in a fatalistic and necessary way, by the exigency of convergent evolution, which would demand a universe with one head and not a two-headed one[1018]. And for the same reason, with the Cosmic Christ as its crowning glory.

[1016] See my book, *Teilhard de Chardin or the Religion of Evolution*.
[1017] *Comment je vois*, no. 30, quoted by Claude Tresmontant, p. 86.
[1018] *Super humanité*, quoted by Claude Tresmontant, ibid, p. 63.

Thus, the Creation, the Incarnation and the Parousia will be three moments of one and the same evolutionary progress.

Both the Kabbalah and the various Gnostic systems give us an explanation of the world and of man which does not derive from a plan which, chosen from among many other possible plans, God has freely willed to carry out. Things unfold by the intrinsic force of themselves, in a rigorous and fatalistic rhythm, which is enriched by the accumulative process itself, and which also enriches God. Moreover, both the Kabbalah and the Gnostic systems look not so much to the perfection of God, from which out of mercy and love the universe comes forth, to return to Him after a period of probation, but they look to the Perfection of God enriched and finished with the universe which is incorporated into Him and which becomes a thing in Him. In these gnosis, the creature perfects and liberates itself by its own effort and perfects and liberates its Creator. Such conditions are rigorously fulfilled in the convergent evolutionism of Teilhard de Chardin.

CONCLUSION

The conclusion of the present book is clear and firm. Throughout all of human history there are only two fundamental forms of thought and life: Catholic and Gnostic.

The Catholic tradition professes the certain knowledge in a most perfect Being, who freely and in time brought the world out of nothingness and to which the creature must return. Before there is a history of the world there is from eternity a metahistory, on which it depends as the effect depends on its cause. Between metahistory and history, between God and the creature, there is an unfathomable gulf in the very structure of being, inasmuch as God is by essence, whereas the creature is by participation. God is fully self-sufficient, while the creature requires absolute dependence on its Creator. The creature must return to God, from whence it came, but by a grace, by a gift freely given to it, which must make it divine. The guilt of the creature brought about a catastrophe in creation, for the reparation of which the Son of God came, and for this purpose he took on human nature. Since then, Jesus Christ, and humanity around Jesus Christ alone, is the sign of salvation for the world.

The Catholic faith is a root that determines a psycho-socioculture. On the individual level it produces the saints and on the social level a whole cultural way of life which reached its summit in the politics of a St. Louis, King of France, in the art of a Fra Angelico and in the philosophy of a St. Thomas. But Catholic psycho-socio-culture comes from faith. If thought is not permeated by faith, a Catholic culture is not possible. Because Catholic culture, like faith, is a grace. And grace is given freely by God, without nature alone being able to do anything to merit it. And the first grace is that of faith, which is the root of all other graces and virtues. Therefore, there can be no Catholic psycho-socioculture without the Catholic faith.

Grace presupposes nature and faith presupposes the value of reason. Catholic tradition involves supernatural truths, but it presupposes purely natural truths as the foundation of those truths. Strictly speaking, man can have access to these natural truths without grace, but he cannot acquire them in an expeditious and convenient way without the grace of Revelation. Hence Thomism, even in the profession of purely natural truths, is a grace. Christian metaphysics would never have succeeded in discovering the transcendence of esse if Christianity had not succeeded in discovering that esse is the constitutive of the divine Essence.

Without the grace of Christianity, reason could not have avoided the confusion and darkness that accompany the cabalistic and Gnostic tradition in the problem of the relations of nature and grace, of world and Church; and even, within reason itself, those between the senses and the intelligence, between the forces of appetite and those of knowledge, between Physics and Metaphysics, between the world of essences and that of esse.

Hence, with the Gnostic fall, man has been deeply affected in the integrity of his human nature and faculties. His natural inclination to goodness and virtue has been sensibly diminished. This is expressly taught by St. Thomas[1019]. In the original justice, man, as he came from the hands of God, moved virtuously, and this in a purely spontaneous and natural way. Lust and anger, which are the fundamental passions of the human being, were subject to reason, and reason was subject to God. Man was governed by the cardinal virtues: fortitude, temperance, justice and prudence[1020]. Since he did not experience any disorder in his practical life, it did not turn him away from it, but on the contrary, it pushed him towards contemplation.

With the Gnostic fall, man has become incapable of contemplating the truths that are above him, and has become a homo faber inclined and prone to look only to his material needs. Hence the Gnostic errors enter preferentially through psycho-socio-cultural life, while the Catholic tradition penetrates through faith and from it extends to the whole psycho-socio-cultural reality. With the Gnostic fall man is imprisoned by the cultural milieu and becomes incapable of exercising his freedom over the sociological determinations that imprison and determine him. This is the case with ancient man, especially with the man of Eastern civilisations, and with modern man, the man of technology. The ancient human being absolutises the psycho-socio-cultural reality of natural forces, and the modern human being, on the other hand, that of technical

---

[1019] 1-2 85, 1.
[1020] 1-2 85, 3.

forces. Thus, ancient man divinises and sacralises nature, while modern man in the process of secularisation divinises the whole technical endeavour. Technology becomes technocracy and technolatry.

The Greco-Roman miracle, which, by valuing reason and the natural law, is in a certain way independent of Gnostic errors, occurs as a providential preparation for the Gospel.

The grand theological vision of the Middle Ages would not have been possible without the vast work of systematisation undertaken by Aristotle, who brought to its ultimate point the Greek idea of a world ordered like a chorus. The cosmos suspended by the love of a supreme Good, which is God. The medieval spirit will be employed to make appear as the Greek spirit, the convergence of all beings, of all goods, towards the Good, of all material, intellectual and spiritual interests, towards total harmony. The Christianity of the Middle Ages is, in this sense, the direct heir of the Greek cosmos and its transposition on the higher level of the supernatural.

But the relapse of the modern age into Gnostic errors can no longer take place in pagan innocence. Paganism is vanquished with the advent of Christianity. And the world will no longer know the innocence of the nature of the pagan world. It may apostatise from Christianity and return to paganism, but it must be to a paganism placed under another sign, in a certain supernatural way. After Christ the struggle is between two typically supernatural forces: the one, a carnal supernaturalism and messianism; the other, a spiritual supernaturalism.

The struggle is between the Synagogue and the Church. Paganism returns, but now under Jewish management. Hence also the Gnostic relapse of the modern age is a relapse into a Judaic or cabalistic gnosis.

After the advent of Christianity, the whole dialectic that shakes the Christian world moves between the Church-Synagogue poles. Christ defeats the Synagogue. And the era of the martyrs of the first centuries of Christianity, when the Synagogue incites the pagan world to torture the Christians, will only serve to water the Christian seed, which, vigorous, will shine with the Church of the Fathers and Doctors, over the Synagogue. The medieval splendour of the Church was to reduce the Synagogue to ghetto life. But in the modern age the Synagogue must avenge the exile to which the Christian world reduced it, and the Cabal penetrates into Christianity to the point of secularising it and threatening it with the secularisation of Christianity itself.

It is the latter phenomenon that we are facing today. With the tactic of "friendship" and of "Jewish-Christian dialogue", the Synagogue is gaining a triumph over the Church. It is clear that, in God's hands, this triumph can ultimately become a triumph for the Church.

The Synagogue-Church dialectic is finally resolved in a more central and luminous mystery, in the mystery of Christ. Christ is the key point of history. The Synagogue prepares Christ in the flesh. The Church continues him in spirit. But, one in fleshly supernaturalism and the other in spiritual supernaturalism, both complete in the dialectical play of the forces of good and evil the whole mystery of Christian redemption. And the mystery of redemption, although it has only one salvific fruit, is fulfilled only by the intervention of the two forces, the evil and the good.

History, in order to be complete, brings together in its bosom, in a mysterious alliance, these two forces which can only be resolved in eschatology. Thus, in time, men, and with them History, are energised by God and Satan, by Christ and the Antichrist, by the Church and the Synagogue, by the City of God and the City of the Devil. Everything is mixed in one and the same individual, whether saint or sinner. And every free act of every man ultimately seeks either Christ or Antichrist.

One of the most sinister errors of Christian progressivism and the Kabbalah is the tendency to homogenise the actions of men, as if the world of evil did not somehow have its own consistency and would not have to be separated and finally expelled at the eschatological hour from the kingdom of God. The intention is to make evil a purely residual reality of the Kingdom of God. And evil, in an enlightened and perfectly deliberate malice, takes its place in history. The evil angels sinned in an act of perfect lucidity. The man Adam sinned in an act also of perfect lucidity. And in all human generations there are men who sin, knowing perfectly well what they are doing and wanting to do evil with perfect lucidity. Evil must not be denied in order for good to shine forth. It must be shown in its full malice and wickedness so that divine mercy, which ultimately must triumph over man's malice and weakness, may shine more brightly.

History, with evil and with good, with profane deeds and with sacred actions, must serve Jesus Christ and the elect. The course and the end of History is determined by Metahistory. And in Metahistory the final act of the contemplation of the glory which is called eternal life. For this reason, history runs towards the final stage which will take place after the resurrection of the bodies and the final judgement. There Jesus

Christ, the Lord of Time and History, will pronounce the final and definitive verdict on the history of peoples and mankind. There it will be seen in an all-embracing and total intuition of the actions of men what is God's final thought on human history. It is there that the true lesson of the Theology of History will take place.

Progressivism, and with it all messianism and millenarianism, wants to confine the judgement of history itself within history. The world is moving towards a happy city, towards a third age of happiness and peace. Whether it is conceived in the manner of Hegel's absolute spirit or Marx's communism, it must always be a new event which will bring about a radical change in human behaviour.

The theology of history of St. Augustine and St. Thomas has stupendously seen that after the advent of Christ on earth nothing new will happen that can alter the ordinary course of events. As Ecclesiastes teaches[1021]:

> "For everything there is a season, and everything under heaven has its season;
> "A time to be born, and a time to die; a time to plant, and a time to pluck up that which is planted;
> "A time to kill, and a time to heal; a time to destroy, and a time to build;
> "A time to weep, and a time to laugh; a time to mourn, and a time to dance;
> "A time to scatter stones, and a time to gather stones together; a time to embrace, and a time to cease to embrace;
> "A time to lay hold of, and a time to lose; a time to keep, and a time to cast away;
> "Time to break, and time to sew; time to keep silence, and time to speak;
> "Time to love, and time to hate; time for war, and time for peace".

We have now entered the sixth age of the world, in which Christ initiated the new way for us. After the natural and Mosaic law, the law of the Gospel. What course the peoples will follow in their folly, man cannot know. For Revelation only makes known to him "ea quae pertineht ad necessitatem salutis" [1022]. Man can only glimpse

---

[1021] 3, 1-8.

[1022] Only those things which are necessary for salvation (St. Thomas, Summa Theol., 1-2, 106, 4, ad. 2).

generalities about the course of events and the density of history. This density is to be measured by a greater or lesser closeness to the norm of Christ, who is the centre and axis of history. History must conform to the cabalistic tradition or to the catholic tradition. It does not take much sagacity to see that for five centuries the world has been conforming to the cabalistic tradition. The world of the Antichrist is rapidly advancing. Everything contributes to the totalitarian unification of the son of perdition. Hence also the success of progressivism. Christianity is secularised or atheised.

How the promises of the Divine Spirit's assistance to the Church are to be fulfilled in this cabalistic age, and how the portae inferi non prevalebunt, the gates of hell shall not prevail, is to be verified, is beyond the human mind. But, just as the Church began as a very small seed[1023], and became a tree and a leafy tree, so it can be reduced in its luxuriance and have a much more modest reality. We know that the mysterium iniquitatis is already at work[1024]; but we do not know the limits of its power. However, there is no difficulty in admitting that the Church of publicity may be won over by the enemy and be converted from a Catholic Church into a Gnostic Church. There may be two Churches, one the Church of publicity, a Church magnified in propaganda, with bishops, priests and theologians who are publicised, and even with a Pontiff of ambiguous attitudes; and another, the Church of silence, with a Pope faithful to Jesus Christ in his teaching and with some priests, bishops and faithful who are addicted to him, scattered like "pusillus grex" all over the earth. This second Church would be the Church of promises, and not the first one, which could fail. One and the same Pope would preside over both Churches, which apparently and outwardly would be but one. The Pope, with his ambiguous attitudes, would give rise to the ambiguity. For, on the one hand, by professing an unimpeachable doctrine, he would be the head of the Church of Promises. On the other hand, by producing equivocal and even reprehensible deeds, he would appear to be encouraging subversion and maintaining the Gnostic Church of Publicity.

Ecclesiology has not sufficiently studied the possibility of such a hypothesis as the one we propose here. But if one thinks about it, the Church's Promise of Assistance is reduced to an Assistance which

---

[1023] Mt., 13; 32.
[1024] 2 Thess. 2:7.

prevents error from entering the Roman Chair and the Church itself, and also prevents the Church from disappearing and being destroyed by its enemies[1025].

None of the aspects of this hypothesis proposed here are invalidated by the promises recorded in the various places in the Gospel. On the contrary, both hypotheses become more plausible if one takes into account the scriptural passages that refer to the defection from the faith. This defection, which will be total, will have to coincide with the perseverance of the Church to the end. The Lord says in the Gospel: "But when the Son of Man comes, will he find faith on earth?"[1026].

St. Paul[1027] calls this defection from the faith a universal apostasy, which must coincide with the manifestation of the "man of lawlessness, the son of perdition".

And this universal apostasy is the total secularisation or atheisation of public and private life into which today's world is heading.

The only alternative to Antichrist will be Christ, who will dissolve him with the breath of His mouth. Christ will then perform the final act of liberating history. Man will not be alienated under the wicked one. But it is not announced that Christ will save multitudes. He will save His Church, "pusillus grex"[1028], the little flock, to whom the Father has been pleased to give the Kingdom.

[1025] The promises are contained in a particular way in: Mt., 16, 13-20; 28, 18-20; John, 14, 16-26.
[1026] Lk., 18, 8.
[1027] II Letter to the Christians of Thessalonica, 2, 3.
[1028] Lk., 2, 32.

Other titles

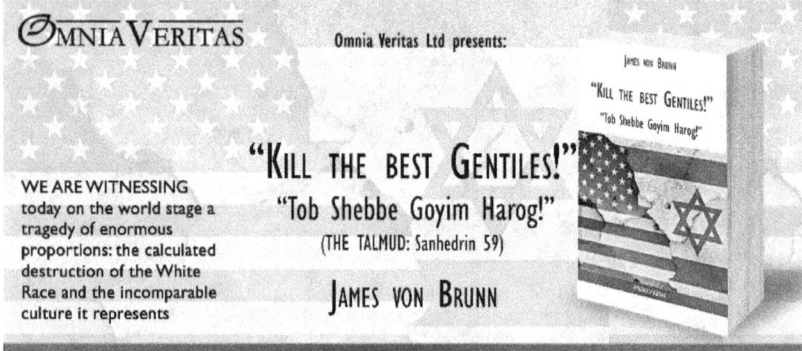

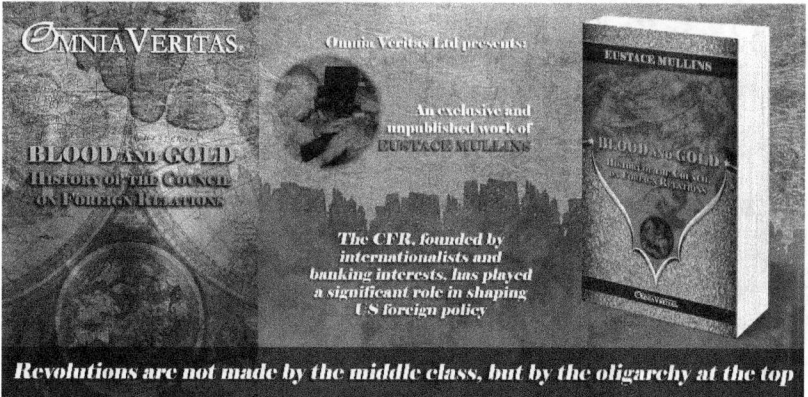

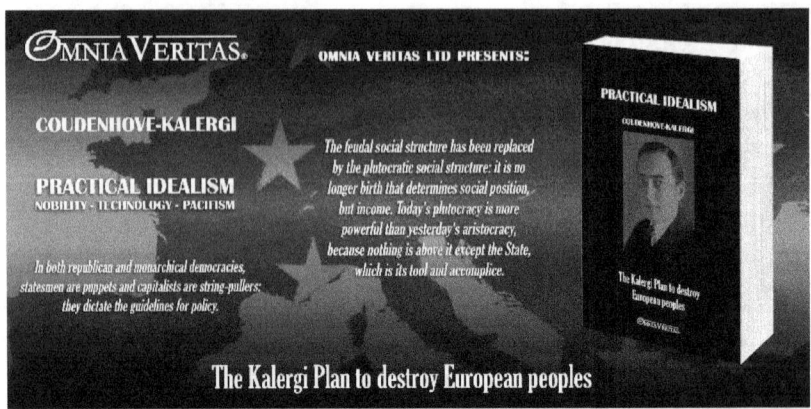

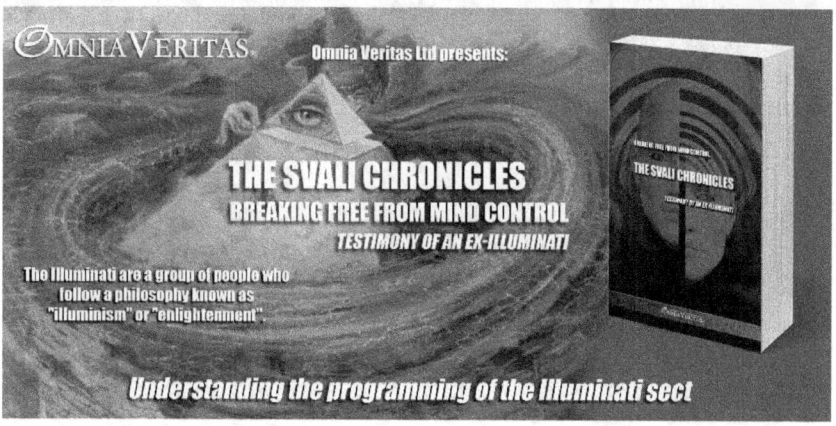

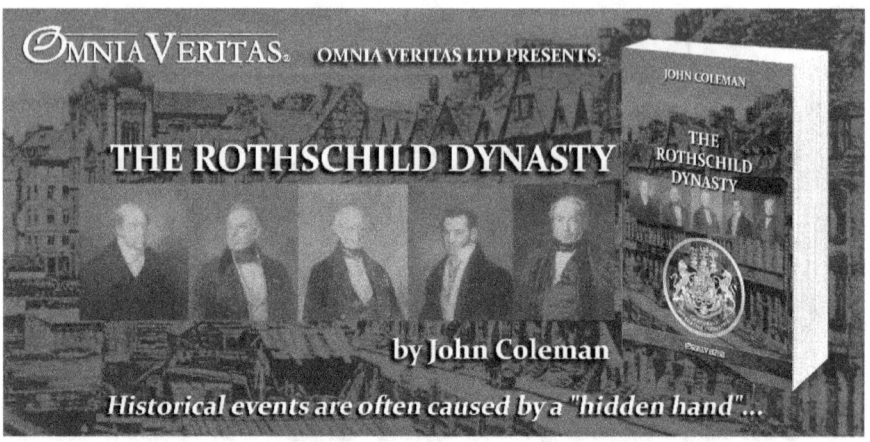

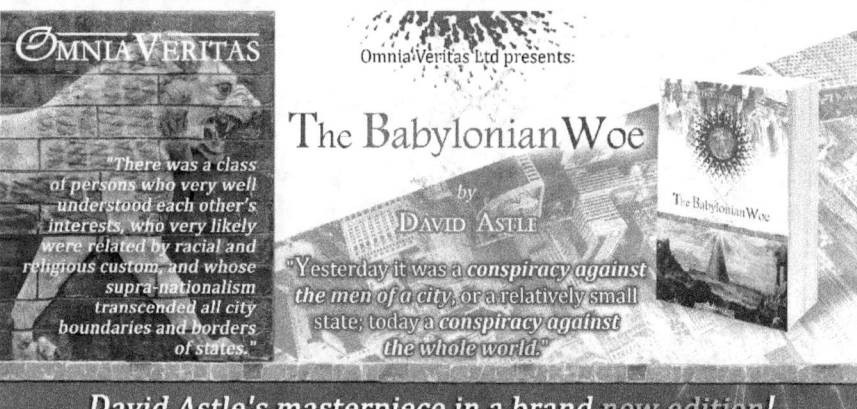

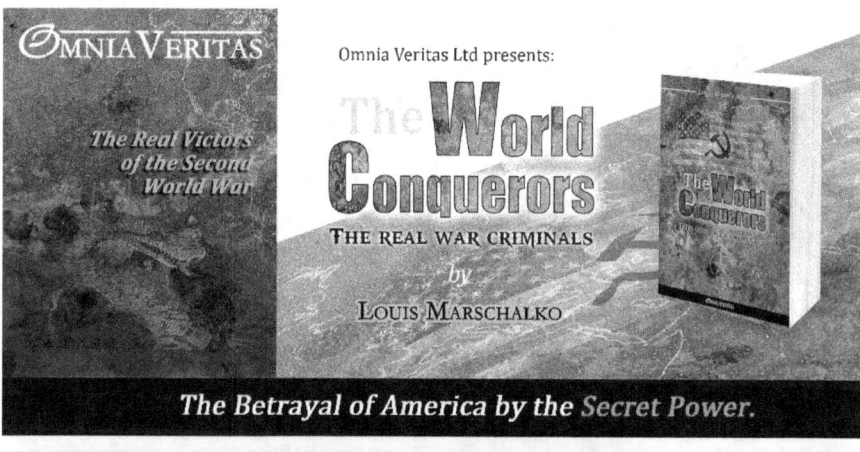